Praise for *Everything Is Grace*

"Joseph Schmidt's skillful blending of the events in Thérèse's life with reflections from her autobiography, poetry, and letters creates a perceptive portrait of this modern-day saint, who realized that everything is God's grace given and to be shared."

Most Reverend Robert Donnelly
Auxiliary Bishop of the Diocese of Toledo, Ohio

"Joseph Schmidt has been deeply rooted in Thérèse's Little Way for many years. His depth of perception highlights aspects of Thérèse's interior sufferings and her growing understanding of God's love through her own experiences."

Sr. Mary Lavin, OCD
Former Prioress, Carmel of the Holy Family, Cleveland Heights, Ohio

"John Paul II's words that Thérèse is a model for living the gospel today are confirmed in the author's reflective presentation. *Everything Is Grace* is written with such insight that Thérèse steps off the pages into the twenty-first century. Joseph Schmidt's book is both erudite and accessible to the general reader. The author engages the heart as well as the mind."

Sr. Patrice Kerin, OSF
Former General Superior, Sisters of St. Francis of Sylvania, Ohio

"In a world where so many paths lead us to violent ways of relating, Thérèse's 'Little Way' shows clearly that love is the only path that can save us from destruction—personally, communally, and institutionally. Joseph Schmidt's biography of Thérèse shows her universal relevance, especially in the way her nonviolent love offers an antidote to the violence that too often reigns in, among, and around us. I believe this book will become a classic."

Fr. Michael Crosby, OFM Cap
Author of *Spirituality of the Beatitudes*

"*Everything Is Grace* is an insightful psychological reflection as well as a penetrating theological reflection on Therese's life and writings, and demonstrates the possibility for deep gospel living—for holiness right within the ordinary events of our own lives."

Sr. Vilma Seelaus, OCD
Author of *Distractions in Prayer: Blessing or Curse? St. Teresa of Avila's Teachings in The Interior Castle*

"Make no mistake about it—this book deserves a place as a modern classic. Written from the perspective of the twenty-first century, *Everything Is Grace* is destined to be the way new generations meet Thérèse of Lisieux. Joseph Schmidt has made a striking addition to the notable biographies of Thérèse."

Doris Donnelly
Professor of Theology, John Carroll University, and author of *Mary, Woman of Nazareth* and *Seventy Times Seven*

"In these times of violence and war, St. Thérèse teaches the wisdom and practicality of interpersonal nonviolence and unconditional love. Joseph Schmidt's beautiful study of her life and spirituality urges us to surrender ourselves to God with love and gratitude, like Thérèse, so that we too can participate in God's disarmament of the world and discover the transforming truth that 'everything is grace.'"

Rev. John Dear, SJ
Author of *Living Peace, Disarming the Heart,* and *The Questions of Jesus*

Everything Is Grace

The Life and Way of
Thérèse of Lisieux

Joseph F. Schmidt, FSC

the WORD
among us®
press

The Word Among Us
9639 Doctor Perry Road
Ijamsville, Maryland 21754
www.wordamongus.org

ISBN: 978-1-59325-095-9

11 10 09 08   4 5 6 7

Cover Design: DesignWorks Group
Book Design: David Crosson

Cover Image: This photograph of Thérèse was taken in late 1894 or early 1895,
about two and a half years before her death.
Copyright © Office Central de Lisieux

Made and printed in the United States of America

Library of Congress Cataloging-in-Publication Data

Schmidt, Joseph F.
  Everything is grace : the life and way of Thérèse of Lisieux / Joseph F. Schmidt.
     p. cm.
  Includes bibliographical references.
  ISBN-13: 978-1-59325-095-9 (alk. paper)
  1. Thérèse, de Lisieux, Saint, 1873-1897. 2. Christian saints--France--Lisieux--
Biography. I. Title.
  BX4700.T5S34 2007
  282.092--dc22
  [B]
                              2006030340

A Note about Thérèse's Words

The words that Thérèse said or wrote are printed throughout the book in italics. They come from her autobiographical manuscripts *Story of a Soul* and her letters, poems, and prayers, as well as from words attributed to her in *St. Thérèse of Lisieux: Her Last Conversations,* in the memoirs of her sister Céline, and in the testimonies given during the process of her beatification and canonization.

List of Illustrations

Contents

Source Abbreviations

CCC *Catechism of the Catholic Church*

CP *Collected Poems of St. Thérèse of Lisieux*, translated by Alan Bancroft

DAS *Divini Amoris Scientia: Apostolic Letter of His Holiness Pope John Paul II*

FGM *Saint Thérèse of Lisieux: Her Family, Her God, Her Message by* Bernard Bro, OP

GC *General Correspondence.* Volumes I and II, translated by John Clarke, OCD

HF *The Hidden Face: A Study of St. Thérèse of Lisieux* by Ida Friederike Görres

HLC *St. Thérèse of Lisieux: Her Last Conversations*, translated by John Clarke, OCD

MSST *My Sister St. Thérèse* by Sister Geneviève of the Holy Face (Céline Martin)

PF *The Practice of Faith* by Karl Rahner

PSTL *The Prayers of St. Thérèse of Lisieux*, translated by Aletheia Kane

SL *The Story of a Life* by Guy Gaucher

SS *Story of a Soul*, translated by John Clarke, OCD

STL *St. Thérèse of Lisieux by Those Who Knew Her*, edited and translated by Christopher O'Mahony, OCD

TLMT *Thérèse of Lisieux and Marie of the Trinity* by Pierre Descouvemont

Foreword

Whenever a nun in a Carmelite monastery dies, her obituary goes out from her Carmel to all the others in the world. In a brief page or two her life in the community is described, her accomplishments mentioned, and her virtues praised. Most important of all, prayers are implored for her departed soul. The tradition is a touching one and binds all Carmelites together.

When Thérèse died, her Lisieux Carmel, instead of this brief notice, chose to send a copy of her autobiography. All Carmelites should know that one of their own had left behind a priceless treasure. They should learn the story of her remarkable life and profit from the wisdom of her spirituality. It took a year to assemble it from her writings and to print sufficient copies for all the Carmels.

Inevitably, Carmelite sisters shared Thérèse's autobiography with friends outside the Carmel walls, who read it with astonishment and passed it on to others. More editions quickly followed, and in the century since Thérèse's death, this fascinating book has been read by countless millions in sixty languages. More than five thousand books have been written about her, some of them deep studies by scholars of renown. Since Pope John Paul II proclaimed her the thirty-third doctor of the church, more books than ever are appearing, for there is always something new to say about this extraordinary saint.

This latest book, *Everything Is Grace* by Joseph Schmidt, presents Thérèse in a fresh manner. Part One is brief—only twenty-eight pages—but is distinguished by the manner in which the author relates Thérèse's teaching to the issues and values of modern Catholicism.

Joseph Schmidt points out that Thérèse prayed that God would raise up a legion of little souls like her and that this reality has happened and continues to happen in the lives of all those who have tried to fulfill God's will at each successive moment. This legion of little, simple, for the most part weak, inconspicuous, souls struggling in their daily lives for love and meaning by doing what God asks of them has found its voice in Thérèse's teaching.

Thérèse was herself a little soul. To take but one example, she had constant distraction in her prayers and often fell asleep when she tried to say them. She saw herself as a child who could dream of heroic achievements, but she knew that she would never actually accomplish them. She would be a little soul to the moment of her death, when she would appear before God with empty hands.

Her genius was to see the value of her littleness and cast herself into the arms of a God who is "nothing but mercy and love." What pleases him, she said, is that he sees her loving her littleness and wanting to be "more and more little." It is confidence and nothing but confidence that must lead us to love. Love was everything to Thérèse. She knew for certain that God loved her, and she returned this love with the utmost passion. "I want to love him," she wrote, "more than he has ever been loved before!"

This was the message that she called "my way," now known as the "Little Way." From her place in heaven she wants to teach it to the army of little souls who struggle through life in this world in the fervent hope of reaching at last the kingdom of the one who is love itself.

It is the second part of the book that I found most fascinating. In almost every one of its forty-six chapters, the author chooses significant moments in Thérèse's life and sets against them the writings they evoked from her *at the time she was writing*. This interplay of experience and writing greatly enhances one's understanding of both. For example, when Thérèse entered the Carmel at fifteen after a rich experience of strongly felt devotion, her prayer suddenly became dry and distracted. Drowsy during the long hours in the chapel, she often fell asleep. One would expect this to upset her. When we read what she wrote at that time, we may find it surprising that she makes so little of her lack of devotion. She *expected* it. She did not enter Carmel to gratify herself but to please Jesus.

Similarly, in the last eighteen months of her life Thérèse went through a terrible trial of faith. Her inner voice kept taunting her about her hope of soon beholding the beloved face of Jesus. "When you die," the voice kept repeating, "*you will see nothing*, for after death there *is* nothing. Death is the end of the human adventure." That "doubt" lasted until her last moment. She dug her nails into the palms of her hands and clenched her teeth. "I made more acts of faith in that period than in all the rest of my life," she wrote. She never lost the peace that remained, *unfelt*, at the deepest level of her soul.

Meanwhile, her beautiful young body fought fiercely against the devastation of tuberculosis. The pain was unbearable. She thought of suicide. Three times she mentioned it. She cried out in agony, asking if she was ever going to die. At the last moment she sat up in her bed, and choking to death, she spoke her final words: "My God, how I love you!" How full of passion they are, these famous last words! When she had lain back down she was dead.

Thérèse's two sisters Pauline and Céline kept notes on the things she said in her final days. They are to be found in *Her Last Conversations*, published after her death. Her words take on a new poignancy when we realize that they were uttered with the last bit of air left in her lungs.

It should be noted that the De La Salle Christian Brothers—the Brothers of the Christian Schools—have a close bond with the Carmel of Lisieux. They taught in two schools in Alençon, where Thérèse was born, and in one in Lisieux, where she spent most of her life. Her father, Louis Martin, was very fond of the Brothers of the Christian Schools and fostered their apostolate. It was they who put him in touch with their Br. Siméon in Rome, who is mentioned prominently in the autobiography and who became dear friends of Thérèse and her family. Since he was close to the priest-secretary of Pope Leo XIII, he had influence at the Vatican. Br. Siméon became a heartfelt supporter of Thérèse's canonization, and had an extensive correspondence with Céline after Thérèse died.

Joseph Schmidt, a member of the De La Salle Christian Brothers, does a great service by putting Thérèse's words in the context of her life, and for this service we shall remain indebted to him. This fine book very much deserves to be read and will deepen our understanding of Thérèse's life and her wisdom.

Patrick V. Ahern
Auxiliary Bishop Emeritus of New York
and author of *Maurice and Thérèse*

Introduction

Everything Is Grace, a reflection on the life and spirituality of St. Thérèse of Lisieux, is intended to serve as an introduction for those who know little or nothing about Thérèse, as well as a further study for those who are more acquainted with this "greatest saint of modern times," as Pope Pius X called her (*Divini Amoris Scientia: Apostolic Letter of His Holiness Pope John Paul II,* 10). It is also intended to be a corrective for those who consider the spirituality of Thérèse to be merely sentimental and syrupy, basically focused on trivialities, perhaps a passing fad of interest, but mainly irrelevant for those who live in this world of harsh realities and complex issues.

Including material from the autobiography of Thérèse, her poems, and her correspondence, as well as references to the testimony presented during the process of her canonization, this reflection also addresses the concerns of those who were surprised that "the Little Flower," as Thérèse has been popularly known, was proclaimed a doctor of the church by Pope John Paul II in 1997. And finally, it may also address the unspoken questions of those put off by the very label "the Little Flower."

Following a brief overview of some of the aspects of Thérèse's spirituality, the main body of *Everything Is Grace* will explore the life of Thérèse, as her unfolding experience revealed to her a fresh view of the spirituality of the gospel.

Thérèse's spirituality, which Pope John Paul II called a revelation of the *"fundamental mystery,* the reality of the Gospel," is inseparable from her life (DAS 10). It is displayed by the way she actually lived, and cannot really be understood outside of her life. She did not write a spiritual treatise that can be read independently of her life; rather, she lived a relationship of love, and as she came to understand God's ways with her, she put that spiritual wisdom into words—words that were mostly autobiographical.

In her correspondence, in her poems, prayers, and plays, in her teaching to the young sisters who were under her care, and in her autobiographical writings, Thérèse spoke about her way of living a life of love. She also warned that some of what she said could be misinterpreted if not put into the larger context of her life.

To understand and appreciate Thérèse's spirituality, there is no better way than to see it lived out by Thérèse herself. Yet her life contains nothing extraordinary; in fact, many of the details are similar to the details of the lives of multitudes of common holy men and women who, at their deaths, are quickly forgotten because their lives were so ordinary. This is especially true of the details of Thérèse's inner distress. She suffered a great deal from her *excessive sensitivity,* as she expressed it, but her sufferings, emotional and physical, while filling her subjective capacity, were not more than many ordinary people suffer. Her own mother, who died of breast cancer, suffered extraordinary physical pain, and her father, who was committed to an insane asylum for three years at the end of his life, suffered extraordinary emotional pain. Some of the saints suffered for years the darkness of faith that Thérèse suffered for the last eighteen months of her life.

Thérèse's virtue and prayer were also ordinary in many ways. She lived the last years of her life in a convent with sisters who rarely noticed that she was acting beyond what was usually expected of the members of the community and what was accomplished by every good nun. Shortly before Thérèse's death, one sister said, "My sister Thérèse of the Child Jesus is going to die soon; and I really wonder what our mother [superior] will be able to say after her death. She will be very embarrassed, for this little sister, as likeable as she is, has certainly done nothing worth the trouble of being recounted" (*Saint Thérèse of Lisieux: Her Family, Her God, Her Message* by Bernard Bro, 9). Another sister who had also lived with Thérèse for seven years expressed what several of the other nuns thought as well: that there was nothing to say about her; that she was very kind and very retiring; that there was nothing conspicuous about her and that no one would have suspected her sanctity. And when first approached about the possibility of canonizing Thérèse, Mother Marie de Gonzague, the prioress of the convent, laughingly remarked, "In that case, many Carmelites would have to be canonized" (*The Story of a Life* by Guy Gaucher, 210).

Thérèse's sanctity is not really the blossoming of rich human potential. It is not the result of the cultivation of extraordinary precociousness. Some saints have been humanly gifted with skills and capacities that are brought to fruition as part of their holiness. A talent for organization, an ability to envision reform, a bent for leadership, a flair for teaching, or even unusual psychic powers are among the natural gifts that contribute to the human base of holiness for some saints and founders of religious communities. Thérèse was gifted with none of these.

The one capacity Thérèse possessed is actually often an obstacle to holiness rather than a contributing factor—namely, a capability to be self-preoccupied and self-reflective. Thérèse noticed everything about herself, and she was willing to share that not as a display of ego-centeredness, but as a manifestation of God's work in her. The difference between these two attitudes constitutes a very fine line, and the temptation to cross the line is always lurking. Thérèse's glory is that she did not give in to that temptation. Her capacity for self-preoccupation finally became her greatest gift, for it allowed her to be attentive to the working of God in her.

Thus, by her personal reflection and in her writings, Thérèse has given us a glimpse into the working of the Holy Spirit in a very ordinary, and in some ways, a very limited soul. A challenge of the life of Thérèse—the essence and challenge of her "Little Way" of spirituality—is that if God could raise her to such a state of holiness, then any soul who is as willing and available as Thérèse could also be raised to sanctity. Thérèse's life was a manifestation of the gospel truth that the good tidings are for the "poor in spirit."

Devotion to Thérèse

Devotion to Thérèse of Lisieux has had a rather curious history in the Catholic Church. It actually began well before she was beatified and canonized. Within a few years of her death in 1897, she was the object of veneration and was already fulfilling her promise to shower graces on those who asked her help. By the time Pope Pius XI canonized her in 1925, devotion to Thérèse was already widespread among Catholics throughout the world. Missionaries were proclaiming her name and teachings as part of their evangelizing efforts, particularly in Asia and Africa. In Europe and North America she was quickly becoming the most popular saint among ordinary people. Statues of Thérèse were proliferating, stained-glass images were appearing, and holy pictures were widely distributed in Catholic schools and churches. Novenas to Thérèse were becoming more and more popular as well.

Then, in the 1940s and early 1950s, devotion to St. Thérèse met with obstacles. Freudian psychology had just emerged. Freud himself was a contemporary of Thérèse. As she was writing the manuscript that has come to us as her autobiography, *Story of a Soul*, Freud was writing his book on dreams. In the context of Freudian psychoanalysis, not many of the saints did well. Thérèse fared worse than most: she was more often than not diagnosed and dismissed as neurotic, or even as psychotic. Some Catholics began to have second thoughts. By the late 1950s and into the 1960s, fewer girls were receiving the name of Thérèse at baptism or confirmation, and novenas to Thérèse were subsiding, although she was still counted one of the most popular saints worldwide. By the late 1960s and 1970s, even the title "Little Flower" was drawing some criticism and seemed to trivialize her teaching and relegate interest in her to pious schoolgirls or to sentimental old women.

Devotees, however, of this young woman who had lived only twenty-four years—her last nine years in a Carmelite convent secluded from the world— have included such diverse personalities as Dorothy Day, Edith Stein, George Bernanos, Paul Claudel, Gustavo Gutierrez, Mother Teresa of Calcutta, and Thomas Merton.

Thomas Merton never wrote a biography of Thérèse, but he attributed his vocation to her inspiration and introduced his novices to her spirituality. He saw the Little Way as a call for the "democratization" of holiness and as "an explicit renunciation of all exalted and disincarnated spiritualities."

Edith Stein wrote of Thérèse, "My only impression when thinking about her was that I was faced by a human life uniquely and totally driven until the very end by the love of God. I know nothing greater than this, and it is a little of this which I would like as far as possible to carry over into my life and into the lives of those around me."

Dorothy Day at first thought that Thérèse really had nothing to teach her. Yet later, twenty-five years into her ministry with the Catholic Worker Movement, she returned to Thérèse, noting that she was the saint needed for our time. Dorothy Day eventually focused several years of her life on writing a biography of Thérèse—so impressed was she with Thérèse's Little Way of spirituality. In concluding the biography, she compared the power of the Little Way with the force of the atom and the atomic bomb:

> Is the atom a small thing? And yet what havoc it has wrought. Is her little way a small contribution to the life of the Spirit? It has all the power of the Spirit of Christianity behind it. It is an explosive force that

can transform our lives and the life of the world, once put into effect. (*Thérèse* by Dorothy Day, 175)

Dorothy Day experienced Thérèse's Little Way as a force more dynamic in its nonviolent love and its spiritually transforming energy than an atomic bomb or a nuclear weapon is powerful in its ravaging and destructive capacity.

Since the Second Vatican Council, devotion to Thérèse has again surged. The extensive outpouring of devotion by lay Catholics as well as by the hierarchy during the worldwide pilgrimage of Thérèse's relics, beginning in the mid-1990s, testifies to the universal esteem in which Thérèse continues to be held.

Interest in Thérèse over the years and throughout the world has continued even to the present day at an extraordinarily high level; indeed, since 1925 there has continued to be published worldwide, on average, a book a month dealing with her life and teaching.

On October 19, 1997, one hundred years after Thérèse's death, Thérèse was proclaimed a doctor of the church. To be named a "doctor" is an enormous honor for any saint; for Thérèse, it affirmed all that the ordinary faithful had understood about her, as well as all that the theologians and hierarchy had come to respect about her teaching. Pope John Paul II's declaration affirmed that Thérèse's teaching carries the depth of authentic Catholic spirituality, revealing the essence of the gospel with new freshness.

Everything Is Grace

The title of this book, *Everything Is Grace*, refers to a remark that Thérèse made just a few months before she died. She knew that she was entering her last days. *If you find me dead one morning, don't be troubled*, Thérèse told her sisters. *It is because Papa, God, will have come to get me.* Then she added a comment that responded to her sisters' expectations that she would have a beautiful death. They imagined that, at the end, she might die in an ecstasy of grace, or at least she would certainly receive Holy Viaticum in much peace and joy, befitting a saint. But Thérèse wanted to prepare them in case her death was sudden or that she would not be able to receive the last sacraments. In fact, because of her inability to retain food during the last weeks of her life, she could not receive the Eucharist as she was dying. She told her sisters quite simply, *Without a doubt, it's a great grace to receive the sacraments; but when God doesn't allow it, it's good just the same; everything is a grace* (*St. Thérèse of Lisieux: Her Last Conversations*, translated by John Clarke, 57).

The remark reveals much about Thérèse. On the emotional level, even as she was in agony on her deathbed, she was concerned about her sisters' feelings and how they would experience her death. She wanted to please and accommodate them. They hoped that she might die "like a saint," on a special Marian feast day or on another significant religious day. They wanted her to receive the last rites of the church, in saintly fashion, and to receive Communion. In her pain she responded to their expectations as best she could, but knew that she might not succeed in fulfilling their image of her dying like a saint. And their feelings of disappointment, even at this late time in her life, concerned her.

Also, from a more spiritual point of view, she was speaking words that she had learned from St. Paul, her most important scriptural teacher. She wanted to help her sisters understand that God's grace was not limited to the sacraments or to projects of human choosing. From her own experience she knew that she had received some of her most important graces in the ordinary and unbidden events of life.

And finally by her comment that *everything is a grace,* she was also sharing her spirituality of the Little Way—the spiritual way of accepting with loving surrender and gratitude all the happenings of life as sent by divine providence. If the experiences of life, even the ordinary and trivial, are received in this attitude of surrender and gratitude as gifts of God, then not just appropriate religious devotions and sacramental activities communicate grace, but surely *everything is grace.*

Part One

CHAPTER 1

The Spirituality of Thérèse of Lisieux

The spirituality that St. Thérèse of Lisieux lived and taught is nothing other than the very heart of the gospel made convincing and accessible to modern people. Thérèse's way of holiness, the way of spiritual childhood, the Little Way, is the gospel way, the way of Jesus. As such, ordinary Christians will recognize it as resonating with the deepest truth of the gospel—truth they have learned from meditating on the Scriptures, from their contact with the rich tradition of the church, from their involvement in the liturgy, from their religious education, and from their own grace-filled intuition and experience.

Pope John Paul II spoke of this fundamental gospel mystery as the reality that God is the loving Father and we are the beloved. The pope confirmed that this is Thérèse's fundamental teaching when he noted in his apostolic letter making her a doctor of the church, "The core of her message is actually the mystery itself of God-love. . . . At the root, on the subjects' part, is the experience of being the Father's adoptive children in Jesus; this is the most authentic meaning of spiritual childhood. . . . At the root again and standing before us, is our neighbor, others, for whose salvation we must collaborate with and in Jesus, with the same merciful love as his" (DAS 8). Thérèse explores, elaborates, and unfolds this mystery with a rich freshness, originality, and simplicity, making it clearly available to modern people.

Thérèse's spirituality was described by one of her novices, Sr. Marie of the Trinity, who learned of it directly from Thérèse's instructions and example:

[She] has done nothing extraordinary: no ecstasies, no revelations, no mortification which frighten little souls like ours. Her whole life can be summed up in one word: she loved God in all the ordinary actions of common life, performing them with great faithfulness. . . . She took everything as coming from God; . . . to abandon yourself to God and to think of yourself as little as possible, not even to seek keeping an account of whether you make [spiritual] progress or not. That's not our business. We have only to try to perform all the little acts of daily life with the greatest possible love, to recognize humbly but without sadness, our thousand imperfections which are always resurfacing and to ask God with confidence to transform them into love. (*Thérèse of Lisieux and Marie of the Trinity* by Pierre Descouvemont, 121, 118)

As "the greatest saint of modern times," Thérèse addresses the modern dilemma: not only the issue of our fundamental human limitations, our sense of guilt, the depth of suffering inherent in human life, and our fear of annihilation—but more so, our sense of alienation, our tendency to self-hatred and violence, our quest for meaning in life, our search for authentic existence, our complete divorce from any sense of hope, our loss of the security of truth, and our fear of "eternal solitude," as Nietzsche put it. A contemporary of Thérèse, Nietzsche, having proclaimed the "death of God," asked the question that reverberates down the years even to today, Where could I feel at home? This was Thérèse's question, as well.

Thérèse says to modern people, burdened with a sense of homelessness in life and suffering a sense of quiet despair, You are searching in the face of death for meaning in your life, for authentic existence, for liberation, for happiness, for freedom, and for truth; you are looking for love and transcendence, for connectedness and companionship, for affirmation and a sense of fulfillment. I have discovered what you search for: it is God, it is divine love stooping down to embrace you. And I know a way that will lead you out of your darkness and suffering. The way is the path of accepting divine love into your life, of willing to be available to the beloved God even in your weaknesses and despair. It is the way of being aware of your need for love, willing to give yourself to God's loving embrace like a child abandons itself with confidence and love into the arms of its loving parent, and then freely sharing love with others in creative good works of peace and justice. It is the willingness to be the person God calls you to be.

I know a way—Thérèse would continue—a Little Way to the fullness of life that you seek, a way to joy, to happiness, to peace, indeed, to eternal life. The way is short, and you have access to it in your present state, in the reality of your present task, whether small and trivial or big and complex; you have access to it in the immediacy of the here and now. It is a matter of awareness and willingness, of surrender and gratitude, of confidence and love. If you are entangled in the vicissitudes of life, in the messiness of your own weaknesses, in the distress of feelings, this way is for you. Everyone desires to love and to be loved, and it is a matter of awakening to this desire and directing it to its true source, its divine source.

Thérèse, like all the great saints and teachers of wisdom, does not propose a blueprint that would help modern people solve all the distressing social and human problems of life, but she does offer a way that will transform the lives of modern people and allow them to address these problems with peace, creativity, compassion, and justice.

A Gospel Way of Holiness

On one occasion, Thérèse spoke of her way as *totally new* (*Story of a Soul*, translated by John Clarke, 207). However, the way of spirituality Thérèse expressed has been within the church from its beginning, flowing from the gospel and founded in the best of Christian spirituality. She understood her way from her own experiences, which were confirmed by the light of the Scriptures. It is really the gospel way, the way of the Holy Spirit, which had been lived before Thérèse by countless ordinary, hidden, holy men and women through the centuries under the Spirit's influence and will be lived by countless more in the future who may never hear of Thérèse. Thérèse herself prayed that God would raise up a legion of little souls like her. In a sense, that has already happened in the countless people who have lived their lives fulfilling the divine will by their inconspicuous acts of fidelity, justice, peace, and love.

Thérèse's Little Way is really a way that had been dormant and hidden rather than a completely new way. God raised up Thérèse to proclaim and confirm the hidden, authentic gospel way. "The Spirit of God," Pope John Paul II said, "allowed her heart to reveal directly to the people of our time the *fundamental mystery*, the reality of the Gospel" (DAS 10). Thérèse lived and taught in a manner that reveals this very traditional gospel way to modern people who might not otherwise know the way. And for those already on the way under the inspiration of the Holy Spirit, Thérèse's life and teaching provide confirmation and validation, giving confidence to those who might otherwise doubt. This makes Thérèse and her teaching a great gift to the modern church and to modern people.

A Traditional Way

As Thérèse came to understand the gospel way, her Little Way, she was greatly influenced by many people. We cannot say that Thérèse was some kind of independent, precocious spiritual genius. She learned the spiritual life as we all do, basically from the holy people with whom we associate. Chief among her mentors were her own saintly parents, Zélie and Louis Martin. By their example, they sowed the seeds of the Little Way in a family life steeped in simple reverence and love for God and for one another, a family life that embraced many liturgical and devotional expressions of faith as well as a spirit of prayer, detachment, surrender to the divine will, and dedication to gospel values. Among Thérèse's four sisters, all of whom had some influence on her, Pauline was particularly important in forming Thérèse's vision of holiness and in providing her with devotional piety, even from the earliest days of her childhood. Thérèse, however, had to make her own way, and she significantly modified some of Pauline's ideas, especially her idea about the role of one's own effort in the path of holiness.

In the gospel Thérèse found her fundamental vision. She was inspired especially by Mary Magdalene's audacity to love Jesus in the face of her own weaknesses, and she was enlightened particularly by the teaching of St. Paul.

In the history of spirituality we also find those who were precursors to Thérèse's way, as well as those who modeled it for her. Thérèse admired and was influenced by various saintly people of history. Joan of Arc, not yet canonized in Thérèse's time, was among her favorites. Thérèse was attracted by Joan's heroism and courage in the face of wrongs committed against her, personal pain, and internal distress, as well as by her simplicity, inner strength, faith, and confidence in the divine call. Thérèse also admired a young missionary priest and martyr not yet canonized, Théophane Vénard, *because he was a little saint* and for his courage, trust, and apostolic spirit. Faith, love, courage, boldness, inner strength, and zeal—these were the characteristics of spirit that resonated with Thérèse, even as a little child.

Among other precursors who inspired Thérèse was St. Francis of Assisi, who lived the same spiritual poverty and nonviolent love that we find at the heart of the Little Way. Thérèse was influenced by her aunt, Sr. Marie-Dosithée, a religious of the Sisters of the Visitation community, which lives the spirituality of its founder, St. Francis de Sales. We find Francis de Sales' way of holy simplicity, abandonment, trust, gratitude, gentleness, patience, and love in the essence of the Little Way.

The great founding saints and doctors of Carmel, Teresa of Avila and John of the Cross, were the mother and father of Thérèse's spiritual teaching. Mother Geneviève, a founder of the Carmelite convent in Lisieux in which Thérèse lived, practiced the ordinary virtues in an inconspicuous way of holiness in total self-surrender that Thérèse much admired. Fr. Pichon, a Jesuit whom Thérèse considered her confidant and confessor, and Fr. Alexis Prou, a Franciscan who preached the one retreat that Thérèse most appreciated and *launched* her on the path of *confidence and love,* were among others who helped Thérèse on her way.

When Thérèse speaks of her way as *totally new,* she does not deny that she has taken a deep drink at the well of that ever-pervasive and profoundly rich spiritual tradition flowing directly out of the gospel through the lives of both ordinary and extraordinary Christians. Yet, for Thérèse, that rich tradition was not always available, and sometimes was misrepresented. Thérèse lived at a time, for example, when it was taken for granted that to be a holy person, one had to be an extraordinary person who had achieved some exemplary works, had attained a high state of prayer and asceticism, and perhaps even had had visions and ecstasies.

Thérèse's era was also a time when perfectionism was thought to be the ideal of Christian life. Jansenism, a heresy that promoted a false image of God as punitive and vindictive, had been condemned two centuries earlier, but was still sending out roots and tendrils into Catholic teaching. Pelagianism, an even earlier heresy that taught that people could successfully strive to merit God's love, also contaminated Catholic life. As a child and then as a nun in Carmel, Thérèse heard preaching purporting to be gospel truth that advocated perfectionism as the ideal, fostered human effort as the basis of hope, and represented Jesus' Father as a God of vengeance and wrath, of limited patience and punitive justice. Thérèse had no theological or scriptural education to counter such teaching theoretically, but she did have her own experience of human love and the gospel teaching of Jesus, "If you, with all your sins, know how to give your children what is good, how much more will your heavenly Father give good things to anyone who asks him" (Matthew 7:11).

From a contemplation of the gospel and from reflection on her own experiences, Thérèse knew that the Father of Jesus was not correctly represented by a Jansenistic image. She knew also that she had been called to holiness, but that she could not reach perfectionism, or accomplish great works, or attain high levels of asceticism. She knew from her own experience that the peace that Jesus gives is different and much more merciful than the peace of this world. Furthermore, she knew that the justice of God would also be different and much more compassionate than the justice of this world. She knew that she could reach holiness by grace even if she did not have the capacity or the achievements of the great saints.

In the face of Jansenism, perfectionism, and Pelagianism, Thérèse's teaching was something of a purification of doctrine, bringing the church back to the gospel holiness that is accessible to everyone. This purification Thérèse achieved in her Little Way, without being against anything, without trying to reform anything, but being for a life of nonviolent love. Her teaching is a fresh and creative expression of the traditional gospel teaching.

A New and Contemporary Way

In many aspects traditional, Thérèse's presentation of the gospel way might be considered "new," however, in the sense that Thérèse is our contemporary. Had she lived to be ninety years old, an age that two of her sisters, Pauline and Céline, each attained, Thérèse would have died in 1963. That the fundamental mystery of the gospel has been newly revealed to us by a young woman who died just over a hundred years ago necessarily gives that revelation a certain contemporary quality. Thérèse's Little Way has a newness about it simply because it presents to people of modern times a way to understand God and gospel holiness by a woman who is a contemporary.

Thérèse struggled, just as do modern people, in the search for truth and integrity in life. She faced the challenge of living with the inner conflicts of her own self-centeredness and willfulness; with the tension to remain true to herself while carrying the burdens of the expectations of others, personal feelings of animosity, and vain self-love. She knew the inner distress of loneliness and abandonment; the struggle of scrupulosity and self-doubt; the sort of helplessness that men and women today feel in the face of psychosomatic illness, addictions, and obsessions; the physical pain and inner darkness that make suicide a viable option. She was confronted with the religious questions of whether God and the afterlife of heaven really exist; with a felt experience of atheism; with the tension between faith and feelings; with the uneasy gap between science and religion; with the profound difference between violence and nonviolence as a way of dealing with evil.

These issues and tensions Thérèse resolved from the point of view of a mature woman—within a feminine perspective—in the workings of her own mind, with the light of the Scriptures—and in doing so has offered modern people the personal and social possibility of doing likewise.

Thérèse's teaching may also be considered new in that Thérèse brings to the understanding of the gospel a spirit of delight and awe that we associate with newness. Thérèse sees the Scriptures with the audacity and boldness, the freshness and hope, the directness and bluntness, the astonishment and utter trust of a child who looks for the first time at infinite possibilities and promises.

When the gospel speaks of our being called to be like God and tells us that God is love, Thérèse accepts this as a truth to be lived brashly. When Jesus assures us that the two great commandments are really one commandment, she accepts that as a truth to be lived selflessly. When Jesus speaks of having come not for the righteous but for sinners, she embraces that as a truth to be lived gratefully. When Jesus requests mercy and not sacrifice, she welcomes that as a truth to be lived personally and socially. When Jesus assures us that he will draw everyone and everything to himself, she rejoices in that as a truth to be lived literally. When Jesus commands love of the enemy, Thérèse applies that in an all-embracing way, to the enemy within ourselves as well as to the enemy outside ourselves. And when Jesus tells us that the reign of God is at hand and that all are welcome, especially the poor, the weak, and the suffering, Thérèse realizes that the opportunity to participate in the call to holiness is to be found in every experience of daily life, especially in suffering, and even in her own imperfect, weak response to grace. In the evening of life she will come before God, Thérèse says, *with empty hands*, confident that she will be clothed in God's own justice and goodness (SS 277). This is the same "old" gospel, but seen through the eyes of a young woman who is dazzled with the promise of the gospel message.

Thérèse's Everyday Mysticism

Thérèse's teaching is also contemporary in that it addresses a very modern problem. Until relatively recent times, even with the decline in faith among academics and philosophers, there had been an enduring undercurrent of religious values and belief permeating the lives of simple, ordinary people in Western culture. But this religious culture, more specifically this Christian, Catholic culture, has begun to fade completely as a context for life in modern times. The decline of cultural support for traditional religious values and Christian beliefs is a recent phenomenon that led the eminent modern theologian Karl Rahner to remark that the Christians of the future will be mystics or they will not exist at all.

What exactly could it mean that the contemporary Christian's baptismal call and challenge is to be a mystic in a modern world suffering the loss of cultural religious faith? The mystic has often been equated with the person who has had transcendent religious experiences that are far beyond the ordinary events of life. Such a person might have had extraordinary prayer experiences as did St. John of the Cross. Or as did St. Teresa of Avila, such a person might have recurring visions of Jesus, as well as unusual spiritual accomplishments or experiences of levitation. Even some modern saints have had the remarkable religious phenomenon of bearing the wounds of the crucified Christ, the stigmata.

But to limit the notion of the mystic to those who experienced unusual spiritual gifts would hardly allow many of the Christians of the future to qualify to be numbered among Rahner's mystics. In the past there have been very few reported mystics of the stature of St. John of the Cross or St. Teresa, and it is hardly likely that there will be many more in the future. Rahner encourages an expansion of the notion of "mystic" to include the "mysticism of everyday life."

Lacking the support of a culture that respects Christianity, the future Christian, to be secure in faith, will need to have personally experienced God's existence, love, and providence in the ordinary circumstances of life. Secondhand faith will no longer be enough to safeguard the Christian of the future from being swallowed up by an atheistic and materialistic culture. No longer will it suffice for the Christian to know about God's existence and about divine love from a sermon or a book. The Christian of the future will need to know God through personal experience.

A personal encounter with the Divine, however, does not need to happen through extraordinary events such as unusual prayer experiences, visions, or levitations. And that is just the point of Thérèse's life and teaching. Thérèse herself is regarded as a mystic, but she did not have what is usually understood to be extraordinary mystical experiences. She did report what were for her subjectively profound, albeit momentary, spiritual insights and experiences. Among these, she spoke of her exhilaration at first seeing the majesty of the ocean; she spoke of the sense of being united with God at her First Communion and also on other occasions when she received the Eucharist; she mentioned the importance of the grace of her reception of the Sacrament of Confirmation as well as the blessing of the smile that appeared on the face of a statue of the Virgin Mary and freed her from a youthful psychosomatic illness. She also wrote of a prayer experience of profound passionate love for God, the effects of which lasted for about a week, and another prayer experience that lasted for a very brief time. But these are the kinds of experiences that many ordinary Christians, as well as other religious people, report frequently. They seem to be the kinds of experiences that Rahner had in mind when he spoke of the Christian mystic of the future (cf. *The Practice of Faith* by Karl Rahner, 57–64, 69–70).

Besides the experiences that Thérèse recounts, the "everyday mysticism," "the experience of the Spirit" that Rahner refers to might include experiences similar to what Rahner himself suggests—for example, an occasion of fulfilling a duty that required complete self-forgetfulness without any affirmation; a comforting or confronting insight into ourselves that reveals a truth that liberates us; a time of silent peace and joy flowing from a brief prayer; quiet awe in the beauty and majesty of nature; an experience of profound happiness without any particular thing being the source of that happiness, that is, happiness at simply existing and living; a moment of freedom, for no apparent reason, from an emotional or physical burden.

"Everyday mysticism" might also include an encounter with a beloved person who gratuitously embraces and affirms us; an experience of beauty in the presence of music or art; a time of desperate longing that opens out into a mysterious certainty and peace; a moment of participating with awe in the wonder of a child; or an experience of freely forgiving someone without needing anything in return.

"The experience of the Spirit" could also include an occasion when we were able to remain tranquil and not retaliate in the face of an unjust accusation; an event of meaninglessness, borne in patience and suddenly yielding meaning; the spontaneous goodness of a stranger to us in a time of need and our spontaneous recognition of the deep goodness of human nature; a personal sacrifice we made solely because we believed it needed to be done and without concern about whether it was even noticed.

We also know God in an experience of being held in existence during a period of personal weakness and desolation; a series of chance happenings leading to physical or emotional healing and well-being; the ability to maintain patience and inner freedom in a time of personal diminishment, loneliness, and suffering; the capacity to respond to personal hurt with forgiveness and without violence; faithful and honest perseverance in a situation in which compromise would lessen personal suffering.

"Everyday mysticism" might also include the capacity to bear serenely trials and pain that had previously seemed impossible to endure; the ability to trust, surrender, and yet act lovingly without cheaply or cowardly giving up even in the face of confusion, fear, and mystery (cf. PF 82–84).

These "experiences of the Spirit," "everyday mystical experiences" are both ordinary and extraordinary: ordinary in that they happen often in daily life and that sociological surveys have documented their frequency. But they are extraordinary in that they open out into the experience of the reality of divine mercy and love. God is present in these experiences, as if slightly under the surface, awaiting our notice. They are called, in the Catholic tradition, experiences of divine providence and grace. When anyone at that moment allows the thin veil of ego-centeredness to part and permits the full depth of the meaning of the moment to enter consciousness, mysticism happens—and then one not only knows about God but also knows the divine reality in the experience of that moment. They are examples of "mysticism in everyday life."

One of the most highly respected spiritual teachers of our time, Thomas Merton, also speaks of "real mystics" who are "hidden contemplatives." Merton speaks of ordinary people who have "abandoned themselves to the will of God, seeking only to keep in touch with the . . . inner and spiritual realities" of the present moment. These mystics simply live life as a "walk with God," "not seeking anything special or demanding any particular satisfaction," living truthfully each day in great simplicity and inner freedom, doing "what is to be done," "not worried about the results of what is done," "content to have good motives and not too anxious about making mistakes." These hidden contemplatives are focused primarily on the divine will in "the living stream of life," finding the "extraordinary in the ordinary," and remaining "at every moment in contact with God, in the hiddenness and ordinariness of the present moment with its obvious task."

Merton gives examples. "At such times, walking down a street, sweeping a floor, washing dishes, hoeing beans, reading a book, taking a stroll in the woods—all can be enriched with contemplation and with the obscure sense of the presence of God. This contemplation is all the more pure in that one does not 'look' to see if it is there. Such 'walking with God' is one of the simplest and most secure ways of living a life of prayer, and one of the safest. It never attracts anybody's attention, least of all the attention of the one who lives it." "A genuine mystical life," Merton assures us, "may be lived in this condition" (*The Inner Experience* by Thomas Merton, 66). This is Thérèse's kind of contemplation and mysticism: the awareness of the divine love in the usual events of daily life, "everyday mysticism," "hidden contemplation," the kind of mysticism and contemplation that will be needed by the Christian of the future.

Thérèse's Little Way

Thérèse teaches that the call to sanctity is extended to everyone, even to the psychologically and spiritually weak, because divine love is actively present here and now in the ordinary experiences of life, loving us, healing us, empowering and uniting us with God's own love. Thérèse through her own experience was convinced that sanctity was available because divine love is always available.

Thérèse died at the age of twenty-four. She is not so much a spiritual genius or spiritually precocious, but more a living gift to the church through whom the Holy Spirit "reveals" the essence of the gospel anew. She manifested once again for our time the reality that gospel holiness does not require, as the mix of Jansenism, perfectionism, and Pelagianism pretended, extraordinary experiences in prayer or virtue, or sinless perfection, or fear of God, or penitential violence to oneself, all of which we could achieve with a bit more effort. Her message is simply Jesus' message of love: that we receive divine love and ought to share that love in acts of justice and charity. Thérèse lived this truth with such freshness and simplicity that she is a blessing for modern people.

The Little Way of Thérèse is not new or original in the sense that it presents newly discovered techniques or formulas of prayer; nor is it new in the sense that it attempts to explain a new theology, or that it directs us into new devotional activities. Nor is the Little Way a new outline of spiritual practices, nor a new model of stages of spiritual growth.

Rather, the Little Way, paraphrasing Thérèse herself, is an attitude, a disposition of heart, a way of awareness and willingness. It is a way of accepting and reciprocating God's love, available in all life's experiences. It is a way of responding, under the impulse of the Spirit, to divine love with confidence, abandonment, and trust, and sharing that love with others in justice and peace. It is the child delighting in and sharing a gift with the giver and those around it. Thérèse's way, just as the gospel way, does not require a prior attainment of a degree of perfection to receive God's free and merciful love, but requires only, within our human condition of weakness, a spirit of abandonment and a willingness to receive and to share that love.

O Jesus! Thérèse wrote at the end of her life, *why can't I tell all little souls how unspeakable is Your condescension? I feel that if You found a soul weaker and littler than mine, which is impossible, You would be pleased to grant it still greater favors, provided it abandoned itself with total confidence to Your Infinite Mercy. . . . I beg You to cast Your Divine Glance upon a great number of little souls. I beg You to choose a legion of little Victims worthy of Your LOVE!* (SS 200).

Thérèse's Little Way of holiness assures us that intimacy with God is available to all of us in the ordinary experiences of the here and now of life. Yet not everyone willingly receives the divine love fully. She noted one reason for this: *Ah! How many souls would have reached sanctity had they been well directed,* she wrote. For us, Thérèse's own life and teaching now provide that kind of necessary direction in the spiritual way, the "mystical" life of everyday experiences.

CHAPTER 2

The Treasure of Thérèse's Teaching

Thérèse lived in relative obscurity: she grew up in a very sheltered family, entered the religious community of Carmel at the age of fifteen, and died nine years later. During her life she had come to know very few people other than her relatives and the sisters in the Lisieux convent with whom she lived her final years. About thirty people attended her funeral. She should have disappeared from history, like so many other religious people who have lived in simplicity and poverty, in faith and commitment, but are considered, by all measure, of little consequence.

Thérèse, like those countless others, had fallen in love with Jesus and had acted in fidelity and charity, fulfilling her responsibilities inconspicuously and with the intention of doing God's will. At her death, with the exception of her blood sisters, the very nuns with whom she had lived and who admired her spoke of her as they would of any other faithful nun. They did not notice anything out of the ordinary about her life. Thérèse would have dropped out of history if not for her writings, the miracles that occurred after her death through her intercession, and the groundswell of devotion among those for whom her Little Way resonated. Through her writings, ordinary Catholics learned of her spirituality, and they found it congruent with their best Christian instincts. They also learned that she had hoped to spend her heaven doing good on earth. They, therefore, prayed to her—and then the miracles began to happen.

Story of a Soul

Thérèse's major writing has come down to us as a single book, an auto-biography: *Story of a Soul*. It is actually three manuscripts written to three different people, now joined into a single text. Thérèse wrote these works in response to the requests of others. Two of those persons were her superiors, her blood sister Pauline, then the prioress, and the subsequent prioress, Mother Marie de Gonzague. The third text was written at the request of another blood sister, Marie, who was also with Thérèse in Carmel and who asked Thérèse to explain her spirituality. Thérèse wrote her manuscripts out of a sense of obedience, with no thought or intention that they be published or even read by anyone beyond those to whom they were addressed. As a result, they do not have what many autobiographies seem to have, that quality we might call "spin."

Thérèse's text is straightforward, and she does not try to justify herself or nuance the text to appear proper. In fact, just the opposite. The writing is filled with a directness that is disconcerting, with stories and expressions of feelings that are written in a spirit of complete simplicity. Thérèse did not produce an exceptional piece of literature, except perhaps in its sentimental approach. The pages that make up *Story of a Soul* are written like other spiritual autobiographies of nineteenth-century Europe. Even though over the last one hundred years the book has gone into more than eighty-nine editions, has been translated into more than sixty languages, and has become a religious best seller, the impact that it has had on readers cannot really be explained in literary terms.

The power of the text seems to lie more in the reader's being confronted with the reality of the gospel lived in the life of a very simple young woman who had a profound depth of authenticity in her love for God. Thérèse's expression of faithful love touches the heart and brings healing to any area of callousness or lack of hope that we, her readers, might have. It rekindles that original spark of devotion that may have flashed in our heart at an early point of our spiritual journey. It melts the ice that caps the cynicism covering the original hope that perhaps, just perhaps, we could be close to God and that we could become a saint; not, certainly, the saint that we had first imagined and that expressed our own agenda, but a saint of God's own making.

The reader witnesses the Holy Spirit's work in a very docile soul. Thérèse's clarity about her interior sentiments and dynamics offers an insight into the unfolding of a soul who is willing, in the face of human weaknesses, to follow that original desire to be united with God. Reading Thérèse, we are connected again with our original awareness, that deep truth that we are loved, that we are capable of loving, that we are really called to live the life of the Spirit.

One of Thérèse's biographers and defenders has raised the questions,

Let us be honest with ourselves: Who among us normal Christians of the twentieth century has ever read *The Story of a Soul* for the first time without being disappointed? Who among us has really liked the book spontaneously, without the aid of an uneasy conscience which leads us modestly to ascribe our discontent with this famous work to our own inferiority? . . . For at first the book displays not a trace of greatness. *At first, we say!* How small everything is, how painfully little. It is as though we must stoop to enter into a world where everything is . . . sweet, pale and fragile. (*The Hidden Face: A Study of St. Thérèse of Lisieux* by Ida Friederike Görres, 15)

Yet with willingness to get beyond the sentimentality of expression, to enter into the mindset of the author, and to respect the simplicity of the presentation, the reader enters a world of simple holiness, courage, and profound gospel wisdom; "a confession of the Church's faith, an experience of the Christian mystery and a . . . mature synthesis of Christian Spirituality" (DAS 7).

No strictly human logic seems to be adequate in explaining the impact this book has had on all kinds of readers from many diverse religions, nationalities, and ways of life. Perhaps the explanation is hinted at by a remark once made by St. Francis de Sales, whose spirituality is not unlike Thérèse's: "There is between the Gospel text and the lives of the saints as much difference as between musical notation and sung music." By reading *Story of a Soul,* many people have begun to hear the music.

In addition to *Story of a Soul,* Thérèse also wrote many letters, some poems and prayers, and several religious plays that were performed as part of the convent's pious recreations. It was the autobiographical manuscripts, however, originally circulated to the various Carmelite convents in France as a kind of extended obituary notice and then passed on to the chaplains as well as the families and friends of the communities, that brought attention to Thérèse. A year after her death, the manuscripts were published by the Lisieux Carmel and more widely circulated.

The Miracles

Then the miracles began, literally around the world. However, we might say that the first miracles were more "in-house." When the sisters of the Lisieux Carmel as well as of Carmels throughout France read Thérèse's writings after her death, they were astonished at her deep love for God and for others, the creative way she dealt with her experiences, her stand against violence to herself or others, and the loving way she responded in her many interior and exterior trials. The sisters she had lived with had not noticed Thérèse in this way, so inconspicuously had she lived among them. Now, on reading her words, they were most impressed with the truth and richness of Thérèse's comprehension of the gospel message and the simplicity with which she had actually lived it. The community itself was gradually transformed. Céline, one of her older sisters and also a Carmelite of Lisieux, testified at the beatification process that Thérèse's first miracle was the conversion she wrought in the spiritual life of the community in which she had lived.

Another and an allied "in-house" miracle followed shortly. During her life, Thérèse had wished to receive Communion daily but was prevented from doing so, as were all the sisters of the community, by a decision of Mother Gonzague. She once told the prioress, *Mother, when I'm in heaven, I'll make you change your opinion* (HLC 262). After Thérèse's death Mother Gonzague's opinion did change. She came to respect Thérèse's view that the Eucharist *is not to remain in a golden ciborium; that He comes down to us each day from heaven . . . to find another heaven, infinitely more dear to Him than the first: the heaven of our soul, made to his image, the living temple of the adorable Trinity* (SS 104). Mother Gonzague, previously objecting to the possibility of daily Communion for the community, now became "very happy about it," Marie, another of Thérèse's blood sisters, testified at Thérèse's beatification process.

Thérèse had promised to spend her heaven doing good on earth, and this message was now communicated by missionaries to all parts of the world. With the spread of her message of promise, people took her at her word and asked her intercessory help. Thérèse responded. Many of the "miracles" were not noteworthy, except to the recipients themselves. They were coincidences that affected the lives of the people who prayed. But many were extraordinary cures attested by medical professionals as well beyond the realm of the natural.

Shortly after Thérèse's death in 1897, the Lisieux Carmel began receiving an average of fifty letters daily testifying to favors received through her intercession. That continued after her canonization in 1925. Thousands of people worldwide reported back each year to the convent that Thérèse had, indeed, fulfilled her promise. They reported favors received in the form of reconciliation of relationships, healing of personal pain and distress, cures of physical and mental illness, clarification in times of discernment, conversions of heart among relatives and friends, monies received at crucial times—all kinds of large and small occurrences just when they were needed most.

There were more than enough "great" miracles with proper official affidavits available to be used for the process of beatification and canonization. Three were needed; many more than that could have been supplied.

Thérèse's Canonization

The process of canonization for Thérèse was begun in 1909, well in advance of the fifty years that canon law at that time prescribed must elapse after the person's death before such proceedings could commence. But the ordinary faithful were in advance of the church, and the Vatican did not want to be "anticipated by the voice of the people," as the prefect of the Sacred Congregation of Rites, who fostered Thérèse's cause, remarked. She was beatified by Pope Pius XI in 1923 and canonized in 1925. Thérèse's was the most rapid canonization of any saint subjected thus far to the canonical process. In 1927 Pius XI also proclaimed St. Thérèse patroness of the missions with St. Francis Xavier; in 1944 Pius XII named her, together with St. Joan of Arc, patroness of France.

The "voice of the people" calling for Thérèse's canonization had arisen from around the world. They saw in her life the truth that holiness is possible even for "little souls" who do not have the capacity of personality and character or the situation in life to do great things but who live ordinary lives, as best they can, in faith and charity. Thérèse's life confirmed the truth that gospel holiness was available to everyone, especially to little souls, to the poor in spirit, and people were filled with hope.

After Thérèse's death, her three blood sisters who had lived with her as nuns in the Lisieux Carmel, believing that her Little Way would benefit the church, advanced Thérèse's reputation as a saint, as did many priests and religious persons who came to know of her. Thérèse herself had confided to her sisters that her teaching would be useful to all little souls. However, Thérèse's popularity among the faithful quickly exceeded anything that could be explained as the result of human effort. Even the effect on those who read *Story of a Soul*, and more so, the numerous great and small miracles that have come through her intercession are basically inexplicable except as God's work. No human agency can really explain the tremendous impact of Thérèse's life and writings, and no human agency controls miracles.

Thérèse and the Second Vatican Council

During the years following the Second Vatican Council, devotion to Thérèse was given an impetus by the interest in her teachings at the council itself. Her name and her teaching were frequently invoked during the interventions on the council floor and in the committee meetings that drafted the documents, as well as in the informal exchanges among the participants at the water coolers and coffee bars. Those who had access to such information reported that Thérèse was the saint most frequently mentioned by the participants of the council during their formal and informal sessions.

Scholars have become aware that some of the particular emphases in the documents of the Second Vatican Council would not have been possible or would have had to take a different tone if Thérèse's teaching had not permeated the thinking of the ordinary Catholic during the years between her death and the days of the council. Her teaching providentially prepared ordinary Catholics for some of the teaching of the council.

Thérèse's life, teaching, and insights could have offered testimony and affirmation—and clarification as well—to the participants of the Second Vatican Council as they discussed any of the following issues:

- reestablishing the authentic image of God as the loving, merciful Abba, Father of Jesus, and that no evil is beyond the reach of divine mercy;
- encouraging a deeper study of the sacred Scriptures in dialogue with the present human situation and making the sacred Scriptures more available to the ordinary Catholic;
- reestablishing authentic devotion to Mary as the exemplary member of the community of faith and the model of Christian life;
- affirming that holiness is not relegated to priests or those in religious life but is a call to all the baptized, and that holiness, available to the little ones, is not necessarily a matter of great actions, but of letting the Lord work in us and through us in the ordinary experiences of life;
- rejecting again Jansenism, perfectionism, and Pelagianism as part of gospel holiness;

- fostering the church's engagement in a deeper spirit of ecumenism, and a more open dialogue with other religions as well as with agnostics and atheists;
- separating the notion of Christian sacrifice and penance from the notion of violence and making it clear that no violence, even violence that attempts to overcome evil, has any place in authentic gospel spirituality;
- establishing the climate for more frequent reception of Communion and clarifying the meaning and significance of the Divine Office as the official prayer of the church;
- proclaiming the importance of the reality of the communion of saints and identifying once again the mystery of the church as the living Christ continuing the work of redemption in the world today;
- emphasizing that love is at the heart of the church and reaffirming the mission of evangelization as primarily sharing God's love with those who do not experience the reality of that love;
- refocusing Christian priority on a way of living lovingly rather than on only a way of thinking properly;
- searching for a deeper understanding of the eschatological mysteries of death, judgment, purgatory, hell, and heaven;
- reemphasizing the unity of the love of God and love of neighbor, denying any dichotomy between contemplation and action, and affirming the contemplative and apostolic calling by baptism of every Christian;
- affirming that the image of God as a loving father could be balanced with Isaiah's image of God as a compassionate mother (cf. SL 215).

Doctor of the Church

During these last one hundred years, as Thérèse's teaching has become increasingly well known by ordinary people and has been studied in depth by scholars, it has also become clearer that her approach to spirituality is an expression of holiness that brings the gospel up to date. Each generation and each age needs an expression of the gospel that addresses the current mentality and needs. Some saints continue to be significant many centuries after their canonization; some drop out of significance as the culture and the church change over the years. The fact that Thérèse was named a doctor of the church in 1997 confirms that she offers modern people a modern and needed insight into the gospel.

A movement among theologians and bishops to petition the Holy See to proclaim Thérèse a doctor of the church began as early as 1932, just five years after her canonization. That a woman would be named a doctor was, of course, unheard of at that time. In 1923 Pope Pius XI had already turned down a similar request to declare Teresa of Avila a doctor; he could not then raise Thérèse to that honor, bestowing on "little" Thérèse the precedence over the "big" Teresa of being the first woman doctor. The petition for Thérèse's doctorate was not only rejected, but word also came from Rome that no one was to discuss the matter further; the following year, the Sacred Congregation of Rites forbade any further collection of signatures for petitions in favor of the doctorate of Thérèse.

Thérèse's teaching, however, was not dismissed. In fact, the same letter forbidding further discussion of Thérèse's doctorate announced that Thérèse's spirituality "does not cease to be a light for the souls who seek to know the Spirit of the Gospel." Scholars and the ordinary faithful began to study her spirituality more attentively.

It was not until first Teresa of Avila and then Catherine of Siena were named doctors of the church, both in 1970, that hope for Thérèse's case was rekindled.

"Doctor of the Universal Church" is a title reserved for a saint who has not only lived a holy life and has been officially canonized, but who also has made a significant contribution—which is already being extensively recognized by the faithful—to the development of the church's understanding in the area of theology and spirituality. In other words, the title "doctor" refers most especially to the saint's capacity to teach the authentic doctrine of the church issuing from the gospel itself, as well as to the fact that the saint's teaching has actually begun to permeate extensively throughout the church's teaching.

The declaration of Pope John Paul II naming Thérèse a doctor, therefore, endorses her teaching as participating, with the teaching of only thirty-two other doctors over the entire history of the church, in the church's official proclamation of the faith. "When the magisterium proclaims someone a doctor of the Church," the pope said in his homily at the Mass of proclamation, "it intends to point out to all the faithful, particularly to those who perform in the Church the fundamental service of preaching or who undertake the delicate task of theological teaching and research, that the doctrine professed and proclaimed by a certain person can be a reference point, not only because it conforms to revealed truth but also because it sheds new light on the mysteries of the faith, a deeper understanding of Christ's mystery" (*Saint Thérèse of Lisieux: Doctor of the Universal Church* by Steven Payne, 159).

As a doctor of the church, therefore, Thérèse can be regarded as a teacher of the church's official doctrine for modern people. By making Thérèse a doctor, the church has made it clear that her teaching is not just of passing interest, much less a kind of fad. Her Little Way is not transitory, nor is it limited to some special school of spirituality or intended only for a special group such as cloistered religious nuns or young adults. Thérèse's spirituality, rather, is a modern proclamation of the gospel directed to every Christian.

Thérèse is "one of the great masters of the spiritual life in our time," Pope John Paul II said (DAS 3). She did not have extensive theological training, but she lived in the monastic tradition that emphasized the truth that a theologian is a person who prays, and the person who prays is truly a theologian.

She has a "special charism of Gospel wisdom," Pope John Paul II also wrote, and clearly she became wise by getting close to the source of wisdom (DAS 1). "Her teaching not only conforms to Scripture and the Catholic faith, but excels for the depth and wise synthesis it achieved" (DAS 7). So Thérèse is a "master" not in the sense that she dominates, but rather in the sense that she is a great teacher who learned the way of God from the gospel, by prayer and her own experience, and guides by the brilliance and clarity of her teaching and the simple example of her own life. "She became a living icon of that God who, according to the Church's prayer, 'shows his almighty power in his mercy and forgiveness'" (DAS 8).

When John Paul II proclaimed Thérèse a doctor, he noted, "In the writings of Thérèse of Lisieux we do not find perhaps, as in other doctors a scholarly presentation of the things of God" (DAS 7). Thérèse, in reality, had no real academic resources by which to formulate and present in any scholarly fashion her understanding of theology or spirituality. Her formal education was limited to elementary schooling. So, although Thérèse did not write a treatise on theology, she has given us a description of her spirituality by the way she lived her life, in the manuscripts she wrote that comprise *Story of a Soul* and in passages of her other writings. "A particular radiance of doctrine shines forth from her writings," the pope said (DAS 8).

Thérèse wrote a considerable volume of material for a person who lived only twenty-four years, who never intended to be a "writer," and who had such limited formal education. The amount of her extant writings includes the 240 pages of her autobiography, *Story of a Soul*, together with some 266 letters, fifty-four poems, eight pious recreational plays, and twenty-one prayers. This amount of published writings exceeds, for example, that of St. John of the Cross. Yet, it is true, as Pope John Paul II noted, that we would search in vain in Thérèse's work for a scholarly, theological presentation of her Little Way, this gospel way of holiness.

Thérèse's teaching is clear and certain but not dogmatic; it is sometimes sentimental; it is descriptive and in its simplicity, inviting. She does not speak against anything; rather she speaks on behalf of God's love. Her way is presented most compellingly in the context of her autobiography, and so is manifested in the experience of someone who is nonthreatening in stature and with whom we can identify as being imperfect, weak, and struggling. Thus, in Thérèse's case the title "doctor" also takes on a more extended, richer meaning. It refers not only to her charism of wisdom and her capacity as a teacher, but also to her role as a healer. Thérèse has had enormous power to bring healing to those who are in relationship with her. At the essence of her teaching is a nonadversarial, nonviolent, noncombative, and nonjudgmental quality that is disarming.

Her capacity to present the gospel in the lived reality of her own experience makes the gospel truth so clear and compelling, and yet so simple and accessible, that many find it reassuring to know that holiness is truly available even in personal limitation and emotional weakness. This does not diminish the challenging nature of the gospel call, but Thérèse's teaching challenges while simultaneously consoling. It takes into account human weaknesses and limitations, and does not terrorize. That is a much needed healing reassurance in modern times.

Thérèse is also a healing presence in the church today in the sense that she is the one person who seems to be able to bridge the many factions and divisions presently besetting the church. She has a following among elderly Catholics, who remember when their parents prayed to Thérèse and when they were introduced to her as children. She has a following among the young, who identify with her in their youthful, enthusiastic struggle to find security, self-worth, and meaning in their lives. She has a following throughout the world, among the rich and the poor, among the sick and the well, among the liberals and the conservatives, among the hierarchy and the laity, among men and women, among priests and religious.

Her popularity and healing also extend beyond the Catholic Church. Her healing presence reaches to all those who respect her as a woman of great holiness and wisdom. She is known and revered by the Orthodox Church, by numerous Protestant churches, by Muslims, Hindus, and Buddhists. Because she is appreciated by so many other traditions, her spirituality becomes a bridge among those traditions and between those traditions and the Catholic Church. She is even respected by agnostics and atheists. Indeed, her spirituality manifests the reality of the healing Spirit present and active throughout the world.

As an expression of gospel holiness, her spirituality is founded on love, and so is without a trace of violence. She offers hope to modern people so much in need of a way of addressing personal and social issues without violence. The Little Way of Thérèse has no place for any kind of so-called "positive" violence either to oneself or to others. Thérèse never suggests that those seeking God need to be violent to themselves in order to address their own evil, or violent to others to address the evil that others may be perpetrating. Violence as a means to achieve righteousness or to address weakness and evil in oneself or others has no part in Thérèse's teaching. This is truly the healing gospel message needed for our time, which so emphasizes violence as a way of overcoming evil.

Thérèse's Contribution to the *Catechism of the Catholic Church*

The *Catechism of the Catholic Church* appeared in 1994 as the reference text for the catechetical renewal following the Second Vatican Council. As the woman most quoted in the text, Thérèse has made a significant contribution to the church's understanding of the renewal envisioned by the council.

In the article "Grace and Justification," which deals with the doctrine of merit in the Christian life, the *Catechism* quotes from Thérèse's prayer, her *Act of Oblation to Merciful Love*. Flowing from Thérèse's spiritual maturity and as a revelation of her Little Way, this prayer expresses her understanding of God's gracious mercy in her sanctification and salvation as well as the role of her weak human response to grace. Thérèse understands grace not as something that God gives, but as the divine, loving presence at the core of her being. By the end of her life she came to the point of abandoning herself completely into the arms of God, her loving Father, knowing her weakness and placing no emphasis whatsoever on her own merits.

A part of Thérèse's *Act of Oblation to Merciful Love* is quoted in the *Catechism*:

> *After earth's exile, I hope to go and enjoy you in the father-land, but I do not want to lay up merits for heaven. I want to work for your love alone. . . . In the evening of this life, I shall appear before you with empty hands, for I do not ask you, Lord, to count my works. All our justice is blemished in your eyes. I wish, then, to be clothed in your own justice and to receive from your love the eternal possession of yourself.* (Catechism of the Catholic Church 2011; cf. SS 277)

The *Catechism* uses these words of Thérèse's prayer to express the church's understanding of the role of human effort and the role of God's grace in our sanctification. Thérèse's prayer is the capstone in the section of the catechism on the doctrine of merit.

The *Catechism* also quotes Thérèse in the section "The Church Is Holy." Love is the foundation of the holiness of the Christian and the heart of Christ's mystical body, the church. Thérèse, at the end of her life, in meditating on this fundamental truth, expressed her understanding, which is recorded in the *Catechism*:

> *If the Church was a body composed of different members, it couldn't lack the noblest of all; it must have a Heart, and a Heart BURNING WITH LOVE. And I realized that this love alone was the true motive force which enabled the other members of the Church to act; if it ceased to function, the Apostles would forget to preach the Gospel, the Martyrs would refuse to shed their blood. LOVE, IN FACT, IS THE VOCATION WHICH INCLUDES ALL OTHERS; IT'S A UNIVERSE OF ITS OWN, COMPRISING ALL TIME AND SPACE—IT'S ETERNAL!* (CCC 826; cf. SS 194)

In this reflection, Thérèse understood her own vocation. She could not be a martyr, or a priest, or an apostle—all important members of the mystical body—but she could be the heart; she would be love in the mystical body. *My vocation is love!* she exclaimed. *Thus I shall be everything* (SS 194). She would thereby fulfill the essence of all the vocations. The *Catechism* proposes that all Christians participate in Thérèse's vocation to be love at the heart of the church.

In the section "The Communion of Saints: The Communion of the Church of Heaven and Earth," the *Catechism* also cites some of Thérèse's final words, encouraging all Christians to be assured that the saints intercede for the whole church. In this regard, the *Catechism* mentions Thérèse's promise as she lay dying: *I want to spend my heaven in doing good on earth* (CCC 956; cf. HLC 102).

Thérèse's understanding of death also becomes a source of encouragement and hope. *I am not dying; I am entering life*, she said (CCC 1011; *General Correspondence. Volumes I and II*, translated by John Clarke, II 128). Quoting Thérèse in the section dealing with the meaning of Christian death, the *Catechism* suggests that these words can truly be on the lips of every dying Christian.

Thérèse is also quoted in the *Catechism* in the section "The Canon of Scripture." Thérèse never had access to a complete Bible, but she made the sacred Scriptures, particularly the gospel, a fundamental source for her prayer. Her words treasuring the gospels are cited in the *Catechism: But above all, it's the Gospels that occupy my mind when I'm at prayer; my poor soul has so many needs, and yet this is the one thing needful. I'm always finding fresh lights there, hidden and enthralling meanings* (CCC 127; cf. SS 179). The *Catechism* invites all Christians to find a source of prayer in the sacred Scriptures, especially the gospels.

Thérèse's contribution to Part Four of the *Catechism*, "Christian Prayer," is probably her most important. Until the publication of the *Catechism of the Catholic Church*, the ordinary definition of prayer, which influenced most of the catechetical teaching in the church through the centuries, was that of St. John Damascene. His definition, formulated at the beginning of the eighth century, was ordinarily presented in this simplified form in earlier catechisms: "Prayer is the lifting up or raising up of the mind and heart to God." His full definition is retained in the current *Catechism*, but is now placed after Thérèse's expression of prayer that she wrote in her autobiographical manuscripts (cf. CCC 2559). The question is asked in the *Catechism*, What is prayer? Significantly, Thérèse's description of prayer is given as the answer: *For me, prayer is a surge of the heart; it is a simple look turned toward heaven, it is a cry of recognition and of love, embracing both trial and joy* (CCC 2558; cf. SS 242).

Thérèse's description of prayer is remarkable in at least six specific ways.

In the first place, it typifies Thérèse's personal and invitational way of expressing her teaching. She does not didactically define prayer, but suggests what prayer is *for me*. Her understanding of prayer comes from her own experience, and she shares her insight into prayer as a very personal statement that might also be of assistance to others. This is the form prayer takes for Thérèse; she is willing to offer her experience of prayer, but she is not willing to be dogmatic about her teaching. She knows, as she says, that *there are really more differences among souls than there are among faces* (SS 239). By retaining Thérèse's phrase *"for me"* as part of its definition of prayer, the *Catechism* suggests that the church respects the deeply personal and unique quality of the Holy Spirit's prayer in each person.

Second, in this definition of prayer, Thérèse has inconspicuously and successfully combined in simple language the three traditional forms of prayer: affective prayer, contemplative prayer, and reflective prayer. Thérèse refers to the experience of affective prayer as *a surge of the heart*. She describes contemplative prayer as *a simple glance turned toward heaven*, and identifies reflective prayer as *a cry of recognition and of love, embracing both trial and joy*.

Third, Thérèse has, by her suggestion that prayer is a *surge of the heart*, shifted the metaphor of prayer. From John Damascene's more humanly effortful, even "stereotypically masculine," image of "lifting up or raising up of the mind and heart to God," Thérèse has moved to the more willing and cooperative attitude, even "feminine stereotypical" stance of allowing the heart, having been empowered by the action of the Holy Spirit, now to surge with the inner energy of the divine impulse.

Fourth, while not excluding the possibility that reflective prayer would include reflection on the sacred Scriptures, a practice dear to her own heart, Thérèse does not refer to Scripture in her definition. Rather, she alerts us to the fact that in her reflective prayer she has also embraced her lived experiences of pain and happiness, *trial and joy*. She has used her ordinary experiences as the base from which to deepen her relationship with God, as the context for her search for God, and as the place on which to stand in her cry to God. In this way, she includes in her description of prayer a faith-filled attitude of acceptance and a grace-filled attitude of surrender in the usual trials and joys of everyday life.

Using one's own experiences as the place from which prayer surges is, of course, the way of prayer pictured for us in the lives of the holy men and women of the Scriptures, of the prophets, and indeed of Mary and Jesus, searching for a deeper understanding of the mystery of divine love. It has been the way ordinary Christians throughout the centuries have intuitively prayed, reflecting on their lived experiences, searching for divine providence in the unfolding of their lives. Thérèse's description of prayer more explicitly validates this way of praying our own experiences as *a cry of recognition and of love embracing both trial and joy* in our ordinary daily life.

Fifth, by including the notion that loving and honest reflection on her ordinary life experiences has been for her a form of prayer, Thérèse shifts the understanding of prayer away from the limited notion of "saying prayers" from a prayer book, to the notion that prayer is a matter of "prayerfulness." Thérèse herself, of course, used a prayer book for her prayer. She recited the Divine Office with her sisters in Carmel as the usual form of her community prayer. But when Thérèse prayed privately and alone, she often dispensed with prayers from a book and simply reflected on her own experiences, searching for God's meaning and love in those experiences. She wrote, *Outside the Divine Office which I am very unworthy to recite, I do not have the courage to force myself to search out beautiful prayers in books. There are so many of them it really gives me a headache! And each prayer is more beautiful than the others. I cannot recite them all and not knowing which to choose, I do like children who do not know how to read, I say very simply to God what I wish to say, without composing beautiful sentences, and He always understands me* (SS 242). Her conversation with God extended throughout the day, about the things of the day, in mindfulness and prayerfulness.

Sixth, Thérèse has expanded the notion of prayer to include a whole *legion of little souls* in a remarkable way. She has done this by offering a description of prayer that, while explicitly mentioning the word "heaven," nevertheless does not explicitly mention the word "God" or "Jesus." "Heaven" was, of course, for Thérèse the eternal embrace of her heavenly Father, and

Jesus was her beloved. But by not explicitly mentioning the words "God" or "Jesus" in her description of prayer, Thérèse allows the possibility of prayer to be embraced by those who, although without faith in God or knowledge of Jesus, sincerely search for love and truth in their life. Thérèse's description of prayer welcomes those who, in their longing for meaning in life, search for God without knowing it. Thérèse has expanded the domain of prayer, thereby permitting an interreligious openness that allows the Catholic understanding of prayer to be included in any dialogue on prayer or religion, even with unbelievers. It extends the common ground on which spirituality can be discussed, an extension very much needed in our day.

These six nuances in the new description of prayer contained in the *Catechism of the Catholic Church* are all significant contributions to our understanding of prayer today. St. John Damascene died in about the year 750, so his definition of prayer has had an influence on the teaching of the church for the last 1,250 years and still remains an important way of understanding prayer. If Thérèse's definition has the same lifetime of influence before a new definition is needed for new Christians, those new Christians will be living in the fourth millennium, about the year 3250. Of course, Thérèse's definition of prayer is a small part of her spiritual legacy, but even that small part may be more enduring than many would imagine.

The Gospel Message

In his apostolic letter proclaiming Thérèse a doctor of the church, Pope John Paul II noted that through Thérèse's life and writings, "God has offered the world a precise message . . . the 'Little Way,' which everyone can take because everyone is called to holiness" (DAS 6). The pope, expressing rare praise for the spirituality of a particular saint, said that Thérèse's teaching regarding holiness is "a special charism of Gospel wisdom." This Little Way, he added, "is nothing other than the Gospel way of holiness" (DAS 2). Thérèse's Little Way has entered the Christian consciousness as a path of holiness that is simple and accessible to everyone.

In the same proclamation, John Paul II also said, "The Spirit of God allowed her heart to reveal directly to the people of our time the *fundamental mystery*, the reality of the Gospel" (DAS 10). We must acknowledge, then, that if we wish to learn the depth of the gospel message, we will find it not only in the written texts of the gospels themselves and in the other New Testament writings, but we will also discover that message reexpressed with clarity, simplicity, and cogency in the life and writings of Thérèse. By reading the texts of the gospels in light of the teaching of Thérèse, and the teaching of Thérèse in the light of the gospels, we will understand more deeply what the gospel is truly saying.

Today various interpretations of the gospel texts are prevalent, some of which are conflicting and even mutually contradictory. By naming Thérèse a doctor of the church, Pope John Paul II has identified her teaching as an important source of clarification for the preferred understanding. The Holy Spirit has used Thérèse, as the pope said, "to reveal" what we as modern people particularly need to know about the gospel. To understand Thérèse's teaching is, then, to have an important contemporary light shining on the gospel, and her teaching can contribute to any current discussion of gospel texts, enlightening any attempt to probe their deepest, richest meaning.

Thérèse's emphasis on love as the foundation of the gospel serves to reconfirm that nonviolence is the decisive consideration for the interpretation of any passage of Scripture. In Thérèse's nonviolent Little Way, the timeless truth of gospel love has a modern expression in both the personal and social realms. By cutting through the complexity of biblical scholarship and the bias of ideology, Thérèse's teaching is a clear and simple example of how gospel love might be expressed today, and thus is a great gift to the church in modern times.

Part Two

CHAPTER 1

I Shall Begin to Sing What I Must Sing Eternally: "The Mercies of the Lord"

The story of the life of Thérèse contains no great adventures, remarkable occurrences, or notable accomplishments. It is similar to the stories of innumerable men and women searching for meaning in their lives, for spiritual peace and joy, for a life oriented toward love, authenticity, and truth. In short, Thérèse's story is the story of everyone's search for God.

Any desires that we might have to search for God and any capacities we have to live in truth, fidelity, and love are themselves the result of divine inspiration and grace in the first instance. Our wish to seek truth and meaning, love and peace, is itself the manifestation of God's prior seeking of us. Thérèse came to know this reality, and so at the age of twenty-two, as she began to write her own life's story she remarked, *I'm going to be doing only one thing: I shall begin to sing what I must sing eternally: "The Mercies of the Lord"* [Psalm 89:1] (SS 13). *It is not, then, my life properly so called that I am going to write; it is my thoughts on the graces God deigned to grant me* (SS 15).

What may be considered important and unique about Thérèse's life is that she began this search for God so young. And what may be considered remarkable is that the path she finally took was a path that seemed to her and to her contemporaries simple and new.

In the small city of Alençon with a population of about sixteen thousand, not far from the coast in the Normandy area of France, on January 2, 1873, Thérèse was born to Zélie and Louis Martin. She was the ninth child of the family—and would be the last, for at the time of Thérèse's birth Zélie was almost forty-two years old and Louis fifty. Four of the children, two boys and two girls, had not lived beyond infancy. The parents and the surviving four children, all girls, welcomed Thérèse with love. Marie was thirteen; Pauline was twelve; Léonie, ten; and Céline, almost four when their newborn sister arrived.

Thérèse was a healthy, beautiful baby, and the family was delighted. When Zélie had been pregnant, however, she had been concerned. Although she had noted rather self-consciously to her sister-in-law, Céline Guérin, that at her age "one is a grandmother," her misgiving had not been because of her years, but because of the tumor in her breast that had been bothering her during most of the past decade (GC II 1199).

Zélie had bruised her breast as a young woman, and a tumor had developed in 1865; after a brief period, however, the major symptoms had gone into remission. So as not to disturb her husband or family, she had kept her condition secret, seeking the advice only of her brother Isidore, who was a pharmacist. When she finally consulted Dr. Notta in December 1876, three years after Thérèse's birth, the disease had progressed so far that it was too late for any kind of treatment.

Even while she was pregnant with Thérèse, Zélie knew that her poor health could have serious consequences for the newborn. Not being able to properly breastfeed her babies, Zélie had lost three children in early childhood, and one other before that child had reached her sixth birthday. The childhood deaths all followed symptoms of enteritis, and Zélie had a sense that her new child might not survive (cf. GC II 1202).

Zélie sought prayers from her family, in particular from her sister, Sr. Marie-Dosithée, a nun of the Visitation convent at Le Mans. Sr. Marie-Dosithée especially petitioned the assistance of St. Francis de Sales, the founder of the Visitation Community, during Zélie's pregnancy.

Zélie had wanted a baby boy, hoping that he might become a missionary priest. She completely gave up her preference, however, and was simply overjoyed with her gorgeous and lively baby girl. Zélie gave her the name Marie-Françoise-Thérèse Martin, in honor of the Blessed Virgin and of St. Francis de Sales.

The day after Thérèse's birth, Zélie wrote again to her sister-in-law, Céline, "My little daughter was born yesterday, Thursday, at 11:30 at night. She is very strong and very well; they tell me she weighs eight pounds. Let us put it at six; that is already not bad. She seems to be very pretty. I am very happy. However, at first I was surprised, for I was expecting to have a boy! I imagined this for two months because I felt the child to be much stronger than my other children" (GC II 1199).

With her sister Marie as godmother and the family in attendance, Thérèse was baptized on January 4 in Notre Dame Church. It was a church that Thérèse would often visit later with her father as they walked together around their neighborhood.

Less than three weeks after her birth, Thérèse was having difficulties nursing, intestinal problems, and sleepless nights; the infant was showing symptoms of enteritis, just as Zélie had feared she might. Zélie requested more prayers, and Sr. Marie-Dosithée again prayed to St. Francis de Sales. Without Zélie's knowledge she promised the saint that if the child survived, the Françoise part of her name would be the name by which she would be called and not by the name Thérèse. The crisis passed, but when Zélie was told of her sister's promise, she did not agree to the name change, hoping that it would not matter to St. Francis de Sales (cf. GC II 1201–2).

Within two months of her birth Thérèse was so seriously ill that death again seemed imminent. The doctor made it clear to Zélie that she would need to obtain the services of a wet nurse to breastfeed Thérèse or the child would not survive.

For several weeks Zélie resisted the advice. Her last baby girl had died two and a half years earlier due to the negligence of a wet nurse, and she had told herself, "never again"—any future children "would not leave the house." The doctor was adamant, however, and finally Zélie decided to contact Rosalie Taillé, the young woman who had cared for her two infant sons. Even though Rose had not been able to save the boys, Zélie still had confidence in "the little Rose," as the Martin family affectionately called her.

At dawn on the day after her decision, since her husband was away on a trip, Zélie walked by herself the seven miles to Semallé, where Rose and her husband lived on a small farm with their four children, the youngest a one-year-old son. Complying with her husband, Rose agreed to Zélie's request on the condition that Rose would nurse Thérèse for an initial eight days in Alençon, but then the child be brought to live with the Taillé family. Rose also asked that Thérèse remain with her for at least a year.

Zélie reluctantly agreed to this arrangement, and Rose accompanied her back to the Martin home where Thérèse lay pale and weak. When Rose first saw the child, she shuddered, knowing that the little one was almost already dead. She took Thérèse to her breast while Zélie, with tears of anguish and sighs of despair, went upstairs to pray before the family statue of St. Joseph (cf. GC II 1204).

A half hour later, Zélie descended the stairs still weeping and came into the dimly lighted room where she saw Rose silently caressing Thérèse. It was a sacred moment. Thérèse continued to nurse for another hour. Then, succumbing to exhaustion, she fell silent in the arms of Rose. Zélie, however, was not able to see that Thérèse was breathing and became alarmed. She bent over the child, but could see no signs of life. She began to weep again in despair. She had had such great hope just the minute before, but now all seemed lost. She thanked God for at least having let her child die in peace.

But Thérèse had not died. She opened her eyes and smiled! Her mother's tears continued to flow, now in joy. Thérèse slept peacefully in Rose's arms through the night. After eight days, Rose bundled Thérèse against the cold weather and carried her back to the little brick house in Semallé. Thérèse was to live the next twelve months with the Taillé family on their farm.

During those months, Zélie visited Thérèse as often as she could, although the distance made this difficult. Her three older daughters accompanied her when they were not at boarding school. In addition to these visits to the Taillé farm, the Martins saw Thérèse each Thursday when Rose came to the city market in Alençon to sell butter and produce and to buy food and supplies for her family. She brought the baby with her, and Thérèse would stay with her own family in her own home for a few afternoon hours while Rose did her marketing.

As the weeks went by, Zélie saw that Thérèse was getting stronger and more vivacious. "Thérèse is growing splendidly, she weighs almost fifteen pounds," Zélie wrote to her sister-in-law two months after Thérèse had been with Rose. "The wet-nurse has begun to make her eat during this past week. I am well-satisfied with this woman; you hardly see another like her for taking care of children" (GC II 1207).

"Thérèse is a big baby; she is tanned by the sun," Zélie again wrote to her sister-in-law four months later. "The wet-nurse brings her on a wheelbarrow into the fields, on top of loads of grass. She hardly ever cries; 'little Rose' says one cannot see a more darling child" (GC II 1208).

Thérèse later traced back to those days on the farm with Rose and the Taillé children her delight in nature, especially her joy of flowers, *of fields enameled with corn-flowers and all types of wild flowers,* and her love of *the wide-open spaces* and *the gigantic fir trees* (SS 29).

As the months passed and the routine continued, with Zélie and the family visiting Thérèse at Rose's home as well as Rose bringing Thérèse with her on her Thursday market trips to reunite with her mother for a few hours, Zélie noticed that two curious things were happening with her infant daughter. On the occasions when country women—for example, those who were part of Zélie's network of workers in her lacemaking business—were at the Martin house, Thérèse was always attracted to them. She was happier being in the arms of these women who dressed like Rose and had her fragrance and demeanor than she was being with Zélie's wealthy clients. Thérèse even preferred these peasant women to the more familiar arms of the Martin family maid. Zélie concluded in a letter that Thérèse was "afraid of people dressed fashionably," but the issue was deeper than that (cf. GC II 1209).

Zélie also observed that on some of the Thursday visits, Thérèse went into fits of crying and did not want to be with her sisters or even to rest in her own mother's arms. The baby would create such a fuss that the Martin maid was obliged to take Thérèse from her mother and carry her back to the market where Rose was selling her butter and produce. Then, reconnected with Rose, Thérèse would laugh contentedly (cf. GC II 1206–7).

Zélie wrote in one letter, "We saw little Thérèse last Sunday; . . . the nurse arrived with her four children. She put the baby in our arms and left immediately to go to Mass. Yes, but the little one didn't want that at all, and she cried uncontrollably! All the house was upset by it. We had to send Louise [the maid] to beg the nurse to return. . . . The nurse left in the middle of Mass and came running . . . [Thérèse] was instantly consoled."

The Thursday visits to the Martin family were occasions when her mother, her father, and her sisters could delight in Thérèse and love her for a few hours in their home. Then Rose would take Thérèse back to the Taillé family, where she would be enjoyed and loved for the remaining six days of the week. The baby Thérèse felt loved, delighted in, and cared for. But there did arise in this little child the unspoken but deeply felt questions, Who is my mother? and Where is my home? Throughout her life, these lingering questions would surface as subtle, distressful emotions and images.

From the moment of her birth, Thérèse experienced deep love, even if that love was nuanced with some uncertainty by the early separation from her mother. Moving between two loving mother figures, two warm and affectionate homes, Thérèse, however, could not fail to have had feelings of confusion, sometimes anxiety, separation, and abandonment. As Thérèse grew older, issues of connectedness, intimacy, and particularly mother-loss would arise in her heart. At times of crisis she would respond with displays of excessive sensitivity and a need to please others in her efforts to connect.

Thérèse's experiences in these early months had established an area of vulnerability in her foundational sense of personal security and bondedness, and she would continue for the rest of her days to remain vulnerable in those areas of her life. As her life unfolded, however, this vulnerability would itself become a grace in disguise. And for now Thérèse's needs and feelings were safely enveloped in the love of both Rose and Zélie and their families.

CHAPTER 2

The First Memories I Have Are Stamped with Smiles and the Most Tender Caresses

Both of Thérèse's parents were deeply religious. Before marriage each had attempted to enter religious life. Louis Martin, the son of a French army captain, had applied to be a monk at the Augustinian Monastery of Grand-Saint-Bernard, but he was told that he must first finish his studies, particularly in Latin, the language used in prayer by the monks. That proved too burdensome, so he focused on learning the art of watchmaking. After an apprenticeship of several years in Strasbourg and Paris, he bought a house in Alençon, inviting his parents to live with him. With his new skills, and following his natural bent toward the quiet, the reserved, and the meticulous, he set up a watchmaking shop.

Louis lived singly and independently for eight years. His business prospered. It was a quiet life, with few distractions and amusements, affording him time for his hobby of fishing, for some socializing, and especially for solitude, prayer, and pilgrimages. Louis preferred it that way. He was a man focused inward, and by nature simple, reserved, and sensitive, even shy, sometimes sentimental, and melancholic. Although possessing deep inner strength and personal courage, he was without worldly ambition. He had refused one marriage possibility, but his mother schemed a second time to marry him off to a young woman whom she noticed while attending classes at the lacemaking school in the town.

Zélie Guérin, whose father also had served with the army and then with the police, had attempted to join the Sisters of Charity of Saint Vincent de Paul in Alençon when she was about eighteen. The religious superior told her, somewhat vaguely, that she was unsuited for the religious life and that marriage was her real vocation. Zélie accepted the advice without question, without self-doubt, and without self-pity.

Possessing a lively spirit, a quick intelligence, and a depth of skill and courage, Zélie quickly moved into the career of lacemaking, an established industry in Alençon. She was capable, shrewd, and determined—and possessed more than the ordinary share of good sense and sound judgment, as well. With an entrepreneurial spirit, by the age of twenty Zélie had organized a network of some twenty women working in their homes, supplying her with lace-pieces that she meticulously and artistically joined. With a flourishing business, now all she wanted was a large family to give to God. She never fully gave up the idea, however, that divine providence might allow her to end her life as a widow in a religious community.

With a little help from Louis' mother as well as a chance encounter on the St. Leonard Bridge in Alençon, Louis and Zélie came to know one another and understood at once that they were meant for each other. Louis was thirty-five and Zélie twenty-seven at the time of their marriage on July 13, 1858. At first, Zélie, with little knowledge of the "facts of life," and Louis, with a certain religious idealism, agreed to live together celibately. This arrangement continued for ten months; then the couple's confessor, probably influenced by Zélie, dissuaded Louis from this path, and immediately Zélie's ambition for many children began to be fulfilled.

Growing up in a severe and scrupulous family, Zélie had lived through a childhood "shrouded in sadness," feeling unwanted and unloved. "I have never had pleasure in my life," she once wrote to her brother. But now, with her deeply loving husband, she would create "a family of love." "I am madly in love with children; I was born to have them," she wrote (GC II 1199). The couple had nine in thirteen years: seven girls and two boys. Within one period of three and a half years, however, they lost the two boys and a girl in infancy, and another girl before the age of six. Five girls survived. The first child, Marie, was born in 1860, and the ninth was Thérèse.

In 1870, twelve years after their wedding, Louis sold his watch business to his nephew and became an assistant to Zélie in her lacemaking work. He involved himself with the purchasing, bookkeeping, and traveling related to his wife's business. This and his interest in fishing and going on pilgrimages involved enough initiative and decision making for his liking.

On April 2, 1874, after one year and two weeks with Rose Taillé, Thérèse, now fifteen months old, returned to a delighted Martin family. Zélie had found it extremely distressing to be without her little child, although she was also very appreciative of Rose's care. Rose had saved Thérèse's life, loving her into physical and emotional health. The baby had quickly grown "very well and strong," as Zélie noted, and she would have liked to have taken her back sooner, but she respected her original promise to Rose. She wrote to her sister-in-law just a few days before the child's arrival back home, "Little

Thérèse arrives definitely on Thursday; she is a charming child; she is very sweet and very advanced for her age" (GC II 1210).

During the months Thérèse had been with Rose, Zélie had written numerous letters about Thérèse to her daughter Pauline, who was away at boarding school, and to her sister-in-law, who lived in Lisieux. "Strong," "beautiful," and "graceful," were Zélie's favorite descriptions of her little daughter. She had "a sweet smile," her mother noted, and "a charming disposition."

Zélie was, of course, seeing Thérèse through the eyes of a loving mother, but years later, after Thérèse's death, when the early edition of her autobiographical manuscript, *Story of a Soul*, was published, these same traits were included in a description of the mature Thérèse, probably written by her sisters Pauline, Marie, and Céline. "She was tall of figure. She had blonde hair, gray-green eyes, a small mouth, fine and regular features. Her countenance, of the color of the lily, was harmoniously carved, well-proportioned, always sweetly serene, as if stamped with heavenly peace. Her carriage was full of dignity, at once simple and graceful." Later Léonie would describe the color of Thérèse's eyes as being "of a very dark and beautiful blue, but they were flecked with brown, which at times made them seem almost black."

As the months went by, Zélie experienced little Thérèse as being very bright, exceeding in intelligence her other children at that age. "She appears to be very intelligent," Zélie wrote. "I am very happy to have her" (GC II 1210). Later Zélie described Thérèse as "a nervous child, but she is very good, very intelligent, and remembers everything" (SS 23; GC II 1219).

Thérèse was deeply affected by the family atmosphere of union, peace, piety, and love in which she now found herself encircled. The affection of her parents for one another and for the children flowed down into the reciprocal and mutual love among the children. Thérèse's four sisters had all embraced her with tenderness. The oldest, Marie, was Thérèse's godmother. "The diamond," as her father nicknamed her, Marie was a nonconformist and a rather independent child.

Pauline was her mother's favorite; "the fine pearl" was the pet name her father gave her. She was currently a boarder at the school attached to the Visitation convent at Le Mans where Sr. Marie-Dosithée, her aunt, resided. Pauline, intelligent and resourceful, with a gifted and powerful personality, became her mother's confidante and support. She would become Thérèse's "second mother," as well as her prioress at Carmel for a time. Marie, and especially Pauline, contributed significantly to Thérèse's psychological and spiritual formation.

Léonie, the middle child, was "good-hearted Léonie" to her father. She had almost died in infancy, and was prayed back to life by her aunt, Sr. Marie-Dosithée, on condition that the child would become a saint. Léonie's survival was regarded as a miracle by the family. She turned out to be the "black sheep" among the children. Relatively unsociable, slow at studies, and sometimes obstinate and lacking good judgment, she was considered a problem by her parents. She would be on the periphery of Thérèse's life, her only sister not to be with her in Carmel, but Thérèse had a special appreciation for her. Léonie, in turn, came to imbibe and value her younger sister's spirituality to a significant degree, living a saintly life.

Céline, closest in age to Thérèse, was bright, lively, accommodating, somewhat perfectionistic and assertive. She was "the dauntless one," "the intrepid," to her father; the jewel of her mother's heart, and a constant companion and faithful confidante to Thérèse. Thérèse would consider her *the sweet echo of my soul* (GC I 557).

Many years later Thérèse herself would recall these early years and write, *God was pleased all through my life to surround me with love, and the first memories I have are stamped with smiles and the most tender caresses* (SS 17). Thérèse experienced her days as filled with joy, and she responded with spontaneity and delight. *Although He [God] placed so much love near me; He also sent much love into my little heart, making it warm and affectionate* (SS 17).

CHAPTER 3

I Wonder How You Were Able to Raise Me with So Much Love without Spoiling Me

The atmosphere of the Martin home was at once filled with religious piety as well as human security and love. Louis and Zélie were exemplary in their charity and Catholic faith, and Thérèse's sisters were truly interested in one another and cared for one another. There were humorous times in the family and exchanges of clever nicknames; Thérèse, as a child, was often described by her mother as a "little rascal" who would play little jokes on her older sisters. There were also some times of misunderstanding, getting on one another's nerves, and exchanges of anger, but no holding of grudges, no jealousy, and no bitterness.

Because of all the love and support that flowed among its members, Thérèse's family could be viewed as ideal. Through the experience of family love, Thérèse learned about human love, which became the basis for her understanding of divine love and mercy. She also learned about sharing love with others, particularly with family members, but also with the poor and needy.

The Martin family's religious sense was rooted solidly in the best of the Catholic spiritual tradition and managed to avoid being contaminated by Jansenism, one of the most dangerous religious tendencies in France at the time. Although condemned as a heresy more than two centuries before, Jansenism still survived in subtle ways. One of the indications of Jansenistic influence in Catholic spirituality in Thérèse's day was the common emphasis on God as a punitive judge and a violent enforcer of law and order. Jansenism, intertwined with Pelagianism, taught a false perfectionistic state attainable by human effort alone that allowed for no mistakes; it also stressed a rigorous spirit of penance for sins and inevitable mistakes as well as a constant fear of divine wrath. Thanks to her family's affection, these attitudes never took root in Thérèse's spirit.

Thérèse's idea of divine love was deeply influenced by her family's love and religious faith as well as by the love she had received from Rose Taillé. Thérèse knew that she had been loved first and constantly from the very beginning, with a love that was not merited. Her parents, and especially her older sisters Marie and Pauline, were appropriately firm with Thérèse, but they did not measure out their affections in meager servings, fearing that too much love would be dangerous.

During the process of beatification for Thérèse, the older Martin daughters were asked how they would describe their parents and the family home in which Thérèse grew up. They responded that their parents were saints in their charity, and that they had practiced many family devotions together, keeping a clear separation from the world. Thérèse herself had written, *The good God gave me a father and mother more worthy of Heaven than of earth* (GC II 1165).

Zélie and Louis modeled for the children a quiet, detached, and respectful love. The family was, in some ways, organized like a small religious community. The devotional practices included conformity to all the church's laws of fasting and abstinence, membership in various pious societies, and refraining from any work on Sunday. Louis also read pious books to the family each evening.

The parents and older children often attended the 5:30 morning Mass. There were daily family prayers together as well as time, direction, and encouragement for personal prayers. Sundays included more family quiet time in addition to an opportunity to visit their cousins, the Guérins, and their aunt, Sr. Marie-Dosithée, in the Visitation convent. Often on Sunday afternoon the family also visited the parish church to adore the Blessed Sacrament and to participate in the prayer of Vespers.

As part of their Christian expression, Zélie and Louis were concerned about aiding the needy and elderly. Zélie looked after some poor people of the neighborhood, visiting them in their homes and on occasion housing them with her own family. For the Martin family, living the Christian faith was a matter of sharing their family's wealth with the least members of Christ's body. Little Thérèse was the family member delegated to give alms to any poor person they might encounter on their walks through the town.

The Martin family kept a clear separation from the "world" at a time when Catholic families were identified as "Catholic" almost solely in terms of this withdrawal from worldly interests together with a focus on devotional activities. The Martins did not involve themselves in the fashions of the time, did not think of life as an opportunity for social advancement, and had no intention of accumulating wealth. Today the family would be labeled as religiously conservative and devotional, without being rigorously strict.

Since baby Thérèse's homecoming, the entire Martin family had done all they could to make her feel welcomed and loved. Even though she was now in her own warm and permanent home with her own seven-day-a-week mother, at first she was distressed. She naturally experienced feelings of confusion at being in new surroundings; she also felt loss in having left "her mother" Rose, "her home" with the Taillé family, and the familiar environment of the farm. She was experiencing the intolerably frightful feelings of separation.

Thérèse made small, childish efforts to resolve these deep, difficult feelings. With the usual baby crying and fussing as well as with some childhood tantrums—"frightful furies," as her mother called them—she tried demanding attention. Her particularly sensitive and conscientious nature, however, quickly moved her from demanding attention to actively reaching toward those who loved her and cared for her, bonding with them by trying to please them. Her need for security was satisfied by her move toward closeness and connectedness.

In a letter dated about three months after Thérèse arrived home, Zélie described Thérèse as "a little burden." "She is continually at my feet, and it is difficult for me to work. So to make up for the time lost, I continue my lace-work up until ten o'clock at night, and I rise at five o'clock. I still have to get up once or twice during the night for the little one. However, the more trouble I have the better I am!" (GC II 1210).

Identifying Thérèse as "a little burden" was a telling way for Zélie to express her own feeling of being the object of the child's excessive neediness. From an experienced mother's point of view, the little child's clinging made her "a little burden," but Thérèse's need was real. Having suffered the distress and confusion of being shuttled back and forth during her first year of life and now her separation from the comfort of Rose, Thérèse needed the assurance that closeness to mother brought. She needed to know that she was really with "mother" and was really "home."

The next day Thérèse's mother wrote another letter describing Thérèse's behavior in more detail: "The little baby has just passed her little hand over my face and kissed me. The dear little thing does not want to leave me, she is continually with me; she loves going into the garden very much, but if I am not there, she does not want to remain and cries until someone brings her back to me. . . . I am very happy that she has so much affection for me, but sometimes it is troublesome!" (GC II 1211). In another letter, Zélie noted simply, "She prevents me from working" (GC II 1212).

Again, Zélie, the practiced and observant mother, found it troubling not only that her work schedule might be interrupted but that the little child had such a need for closeness and tried so hard to be near and to please her. Having been the mother of eight children before Thérèse, Zélie had a sure intuition about the behavior and feelings of babies.

She wrote to Pauline at the Visitation boarding school, describing Thérèse's emerging style of pleasing others: "Marie loves her little sister very much, she finds her very darling; . . . the poor little thing greatly fears causing her any trouble" (GC II 1224).

When Thérèse was two and a half, her mother wrote to Pauline, "I hear Thérèse calling me: 'Mamma!' She does not go upstairs alone without calling at each step: 'Mamma! Mamma!' So many steps, so many 'Mammas!' And if, unfortunately, I forget to answer a single time: 'Yes, my little girl!' she remains there without going forward or backward" (GC II 1218).

Thérèse described herself as possessing from her earliest years a sensitive and loving nature. Building on her graced nature and in the loving atmosphere of the family, Thérèse calmed the weakness of her difficult feelings of separation by little acts of affection and accommodation that moved her to closeness and bondedness. She began to develop a style of feeling secure and bonded by pleasing others.

Thérèse acted in ways that were pleasing to the members of her family and were rewarded with family affirmation and approval. As a small child she could hardly have done otherwise. She was following the giftedness of her nature. She became part of a family that was constantly interacting in loving ways, supporting one another, protecting one another, pleasing one another. The family atmosphere, in a sense, conspired in Thérèse's way of coping with her difficult feelings by encouraging her to please as a virtuous activity. No one would have known if Thérèse's acts of pleasing others were coming from anything less than real love. Only Thérèse herself would have known—and, of course, during her early years she was not aware.

Over the years, however, with the grace of insight, Thérèse came to see that while pleasing others could be a good thing, the motive of calming her disturbing feelings might not be a worthy one. If that motive fully replaced the motive of real love, then her feelings would be dictating her behavior, and that could become a serious personal weakness, undermining her authentic sensitivity and loving spirit. It could move her to compromise her personal integrity and to lose her true self for the sake of feeling good, and then she would be living out of sham love. But, from her earliest memories, it was out of real love that she wanted to live.

In the protected family milieu a noble characteristic of Thérèse's nature that did quickly emerge was her spontaneous sense of honesty and integrity. Thérèse had no tendency to self-justification, dishonesty, or deceitfulness. Her mother noted simply that she "would not lie for all the gold in the world" (GC II 1233).

Nor was she afraid to admit her mistakes. The loving support within the family helped Thérèse to respond to her failings without fear. She felt assured that she would be loved even with her faults. When she had done something wrong, she quickly responded with an acknowledgement of her mistake and a sense of repentance. This quality also helped her to become close to those who loved her by winning their approving response. "As soon as she had done some wrong," her mother described the three-year-old, "everybody must know it. Yesterday, without willing to do so, she knocked off a little corner of wallpaper, and she was in a state to be pitied, and her father must be told very quickly. . . . She has in her little mind that we will pardon her more easily if she accuses herself" (GC II 1224; cf. SS 18–19 for a slightly different translation).

"She has a heart of gold;" her mother noted, "she is very lovable and frank; it's curious to see her running after me making her confession: *Mamma, I pushed Céline once, I hit her once, but I won't do it again.* (It's like this for everything she does)" (GC II 1223).

Thérèse, as any child, wanted to have her own way and so often enough acted in a self-centered and willful manner. In this she sometimes succeeded, especially with her father, who regarded her as his "little queen," but her older sisters were quick to check her self-indulgence.

Zélie, as a young mother, had written to her brother about her own sad childhood: "My childhood, my youth were as sad as a shroud. . . . My mother was too strict with me. Although she was so good herself she did not understand me and I suffered from this very much" (SL 9). Zélie consciously refused to pass that experience on to her children. She gave them the understanding and love that had been denied to her.

Nor was Zélie's love for her children soiled by any prolonged grief over her little ones who had died in infancy. She had told little Thérèse of her love for these deceased children, had prayed with Thérèse to these "little angels," and then had allowed them to rest in peace. She did not compare her living children with those who had gone before or pamper herself with her loss.

In these early years under the direction of the family members, Thérèse began to develop an interior watchfulness and an inner self-discipline. These qualities, together with her sensitive conscience and her sense of obedience flowing from it, protected her as a child from being spoiled. Later, as she wrote about her childhood, she expressed thanks that she had been raised so lovingly but firmly. To her sister Pauline she wrote, *I wonder at times how you were able to raise me with so much love and tenderness without spoiling me* (SS 44).

Thérèse at three and a half, July 1876

CHAPTER 4

I Was Far from Being a Faultless Little Child

In the atmosphere of a loving family nest, Thérèse did not need to be perfect; she did not need to be afraid. Nor did she need to be concerned about punitiveness or vengefulness. She could acknowledge her mistakes and run to her parents and her sisters for forgiveness, correction, and affection; and all was well again. She equated being good with following her conscience, pleasing God, and pleasing others. Formalism and law-keeping were never the primary way of goodness for Thérèse.

Only a person who had experienced a glimmer of divine love through immersion in human love would be able to proclaim God's love convincingly. Only a person who had known personal human weakness and experienced a taste of divine mercy through the experience of human forgiveness could assert and manifest God's mercy and forgiveness in a compelling way. Only a person who had lived the deep human desire to be connected, to be loved, and to love in return could announce with conviction God's own longing to love and be loved. And divine providence was preparing Thérèse from her earliest years to be just that person.

Thérèse later remembered that by the time she was three, she had had the intention of refusing *nothing He was asking from me* (HLC 251). She was also at a very early age vaguely considering in some way giving her life to God, her loving Father, in a religious community. Yet even as Thérèse was moving through childhood in so protected and destined a way, she was not free from her own inner conflicts. Two childhood incidents, both occurring when she was about three or four years old, indicated disturbances that she experienced within herself. These disturbances flowed from the early difficult feelings of insecurity and separation, as well as from her emerging anxiety about the way she was compensating for these difficult feelings. Both incidents occurred while Thérèse was asleep, so she did not consciously control them.

The first, a physical reaction as she slept, manifested the inner struggle she experienced around her self-image as a child. The second, a dream, spoke to her about a path that would help her resolve that inner struggle. It would be a path that included honest self-appreciation, courage, and truth. At the end of her life, she identified truth as a way she had always tried to follow.

This first incident flowed from Thérèse's image of herself as *far from being a faultless little child* (SS 24). She, "the little burden," recognized in herself, even as a child, that she had a need for attention and closeness—a need that led her into self-centeredness, self-will, and an excessive sensitivity. She spoke of herself as being inclined to *an excessive self-love* (SS 25).

Thérèse understood even in the infrequent annoyances and corrections of her parents and sisters that she was *far from faultless*. When she heard the family speak of her as "the little imp" and "the little rascal," she experienced these not only as terms of endearment, but also as terms that alerted and warned her that she was not yet good enough (cf. GC II 1222).

Recalling her childhood years later, Thérèse remembered,

They weren't even able to say about me, "She's good when she's asleep" because at night I was more restless than during the day, throwing off the blankets and sending them in all directions and (while still sleeping) banging myself against the wood of my little bed. The pain would awaken me and I'd cry out: "Mamma, I bumped myself!" Poor little Mother was obliged to get up and convince herself I really had bruises on my forehead, that I really bumped myself! She'd cover me up and then go back to bed, but in a short time I would begin bumping myself again, so much so they had to tie me in bed. And so every evening, little Céline came to tie me up with a lot of cords which were to prevent the little rascal from bumping herself and waking up her Mamma; this was so successful a means that I was from then on, good when sleeping. (SS 24)

It would be some time before Thérèse matured from the self-violence implicit in this behavior into a personal sense of security and self-appreciation that did not require her to harm herself to gain attention and closeness, nor require her to punish herself for what she perceived to be her faults and inadequacies.

The second incident, a dream, occurred at about this same time and suggests her inner struggle to establish a sense of self-appreciation founded on a courageous, truthful acceptance of every aspect of herself, and not needing to compensate for her difficult feelings:

I dreamed one night I went to take a walk all alone in the garden. When I reached the foot of the steps leading to the garden and which have to be climbed to get into it, I stopped, seized with fright. In front of me, near the arbor, there was a barrel of lime and on this barrel two frightful little devils were dancing with surprising agility in spite of the flat-irons they had on their feet. All of a sudden they cast fiery glances at me and at the same moment appeared to be more frightened than I was, for they jumped from the barrel and went to hide in the laundry which was just opposite. Seeing they weren't so brave, I wanted to know what they were going to do, and I went up to the window. The poor little devils were there, running on the tables, not knowing what to do to hide from my gaze. Sometimes they approached the window, looking out to see if I was still there and seeing me there they began running like madmen. (SS 28)

Thérèse pondered the dream and believed that *God permitted me to remember it in order to prove to me that a soul in the state of grace has nothing to fear from demons who are cowards, capable of fleeing before the gaze of a little child* (SS 28). Ultimately this insight became a significant aspect of Thérèse's spiritual path: her willingness to face the realities of her own inner demons with the honest, forthright gaze of a little child, courageous in the truth that even with her inner demons she was in the arms of a nonvindictive and loving God. She had nothing to fear and could ultimately be at peace in her search both inwardly and outwardly for the truth.

In the hands of Jesus, the good shepherd, in the arms of the Father welcoming the prodigal son, and under the longing gaze of the mother sweeping the house looking for the lost coin, Thérèse, "the little rascal," would finally come to know in her deepest self that she had nothing to fear. She could move along the path of honest reflection on her own life, become aware of her faults and weaknesses, be forthright in admitting and repenting of them, and still know that God loved her.

To walk this path Thérèse would need an inner strength of will—and it was precisely this strength that Zélie had noticed in the infant Thérèse. Zélie called it stubbornness. Not having experienced this willpower quite so strongly in her other children, she sometimes actually found Thérèse's determination frightening.

When Zélie observed Thérèse and Céline interacting, she saw that Thérèse had a more spontaneous and unrepressed spirit than did Céline. Of the two, Thérèse was more comfortable and uninhibited being herself; but it was especially Thérèse's strong will that drew Zélie's attention and concern.

Céline was almost four years older than Thérèse, but little Thérèse seemed to have both a quicker intellect than Céline and a more indomitable resolve. "As for the little ferret," Zélie wrote of Thérèse at about three and a half, "I do not know too well how she will turn out; she is so little, so thoughtless, she has an intelligence superior to Céline's, but she is less gentle and has in her an almost invincible stubbornness; when she says, 'no' nothing can make her give in. I could put her all day in the cellar and she would sleep there rather than say, 'yes'" (GC II 1223).

Thérèse became at times so willful and emotional that her mother had reason to be alarmed. "Céline is playing blocks with the little one," Zélie wrote to Pauline, "and they argue every once in a while. Céline gives in to gain a pearl for her crown. I am obliged to correct this poor little baby, who gets into frightful tantrums; when things don't go just right and according to her way of thinking, she rolls on the floor in desperation like one without any hope. There are times when it gets too much for her and she literally chokes" (SS 23; GC II 1219). Thérèse's strength of will became an enduring aspect of her character.

Reminiscing about her childhood, Thérèse also recalled her own strong will. *One day,* she remembered, *Mamma said: "Little Thérèse, if you kiss the ground, I'll give you a sou." A sou was a fortune at the time and to get it I didn't have to lower my dignity too much, my little frame didn't put much of a distance between my lips and the ground. And still my pride revolted at the thought of "kissing the ground;" so standing up straight, I said to Mamma: "Oh! No, little Mother, I would prefer not to have the sou!"* (SS 24).

Thérèse would have kissed the ground out of obedience to her mother; but she believed her *excessive self-love* prevented her from performing an arbitrary act of humiliation and loss of self-dignity.

Thérèse remembered another incident of her childhood that was expressive of her strong will. Thérèse and Céline were playing together and their older sister Léonie held out to them a basket of little dresses and materials for dolls: "Here my little sisters, choose; I'm giving you all this." Céline took a little ball of wool. Thérèse reached out, saying, *I choose all!* and snatched the whole basket (SS 27). It was a bold, powerful, and spontaneous gesture for little Thérèse, one that must have surprised Léonie and Céline and perhaps startled Thérèse herself.

As Thérèse reflected on this experience, she came to know her capacity to be both singular in her focus of will and passionately determined in her desire. Later she spoke of herself as capable of *immense desires* even *infinite desires,* and she remembered this incident of choosing all as *a summary of my whole life* (TLMT 86; cf. GC I 622 and GC II 1102, note 4; SS 27). She passionately and boldly desired to be a saint, and she directed the singular focus and depth of her desire to God.

Later on, Thérèse reminisced, *I understood there were many degrees of perfection and each soul was free to respond to the advances of Our Lord, to do little or much for Him, in a word, to choose among the sacrifices He was asking. Then, as in the days of my childhood, I cried out: My God "I choose all!" I don't want to be a saint by halves. I choose all that you will!* (SS 27). Compromise or mediocrity was not an option (cf. GC II 1133).

Thérèse even as a child wanted to be a saint, but during the next years another important awareness would break in upon her. She would progressively understand that her striving to be good could hide a tendency toward self-centered willfulness. She became aware not only that her willpower could be misdirected in terms of what she actually chose, but that even by choosing good she could be on the wrong path if she willfully chose good in a self-centered or self-righteous way. The very act of willpower even directed toward sanctity, she understood, could be tainted by the self-love that could drive her to try to make herself the saint she wanted to be rather than allowing God to make her the saint she was created to be. She recognized that in the use of her willpower she could sometimes be self-serving or even violent to herself or others in her efforts to be good. She was beginning to glimpse that holiness, while needing her cooperation, was really a matter of God's doing.

CHAPTER 5

It's Pauline Who Will Be My Mamma!

In her family life, through all her ordinary experiences, Thérèse was being prepared for a way of envisioning and relating to God that she would later find validated in the Scriptures themselves. The elements that she found in her family and that she would integrate as part of her way of spirituality included confidence in divine love, generosity and concern for others, patience, kindness, truth, simplicity, detachment, fidelity in small things, trust, and gratitude. Above all, she was learning silently and imperceptibly that divine love and mercy were more than she could have ever imagined. She would need the strength of this truth in the disturbing months ahead.

Zélie's health continued to deteriorate, especially after the early weeks of 1877. Thérèse could only stand by helpless. Then Thérèse's aunt, Sr. Marie-Dosithée, died in February. The last time Zélie spoke to her dying sister, she asked her prayers for herself, knowing that she too was not far from death. She also asked her sister to pray for Thérèse and the family, but especially for Léonie, who had become more and more withdrawn, moody, and recalcitrant during the last several months.

A few weeks after Sr. Marie-Dosithée's death, as if in answer to prayer, but specifically due to the vigilance and detective work of Marie, the most significant factor contributing to Léonie's intractable behavior was discovered. The Martins' maid, Louise, in attempting to gain control over the turbulent Léonie, had for many months been secretly terrorizing her, doing physical and emotional violence to the naturally sensitive thirteen-year-old child. Louise was at once confronted, corrected, and informed of her dismissal. Only her display of sincere repentance, her previous fidelity, and her willingness to assist Zélie as she became increasingly ill gave her a brief reprieve.

Zélie was greatly disappointed in Louise and felt betrayed, but she managed to control the maid's behavior, to forgive her, and to continue to bring out the best in her. Thérèse must have noticed, but, of course, couldn't have fully understood the implications of the fact that her mother and the family handled this difficult situation with truth, love, and justice rather than with retaliation. Her mother's way of strength and charity would resonate with Thérèse's own way of addressing some troublesome personalities years later.

Louise was dismissed after Zélie's death but always retained a respect for Zélie and the Martin family.

Léonie had responded to Louise's violence to her by bonding with her victimizer and becoming increasingly dependent on her, while being deceptive and rebellious with her family. Once Louise's behavior ended and Léonie was safely enveloped in the family's acceptance, and particularly in Zélie's motherly tenderness, the young child began to change immediately. Within weeks Léonie's true expansive and generous personality began to emerge. Her transformation became a deeply consoling grace for Zélie in her final days.

Now knowing that only a miracle could save her, Zélie embarked on a pilgrimage to the shrine of the Blessed Mother at Lourdes with Marie, Pauline, and a more-cooperative and peaceful Léonie. Almost nothing, however, went well on the trip; delays and mishaps of all kinds conspired to make the journey totally unpleasant. As for the experience at the shrine itself, it was to no avail. The sufferings Zélie endured while on the pilgrimage may have even hastened her death.

Zélie's pain increased during the next two months, and the doctor could prescribe no treatment. She was almost forty-six years old. Having a great capacity for self-denial and endurance, Zélie did not complain, making as little disturbance as possible for the family as her condition grew worse. In the final weeks of her life, she took a remote room in the home so that her sobs could not be heard by the family at night. In the early morning hours of August 28, 1877, Zélie passed away. At the age of four and a half, Thérèse had lost her mother, the foundation of her life.

Even though Thérèse and Céline had spent time during the final days of their mother's life at a relative's house and so had been sheltered from the details of their mother's condition, the reality of their mother's impending death preoccupied them. They attended the ceremony of the last anointing, and Thérèse witnessed her father's sobbing. Thérèse felt terror as the foundations of her life began to shift. In the arms of her father, she kissed the cold forehead of her mother, but, *I don't recall having cried very much, neither did I speak to anyone about the feelings I experienced. I looked and listened in silence. No one had any time to pay any attention to me* (SS 33).

In losing her mother and momentarily not feeling securely held by the family, Thérèse was deeply hurt in three areas of her heart. The death of her mother evoked all the child's earlier feelings of separation and being abandoned; at the same time, Thérèse experienced a certain loss of self-confidence and was plunged into the darkness of personal insecurity and melancholy. In addition, she was enveloped in a shadowy fear of the mystery of death. Each of these areas would take years to heal.

Her mother's passing was a decisive turning point in Thérèse's life. The childhood years before her mother's death were the foundation of her life. She had opened to life with a sense of spontaneity and joy. Everything smiled at her, and in delight she smiled back. She overflowed with energy, humor, and playfulness. She was "the little imp," "the monkey," "the little demon." In the loving care of her family, she had grown quickly, physically, intellectually, and spiritually.

Her mother's death ended Thérèse's early period of self-confidence and pervading joy. *My happy disposition completely changed after Mamma's death. I, once so full of life, became timid and retiring, sensitive to an excessive degree. One look was enough to reduce me to tears, and the only way I was content was to be left alone completely* (SS 34–35). Feelings of loss and separation that had somewhat quieted during the last years again erupted in her, and sorrow filled her heart.

Thérèse now turned inward to calm her feelings and to find her way. She became timid, shy, and retiring, entering into a state of melancholy and excessive sensitivity that she later would call *the winter of my soul*. The spontaneous joy and peace that had filled Thérèse's early years were covered over with a misty cloud of sadness. Everything—a look, a word—made her cry as she began the second period of her life, *the most painful of the three*, Thérèse remembered. *This period extends from the age of four and a half to that of fourteen, the time when I found once again my childhood character* (SS 34).

With her mother's passing, Thérèse had the immediate need to relate to someone who would provide the warmth and security, the affirmation and caring of a mother—someone who would not leave her again. Following the funeral Mass, the day after Zélie's death, the five Martin daughters were gathered in sorrow. Louise, still present in the household, turned to Céline and Thérèse and said, "Poor little things, you have no mother any more!"

Céline responded by throwing her arms around Marie, saying, "Well, you will be my Mamma!" Accustomed to following Céline's example, Thérèse threw herself into Pauline's arms, crying, *Well, as for me, it's Pauline who will be my Mamma!* (SS 34). The importance of this exchange for Thérèse cannot be overestimated. Although Marie, Thérèse's godmother, would continue to play an important role as Thérèse's life unfolded, Pauline would emerge as the main focus of Thérèse's attention and the major formative influence in her life.

Apparently Louis Martin had not been present at this bonding ritual between his daughters, and Léonie had remained withdrawn—perhaps intimidated by the presence of Louise. Shortly before Zélie's death, however, Marie had promised her that she would especially look after Léonie, and in this Léonie was blessed.

Louis was tremendously grieved by his wife's death; shattered in his sense of stability, he felt isolated and overburdened. Although he was courageous and forthright, assertiveness had never been his natural tendency, and his leadership role in the family took the form of a *truly maternal love,* as Thérèse expressed it (SS 35).

Now fifty-four years old and with five children to raise, Louis agreed, on the advice of Marie and Pauline, to follow the recommendation of Zélie's brother, Isidore Guérin, and his wife, Céline. He quickly took steps to sell the lace business and move his family to Lisieux, where he would be near the Guérins. He had hoped not to leave his friends in Alençon, but he knew that the proximity of the two families would provide support for his daughters and himself.

In Lisieux, through the efforts of Isidore, Louis leased a house near the Guérin home. Isidore and his wife, together with their two daughters, Jeanne, nine years old, and Marie, seven, welcomed the Martin family to Lisieux in November. The two families became very close, with much visiting back and forth as well as vacationing together. Marie Guérin, although almost three years older than Thérèse, became a companion for Thérèse, particularly when they later attended school together.

Years later Thérèse remembered that she *experienced no regrets whatsoever at leaving Alençon; . . . and it was with pleasure* that she moved with the family to Lisieux (SS 35). The entire Martin family delighted in "Les Buissonnets," as the girls called the three-floor spacious house with four bedrooms, three attics, and a belvedere on the third floor that had a beautiful view overlooking Lisieux. Situated adjacent to a park and surrounded by a wall, the property had many beautiful trees, an English garden in front, and a large vegetable garden in the back, with a laundry, a shed, and a greenhouse. The belvedere became Louis' study and a place where Thérèse and Céline would later sometimes sit to talk, sharing their friendship while gazing over the town and at the evening sky.

Thérèse, who now *could not bear the company of strangers,* found her joy *only within the intimacy of the family* (SS 35). Her life continued to be sheltered by the love of her sisters and father as the family slowly adjusted to Zélie's absence. Louis gladly allowed Marie, seventeen, and Pauline, sixteen, to become the household managers and the parental figures for Céline and Thérèse. Thérèse became her father's little queen, and he, her admirable king. Even though emotionally Thérèse continued to experience a pervading sense of melancholy and shyness, intellectually she developed considerably in the next months. Léonie remained in the background as life returned to normal and the family adopted a daily and weekly routine.

Marie and Pauline extended their role as the resident tutors for Céline and Thérèse, while Louis presided and distributed prizes at the various academic rituals and ceremonies that the elder daughters devised. *I enjoyed no great facility in learning,* Thérèse later recalled with some false modesty, for even earlier she had outpaced Céline in grasping concepts. *I did have a very good memory,* Thérèse acknowledged. *Catechism and sacred history were my favorite subjects and these I studied with joy. Grammar frequently caused me to shed many tears* (SS 36).

Later Thérèse remembered that it was at this time that she first understood a sermon on Christ's passion delivered during a Mass that she attended with her father. It was also during this period that, on one of her many afternoon walks with her father, Thérèse noticed a man with crutches. Prompted by her father, and with her own feelings of sensitivity and compassion, she offered the man alms. He would not take the coin, so in her heart Thérèse promised to pray for him on her First Communion day, a day, she had been told, on which all prayers were answered. *I said, "I'll pray for this poor man on the day of my First Communion." I kept my promise five years later, and I hope that God answered the prayer he inspired me to direct to Him in favor of one of his suffering members* (SS 38).

Thérèse was by nature a very sensitive, compassionate, and self-aware child. She had never been robbed of her feelings by her parents or her sisters; her feeling had not been diminished or disrespected, and they played a significant role in the way she experienced life. In addition to the ordinary sensitivities of any young child, feelings of anxiety often evoked by deeper feelings of separation and being abandoned were common with Thérèse in her early years and throughout her life. As she matured, however, she was able to manage her feelings with more and more self-awareness and self-discipline, finally putting them in dialogue with faith. In the context of awareness and faith, her feelings became a way of self-knowledge and spiritual growth.

CHAPTER 6

This Time I Had No Repentance

As a child Thérèse most often responded with tears to her anxiety around separation or to the frustration of not getting her way. At first her frustration took the form of childhood tantrums; later, on occasion, her anxiety and frustrated feelings evoked excessive anger that simply overwhelmed her. One such occurrence involved Victoire Pasquier, the young maid her father had employed to assist the older girls in the management of the home after the dismissal of Louise and the family's move to Lisieux.

Thérèse seems to have usually gotten along well with Victoire. They had a fondness for one another, and Thérèse records two instances when Victoire rescued her from minor predicaments. One time when Victoire was ironing the family laundry and Thérèse was swinging on a chair, the chair slipped and she fell into the bucket of water that Victoire was using to sprinkle the pieces. Thérèse was so wedged into the bucket that Victoire had to extricate her. Humorously recalling the incident Thérèse wrote, *I filled the bucket like a little chick fills an eggshell!* (SS 40). On another occasion Thérèse fell into the cool ashes of the fireplace, and Victoire again rescued her. Later Thérèse also saw a good bit of humor in the situation.

But one time just after the family had moved into Les Buissonnets, she had an encounter with Victoire in which she found no humor at all. Thérèse, about five years old, was completely overcome by her angry feelings, losing her temper, and replicating one of her baby tantrums.

At the time Thérèse was too young to join her older sisters as they attended the May devotions in the parish church in honor of Mary. With the family out of the house, Thérèse was in charge, having her own way and enjoying her power as queen of the scene. She customarily performed her own religious devotions to the Blessed Mother at the altar she had set up at home. Victoire would sometimes accompany Thérèse in these devotions and would occasionally delight Thérèse by further dressing the altar with little candle stubs.

On this occasion Thérèse had meticulously arranged her May altar with the little statue of Mary, little flowerpots, and candlesticks. She began the service by lighting the two tapers on the altar and asking Victoire to begin saying the Memorare. The tapers were small and precious, and the prayer had to be said while the candles were burning. Victoire pretended to begin the prayer, then fussed with this and that and began to laugh as Thérèse watched her *precious tapers burning away rapidly* (SS 39). Thérèse herself began to burn. She again tried in vain to get Victoire to start reciting the prayer. Victoire just kept giggling. That was when anger and frustration overcame Thérèse, and she completely lost control.

Then rising from my knees, Thérèse remembered, *I shouted at her and told her she was very wicked. Laying aside my customary gentleness, I stamped my foot with all my might. Poor Victoire stopped laughing. She looked at me in amazement and then showed me the two candle stubs she'd brought along* (SS 39). Victoire had been playing a little game with Thérèse, and Thérèse was furious.

The enormity of Thérèse's anger must have surprised even herself. She may have thought she had gotten over the power of the angry feelings that had moved her into the frightful tantrums of her first years, but clearly she had not. After she had calmed down, Thérèse *poured out tears of repentance, having a firm purpose of not doing it again! I committed a fault which merits the penalty of being confessed. It gave me good reason to humble myself* (SS 39). The experience taught her that feelings of distress and anger could become so strong in her that they could control her, driving her in a compulsive way into an action that needed repentance.

Immediately after telling this story about Victoire in her manuscript, *Story of a Soul,* Thérèse recounts another incident that is even more revealing about her self-awareness as a child and her capacity to deal with her feelings.

This experience also involved Victoire, and it again resulted in anger on Thérèse's part. She wrote about the incident some seventeen years later with a certain delight in remembering how little Thérèse, her energy of will fortified with anger, calmly acted with a degree of childhood creativity to address the situation:

Another time there was another incident with Victoire, but this time I had no repentance because I had kept calm. I wanted an ink stand which was on the shelf of the fireplace in the kitchen; being too little to take it down, I very nicely asked Victoire to give it to me, but she refused telling me to get up on a chair. I took a chair without saying a word but think-

ing she wasn't too nice; wanting to make her feel it, I searched out in my little head what offended me the most. She often called me "a little brat" when she was annoyed at me and this humbled me very much. So before jumping off my chair, I turned around with dignity and said: "Victoire, you are a brat!" Then I made my escape, leaving her to meditate on the profound statement I had just made. (SS 39)

The child Thérèse knew that Victoire would now be offended and angry, and that Victoire herself would act in a driven, compulsive way. Little Thérèse could easily predict that Victoire would report her to her older sister. *The result wasn't long in coming, for soon I heard her shouting: "M'amz'elle Marie, Thérèse just called me a brat!" Marie came and made me ask pardon.* Thérèse, of course, obeyed Marie and did not try to justify herself or act in any deceptive or blaming way. So she apologized, but added in recounting the incident, *and I did so without having contrition* (SS 39).

On this occasion the child Thérèse knew that she did not need to repent. She had legitimate anger, and the anger did not cause her to lose her true self. The energy of her appropriate anger had not become excessive, and she had not become driven or compulsive. She had retained her inner freedom. She had acted even with some humor and creativity, if also with some rudeness. She had learned that she could deal with difficult feelings, stand her ground emotionally, and be true to herself even if it meant displeasing someone.

In the first incident with Victoire, Thérèse had known when she had let her anger get out of hand. In the second incident, she knew that she could act with anger in a way that was not a fault needing contrition. Remembering this second incident many years later, she added, delighting in the energy of little Thérèse, *I thought that if Victoire didn't want to stretch her big arm to do me a little service, she merited the title, brat* (SS 39). Thérèse in her maturity could not fault the intuitions of the little child.

Three months later, in August, Thérèse would have another emotional experience that she remembered with some delight. Now just one year after her mother's death, she and the Martin family spent the summer holidays with the Guérin family at the seaside resort of Trouville, where Uncle Isidore had leased a villa.

One day as the five-and-a-half-year-old Thérèse walked with her father on the seashore, she noticed that a man and a woman nearby were look-

ing at her. As I ran ahead of Papa they came and asked him if I were his little daughter and said I was a very pretty little girl. Papa said "Yes," but I noticed the sign he made to them not to pay me any compliments. It was the first time I'd heard it said I was pretty and this pleased me as I didn't think I was (SS 48).

The family had avoided complimenting Thérèse on her beauty as a child to avoid promoting any kind of vanity. Now she got a glimpse of knowing that although she may have been loved by the goodness of her parents into being the little queen, she was also beautiful and lovable in herself, and that to be lovable in oneself was a grace and not necessarily a reason for pride. The compliments of the strangers did not evoke vanity in Thérèse, but she was certainly delighted at knowing that she had been given spontaneous attention and had pleased someone simply by her own beauty.

Besides knowing her beauty for the first time, this walk with her father also provided her with a vision of the sea for the first time.

Never will I forget the impression the sea made upon me; I couldn't take my eyes off it since its majesty, the roaring of its waves, everything spoke to my soul of God's grandeur and power. . . . In the evening at that moment when the sun seems to bathe itself in the immensity of the waves, leaving a luminous trail behind, I went and sat down on a huge rock with Pauline. . . . I contemplated this luminous trail for a long time. It was to me the image of God's grace shedding its light across the path the little white-sailed vessel had to travel. And near Pauline, I made the resolution never to wander far away from the glance of Jesus in order to travel peacefully towards the eternal shore! (SS 48–49)

The image of the vast, majestic sea became an image of life itself for Thérèse. She was in a small boat, often alone, on this vast majestic expanse traveling toward a shore she could not see, following that luminous trail.

I repeated these words which always gave rise to a new peace and strength in my heart: "Life is your barque not your home!" When very little, these words gave me courage, and even now, in spite of the years which have put to flight so many impressions of childish piety, the image of the barque still charms my soul and helps it put up with its exile. Doesn't Wisdom say: "Life is like a ship that plows the restless waves and leaves after it no trace of its rapid passage"? [Wisdom 5:10]. *When I think of these things, my soul is plunged into infinity, and it seems to me it already touches the eternal shore.* (SS 87)

All nature enthralled her. During an evening walk with her "king" she had seen the stars forming the letter T. *I pointed them out to Papa and told him my name was written in heaven* (SS 43). This may have been an occasion for some feelings of vanity, but also of another grace, because she immediately knew that while the T was special to her, *the star-studded firmament* was the work of the Creator and deserved her awe and contemplation.

Thérèse found a sanctuary in the wide, open spaces as she listened to the murmuring of the wind in the gigantic fir trees, admired the clouds, and even delighted in the flash of lightning. She cultivated little flowers in the front garden, and she loved going alone to visit the wildflowers in the field.

After her home classes in the afternoons, Thérèse walked with her father to visit the Blessed Sacrament, going to a different church each day. They also walked together in the countryside, and on his serious fishing ventures, she sat beside him, casting her own little line into the stream. Sometimes she wandered off into the wildflowers and simply sat and thought. She was becoming closer and closer to her father, treasuring his motherlike love. As king and little queen they lived in complete harmony. That was a great consolation for Thérèse, but even her relationship with her father could only occasionally pull her out of her pervading mood of melancholy.

Withdrawing at times even from her king as he sat fishing to be silent by herself, Thérèse remained sad, isolated, and brooding. She remembered that when she took *the lunch I had brought in my little basket, the beautiful bread and jam . . . had changed its appearance; instead of the lively colors it had earlier, I now saw only a light rosy tint and the bread had become old and crumbled. Earth again seemed a sad place and I understood that in heaven alone joy will be without any clouds* (SS 37). Life, Thérèse was understanding, was filled with disappointments.

When she was six years old, Thérèse had an experience that deeply disturbed her and brought to the surface once again feelings of loss and separation, this time about her father. He was on a business trip to Alençon and was not expected to return for several days. The afternoon was bright, and

Thérèse was looking pensively out from the attic window of her room onto the large garden area below. She saw a man dressed exactly like her father, wearing a hat similar to his, and having his same build and gait. But the man was old and stooped, and had a cloth covering his face, so she could not recognize him. *Immediately a feeling of supernatural fright invaded my soul, but in an instant I reflected that surely Papa had returned and was hiding to surprise me; then I called out very loudly* (SS 46). The figure appeared not to hear and continued to walk through the garden, passed behind some shrubbery and trees, and disappeared.

Thérèse cried out in alarm and fear. She, Marie, and Victoire searched the area but found no one. The vision resurrected her feelings of separation and being abandoned. Was she going to lose her father also? Anxiety, insecurity, and melancholy were ever present just under the surface. She needed desperately to hold on to her father.

Thérèse (right) at eight years old with her sister
Céline in 1881

CHAPTER 7

I Too Will Be a Religious

At eight and a half, Thérèse entered the Benedictine Abbey school as a day student. *I have often heard it said that the time spent at school is the best and happiest of one's life. It wasn't this way for me,* she recalled (SS 53). Up until this time she had been homeschooled by Pauline and Marie. With her quick intellect, she had delighted in learning in the security of home, spontaneously interacting with her sisters. Now at the abbey school in her state of timidity and melancholy, Thérèse was overwhelmed by the imposing manner of her peers. She was the youngest among her classmates and intellectually could match and excel any of them. She won all the academic prizes, but she did not have the social skills that she needed.

Thérèse had never before associated for any extended period with peers who were not preselected by her family. She had no experience playing rough playground games; no practice in the give-and-take of childhood banter and teasing. These interactions with her classmates were the first time she experienced outright petty malice and cruelty. She was not prepared for the jealousy and bullying that she encountered. *I didn't know how to defend myself,* she remembered, *and was content to cry without saying a word and without complaining* (SS 53).

Thérèse was a goldfish among the sharks. One of her classmates, she remembered, *was about thirteen or fourteen and she wasn't too intelligent, but she was really adept at influencing the students and even the teachers. When she noticed I was so young, almost always first in the class, and loved by all the Sisters, she experienced a jealousy pardonable in a student. She made me pay in a thousand ways for my little successes* (SS 53).

In this setting her sisters Pauline, Léonie, and Marie were not present to be supportive. Now Thérèse leaned for help mainly on Céline, who together with their cousins Jeanne and Marie Guérin, also attended the school. Céline *was always a ray of sunshine for me,* Thérèse remembered, *giving me much joy and consolation. Who can say with what intrepidity she defended me at the Abbey when I was accused of something?* (SS 55).

Thérèse's survival style of getting close to people by pleasing them did not, could not, work with classmates who simply would not be pleased by her. She could not engage in their kind of behavior; she preferred helping the younger children, or burying dead birds, or telling stories. She was shy; they were boisterous. She was obedient and reserved; they were aggressive and mischievous. She may have seemed to them as a kind of silent reproach to some of their conduct. Her strategies of personal relationships utterly failed.

She continued to do well academically. She had all the right answers in the formal setting of the classroom, but all the wrong moves in her social interactions. All she could do was endure, bearing the emotional pain. She was beginning to learn just how naturally sensitive, self-conscious, and self-centered she really was. She could not, as her classmates so easily could, deflect with an emotional shrug the thoughtless comments, the teasing banter, or the pointed remark. She could not demand her rights or counter a sharp retort. She scanned everything with an emotional sensitivity and evaluated in a personal way every comment and gesture of her classmates.

At the same time, Thérèse was learning another truth: for all her inner weakness, she was capable of enduring great emotional pain and distress. She was tapping a deep reservoir of inner strength, courage, and endurance that she had not touched before. She could, at a deep personal level of integrity, stand her ground against the battering that, for a lesser person, would have resulted in outbursts of violent anger and lingering resentment.

But this awareness of inner strength developing secretly in her soul did not lessen the emotional suffering and weakness she was experiencing. If it had not been for the presence and support of Céline and the companionship of her cousin Marie, Thérèse would not have been able to remain at the school. She knew that she would have simply become sick, so difficult was the stress. *The five years I spent in school were the saddest in my life* (SS 53).

Thérèse returned home at the end of each school day to the safety and security of the family. Her father was there to praise her and to lavish affection on her, and her heart expanded. Yet she never shared with him her struggles at the school, perhaps because, following the example of her mother, she did not want to disturb him. But there was certainly another reason as well. By the influence of sheer grace, Thérèse, when she was five, had adopted a religious attitude that she noticed glowing in the gospel account of the life of Mary and Joseph—the same attitude she also saw glimmering in the lives of her own parents. She had decided at that time that she would never complain about anything, even when things were taken from her or when she was accused unjustly (cf. SS 30).

Although Thérèse herself considered this disposition as having little merit since usually it did not cost her much; it was an attitude that contributed enormously to her blossoming pleasant and agreeable disposition. Years later in the convent of Carmel, Thérèse' ability to manage the arbitrariness of the nuns with this uncomplaining, nonaccusatory, and nondemanding disposition made her presence a balm amid the difficult relationships that arose among them. Sometimes it contributed to making her appear Pollyannaish, and having *a weak character*, but it was an important religious disposition that opened her to the graces of humility, detachment, and self-forgetfulness, which she needed so badly and which grew to eventually become the fundamental virtues in her life (SS 91).

She was now applying this religious disposition in recounting to her father the events of the school day. She did not complain about her classmates nor did she let their poor behavior become a source of justification for a sense of self-righteousness. This attitude demanded of her enormous vigilance, courage, and inner strength.

She was uncomplaining and nonaccusatory even as she talked with her sisters Marie and Pauline about the school day. Céline could not be with Thérèse much of the time at school and so she failed to grasp how disturbing the situation was for her little sister. Thérèse began to have a physical reaction to the stress. She began to get severe and prolonged headaches.

A little less than a year after Thérèse had entered the school, and while the stress of the situation was at its most intense, an event occurred that disturbed her supportive relationship with Pauline and evoked again the lingering feelings of separation, being abandoned, and mother-loss. Thérèse thought that she had had a mutual understanding with Pauline that the two of them would someday go together to a *far-away desert place* and become hermits. To her little sister's silly scheme Pauline had *answered that my desire was also hers*, Thérèse remembered, *and that she was waiting for me to be big enough for her to leave* (SS 57).

Pauline's answer had meant almost nothing to herself, but to Thérèse it had been a solemn promise as well as a maternal endorsement of her childish desire. So when she overheard Pauline telling Marie that she was going to enter the Carmelite cloistered community, although Thérèse did not know exactly what Pauline meant, she did know that her "second mother" was abandoning her. Thérèse was filled with anguish. She understood in an instant, again under the influence of sheer grace, that life was nothing but one continual suffering and separation. She shed bitter tears. *It was as if a sword were buried in my heart*, she remembered sadly (SS 58).

Attempting to comfort Thérèse with descriptions of the cloistered convent, Pauline managed to help her little sister imagine that Carmel was the real *desert where God wanted me to go also to hide myself. . . . I felt this with so much force*, Thérèse later recounted, *that there wasn't the least doubt in my heart; it was not the dream of a child led astray but the certitude of a divine call; I wanted to go to Carmel not for Pauline's sake but for Jesus alone* (SS 58).

Thérèse was convinced that she was experiencing a real call from God. Even as early as the age of three, when she had heard Pauline then talking about becoming a religious, she had thought, *I too will be a religious.* At that time, she had not known fully what that meant, but now things were clearer. She knew that she wanted to enter Carmel as soon as possible—and *for Jesus alone.* A great peace filled her soul.

Even Pauline now agreed that her little sister might have a budding vocation and, wanting to further console her, took her to visit the mother superior of Carmel. A cultured woman and immediately attractive to Thérèse, Mother Marie de Gonzague quickly put the young girl at ease. She believed that the grace of a religious vocation could be given to a nine-and-a-half-year-old child, and she concurred that Thérèse should continue to nourish her desire. Thérèse felt a glimmer of joy. To add to her delight, *it was on this day I received compliments for the second time.* One of the sisters of the convent, Thérèse remembered, *did not hesitate to say that I was pretty* (SS 59).

Thérèse's sense of her own vocation did not diminish the pain of losing Pauline. Thérèse had not wept at her own mother's death, yet now, during the days before Pauline's departure, she wept continually. She imagined that her world was again crumbling around her. She was actually astonished that the sun was still shining. Only Thérèse's deep, latent feelings of being abandoned and separated, together with her very sensitive nature, would have had the power to evoke such images.

During the next months when she visited Pauline in Carmel, Thérèse's feelings of mother-loss and grief resurfaced. Always accompanied by her family during these visits in the convent parlor, she never had an opportunity to personally reconnect with Pauline, the "mother" she had chosen for herself. Marie, who monopolized most of the conversations during the visits, remembered that during one visit when no one was paying any attention to her, Thérèse said in a kind of sorrowful desperation, *Look, Pauline, I'm wearing the little skirt that you made for me* (GC I 151, note 2). But Marie continued talking, and no one took notice.

Thérèse's heart felt like it was continually breaking. She believed that *Pauline is lost to me*, and over the months and years came to experience Pauline's absence *almost in the same manner as if she were dead* (SS 60, 88). For the third time she had lost a mother figure; an intimate maternal bonding had been severed.

At this time another interaction with her sister Marie proved distressing to Thérèse. Her father had invited Céline to take art lessons from a private tutor. Thérèse was present, and Céline saw her little sister's eyes light up, hoping to be invited also. Turning to Thérèse, her father said, "and you, my little queen, would you like to learn how to draw?" Céline remembered that Thérèse was about to answer when Marie thoughtlessly interrupted and said, "That would be a waste of money, Thérèse has not got the same aptitude as Céline" (*St. Thérèse of Lisieux by Those Who Knew Her*, edited and translated by Christopher O'Mahony, 97); and besides, the house "was already cluttered with 'smearings' that had to be framed" (GC I 210). Louis, distracted, did not pursue his invitation to Thérèse, and she never pressed her case. Thérèse later remembered that she had such a strong desire to complain that, even many years afterward, she wondered how she managed to say nothing.

Under the pressure of the situation at school, Thérèse became impatient with Marie, and Céline found her "excessively teary." Now, with her increasing headaches, she began to have occasional cases of insomnia. Her distress was taking a serious emotional and physical toll.

CHAPTER 8

I Had Seen Her Smile at Me

Six months after Pauline had entered Carmel, during the school recess at Easter time, ten-year-old Thérèse was staying with Céline at their cousins' home. Their father had taken his older daughters Marie and Léonie with him on a trip to Paris. On previous occasions when Thérèse had stayed at the Guérins', she had especially enjoyed the company of her cousin Marie, who was so supportive to her at school. But during this visit when Thérèse tried to draw close to her aunt by calling her *Mamma,* Marie thoughtlessly shot back: "My Mamma is not your Mamma; you don't have one anymore." Thérèse was stunned and fell silent (FGM 165; cf. STL 178).

A little later during that same visit, Uncle Isidore asked Thérèse to go for a walk. Although Thérèse knew that her uncle had a deep fondness for her—*he used to call me his little ray of sunshine,* she remembered—she never seemed to feel completely at ease in his presence, and *I didn't like it when he asked me questions* (SS 42). She found him to be brusque at times and blunt, so unlike her mild father. Her father would take her on his lap, gently rock her, and sing *in his beautiful voice, airs that filled the soul with profound thoughts* (SS 43). Isidore, she remembered, placed *me on his knee and sang Blue Beard in a formidable tone of voice* that scared her half to death (SS 42). *He frightened me,* Thérèse wrote, and actually his outspokenness sometimes even frightened her father as well (SS 35). Isidore, meanwhile, thought that Thérèse was weak and sentimental. She was embarrassed by this assessment.

They had not gone far on their walk when Isidore spoke about his sister, Thérèse's mother. Thérèse, recalling the memories of her mother, who had died a little less than six years before, and having just lost Pauline, her other "mother," began to weep uncontrollably. Her uncle was both alarmed and irritated by Thérèse's crying and told her that she was too softhearted. He also announced that he would help her overcome her brooding and melancholy.

Her uncle proclaimed, Thérèse remembered, *that I needed a lot of distraction, and he was determined to give us a good time during our Easter vacation. He and Aunt would see to it* (SS 60). Isidore had decided that that very evening he would take Thérèse, Céline, and his own daughters to the Catholic Circle meeting for some socializing, music, and dancing.

Socializing, music, and dancing were the last things that Thérèse felt she needed in her present state of disturbance and at this time of her growing desire to enter the convent. And, although over the years she had tried to cope with the trauma of losing her mother, and although she was doing her best to adjust to having just lost her mother-substitute, apparently for her uncle her efforts were not good enough. This last year and a half at the abbey school had been emotionally difficult for her. She felt inadequate in that situation, and now she was physically enduring the distress of constant headaches and frequent insomnia. She was sad, deeply sad, and confused. In her emotionally weakened condition, she believed that by upsetting her uncle her inadequacy had been further confirmed. She was a failure by just being herself.

Thérèse was finding that her strategy of overcoming her feelings of loss and separation by pleasing others was not working. It had not worked with her classmates; it had not even worked when she had just tried to get close to her aunt, and now she was displeasing her uncle. She was beginning to lose confidence in her ability to cope. Her joy as a child that had so empowered her and brought her such affirmation before her mother's death had dried up. She recognized that she was being dominated by anxiety and melancholy. She knew that she was brooding and isolated. She knew that she needed help.

Giving her life to God in Carmel and moving out of the school situation would in some way help her regain herself. Intuitively Thérèse sensed, however, that what would not help her at this time were socializing, music, and dancing to "distract" herself. She felt herself sinking into a quagmire and knew that she needed to protect herself from her uncle's ill-conceived plan.

That night, just before the family was to leave for the social event, Thérèse became physically ill. Instead of going to the Catholic Circle, she had to be taken to bed. Her feelings had gotten the better of her. She fell into a state of nervous trembling that lasted throughout most of the night.

The next day Dr. Notta was called to her bedside. He ruled out hysteria and very tentatively diagnosed the disease as St. Vitus' Dance or chorea. He announced that Thérèse's condition, quickly deteriorating, might actually be fatal.

Whatever the disease was, and whatever its organic basis, Thérèse's illness was certainly brought on by the lingering unresolved disturbance of her mother's death, the overwhelming anxiety she was experiencing with the loss of Pauline, the excessive tension and self-doubt in the school situation, the uncertainty she felt about how she needed to act to best please her beloved Lord, and then the upsetting intrusion of her uncle.

Thérèse's father and sisters were called back from their trip, and Thérèse overheard her king being told that his little queen was either going crazy or was going to die. Thérèse was terrified. But remarkably, she knew that, although she was sometimes delirious, she was not losing her mind; moreover, she knew that she would be able to attend the ceremony about a week away at which Pauline would receive the habit of Carmel.

Thérèse did, in fact, recover enough to participate at Pauline's ceremony. However, the very next day she had a relapse, and the illness lasted into the next month. During this time Thérèse found healing in receiving gifts from Pauline, particularly in a doll dressed as a Carmelite. But Uncle Isidore *wasn't too happy, and said that instead of making me think of Carmel, it would be better to remove it from my mind. I am quite convinced, on the contrary,* she remembered, *that the thought of one day becoming a Carmelite made me live* (SS 64).

Marie, replacing Pauline as Thérèse's mother figure and staying long hours at her bedside during the following weeks, recalled that Thérèse would sometimes tumble out of her bed in what seemed to be acts of self-violence. She had seizures of nervous trembling and hallucinations, sometimes would try to speak and be unable to emit a sound, and sometimes would clench her teeth and refuse to eat (cf. GC I 162).

In her complete emotional and physical distress, Thérèse herself recalled that she *appeared to be almost always delirious, saying things that had no meaning.* She knew that *a miracle was necessary for my cure* (SS 62, 65).

Six weeks after the onslaught of the illness, on the feast of Pentecost, the Martin sisters gathered around Thérèse's bed, praying before the family statue of the Our Lady of Victories, the statue before which their mother had prayed often during her life. Thérèse remembered the scene vividly:

All of a sudden the Blessed Virgin appeared beautiful to me, so beautiful that never had I seen anything so attractive; her face was suffused with an ineffable benevolence and tenderness, but what penetrated to the very depths of my soul was the ravishing smile of the Blessed Virgin. At that instant, all my pain disappeared.

The miracle that Thérèse had needed happened, *and it was Our Lady of Victories who performed it* (SS 65–66).

Marie, who was at the bedside, testified later that "I saw Thérèse all of a sudden staring at the statue; her look was radiant. I understood she was restored, that she was looking not at the image of Mary but at the Blessed Virgin herself. She remained in ecstasy for four or five minutes" (GC I 173, note 1).

Thérèse was cured. Instantly all her physical and emotional symptoms simply vanished, and she returned to normal life. The family and the doctor were amazed.

Immediately after feeling the joy of the Blessed Virgin's smile, even as she continued to lie quietly in bed, Thérèse had an important awareness. *Ah! I thought, the Blessed Virgin smiled at me, how happy I am, but never will I tell anyone for my happiness would then disappear* (SS 66). Knowing at once in the depths of her heart that her healing was a private, personal, and intimate exchange between the Blessed Virgin and herself, Thérèse also knew it was not meant to be shared in any detail with her family. It simply was no one else's concern. She needed to protect this experience from prying and curious eyes in order to respect it and properly understand and value it.

Marie had been kneeling beside Thérèse's bed as the healing happened but did not know exactly what had occurred. Overjoyed at Thérèse sudden return to life, she had cried out, "Thérèse is cured!" Later when Marie was alone with her little sister, she asked her out of curiosity to share details of the moment of the cure, because she had sensed that something had passed between Thérèse and the Blessed Virgin.

Although she knew that she was going against the voice of her heart that clearly told her to hold the experience in confidence, the strong-willed, stubborn Thérèse let her feelings of needing to please Marie get the better of her: *I was unable to resist her very tender and pressing questions* (SS 66). She could not refuse Marie, who had been her "mother" throughout the illness, who had prayed for her recovery, and whom she needed close in her life. She could hold her ground in anger with Victoire, but she could not hold her ground in integrity with Marie. Thérèse revealed to her what had happened, and under further prodding agreed to Marie's desire to share the secret with Pauline and all the sisters in the Carmelite convent.

Thérèse knew immediately that she had failed herself, and she came to feel that Marie in some way, without malice, had ceased to protect her as a mother and in a sense had abandoned her.

The sisters of Carmel, on hearing of Thérèse's experience, wanted to know all about the Virgin. Was she carrying the Christ Child? Was she covered with light? Thérèse was deeply troubled at these questions. They were irrelevant and intrusive. All she knew was that *the Blessed Virgin had appeared very beautiful, and I had seen her smile at me* (SS 67).

Without the protection of a mother, Thérèse was being lured into an arena of the spectacular, and she knew there was something false about it. She was being subtly invited into some kind of specialness that was untrue and seductive. The entire matter was becoming an occasion for self-centeredness and self-indulgence. This intimate personal experience was being made the focus of a voyeuristic crowd.

Certain now that she should have listened to her heart and kept all this to herself, Thérèse fell into a state of distressful self-doubt and anxiety about the illness and the cure. She wondered whether she had seriously compromised herself by sharing her secret with Marie, whether she might have actually just imagined the smile of the Blessed Mother, and whether she might have been deceitful, pretending in some way to be ill or actually becoming *ill on purpose. This was a real martyrdom for my soul*, she remembered (SS 62). During the next several years, again in the secret of her own heart, she bore the pain of her weakness and distress, praying to God to heal her.

The misgivings about whether she had just imagined the smile of the Virgin were finally resolved only four years later when in Paris she visited the shrine of Our Lady of Victories. There again in a special way Thérèse encountered the Blessed Mother, who *made me feel it was really herself who smiled on me and brought about my cure* (SS 123).

The self-doubts about her own possible deceptive contribution to her illness and whether she had seriously compromised herself by sharing her secret with Marie were not resolved until five years later, when she made a general confession after entering Carmel. *God, willing no doubt to purify and especially to humble me, left me with this interior martyrdom until my entrance into Carmel* (SS 62).

Through all this, Thérèse matured into a more self-aware, strong, and faith-filled young woman. She came to see this entire painful episode of her illness, the sharing of her secret with Marie, and her bearing the distress in prayerfulness as a disguised grace of divine providence. *Without any doubt, she mused years later, if I had kept my secret I would also have kept my happiness, but the Blessed Virgin permitted this torment for my soul's good, as perhaps without it I would have had some thought of vanity, whereas humiliation becoming my lot, I was unable to look upon myself without a feeling of profound horror* (SS 67).

Knowing now with the certainty of personal experience that her heavenly Mother was the only mother who would not abandon her, Thérèse was also even more convinced that the gift of herself to God in Carmel, Mary's community, was her real destiny. *I understood it was at Carmel I would truly find the Blessed Virgin's mantle, and towards this fertile Mount I directed all my desires* (SS 123). She was also convinced that the Holy Spirit would give her the needed courage and inner strength to take the next steps to respond to the divine call.

CHAPTER 9

If I Were God, I'd Save Them All

Thérèse was back at the abbey school and, at eleven years old, was now preparing to receive her First Communion on May 8, 1884. Four years earlier Thérèse had made her first confession and had to be dissuaded from telling the priest in the confessional that she loved him, because he took the place of Jesus to whom she was really expressing her sorrow and repentance (cf. SS 40).

During that same time of Thérèse's first confession, Céline had received her First Communion, and Thérèse had participated at home in Céline's preparation under the instruction of Marie. Marie's classes were a challenge to both Céline and Thérèse, but Thérèse had actually surpassed her older sister in much of the learning.

Thérèse had found the experience of being with Céline as her sister received her First Communion, *one of the most beautiful days of my life* (SS 57). Now she was preparing for her own First Communion.

Thérèse's official preparatory classes for Communion were held at the school, but Marie was her tutor at home, and Pauline, from Carmel, was her coach. Pauline gave Thérèse a notebook in which she was to make daily entries counting her little sacrifices and her good acts. This was a common spiritual practice at the time, especially for children, and identical to the spiritual training that Marie had given both to the three-year-old Thérèse at the beginning of her religious education classes at home, and also to Céline in her preparation for her First Communion. Even at three or four (cf. GC II 1226), little Thérèse *put her hand in her pocket a hundred times a day to pull a bead of her chaplet every time she makes a sacrifice of some kind* or to note the practice of virtue (SS 25, note 19). At that age she and Céline talked about *her practices*, as she called them as a child, and her mother recalled that "when she's playing in the garden that's all she talks about" (SS 29; cf. GC II 1232–33 for a slightly different translation). Thérèse was being encouraged into a form of self-preoccupying asceticism.

For all the good that pious practices of this kind could effect, they could also be presented in a way that carried a Jansenistic and Pelagian sense. The Pelagian erroneous idea that it was possible to achieve merit and divine grace by human effort alone, however, did make some sense of keeping accounts, since that would be keeping on earth a record of what the Jansenistic god of justice was doing in heaven. The more evidence the judge had for good deeds, the more he would be obliged to reward.

This attitude, Thérèse would later notice, was counter to Jesus' teaching in the parable of the two men who went to the temple to pray (Luke 18: 9-14). The publican, who had accumulated no good deeds, was justified. The Pharisee, who had a complete and accurate list of impressive personal spiritual accomplishments, was not justified. Holiness, Thérèse would recognize, had more to do with "a heart contrite and humbled" (Psalm 51:17), with the desire to be honest, available, and loving, than with credits and debits.

Although potentially feeding into Thérèse's childhood inclination to excessive self-consciousness and self-preoccupation, Pauline's advice did not become the spiritual trap for her little sister that it might have been. Thérèse did, it was true, please Pauline by keeping a record of her spiritual practices, recording over the weeks thousands of acts of penance and virtue, and a thousand more acts of prayer; but she also, under grace, used the notebook in an honest, detached way, without compulsivity or self-promotion. She was not complacent with a high score. She wanted to do everything as an expression of her simple desire to please God. Her Beloved could do the mathematics.

Intuitively focusing her attention primarily on the orientation of her heart, Thérèse used her record-keeping not as a way of achieving some mathematical results, but as a way of noting her actions as an expression of her love. She wanted to give her heart to Jesus. She would later write, *When one loves, one does not calculate.*

Pauline had adorned Thérèse's notebook with playful symbols of flowers: roses, violets, and daises. Thérèse's imagination was captured more by the flowers symbolizing acts of love than by the idea of counting and keeping records. Later she would refer to spiritual practices as *strewing flowers* for Jesus, and on her deathbed she spoke of herself as giving her life to Jesus in the gesture of unpetalling a rose (SS 196).

As Thérèse continued her preparation for the reception of her First Communion, the awareness of her weakness was in her consciousness. She was also, of course, aware of her gifts of nature and grace, of personality and family. She thanked God, her loving Father, for these blessings, but her weaknesses were always before her: her continual inability to manage her sensitivity, the recent nervous illness that had caused such anxiety about being honest and true to herself, her failure to fit in at school, her constant tears, her feelings of sadness and melancholy, her distress around separation, her inability to please others as she would have liked, and her sense of self-centeredness. And none of these weaknesses could she manage even with all the power of good resolutions and strong will.

What kept this so sensitive, so secluded, so pious, yet so weak, self-absorbed eleven-year-old from growing discouraged was simply her confidence that God and the Blessed Mother loved her. It was only in this certainty of love that Thérèse dared to allow herself that deep awareness of her own weakness.

Preparations for First Communion involved the special experience of four days of silence and prayer, with the children participating in the life of the Benedictine community that staffed the school. For Thérèse they were days of sheer delight. Living in the cloistered community, she became a miniature nun, wearing in her belt a large crucifix that Léonie had given her, moving mysteriously along the dim convent corridors from one religious activity to the next, keeping strict silence, not looking to her right or left, making appropriate pious gestures, all in a legitimate withdrawal from her classmates. She had found her niche.

Then there was the most important preparatory activity of all, the retreat talks. These were given by Fr. Domin, the school chaplain for the past forty-one years. His talks had been established over the years and they were not far in spirit from Jansenism and Pelagianism. Purporting to prepare the girls for their encounter with divine love manifested in the gift of the Eucharist, Fr. Domin's talks focused on the ability that these young girls had of making sacrilegious Communions, committing mortal sin, and being eternally damned in hell.

Thérèse had expected to hear about divine love and providence, and to meditate on God's infinite patience and mercy. Instead she was being asked to ponder her ability, and perhaps her inevitability, of being alienated from God in this life and in the next life, eternally condemned to be separated from her Beloved. *Father told us many things that filled me with fear,* she wrote in her notebook.

Talks of damnation and being rejected by God did not inspire Thérèse to virtue; they simply made her distraught. Her delicate conscience was frightened by thoughts of sin, but what especially distressed her was the uncertainty about whether she was pleasing God. Since she had been three years old she had consciously tried to please her loving Father in everything. Thérèse never had obsessive thoughts about divine vengefulness or punitiveness. She was certain that that notion about God was not true, but she did have a concern over whether she needed to do more for her loving Father. She would do anything to please her Beloved. Now she was being told by Fr. Domin that no one knows whether they are worthy of love or hatred. The eleven-year-old broke down and wept.

Years later Thérèse found consolation in understanding that although there might be truth in what Fr. Domin said, there was an even deeper, fuller truth. It was the truth that *Jesus gives us the grace of feeling at the bottom of our heart that we would prefer to die rather than to offend Him* (GC II 729). Certain of her sincere desire to not offend God, Thérèse would come to rely on her clear conscience even as she heard similar notions of "no one knows" proclaimed years later in the retreats at Carmel.

Fr. Domin's talks had unanticipated consequences. In the fear they elicited they did not promote the young listeners to charity; rather in the days that followed the retreat the teenage girls' tongues began to wag. The girls' gossip turned to the theological issue of trying to decide, from among the evil people they knew, whom God should send to hell. The possible candidates might include a harsh teacher, or a cantankerous neighbor, or even, perhaps, one of their own nasty classmates. Overhearing some of this chatter, Thérèse, with her image of a loving God and her unwillingness to condemn others, whispered to a companion she knew would understand. *If I were God*, she said simply, *I'd save them all.*

CHAPTER 10

I Beg of You to Take Away My Freedom to Displease You

Writing about her experience of her First Communion years later, Thérèse used the language of bridal mysticism. She rarely used such language. Most often in describing her religious experiences, Thérèse employed the imagery of a child in the arms of a loving parent. But in describing her First Communion she wrote, *Ah, how sweet was that first kiss of Jesus! It was a kiss of love; I felt that I was loved, and I said: "I love You, and I give myself to You forever!" There were no demands made, no struggles, no sacrifices. . . . That day, it was no longer simply a look, it was a fusion; there were no longer two, Thérèse had vanished as a drop of water is lost in the immensity of the ocean. Jesus alone remained* (SS 77).

Thérèse had prepared herself with sincerity if also with self-consciousness, but as she experienced herself embraced by Jesus in a loving, total union more intimate than that of parent and child, she was overwhelmed and forgot herself in the fusion of love. The immensity of this experience of love she had never known before—and would never know on the human plane. As a drop of water in the ocean of love, she felt herself to be in no way separate from her spouse; the two were one in the merging of love.

There are certain things that lose their perfume as soon as they are exposed to the air, Thérèse later wrote about this experience. *There are deep spiritual thoughts which cannot be expressed in human language without losing their intimate and heavenly meaning; they are similar to "the white stone I will give to him who conquers, with a name written on the stone which no one knows except Him who receives it"* [Revelation 2:17] (SS 77).

The secrecy, the intimacy, the specialness, the feeling of being surprised and inundated by love—all this confirmed for Thérèse the truth and the depth of the reality of her relationship with Jesus. She was flooded in tears of consolation.

Those who saw her thought that she was crying because her mother was not there with her or because Pauline was not present. *They did not understand that all the joy of Heaven having entered my heart; this exiled heart was unable to bear it without shedding tears* (SS 77). With heaven in her soul, Thérèse knew that her mother was also with her at that instant. And as for Pauline, Thérèse would be seeing her that very evening when her older sister would make her profession in Carmel. With Pauline's profession of religious vows and Thérèse's reception of First Communion, the two sisters were united in the gift of themselves to Jesus. Thérèse would remember that, *on that day, joy alone filled my heart and I united myself to her* [Pauline] *who gave herself irrevocably to Him who gave Himself so lovingly to me!* (SS 78).

During that same afternoon she made an act of consecration to the Blessed Virgin, and she remembered as well the suffering man on crutches she had encountered five years earlier. At that time she had promised to pray for one of Christ's suffering members at her First Communion, and now she did.

Her First Communion also prompted Thérèse to make three resolutions. The first was that she would *not become discouraged* (cf. TLMT 119; STL 174). This was a time of great and lingering distress for Thérèse. She was still suffering from the self-doubt of her illness and the mysterious cure by the smile of the Virgin. She was struggling as well with the pain and confusion surrounding her experiences at the abbey school. And also, she was trying to understand how she could have such a great desire to be a saint and yet have so little to show for it. In these three areas of her life, Thérèse walked in a kind of darkness that she knew could easily lead to frustration and discouragement.

She had one great desire, and that was to please Jesus. She had a clear sense that she would die rather than offend him. Her rampart against discouragement would be her sincerity, her bold confidence, her inner certainty that she was loved by the God of love. This certainty of divine love was more sure for her than was the feeling of distress that now surrounded her as she moved into teenage years. It was the certainty founded on her conviction that the love of her parents and family for her was only a faint glimmer of God's infinite love for her. Thérèse was determined to make the reality of divine love the core of her self-understanding and peace. Clinging to that reality, this child of eleven knew, would eventually lead her through the areas of her life that were tangled in weakness and confusion. Her task was to keep from falling into discouragement.

The second resolution Thérèse made was that she would say the Memorare, the prayer to Mary, every day. Since the death of her mother the role of Mary had become decisive in her life. Still suffering from the wound of triple mother-loss, she had deepened her relationship with Mary by the grace of her cure and now by her act of consecration. Mary would be the mother who would never abandon her. Thérèse was certain of that, but she also recognized that she could slip away from Mary. She did not want that to happen, and she resolved to express daily her love for Mary in the traditional prayer of the Memorare. Of course she would do more than that; she would pray the rosary, she would write prayers and poems to Mary, and silently, in short prayers from her heart, she would often express her love and need for Mother Mary.

Last, Thérèse resolved that she would try to humble her pride. She experienced her self-centeredness as an obstacle to her desire to be united to her Beloved. Even as a child of three years old, Thérèse had seen herself as having an excessive self-love. Knowing this tendency to self-centeredness, self-preoccupation, and willfulness, she had been grateful to her parents for having given her opportunities to practice obedience and self-sacrifice. If they had treated her, she recalled, with the leniency with which they had treated Céline, who was less prone to willfulness and self-centeredness, they would have spoiled her.

Fearing the pride of her self-will, Thérèse also asked Jesus at her First Communion to take away her liberty. She felt inadequate and too weak to tame her strong will, so she prayed that God would simply take it away. Even many years later she would continue to pray, *I beg of you to take away my freedom to displease You* (SS 276). She did not know that the resolution she was making to humble the pride of her willfulness and self-centeredness and also her request that God take away her liberty were desires incapable of being fulfilled.

On the one hand, Thérèse's liberty or freedom could not be taken away. Freedom and liberty as part of her free will were part of herself. If she were to continue to remain the human person she was, her will, the center of liberty and freedom, could not be removed. God would, rather, support her will and let grace transform her willfulness into willingness, her self-centeredness into God-centeredness, and her self-preoccupation into a desire to save souls and to assist in her Beloved's work in this world. And that is what happened. Thérèse's Communion prayer would be answered in a way she had not anticipated. Over the next years she became not less free, but more free, more liberated from her feelings. She gradually developed more inner freedom around her sensitivity and was able to let go of her self-will, self-centeredness, and self-preoccupation. Her movement into the grace of more and more inner freedom became an important transformative aspect of her spiritual growth.

On the other hand, Thérèse was mistaken to think that humility was a virtue that could be achieved with a willful decision. As an eleven-year-old Thérèse could not have known that a resolution that would move her into a willful effort to become humble would itself be an egotistical act of pride. But even at this age she did understand a most important counterbalancing truth: that *the nature of love is to humble oneself* (SS 14).

She had reflected on that spiritual truth in the context of God's descending by grace into the hearts of the weak and the lowly, the poor sinners who had no knowledge of divine love. And, more important, she had known the truth of her Beloved's descending grace from her own experience as she received her First Communion. In the Eucharist Jesus had perpetuated his incarnation, continuing to humble himself, stooping down as it were, by becoming one with her.

Thérèse saw that that was what she herself now needed to do. She needed to imitate Jesus. She needed to be available to God and to allow the Holy Spirit, as Mary had done, to descend more and more by grace into her heart. Focusing on receiving divine love and noticing and giving up the weaknesses that blocked that love from coming into her life would be Thérèse's path to humility. The awareness of her brokenness, together with her willingness to bear the humiliation of her weaknesses, would impel her to throw herself into the arms of her loving Father, and that would be enough. Her resolution to be humble would melt into her desire to become a great saint by being loved into holiness by divine love. *I desire to be a saint,* she would later pray, *but I feel my helplessness and I beg You, O my God, to be Yourself my Sanctity* (SS 276).

In Thérèse's time daily Communion, even for monks and nuns, was virtually unknown. Rare also was weekly Communion. Nevertheless, Thérèse boldly sought permission from her confessor and was able to receive the Eucharist again only two weeks after her First Communion. She experienced her second Communion with equal joy and love. She described her sense of union with Jesus in the words of St. Paul, "It is no longer I who live but Jesus lives in me" (Galatians 2:20). She also *felt born within my heart a great desire to suffer, and at the same time the interior assurance that Jesus reserved a great number of crosses for me. I felt myself flooded with consolations so great that I look upon them as one of the greatest graces of my life. . . . I also felt the desire of loving only God, of finding my joy only in Him* (SS 79).

At the end of her life, still regretting that she could not receive Communion daily, Thérèse prayed, *I cannot receive Holy Communion as often as I desire, but, Lord, are You not all-powerful? Remain in me as in a tabernacle* (SS 276).

CHAPTER 11

Jesus Knew I Was Too Feeble to Be Exposed to Temptation

In June 1884, a short time after her First Communion, Thérèse received the Sacrament of Confirmation from Bishop Hugonin, with Léonie as her sponsor. Céline, who supported Thérèse in her preparation for this sacrament, believed that Thérèse was equally ardent and perhaps even more radiant and grace-filled by her confirmation than by the blessings of her First Communion. Thérèse reflected that *I did not experience an impetuous wind at the moment of the Holy Spirit's descent, but rather this light breeze which the prophet Elias heard on Mount Horeb.* That light breeze carried a great grace for Thérèse, a grace that completed the earlier Communion grace of her desire to be willing to suffer for Jesus: *On that day I was given the strength to suffer; strength I was to need for soon afterwards the martyrdom of my soul was about to commence* (SS 80).

That martyrdom was to begin in its full intensity the following year, but during the intervening twelve months, even with the continued tension at school, Thérèse enjoyed an inner peace and experienced many incidents of childhood pleasure as well as some disappointments.

At this time, Thérèse developed a cough similar to the one she had when she was two years old and similar to the more recent one that had sent her to the infirmary at the school. This time the cough lasted several months, but that did not deter her from her vacation with her cousins, the Guérins. In fact, her family hoped that her going on vacation to her aunt's house in a small rural town would help her whooping cough. There she enjoyed the fresh air, taking walks and sitting with Céline sketching the interesting shapes of the farm buildings. Even without formal art lessons, she was becoming skilled for her age at sketching and drawing.

Thérèse asked her father for another pet, for *an animal with hair,* she said playfully. "But, my little queen," he answered with lightness, "you have animals with hair; you have rabbits." *That's true,* she bantered, *but I'd like an animal with hair that follows me everywhere and jumps around me!* (cf. GC I 238). Thérèse's description did not completely preclude rabbits, but her father took the hint and got her a dog, a spaniel. She named him Tom. She had and would have more pets than rabbits and Tom; her father had given her a magpie just before she had entered the abbey school and would give her a baby lamb; she also had a pet linnet. Later she arranged an attic area, Pauline's old painting room, to become her personal indoor garden and aviary, with *a large cage which enclosed a great number of birds*; statues, pictures, books, and special furnishings also abounded there (SS 90).

Thérèse's studies at school continued to go well, and she became Fr. Domin's "little doctor," offering catechism answers that no one else could (SS 81). She even had some original answers of her own. She disagreed with his teaching on the vindictiveness of God and contradicted the common teachings that Communion should be received rarely, that fear and violence were part of the gospel way of holiness, and that babies who died without baptism would be consigned to limbo, never to enjoy the divine vision. Since God can do all things, she reasoned, she wondered about the current opinion on limbo, *if I were in His place, I would show myself to infants* (cf. GC I 175).

All my teachers looked upon me as a very intelligent student, she remembered (SS 82). But her relationships with her classmates and even with some teachers continued to go poorly. She recognized that some of her difficulties were due to her own ineptitude, her excessive sensitivity, and her need for closeness.

Even within her family Thérèse's need for attention became a burden to her. During a vacation with the Guérins when she was twelve, she noticed that her cousin Marie, three years older than she, often whimpered, saying she had a headache. Then her mother, Thérèse's aunt Céline, would baby Marie, *giving her all kinds of endearing names*. Thérèse reminisced in a humorous vein:

> *I, who had a headache almost every day, and didn't complain, wanted to imitate Marie. So one evening, sitting in an armchair in the corner of the parlor, I set about the business of crying. Soon Jeanne and Aunt hurried over to me, asking me what was the matter. I answered like Marie: "I have a headache." It seemed that complaining did not suit me, for I was unable to convince them that a headache would make me cry; instead of babying me, they spoke to me as to an adult, and Jeanne scolded me for lacking confidence in Aunt, for she was con-*

vinced something was bothering my conscience. Getting nowhere for all my trouble I made the resolution never to imitate others again and I understood the fable about "The donkey and the pet dog." I was the donkey. (SS 89)

This incident didn't cure Thérèse of her headaches, but it did give her insight into how she craved attention and closeness. *I did get what I deserved and this cured me for life of any desire to attract attention* (SS 90). It also helped her to understand how important it was for her not to imitate others but to become her own person and to accept her own weaknesses and gifts.

The truth was that at school and at home Thérèse had not yet matured into using her God-given gifts with inner freedom. She was growing in this way, but for now she often used her loving and sensitive spirit, her gifts of courage and honesty, her intelligence, her conscientiousness and natural tenderness, her great capacity to be aware of her inner life, her great strength of will—all these personal gifts of mind and spirit—in a self-centered way simply to calm the insecurity she felt within herself. Her natural sensitivity continued to make her especially vulnerable to the childhood feelings of mother-loss and separation.

Trying to accommodate and please others at school and simply "toughing out" her upsetting feelings had been a strategy that had worked for a while, but now that path was going nowhere. Thérèse was understanding, even more importantly, that there was a falseness in this strategy itself.

She had one budding peer friendship at school that she had hoped to cultivate by her style of pleasing, but her friend, separated from her for a few months, simply forgot about her. *When I saw my companion back again my joy was great,* she recounts, *but all I received from her was a cold glance. My love was not understood* (SS 82). Thérèse's affectionate heart was deeply wounded.

As she reflected on that experience years later she understood that, although at the time it seemed to be only rejection, it had really been a blessing. *How can I thank Jesus for making me find only bitterness in earth's friendships! With a heart such as mine, I would have allowed myself to be taken . . . and then how would I have been able to fly and be at rest. Jesus knew I was too feeble to be exposed to temptation* (SS 83).

Thérèse understood that she could have easily fallen into a kind of infatuation that would have undermined her true self. *My heart, sensitive and affectionate as it was, would have easily surrendered had it found a heart capable of understanding it* (SS 82). She had always had a sense that God was protecting her from the many side paths into which her emotional weaknesses could have diverted her. Her failure at friendship had been another grace in disguise.

As she recalled this experience with her classmate, she compared herself with Mary Magdalene, who had been on the side path of compromising her personal integrity until she met Jesus. Thérèse associated Magdalene with the profligate woman who had washed Jesus' feet with her tears and dried them with her hair. *I know that without Him, I could have fallen as low as Saint Mary Magdalene, and the profound words of Our Lord to Simon resound with a great sweetness in my soul. I know that "he to whom less is forgiven, loves less"* [Luke 7:47], *but I also know that Jesus has forgiven me more than Saint Mary Magdalene since He forgave me in advance by preventing me from falling* (SS 83).

Thérèse's consciousness of God's stooping down to save her before she could fall more deeply into tendencies of self-love and self-indulgence—this appreciation of the prior protection of divine love—was a constant source of gratitude for Thérèse. To explain this awareness, she composed a parable—one of several she wrote—to praise the divine *foreseeing love* and mercy:

Suppose a clever physician's child meets with a stone in his path which causes him to fall and break a limb. His father comes to him immediately, picks him up lovingly, takes care of his hurt, using all the resources of his profession for this. His child, completely cured, shows his gratitude. This child is no doubt right in loving his father! But I am going to make another comparison. The father, knowing there is a stone in his child's way, hastens ahead of him and removes it but without anyone's seeing him do it. Certainly, this child, the object of his father's tender foresight, but unaware of the misfortune from which he was delivered by him, will not thank him and will love him less than if he had been cured by him. But if he should come to learn the danger from which he escaped, will he not love his father more? Well, I am this child, the object of the foreseeing love of a Father who has not sent His Word to save the just, but sinners. He wants me to love Him because

He has forgiven me not much but ALL. He has not expected me to love Him much like Mary Magdalene, but He has willed that I know how He has loved me with a love of unspeakable foresight in order that now I may love Him unto folly! I have heard it said that one cannot meet a pure soul who loves more than a repentant soul; ah! How I would wish to give the lie to this statement. (SS 84)

Thérèse posed to herself the question, *How can a heart given over to the affection of creatures be intimately united to God?* And, in light of her own nature and style, her own gifts and weaknesses, she believed that she would personally have to answer, *I feel this is not possible* (SS 83).

Thérèse understood that this was a personal awareness and discernment about herself. Thus, she did not denounce others who were more capable of legitimate friendships, acknowledging that she had seen others in healthy relationships. But, since she knew she was so prone to attachments, *it was not so for me,* she reminisced, *for I encountered only bitterness where stronger souls met with joy, and they detached themselves from* [any temptation] *through fidelity. . . . I know that without Him, I could have fallen as low as Saint Mary Magdalene* (SS 83). Her sensitivities were both a burden and a gift, and she was noticing her tendency to what has come to be called "codependency."

Years later as she reflected on this time of her life, and after several years of experience in the convent, Thérèse wrote, reminiscent of St. Augustine, *Without having drunk the empoisoned cup of a too ardent love of creatures, I feel I cannot be mistaken. I have seen so many souls, seduced by this false light* (SS 83).

CHAPTER 12

I Considered That I Was Born for Glory

Thérèse had noticed that she had received an important grace on the day of her confirmation: *On that day I was given the strength to suffer* (SS 80). Now, a year later, what she considered the martyrdom of her soul was about to begin.

To celebrate the anniversary of the children's reception of First Communion, the school held another retreat. Fr. Domin, the same priest chaplain whose harsh retreat conferences had sown the seeds of worry in Thérèse the year before, again spoke on the danger of mortal sin, hellfire, and damnation. This time he extended his warnings about the limitations of divine mercy and the perversity of human nature, describing how much God despised a soul in the state of sin. Thérèse, his "little doctor," was again terrified.

Desiring to be a saint yet experiencing herself as weak and inadequate, wanting to please her loving Father in everything yet being admonished to ponder the perversity of her nature, Thérèse was thrown into what she called a *terrible sickness, . . . a martyrdom* (SS 84). As a sensitive child of twelve and a half, she was being gripped by what the spiritual tradition calls "scruples": the fear that any and every thought and act could be bad, even sinful, and that the fires of hell were inevitable. In particular and more significant for Thérèse, she was besieged with the worry that she was not doing enough to please her Beloved.

During the following months terror often overpowered Thérèse's usual clear thinking. She entered a maze of dreadful second thoughts and conflicting feelings, of brooding, of depression, of dark chasms and ever-twisting possibilities of fear and obsession. She was losing confidence in her own judgment of what was right and wrong. She was having self-doubts about her relationship with her loving Father. This state of scruples continued in Thérèse for the next year and a half and impeded the growth of her basic nature to live by love.

Several of the weaknesses Thérèse had experienced over the previous years were also coming together and causing terrible general anxiety in her heart. Her self-consciousness, her tendency to self-love, and her need to be close, together with her tendency to *be taken* in friendships, as she said—all these contributed to her anxiety. Other areas of self-doubt continued. In her concern about her self-compromise following the cure by the smile of the Blessed Virgin, she still could not think about herself *without feeling profound horror. O my good Blessed Virgin,* she had prayed at the time of her First Communion, *grant that your little Thérèse may stop tormenting herself* (*The Prayers of St. Thérèse of Lisieux*, translated by Aletheia Kane, 37).

A further incident three months after the cure had only contributed to Thérèse's developing inner struggle. To celebrate her healing, the family went on a vacation, and Thérèse had the opportunity to revisit some of the places and people of her childhood at Alençon. There her father introduced her with pride to his longtime friends who had known her as a playful, bubbling child before her mother's death. "She is now a fine figure of a girl," her father wrote to a friend. His little queen was, if shy and withdrawn, a very attractive young woman, turning heads with the beauty of her dark blue-gray eyes and quiet smile, her mature bearing, and her long blonde hair that reached to her waist. And she was flattered by the attention. *I must admit this type of life had its charms for me,* Thérèse remembered. *At the age of ten the heart allows itself to be easily dazzled. . . . I began to see something of the world; I was entertained, pampered and admired* (SS 73).

She felt the enjoyments of being the center of attention, but because of her tendency to self-indulgence she experienced these feelings as temptations. She knew that she could have easily been beguiled by the good things and pleasant relationships, the entertainment and admiration, that surrounded her. *The friends we had there were too worldly,* she cautioned herself. *They knew too well how to ally the joys of this earth to the service of God.* She recalled the words of the Book of Wisdom: *"The bewitching of vanity overturneth the innocent mind"* [Wisdom 4:12] (SS 73).

Her father, however, was enjoying himself. Louis was delighted with Thérèse in her *first entrance into the world,* as she described it. Was she being too hard on herself? Was she being overly cautious and unduly fearful of her own weaknesses? She feared and fled, but not without feelings of self-compromise, and not without personal confusion, self-doubt, and inner struggle.

More significant, perhaps, was Thérèse's developing awareness of her beauty and her sexuality. Was she embarrassed when adolescent feelings arose in her? A few years after this experience in Alençon, she prayed to the Blessed Mother when she was in Paris at the Church of Our Lady of Victories on her way to Rome

to keep far from me everything that could tarnish my purity; I was fully aware that on a voyage such as this into Italy I could easily meet with things capable of troubling me. I was still unacquainted with evil and so was apprehensive about making its discovery. I had not yet experienced that to the pure all things are pure, that the simple and upright soul sees evil in nothing since it resides only in impure hearts, not in inanimate objects. (SS 123)

Did Thérèse think that to delight in her physical beauty was in some way a sin? Nature's beauty gave her joy, but no one in her family or at school had encouraged her to take delight in her own beauty and sexuality. The entire matter of sexuality and physical beauty was a taboo subject in the family culture and at school. Later she would write, *When I was very little, I was troubled at having a body. I was not at ease in it; I was ashamed of it* (*The Story of a Family* by Fr. Stéphane-Joseph Piat, OFM, 47, note 2).

Her parents and sisters had taken great care that the little Thérèse, who even as a young child of three *thought within myself that I would look much more pretty with my arms bare*, did not hear any words of admiration from others. She understood that this was to assure *that I heard nothing capable to giving rise to vanity in my heart* (SS 24).

Remembering the incident when she had been complimented at the seashore by a woman who was a total stranger, Thérèse wrote to Pauline, *As I listened to what you and Marie said, and as you had never directed any compliments to me, I gave no great importance to the words or admiring glances of this woman.* Yet in her sensitivity Thérèse had indeed thought about this incident; it remained in her memory for the rest of her life. And *the joy I had putting on some pretty sky-blue ribbons Aunt had given me for my hair* disturbed her so much as a twelve-year-old that years later she would *recall having confessed . . . even this childish pleasure which seemed to be a sin to me* (SS 89).

Now entering her teen years, Thérèse was moving into a period of life that included deeper consciousness of her physical maturity and sexuality, and these areas surely brought feelings of confusion and inner conflict, of distress and particularly of scrupulosity. When she had *chosen all,* she had decided her life for God was going to be all or nothing. She was not going to be a saint by halves. Following Pauline's example, she had especially cultivated her desire to be with Jesus in Carmel, and she thought *perhaps Jesus wanted to show me the world before his first visit to me so that I might choose more freely the life I had promised him to follow* (SS 73). Maybe even the temptations in Alençon and later in Paris were graces in disguise.

Her emotional sensitivity, her style of experiencing good and bad in a somewhat exaggerated way, together with her family's cautions about pride and self-love, seems to have led Thérèse to believe that the admiration of others was for her the doorway into vanity. Disturbed by her so finely honed conscience, every hint of compromise to her desire for holiness raised the fear-filled rebuke of scruples.

Pride and self-love had concerned Thérèse at the time of her First Communion, prompting her to pray for humility. Recognizing her tendency to vanity, she also had experienced in herself the tendency to willfulness and self-centeredness, as well as her capacity to compromise herself and go against her own integrity.

These tendencies and feelings are not unusual in any religiously sensitive young person, but what is remarkable is that Thérèse became aware of them at so early an age and that she recognized that they were undermining her spiritual desires. Also remarkable is that she did not blame anyone for these feelings or for her actions that flowed from them. She was more and more aware that in some way she bore at least some responsibility.

Now her scruples were elicited by the dark warnings and frightful images preached by Fr. Domin as he tried to prepare the young women before him for the anniversary of their First Communion. *What* [Fr. Domin] *told us was frightening,* Thérèse wrote in her retreat notes. *He spoke about mortal sin and he described a soul in the state of sin and how much God hated it* (GC I 226).

For Thérèse the issue was not that God was vengeful or hateful, but whether she was doing all she could to please her loving Father. Pleasing him, she thought, meant for her to become a better person. She had sometimes succeeded in trying to address her weaknesses by using her strong will, but more often she had failed; and when she failed she had become *the donkey.*

She learned, however, that even her most sincere efforts did not allow her to peacefully receive the simple joy of a compliment, or to ignore the teasing of her classmates, or to forego the need to be special and noticed, or to bear without self-indulgence the feeling of loss. The more she tried, the more her failures were a burden to her. *All my most simple thoughts and actions became the cause of trouble for me*, she remembered (SS 84).

Thérèse's efforts to become a better person raised another concern, the matter of self-deception. Was it possible that she was deceiving herself in self-love, trying to be what she wanted of herself, rather than what her loving Father wanted of her? Could she trust her own sincerity? Could it be that she was simply being a hypocrite, letting her motivations be contaminated with self-seeking, trying to be perfect to make herself feel good and not as a way of pleasing God? Was she living out of a kind of sham love? The self-doubt of scruples pervaded everything.

Following the family pattern of the daughters protecting their father from any cause for anxiety, Thérèse never shared any of her concerns about her self-doubts and scrupulosity with him. To her older sister Marie, however, she confided everything about her state of mind and soul. Only Thérèse's innate sense of obedience to Marie, who guided her with consummate skill, would bring her through the eighteen months of scruples.

Thérèse, who could not enjoy playing the coarse games of her classmates, enjoyed reading and *would have spent my life at it*. She liked to read history, tales of chivalry, and in retrospect valued the fact that at this time she did not *always understand the realities of life* (SS 72). Even in this simple joy she was always wary of her sentimentalism, of escapism, of self-indulgence, of possible sexual thoughts, and knew at some level that her heart was easily affected and could have easily been contaminated. But she was thrilled to read the patriotic accounts of the French heroines, and especially Joan of Arc.

At this time Joan became Thérèse's personal heroine. She greatly admired Joan for her boldness in following her lights, for her burning zeal, and for her determination to obey God's will. Joan's courage and greatness found an echo in Thérèse's heart. *Then I received a grace which I have always looked upon as one of the greatest in my life. . . . I considered that I was born for glory* (SS 72). This thought could have been a surge of ego-centeredness or self-promotion, but in Thérèse it was an inspiration similar to the inspirations that had captured Joan herself.

Immediately Thérèse understood that, unlike Joan's call to glory, it was not worldly greatness that she herself would accomplish. Worldly greatness would not be possible for this sensitive and shy teenager. Her greatness and glory would be the kind that God willed for her. *God made me feel that true glory is that which will last eternally, and to reach it, it isn't necessary to perform striking works but to hide oneself and practice virtue in such a way that the left hand knows not what the right is doing* [Matthew 6:3]. She understood that her greatness would consist of her *becoming a great saint*, but a hidden saint (SS 72).

In Thérèse's eyes Joan was a great saint because, in her love of God, she had been willing to pursue the truth of her life without giving in to self-doubt, even in the face of objections, criticism, suffering, and death. Joan, listening to the inner voices of her heart, had been willing to be true to herself. Thérèse knew that she too was called to this, but that she had far to go. She had already failed in this regard when she had violated her inner sense that told her to keep the secret that it was the Virgin's smile that had cured her.

Joan's faith and courage had given her the power not only to lead armies, but also to be able simply to manage her own feelings, to stand her ground emotionally for what she believed to be her calling although she felt distress, confusion, and her own weakness. To this strength Thérèse also knew that she was called; she was beginning to understand that attaining it would be an important part of her growing up emotionally and spiritually.

CHAPTER 13

I Understood That My Mission Was to Get the King of Heaven Loved

Thérèse was beginning to recognize more deeply that she needed the clarity of truth to illuminate her motivations. She was trying to practice virtue, following in the footsteps of the family tradition of being good. She intended to have a singular intention of pleasing Jesus, but she also knew that other intentions found a place in her heart. The intention of pleasing her sisters, of being good in the eyes of her father, of calming her own distressing feelings—these also were motivations that did not exclude pleasing Jesus, but could, if they became dominant, begin to poison her intention to please God alone.

Years earlier her mother had noticed that Thérèse even as a child "would not lie for all the gold in the world" (GC II 1233). But as she entered her teenage years, Thérèse was beginning to understand that there were other ways besides outright lying in which she could compromise the truth of herself. The temptation of not following her call, of not listening deeply to her inspirations, of giving her affections in a selfish, codependent way to others, of condoning a mixture of motivations in her heart—these also were compromises with the truth, and Thérèse wanted to choose all for God.

She equated trying to be true to herself with trying to please her Beloved and knew that her desire for personal integrity and truth would lead her to her loving Father. She came to understand that by holding to the truth she would be moving toward Jesus, who called himself "the truth."

Joan of Arc now became Thérèse's model for this desire to be true to herself and faithful to her personal integrity. Joan also became her model for managing her stubbornness and willpower. Although *timid and sensitive by nature*, Thérèse was really a fighter; she had the will of a combatant, of a warrior, of a crusader.

When I was a child I dreamt of fighting on battlefields . . . [but] *instead of a voice from Heaven inviting me to the fight* [like Joan of Arc] *I heard in the depths of my soul a voice sweeter and stronger still. . . . I understood*, Thérèse wrote, *that my mission was, not to get a mortal king crowned but the King of heaven loved; to submit to Him the kingdom of hearts* (GC II 1085). Her weapon would not be the sword but truth and love. Her spirit of combat would not be the willfulness of conquest, but the willingness to lovingly bear her own petty life issues for her loving Father. In this willingness was a seed of Thérèse's sense of her call to holiness.

Thérèse's image of holiness, beginning to unfold in these early years from her own experience, took on other qualities that were not in the ordinary notion of sanctity in her day. The common idea of holiness was more the one that had inspired Pauline's notebook of accounting for sacrifices and virtues, and the one that had inspired Fr. Domin's frightful conferences. According to this common idea, holiness was to be attained by performing severe and painful penances, by avoiding all sin and acquiring virtues, and even by achieving elevated states of prayer, even visions and ecstasies, all under the critical eyes of a punitive God.

Thérèse knew that Joan of Arc, although not yet canonized and not completely accomplished in this kind of holiness either, still did begin to approach that model better than she herself ever could. Thérèse recognized that she was limited in personality and character. She felt inadequate in every area except in her great desire to please God. This road of great accomplishments in extraordinary achievements and perfection was well beyond her ability. She could not even manage her excessive sensitivity or overcome her tears. She knew that no matter how hard she tried on this path of greatness, she would not succeed.

Her understanding of sanctity now began moving further along another path, one not taught in the school and not heard in the sermons and retreat talks. Her path would be simply loving God by bearing truthfully her own limitations and weaknesses, and focusing on what she could do at each moment with the best motivation she could manage. She would do even little things, especially little, hidden things like inconspicuous acts of charity and enduring little inconveniences, with the intention of pleasing her loving Father.

Emotionally Thérèse continued to feel the need for connectedness and support that had surfaced so strongly after her mother's death. Over the years she had skillfully developed a personal pattern to cope with her feelings, but that pattern sometimes compromised her personal integrity and her singular motivation. Her intention to please Jesus was true, but apparently not the whole truth. She had also been doing quite a bit to feel good about herself, and the ambiguity of her motivation now began to become more conscious. Over the next year and a half her situation would reach a crisis.

Thérèse's cousin Marie had been with her at the abbey school, but Marie was frequently ill and left the school in August 1885, at about the same time that Céline also completed her schooling.

In September Céline and Thérèse again spent vacation time with their cousins Jeanne and Marie at the seashore in Trouville. Isidore believed that the fresh air of the seashore was good for his daughters, especially Marie, who, now at fifteen, was experiencing difficulties in her development as an adolescent. He also thought it would help the teenage Céline as well as Thérèse, who was still being treated for whooping cough.

In October Thérèse returned to the school after vacation, but without the protection of Céline or the support of her cousin Marie. The school year began with another retreat, and although there was a substitute preacher for Fr. Domin, to Thérèse's dismay he too focused on sin, death, hell, and the last judgment. Things did not get any better for her at the school, and within six months, with her scrupulosity, her headaches, and insomnia continuing, her father acted. Thérèse wrote about this very succinctly when she said, *At the end of the year, Céline, having completed her studies, remained home and poor Thérèse was obliged to attend school alone. It wasn't long before she got sick* (SS 85). The stress-related nature of Thérèse's illness must have been clear to her father, but he respected his daughter's weakness and took her out of the school.

Thérèse, delighted with the new arrangement, began private tutoring lessons several days a week in the home of Valentine Papinau, who had also been a tutor for her cousin Marie. Miss Papinau lived with her mother and enjoyed a social life. Many of her friends visited the home and distracted Thérèse, busy with her studies. She overheard some remarks complimenting her own beauty. *These words, all the more flattering since they were not spoken in my presence,* Thérèse remembered, *left in my soul a pleasurable impression which showed me clearly how much I was filled with self-love. It is so easy to go astray on the flowery paths of the world* (SS 86). Thérèse continued to hover on the edge of the pitfall of scrupulosity.

Thérèse, thirteen in January 1886, relieved from the stress of the abbey school, was enjoying the homeschool arrangements, which allowed her to maintain a rather solitary existence. Her love of learning began to blossom, and she set up an area on the upper floor of Les Buissonnets in which to read and study during her free time.

Thérèse's sister Marie, now twenty-six, announced in August that she had decided to enter Carmel, and the date was set for October. Although she had never taken to the idea of marriage, she had not indicated an attraction to religious life, so her announcement was somewhat of a surprise to the family and a complete shock to Thérèse. Fr. Pichon, a Jesuit, had been for some years Marie's spiritual director. He had also become a family friend, having visited the Martin home on several occasions, and had first met Thérèse when she was ten. Fr. Pichon was a significant influence on Marie's decision.

Thérèse was hurt by Marie's sudden announcement. *As soon as I learned of Marie's decision,* she later wrote, *I made up my mind not to look for enjoyment in this world any longer.* Marie had been a pillar of support for Thérèse after Pauline had entered Carmel. *It was Marie who guided, consoled, and aided me in the practice of virtue.* Thérèse noted, *she was my sole oracle. . . . She was indispensable to me. I told my scruples only to her and was so obedient that my confessor never knew my ugly malady. . . . I loved her so much I couldn't live without her* (SS 88). Marie was, in fact, Thérèse's fourth mother figure, and Thérèse was now about to lose her too.

Thérèse and her sisters went again with their father to Alençon for a short visit. Thérèse wanted particularly to pray at their mother's burial place, but that plan was upset and resulted in floods of tears at the gravesite because she had forgotten to bring the cornflowers that she had gathered especially for her mother. During the visit, Léonie stopped to see the superior of the Poor Clares in Alençon. The superior encouraged her to enter the community then and there. Léonie accepted the invitation, much to the dismay of the family, especially to Marie, who was clearly angry about what this precipitous decision would do to their father. It was equally upsetting to Thérèse, who recalled that *I hadn't even the chance to kiss her before her departure* (SS 92). Léonie was to remain with the Poor Clares for only six weeks before deciding that the community was not her calling.

Marie left for Carmel the following week, and Thérèse was now alone in her continual state of inner turmoil. Marie's wise and practical counsel had been invaluable during these eighteen months of scruples, what Thérèse herself described as *a martyrdom* (SS 84). Marie had been deeply empathetic to Thérèse as well as being levelheaded and firm, qualities that made her an excellent guide for her excessively sensitive little sister. Nevertheless, Marie knew that Thérèse would have to learn to work things out for herself. Thérèse would have to begin to manage her feelings and to grow up.

Uncle Isidore had noticed three years earlier that Thérèse was being at some level self-indulgent. Now Thérèse too was beginning to acknowledge that truth about herself. She *desired the grace of having absolute control over my actions* [and feelings], *of not being their slave but their mistress,* but that growth would take many years. Regarding this time she wrote that, yes, *I really made a big fuss over everything! . . . I was still only a child who appeared to have no will but that of others, and this caused certain people in Alençon to say I had a weak character* (SS 91).

Now, w*hen Marie entered Carmel, I was still very scrupulous. No longer able to confide in her I turned towards heaven.* In a kind of desperation to be delivered from this state of the martyrdom of scruples and confusion, Thérèse prayed to her brothers and sisters who had died in childhood. *I thought that these innocent souls, having never known troubles nor fear, would have pity on their poor little sister who was suffering on earth* (SS 93).

Thérèse's prayer was answered as she came to know that *if I was loved on earth, I was also loved in heaven.* She did not need to be a fear-filled child. She could trust God and his divine love. She could trust her own good judgment and her good conscience; she could bear her self-doubts, knowing that God loved her and would not abandon her. Her scruples were over. *Since then, my devotion to my little brothers and sisters has grown* (SS 93).

The grace given to Thérèse at the reception of the Sacrament of Confirmation, the *strength to suffer,* had been her salvation during these past eighteen months. With Marie's guidance she had had the strength to simply endure the pain of her conflicting feelings and her self-doubt. She would continue to need this inner strength as she made fruitless efforts to achieve goodness by managing her motivations, overcoming her excessive feelings, and eliminating her self-love. She would also need her great desire to be true to herself as she saw the first glimmerings of her own complicity in the self-violence inherent in this path of striving to be perfect.

As her guide in understanding the gospel truth that the path to holiness is by faith and love, not effort and striving, St. Paul's wisdom would supersede the advice of Pauline and Marie. On the authentic gospel path of *confidence and love,* Thérèse's emotional and spiritual issues that continued to burden her would, ironically and providentially, as she bore them patiently, become the very stepping-stones of disguised graces for her progress through the darkness and nothingness into which her early adolescent path was vanishing.

CHAPTER 14

God Would Have to Work a Little Miracle

I had a great desire, it is true, to practice virtue, Thérèse wrote as she reflected on this time in her life, *but I went about it in a strange way. It sometimes happened that I tried to make up the bed to please God, or else in the evening, when Céline was away, I'd bring in her plants. But as I already said, it was for God alone I was doing these things and should not have expected any thanks from creatures. Alas, it was just the opposite. If Céline was unfortunate enough not to seem happy or surprised because of these little services, I became unhappy and proved it by my tears* (SS 97). As Thérèse's fourteenth birthday neared, the ambiguous nature of her motivations was now becoming obvious to her.

Thérèse recognized that if she were acting for *God alone*, then whether Céline or anyone else noticed should not have mattered; but that was not at all the case. Céline's approval was quite important for Thérèse.

She also saw something about her sensitivities that extended even beyond her interactions with Céline: *I was really unbearable because of my extreme touchiness; if I happened to cause anyone I loved some little trouble, even unwittingly, instead of forgetting about it and not crying, which made matters worse, I cried like a Magdalene and then when I began to cheer up, I'd begin to cry again for having cried. . . . I was quite unable to correct this terrible fault* (SS 97).

Thérèse saw herself as *still in the swaddling clothes of a child!* Compensating for her upsetting feelings, she needed to be cared for, to be affirmed, even to be pampered; furthermore, she invited these reactions from her family. She had been for some years engaged in a kind of personal pattern that conformed to a family pattern. Everyone in the family thought that Thérèse's behavior was simply excessive sensitivity, a quality that as she got older she would grow out of naturally. Thérèse, however, recognized her own responsibility, and therefore she saw her way of behaving as really a *terrible fault.* Not a minor peccadillo, but a terrible, personal compromise that could infect her heart. Not a slight failing or weakness, but a fault that was moving her along a path that diverted her from the path of truth and inner freedom.

Under the power of pure grace, Thérèse, even at this early age, knew that she was helpless in being able to correct this *terrible fault*. She had tried in vain for ten years now, since the death of her mother, to pull herself out of her present and enduring mire of mixed motivations, melancholy, and self-preoccupation. She had tried also with her best efforts to overcome her self-centeredness and willfulness, and she had failed. She knew that only God could rescue her; that, as she said, *God would have to work a little miracle to make me grow up* (SS 97).

Thérèse had, indeed, not grown up in some ways, and she noticed that *Céline wanted to continue treating me as a baby since I was the youngest in the family* (SS 98). Her father also was enjoying the teenage Thérèse in her role as the baby. Thérèse was too kind and too needy to confront this characterization of herself. It pained her, but she was also benefiting from it. Some of her important needs were met by this role. She was too kind and too needy to object. She could not stand her own ground emotionally, and this weakness was precisely the red flag signaling to Thérèse that she needed *a little miracle* to be true to herself.

Thérèse was too kind; the entire family was too kind, in the sense that an implicit family arrangement tended toward establishing peace at any price. This was part of the arrangement that identified a family member as "good." Thérèse, however, was beginning to sense that her acts of kindness, acts that pleased and accommodated family members, acts that fostered the family pattern, were sometimes motivated by her needs to be connected, to be secure, to be noticed and approved, to be a full family member—rather than motivated by real charity for others.

Her so-called "good" actions could have been examples of what St. Paul spoke of when he said, "If I give everything I have to feed the poor and hand over my body to be burned, but have not love, I gain nothing" (1 Corinthians 13:3). No one told Thérèse this. The truth was actually shrouded in the family pattern. Pondering the awareness of her mixed motives, however, she began to reflect on her personal pattern, and she began to grasp the subtle personal compromise that was threatening her.

For Thérèse, the clue that she needed the little miracle to call her back to her true self was a twofold awareness. First, she experienced that at the deepest part of herself she was not free; she was losing her inner freedom and integrity to the power of her feelings that she could not manage. And second, she began to see that she was moving toward violence.

Being dominated by feelings was not new to Thérèse; that had been a continuing weakness with her since her early years. She had been overcome by feelings when she had lashed out at Victoire and stamped her little foot as hard as she could. Her feelings had also overpowered her following her mother's death and again when she could not resist Marie's request to share the experience of intimacy with the Blessed Virgin.

These were not "sins," perhaps, but they were aspects of that "terrible fault," the loss of her true self. They were for Thérèse indications that by giving way to feelings she was doing violence to herself, to her own integrity. For Thérèse the loss of inner freedom and the movement toward violence, both violence toward herself and violence directed toward others, were compelling red flags.

Even after noticing what was happening within herself, Thérèse could have continued on this path in secret, but two personal and interrelated gifts surfaced to her rescue: her sensitive conscience and her longing for the truth. At some level of consciousness, she knew that the path she was on was not a path of truth. As Thérèse searched for Jesus, her true self—that self at one with the Spirit of Truth—was crying out in the flow of her frequent tears against the pattern she was following. In the delicacy of her conscience, Thérèse was listening.

In her autobiographical writings, Thérèse identifies many personal heroes, Joan of Arc and Théophane Vénard, among them. She compares herself most often, however, with Mary Magdalene, and she thought of Magdalene when she recognized that *I'd begin to cry again for having cried* (SS 97). Mary Magdalene was the saint who had almost sold her soul. In the biblical interpretation of Thérèse's era, Mary Magdalene was considered to have been on a path of falseness, believing that she could establish her security, self-worth, and identity and overcome her feelings of anxiety by the rewards that came through compromising herself. She lived a lie until she met Jesus.

Jesus raised Mary Magdalene to her own dignity as a child of God, as a person called to live her life in personal integrity. Magdalene was portrayed in the common scriptural teaching as having been physically promiscuous. Thérèse was becoming aware that in her efforts to overcome her difficult feelings, she was becoming emotionally promiscuous. Thérèse knew that, like Magdalene, she needed to meet Jesus in a way that would transform her.

This would be the miracle that Thérèse prayed for: that God would move her from the path bordering on compromising herself to the path of personal integrity at a new level. She spoke of this as the need she felt to *grow up*, out of *the swaddling clothes of a child!* (SS 97). It was the need to become more deeply her true self, relating to her Beloved without reservation; to "no longer be tossed here and there, carried about by every wind" (Ephesians 4:14), as St. Paul wrote, but to be carried by the breath of the Holy Spirit. Her security, self-worth, and identity needed to be established in her relationship to God alone; only this would allow her to bear serenely the distressing feelings of separation and loss.

Thérèse's need was not a matter of her avoiding a particular sin or acquiring a particular virtue. She needed a complete change from the path she had entered at the time of the death of her mother. She needed to reclaim her own soul. The experience of her mother's death had put her on the false path of self-indulgence, hypersensitivity, sadness, melancholy, and isolation.

Perhaps her uncle had seen some element of this truth when he regarded Thérèse as too concerned about her mother's death, implying that she was holding on to her pain for her own sake. Up to that point Isidore had been the only one to break the family pattern. On the occasion of his talk with Thérèse about her mother's death, he had implied that she needed to stop her self-indulgence and to get herself together. Through her uncle, the Holy Spirit had told her to reclaim her own spirit.

Her new path needed to be a reclaiming of the path she had traveled before her mother's death, but now with deeper awareness of her weaknesses and gifts, in humility and truth. Thérèse sensed that, with her mother's passing, she had lost her *strength of soul*. Now she realized that she needed to regain that *childhood character*, or she would eventually die spiritually (SS 98, 34). Her real nature had to bud forth with all its childlike simplicity and beauty; with all its originality, spontaneity, and creativity; with all its inner freedom and charity; with all its integrity and loving nonviolence. Then she would be on the path of becoming the person God called her to be.

When Thérèse experienced herself as weak, she thought that she needed the support, recognition, and praise of others. What she really needed was the inner strength—*the strength of soul*—that was founded on her own conscience and her relationship with her loving Father. *God would have to work a little miracle to make me grow up,* she recognized, *and this miracle He performed on that unforgettable Christmas day* (SS 97).

CHAPTER 15

The Grace of My Complete Conversion

When God's little miracle burst upon Thérèse, totally transforming her with spiritual enlightenment and personal empowerment, she referred to it as *the grace of my complete conversion* (SS 98; cf. GC II 1016). Ironically, the person closest to her did not even notice. Her father, her beloved king, could not have imagined that his little queen had even needed a conversion, yet the conversion happened in relationship to him. It was clearly all God's doing within the heart of Thérèse, while on the outside it unfolded in a trivial event precipitated unknowingly by her king.

Thérèse, now just a little more than a week from her fourteenth birthday, attended Christmas midnight Mass with her father. As part of the Christmas celebration *I used to love to take my shoes from the chimney-corner and examine the presents in them,* Thérèse remembered years later; *this old custom had given us so much joy in our youth that Céline wanted to continue treating me as a baby since I was the youngest in the family* (SS 98). Putting shoes by the chimney to be filled with tiny gifts was a custom similar to hanging stockings from the mantel, inviting children to be playful about trivial things while pretending surprise and showing great displays of affection.

After Mass Louis came into the living room, anticipating the customary scenario. Thérèse was going up the stairs to her bedroom to put her hat and coat away. Her father, thinking that she would not hear him, turned to Céline and said in a weary voice, bordering on exasperation, "Well fortunately, this will be the last year!" (SS 98).

Louis had not intended that Thérèse would hear his impatient remark. He was truly not himself; he was tired and was not following the family pattern in his role as a kind, restrained, patient father. Thérèse, however, had overheard the words, and they *pierced my heart* (SS 98). It was as if her father had now abandoned her.

She knew that *Papa had always loved to see my happiness and listen to my cries of delight as I drew each surprise from the magic shoes* (SS 98), but, with her father tired and irritated, this Christmas would be different. She had always tried to please him, especially on joyful occasions like this very Christmas night, and she had always succeeded. This time, however, she had failed, not by some sort of negligence on her part but by simply being herself in her role as the *baby*, the *youngest in the family*.

Thérèse heard her father's remark and was challenged by the ring of truth. Months before, she had heard similar words from her uncle and she had resisted. At that time her whole world had seemed to be threatened by her uncle's reference to her deceased mother and his admonishment to her. She had perceived him as an adversary and had fought any truth in his words. Her efforts to resist had resulted in her nervous disease. But her father was her beloved; she could not make her king an adversary. She listened.

She had also heard similar words in her own conscience: When will you give up being the baby? When will you not need to hold onto your feelings in a self-indulgent way? When will you give up the need to please everyone? When will you get out of the swaddling clothes? Now, in the presence of her king, Thérèse did not need to resist the truth.

Her father's words did not conform to the customary Martin family pattern. Louis had, indeed, with this one remark altered the entire blueprint of the family pattern. He was not supposed to say these words; and if he did, she was not supposed to hear them; and if she did hear them, she was supposed to burst into tears and continue to act like the baby. Her father spoke the words; Thérèse heard them, but she did not cry. Tears came to her eyes, but they did not flow.

Thérèse's sensitivity had been offended, but what of that? Could she not bear the pain of having inadvertently displeased her father, if enduring that pain was necessary to remain true to herself? Originally, in conformity with the family pattern, she had felt that if she did displease her father, she would not survive as the person she was. Her feelings had made her believe that failing to please her father would mean that she was not the good person on which she had staked her identity. Who would she be if she were not the sensitive, pleasing little Thérèse? She felt that she would surely die; it was as simple as that. Her feelings told her that she would simply no longer exist; that she would dissolve, as it were, into nothingness.

The threat of the feelings of separation and being abandoned attendant on Thérèse's displeasing her father were so intimidating that they raised the specter of annihilation. The movement from the path Thérèse had been on with its dimension of falseness to the path of deeper truth to which she was called—a movement of profound transformation—felt like death. That feeling was not unlike the experience of St. Paul, who, in his conversion, had felt the annihilation of having to "forfeit everything" (Philippians 3:8), even his sense of identity.

But Thérèse was not annihilated. She did not die; she did not even get ill as she had at the words of her uncle. She stood her ground emotionally, and taking the next step on the stairway to her room, she experienced an inner strength that resonated with her simple physical strength of climbing the steps. To her profound relief and liberation, she did not fall into nothingness. She survived, and as she continued to climb the stairs, one step at a time, she felt in her soul the strength of the God whom she had received just a few minutes before at the Christmas Eucharist. *He made me strong and courageous,* Thérèse recalled, *arming me with His weapons,* the weapons of God's own Spirit: truth, freedom, and peace (SS 97).

Céline, knowing that Thérèse had overheard her father's remark, ran up the stairs behind her to comfort her. But Thérèse did not need to be comforted. She had immediate feelings of hurt—indeed, it was true, deep hurt—but they were only feelings, and she did not need to harbor them. She was not a baby any longer. She had broken out of the family pattern and had reclaimed her true spirit. She felt a sense of inner freedom surge within her. She felt grace enter into her soul in the form of power, courage, and love.

Céline was astonished. She could not believe her eyes. Thérèse had never been this strong before. Céline had believed that her little sister had always needed to be comforted and treated like a baby, just as she had consoled and reassured Thérèse against her classmates. Now Thérèse did not need Céline. Thérèse had gained a sense of herself that detached her from her feelings of neediness. *Céline believed it was all a dream!* (SS 98).

Having reached her room, Thérèse put her hat on the bed. Tears were in her eyes, it was true, but she ignored Céline's need to comfort her; she turned, and walked down the steps. With a sense of calm and joy she opened the little gifts that were in her shoes. Céline's astonishment grew. Thérèse had *acted* this way each Christmas, but she had never *been* this way before. She had never been the person who could manage her sensitivity, who could stand her emotional ground in the face of powerful feelings; and yet that was exactly what was happening now. Céline, who knew Thérèse so well, understood that something deeply transformative had happened to her. She recognized that, as her little sister said of herself, *Thérèse was no longer the same; Jesus had changed her heart!* (SS 98). Thérèse had regained her soul. She had *found once again her childhood character,* and it was Jesus' Christmas gift to her. *He transformed me in such a way that I no longer recognized myself* (GC II 1016).

As Thérèse opened her little gifts with her usual cheerfulness and expressions of surprise and joy, she delighted her father, eliminated his weariness, and brought him back to his best self. Thérèse was pleasing her father, but not because she needed to please him to make herself feel connected and good. She was pleasing him now because, from the depths of her true self with a deepened sense of inner freedom, she could act in whatever compassionate, creative, and free way she was called to. And pleasing her father was exactly what, on this Christmas night, she was called to do and wanted to do. She could leave behind her own needs and accommodate her father as he needed to be accommodated and supported.

Thérèse was on a new path. Because of her tender nature, her capacity to be empathetic, and her sensitive spirit, she would, of course, continue to please people throughout her life and sometimes makes mistakes, but from this time of her complete conversion she would never walk on the path of accommodating others at the expense of her own true self. That is, she would never please others because in a self-indulgent way she needed to please them for her own sense of security, or closeness, or fear of separation. Now she would accommodate others in a spirit of freedom and creativity, and as an expression of real love. In pleasing others, she would never again act in violence to her own integrity.

By the time Thérèse had entered Carmel, she had become so skilled at pleasing others and accommodating situations that she never insisted on her own way. Out of love and concern for the sisters in Carmel and with the intention of pleasing God, she became so adept at not even manifesting her preferences, that the sisters with whom she lived for many years were never aware of them. The sisters never knew of Thérèse's suffering at not having her own preferences fulfilled, even in such basic areas as food or friendship. What the sisters were noticing was that she never acted out of willfulness. She appeared to have no will of her own. One sister wrote that for Thérèse, virtue must have been very easy because she never complained.

To the end of her life, Thérèse was, however, always aware of the power of the feelings that tried to manipulate her. As she lay on her deathbed, her feelings of needing to please others almost got the better of her. Pauline recounts the story of Sr. Philomena's nephew, who was to celebrate his first Mass at Carmel and was to bring Thérèse Communion. At the time Thérèse was suffering enormous physical and emotional distress. For a while she had been regularly coughing blood, and had not been able to receive the Eucharist. Nevertheless, Pauline asked Thérèse to pray to be able to receive Communion from the hand of Sr. Philomena's nephew.

Thérèse answered, *You know well that I cannot ask this myself, but you ask it for me. . . . This evening, in spite of my feelings* [of physical pain], *I was asking God for this favor in order to please my little sisters and so that the community might not be disappointed; but in my heart I told Him just the contrary; I told Him to do just what He wanted* (HLC 99).

To her final days Thérèse still had strong feelings of needing to please others, but she had become aware that this was a weakness that she needed to resist and willingly submit to divine mercy.

Thérèse's conversion had been God's little miracle. Her only contribution had been the willingness to stand her ground and not be intimidated by her feelings. That reality had been thrust upon her; she had never before thought that she could do it.

Thérèse experienced her Christmas miracle as empowerment. Up until that night all her efforts had been futile. She had been helpless in the grip of her feelings. She had been falling into the compulsion of codependency, of allowing her identity to be established by others, of compromising her true self. Now she was empowered to cope with her feelings and to put them into a proper order, to put them *underfoot,* as she would later say. She did not need to be intimidated by her feelings or think that if she did not follow them she would cease to exist.

On that night when He made Himself subject to weakness and suffering for love of me, He made me strong and courageous, arming me with His weapons, Thérèse wrote. *Since that night I have never been defeated in any combat, but rather walked from victory to victory, beginning, so to speak, "to run as a giant"!* [Psalm 18:6] (SS 97).

The Christmas miracle also enlightened her. That Christmas night, Thérèse said, was a *night of light.* Receiving a new confidence and inner strength, she came to know a God who would supply for her weakness. She became more deeply aware of her own pattern of self-preoccupation and self-indulgence, and now she experienced a divine call *to forget herself and to please others* in real charity.

Thérèse saw also that her spiritual growth was not the achievement of her work, which, after all, she *had been unable to do in ten years.* Since the death of her mother she had attempted to cope with her feelings; she had tried to establish her soul in God; she had tried to move out of her tendency to compromise herself, but she simply, of her own power, had not been able to do any of these. The growth she now experienced was a complete gift *done by Jesus in one instant,* Thérèse reflected. God was *contenting himself with my good will which was never lacking* (SS 98). Her loving Father did not need her "work" but rather her "good will," that is, her "willingness."

Thérèse's knew more clearly that God's power was enfolded in mercy, and that divine mercy was available to her good will. She now could say to Jesus, *like His apostles, "Master, I fished all night and caught nothing"* [Luke 5:5]. *More merciful to me than He was to His disciples, Jesus took the net Himself, cast it, and drew it in filled with fish* (SS 99). She could trust and love, and abandon herself with confidence into the arms of her loving Father.

Thérèse's spirit opened out, and her life changed. She said of her *complete conversion* that she *had discovered once again, the strength of soul which she had lost at the age of four and a half, and she was to preserve it forever!* (SS 98). The next months contained one new liberating experience after another, one new self-awareness after another, as she worked out the deep implications of what had happened.

Actually it took Thérèse the remaining years of her life to explore all the meanings and challenges of that Christmas grace, the deep and rich implications of which gradually unfolded into the Little Way of her spirituality. She was on a new path, and she knew with certainty that it was God's path for her.

CHAPTER 16

I Experienced Transports of Love

The experience of her complete conversion put Thérèse in touch with her soul. She felt a new inner freedom and inner strength. She experienced a new intensity in her spiritual desires, a new burst of energy in her zeal, a new depth of self-confidence, a new openness to truth and self-awareness, a new movement toward learning, a new spirit of love, a new sense of mission, and a more profound sense of her vocation to Carmel. The year 1887, beginning barely a week after Thérèse's conversion, was to be one of the happiest of her life. She was fourteen years old, and as a special source of delight she also experienced during that year a new burst of physical growth that almost took her to the full stature she was to reach at five feet four inches.

At this period of her life, in addition to the gospels, two religious books became especially important for Thérèse. *The Imitation of Christ,* a classic spiritual text from the fifteenth century, had a profound effect on her. It was a book that validated the Martin family lifestyle with its emphasis on the dangers of worldly involvement, on detachment from worldly fashions, and on the importance of the spiritual practices of prayer, mortification, solitude, and charity. Thérèse committed the book to memory.

The Imitation of Christ advised a "disdain" for "vain secular learning." Yet, Thérèse's complete conversion had reduced the clamoring of her feelings, and with her newly found sense of inner freedom she was drawn more deeply into the adventures of the mind. An *extreme desire for learning* had awakened in her. What was she to do? Fulfilling some of the potential of her conversion, she held her ground emotionally and was not intimidated even by the respect she had for *The Imitation.* Knowing that *I was at the most dangerous age for young girls,* Thérèse nevertheless told herself that being *at an age for study, it could not be bad to do it. I don't believe that I offended God. . . . Not satisfied with the lessons and work my teacher was giving me, I applied myself to some special studies in history and science, and I did this on my own.* Reading extensively, *in a few months, I acquired more knowledge than during my years of study* (SS 101).

Thérèse now possessed the self-confidence that she would need in abundance, especially in the face of religious authority, to continue on a new path that would increasingly diverge from the contemporary path of holiness.

The second book that was so important to Thérèse at this time was a collection of conferences by Fr. Arminjon entitled *The End of the Present World and the Mysteries of the Future Life*. It was not a spiritual book of classic dimensions and has not endured, but *this reading,* she said, *was one of the greatest graces in my life* (SS 102). The book had been lent to her father by Pauline from the Carmel library. Thérèse read it and copied a number of lengthy passages. She saved these passages and reread them often. The book touched her heart with its description of the glories of heaven.

Arminjon's book confirmed that the rewards of heaven will not be something like thrones or crowns, or whatever those symbols of prestige might mean. Rather, the reward and joy of heaven will be *someone.* Those rewarded in heaven will, of course, have bliss and happiness, but it will be the eternal love-relationship with God that will constitute the essence of their heavenly joy. Thérèse understood that the beginnings of that relationship are already available in this life, and she wanted more than anything else to develop that relationship in every way she could.

A passage that she copied from Arminjon's book described what God would say to those who opened their hearts to reciprocate divine love. In their final hour of life God would embrace them and say, "Now it is My turn! Can I respond to the gift which the saints have made to Me other than by giving Myself now without limit or measure? . . . Yes, it must be so: I am now the soul of their soul. I must penetrate them with My blessedness, as fire penetrates iron. . . . I must show Myself to their spirit cloudlessly, unveiled, without the medium of the senses, must unite Myself with them face to face" (HF 129). Thérèse was delighted.

This imagery deeply affected Thérèse, and she would return to it again and again in her own prayer and in her spiritual teaching. She would use this imagery to justify and to give meaning to all her pain and suffering. What could all suffering amount to if at life's end her loving Father would say, "Now it is My turn!" (cf. GC I 450–51, note 5)?

Never would Thérèse speak of the soul's weaknesses being purified except in the imagery of the soul's being penetrated and consumed by God as by fire. She would teach that the fire of divine love is more purifying than the fires of purgatory. Her loving Father's embrace consumes and purifies weaknesses and sins. There is no room for a notion such as God's retaliation.

She prayed at the end of her life, *If through weakness I sometimes fall, may Your Divine Glance cleanse my soul immediately, consuming all my imperfections like the fire that transforms everything into itself* (SS 276). She would experience suffering as God's way of consuming her in divine love. She would speak of heaven as *seeing God face to face.*

Thérèse and Céline talked about such matters in conversations in the belvedere of their home, often conversing long into the evening. After Thérèse's conversion the two sisters *could understand each other* more profoundly, Thérèse remembered. *The distance of age no longer existed because I had grown in both height and grace.* Experiencing her little sister as having greatly matured, Céline confided in Thérèse with a new openness about her own spiritual insights and feelings. Céline's confidences were a *sweet echo of my soul,* and Thérèse was greatly consoled. The two, described by their mother when they were children as two peas in a pod, had become *spiritual sisters* (SS 103).

Thérèse now brought to her spiritual conversations with Céline a spontaneous and lively expression that she had lacked before her conversion. They spoke together of heaven and especially of how they could foster their love relationship with God that was to last into eternity. They spoke of the beauty and goodness that divine love had put into their lives through nature, as well as through their parents and their sisters. Thérèse was especially grateful for the experience of her conversion, and the love that then entered her soul. *At the age of fourteen, I also experienced transports of love. Ah! How I loved God! . . . I wanted to love, to love Jesus with a passion, giving Him a thousand proofs of my love while it was possible* (SS 102).

Thérèse was discovering new insights into herself and into the spiritual life. She felt a certainty and a clarity in faith. She tapped the depths of truth and love that, in her expansiveness, she believed made hope unnecessary and doubt impossible. In the glow of the feelings of confidence, peace, and joy, she thought, *I don't know if I'm mistaken, but it seems to me the outpourings of our souls were similar to those of St. Monica with her son* [Augustine] *when, at the post of Ostia, they were lost in ecstasy at the sight of the Creator's marvels!* (SS 104).

She had been granted permission by her confessor to receive Communion more frequently, sometimes as often as four times a week. Thérèse had no hesitation in acknowledging her own unworthiness to receive the Eucharist, but as she said, *It appeared to be Jesus Himself who desired to give Himself to me* (SS 105). She reflected on her weakness and sinfulness and began to understand that reverence for the Eucharist should not mean that it be received infrequently, but just the opposite. The more reverence she had for Communion, she believed, the more often she should receive, because Jesus had come to earth for sinners and now he was offering himself continually to sinners in Communion.

Thérèse recognized that Jesus, in the Eucharist, was lowering himself to her just as he had lowered himself in the incarnation to all sinners. *When Jesus wills to take for Himself the sweetness of giving,* Thérèse would later write, *it would not be gracious to refuse. Let us allow Him to take and give all He wills* (GC II 795).

These spiritual insights came to Thérèse as she contemplated the truths that she had read and as she prayed over the experiences of her own life. She knew that even now *because I was little and weak He lowered Himself to me, and He instructed me secretly in the things of His love.* She was now on a path of spiritual enlightenment, and she believed that Jesus himself was teaching her directly. *Had the learned who spent their life in study come to me,* she wrote in her wisdom at twenty-two years old as she was formulating her Little Way, *undoubtedly they would have been astonished to see a child of fourteen understand perfection's secrets, secrets all their knowledge cannot reveal because to possess them one has to be poor in spirit!* She was convinced that God *willed to have His mercy shine out in me* (SS 105; cf. SS 158).

The life of God that would continue to grow into eternity was surging in Thérèse, and she could feel it in her emotional life as well as in her life of faith. Her inner freedom was deepening, her love expanding, and her vocation to Carmel was now certain. *The divine call was so strong that had I been forced to pass through flames, I would have done it out of love for Jesus* (SS 106).

Pauline, now five years in Carmel, continued to encourage Thérèse in her vocation. Marie, however, knowing intimately of Thérèse's bout with scruples just a short time before, thought she was too young to enter Carmel. At first and with feelings of inner conflict, Thérèse avoided speaking of her desire with her confidante Céline, fearing that she too might object. But Céline received the announcement with graciousness and courage. She became her younger sister's greatest support.

Six months after her conversion, in May 1887, now confident of God's call, Thérèse asked her father for his permission to enter the Carmelite convent. Earlier that month Louis had suffered a slight stroke, which had caused several hours of paralysis. He had recovered, although at almost sixty-four years old he was considerably frailer than before. Thérèse tried to choose the right moment to ask him to sacrifice his third daughter.

On Pentecost Sunday evening, Thérèse found her father sitting in the garden. She had prepared herself during the day, pondering the right time and the right words. Four years before, on this same feast day, she had been cured by the smile of the Virgin. Now, she approached her father, and, weeping, she poured out her desires, asking for his permission. Holding one another, they walked tearfully together in the garden. Her father naturally suggested that she was too young to make such a decision, but the intensity of her desire readily moved him and easily convinced him.

Louis plucked a small white flower that was growing on the low garden wall, its roots still intact. Showing it to Thérèse, he explained to her the providential love with which God had brought the little flower, a symbol of herself, into being and had preserved it to that day. As they wept together, he gave it to her as a sign of her heavenly Father's love and his own tender love, as well. She treasured the little white flower the rest of her life, carefully preserving it between the pages of her copy of *The Imitation of Christ*, at the chapter entitled "One must love Jesus above all things." That, coincidentally, was the chapter that many months later, Mother Gonzague, knowing that Thérèse had memorized the book, would ask her to recite on the day of her entrance into Carmel. Its title echoed Thérèse's fundamental desire.

She had hoped that her entry into Carmel would be in six months time, just as she turned fifteen; or even, more joyfully, on the day of Christmas to commemorate the first anniversary of her complete conversion. Thérèse was convinced that God wanted her to enter Carmel, but she formed her own idea of just when that would occur. Still needing to grow into deeper awareness of her own self-love, and to *forget herself,* she did not see anything particularly willful or self-centered about her determining the exact day.

Three years later she would also set a date, this time for her profession of vows in Carmel. When that date was delayed by the priest-superior, who was convinced that Thérèse was too young to make vows, she then had an insight into her self-centeredness. As she prayed about how distressed she was by the delay, she came to the awareness that her *intense desire to make Profession was mixed with a great self-love* (SS 158; GC II 902–3). That insight was a sign of the spiritual progress that Thérèse would make along her path of awareness and freedom. But now, even with all the enlightenment of her conversion, she was still unaware of her possible mixed motives and she blissfully set the precise date for her entrance into Carmel.

CHAPTER 17

I Felt Charity Enter My Heart

One of the first experiences Thérèse associated with her Christmas conversion was the deepening of her capacity to love. *I felt charity enter my heart*, she said (SS 99; cf. HLC 77). Charity had always been in her heart, but now she experienced it differently. Now charity removed her need to be so preoccupied with herself and with what others were thinking of her, and it challenged her mixed motivations. Thérèse's charity would now have less and less to do with codependency or protecting herself against the frightful feelings of separation, and little to do with feelings at all. She began to understand more deeply that gospel love is all about detachment from self-centeredness so as to be sufficiently *poor in spirit*, receptive enough to accept God's love, and willing to share that love in acts of charity.

A holy picture fell out of her missal, and she gazed on the image of Jesus crucified. She had seen this particular picture or similar ones many times before, but on this occasion the image touched her differently. Seeing that Jesus' blood was falling on the barren ground, she suddenly recognized that Jesus' love was not being received or reverenced; it was not being appreciated or reciprocated. She had an insight into her role in God's redemptive act. *I was resolved*, she wrote later, *to remain in spirit at the foot of the Cross and to receive the divine dew. I understood I was then to pour it out upon souls* (SS 99).

Thérèse heard Jesus' words on the cross, "I thirst," reverberate in her heart. *These would ignite within me an unknown and very living fire*, she wrote. *I wanted to give my Beloved to drink and I felt myself consumed with a thirst for souls* (SS 99). By participating with Jesus in thirsting for souls, she desired to receive Jesus' blood and to share that outpouring of love with those who might otherwise never see God face to face.

She wanted to give him souls, especially the souls of great sinners, so that they would hear God one day say to them what she had read in Arminjon's book: "Thus it must be, that My glory illuminates them, that it breaks forth and radiates from all the pores of their being, that they recognize Me as I recognize them, that they become as gods" (HF 129).

Thérèse was coming to understand that for her to love Jesus was primarily for her to receive Jesus' love. To love was not a matter of her trying to love Jesus or to love others with her own love. She knew she could not do that, simply because her own love was mostly self-love. The charity entering her heart at the moment of her conversion was divine love coming into her in a new way, inviting her to love in a new way.

She was limited and weak, but she could receive Jesus' love. She knew that the attitude itself of receptivity and reciprocity gave Jesus pleasure. Jesus' thirst was the thirst that became for her a thirst to be receptive to Jesus' love and to share his love with others in thought, desire, and action.

Standing at the foot of the cross, Thérèse was aware of being at the point of union with God and the world. In her own life, this was for her the point of the union of receiving and giving, of faith and zeal, of surrender and initiative. She saw herself at the center of divine love, receiving Jesus' love and mediating that love to the world. This self-understanding was a great grace for Thérèse, and by giving this grace to her, her Beloved had, in one bold and stunning stroke, accommodated Thérèse's gifts and weaknesses.

By inspiring her to take her place at the foot of the cross, God had fulfilled Thérèse's desire for intimacy with Jesus and for love of others. This grace redeemed her need to be connected and bonded with others by associating her with Jesus' own role as mediator of divine grace. It healed her fear of abandonment by this deep spiritual bond with Jesus. It purified her need to please others and to be of service; and it gave meaning and significance to her suffering. This grace transfigured her self-centeredness by placing Thérèse at the center of the paschal mystery and transformed her self-preoccupation by empowering her to participate in Jesus' redemptive work.

Thérèse was beginning to discover in a new way the reason for her very existence. She was deepening her sense of identity and self-worth in the security of her relationship with her loving Father. Divine love, she understood from her own family, was primary. God loves us first. Thérèse had heard it also in the gospel; now she was experiencing it at a deeper level in her own personal relationship with God. Having come to clarity about the gospel truth that the primary way for the followers of Jesus to love God is to allow divine love to envelop them, she recognized that her role of praying for sinners was a way of sharing God's love with them.

At this very time there came to Thérèse's attention news of a murderer who was about to be executed. Henri Pranzini, a great sinner in the eyes of all who heard of him, had brutally killed a lady of the court, her child, and her maid. The crime had occurred in Paris, and the murderer was apprehended in Marseille trying to sell the stolen jewels. This was major news in all the secular and religious newspapers throughout France. There was much talk about the viciousness of the crime, the depravity of the criminal, and the rightness of the execution.

Although Pranzini was mocked in the press as "the sinister scoundrel," "the monster," and "the vile brute," Thérèse did not condemn him in her thoughts, nor did she participate in the gossip surrounding the event. Learning that he was unrepentant, she felt a deep surge of compassion for him and experienced a spiritual impulse to save him from damnation. She adopted him as her *first child*. She would pray him into repentance. She knew that this would seem unusual even to Céline, so she tried to keep her intentions a secret. But again, as with Marie, she broke her promise to herself because Céline *asked me such tender and pressing questions* (SS 99). Céline, however, understood immediately, and the two now prayed together for Pranzini.

Standing at the foot of the cross in Pranzini's place, Thérèse offered to God the infinite treasure of Jesus' love that she was willing to accept in herself on his behalf. It was a bold prayer, of a kind she had never prayed before. It came from a new understanding of her role of mediating Jesus' love. She was confident, but at the same time she prayed to God *begging Him for a "sign" of* [Pranzini's] *repentance only for my own simple consolation* (SS 100).

Thérèse began to see how narrow was the circle of self-centeredness in which she had been moving before her conversion. She had been striving to love others mostly with her own love, which was often tainted with the codependent self-love of calming her own difficult feelings. Now she saw that God was moving her in another way: a way of letting divine love be the energy of her desire to participate in Jesus' redemptive work, a way that at the same time moved her to *forget herself*. She asked for a "sign" that her new path of mediating Jesus' love to others was indeed the path God intended for her.

As the time of his execution neared, Pranzini had not received the Sacrament of Reconciliation. He maintained his plea of innocence. He had, in fact, given no sign whatsoever of repentance.

The day after the execution, with the self-confidence and spiritual audacity fostered by her conversion, *in spite of Papa's prohibition that we read no papers,* Thérèse acted on the simple belief that, *I didn't think I was disobeying when reading the passages pertaining to Pranzini* (SS 100).

He had mounted the scaffold, Thérèse remembered reading, *and was preparing to place his head in the formidable opening, when suddenly, seized by an inspiration, he turned, took hold of the crucifix the priest was holding out to him and kissed the sacred wounds three times.* Thérèse's heart pounded as she read. It was the sign that she had asked for. It was also a perfect replication of the grace Jesus had given her just a short time before: the grace of knowing the value of Jesus' wounds from which Jesus' love flowed, and *the lips of my "first child" were pressed to the sacred wounds!* (SS 100).

The picture of Jesus' blood falling unaccepted to the ground had awakened in her the infinite value of Jesus' suffering on the cross and the availability of his love to those who would embrace that cross. Now Thérèse's joy was a participation in that great joy of those in heaven over one sinner who repents. Later she would express in prayer the bold desire to share for eternity the wounds of Jesus crucified: *I hope in heaven to resemble you and to see shining in my glorified body the sacred stigmata of your passion* (SS 277).

Thérèse gradually understood that standing under the cross was also to be in a place of potential personal suffering. It was a place of pain, not self-inflicted, masochistic pain, but the pain of being with Jesus in his suffering; the pain of bearing that daily cross of which Jesus had spoken. The meaning of suffering in the spiritual life began to emerge with more clarity in Thérèse's consciousness.

To catch the blood flowing from the hands of the Crucified and to participate in the suffering and pain of Jesus was, above all, to bear with Jesus the suffering of ordinary life, the pain of the human condition; the pain of being displeasing to oneself in personal weakness, inadequacy, and incompleteness; the pain thoughtlessly or even deliberately inflicted by others. It meant not to retaliate, not to be vindictive or violent; not to be discouraged or self-indulgent. Such were the considerations that became part of Thérèse's spiritual attitude and teaching.

With the experience of Pranzini's conversion, Thérèse had taken an important step in her mission of standing under the cross and mediating divine love to the world. Her full understanding of the implications of her mission would be years in unfolding. The significance and the extent of the role of suffering in her life, as she continued to stand under the cross, would also gradually be revealed. *There still remained many things for me to leave behind*, Thérèse knew; but *the biggest step was taken* (SS 101). She now needed to take the next step to fulfilling her missionary vocation, and that step was to enter Carmel.

When Thérèse spoke to Céline of her desire to enter Carmel, Céline had nobly supported her completely. Céline, now eighteen, knew that their father needed emotional and physical support, especially following his stroke, and she decided to remain with him. She was unusually mature for a girl her age and would receive a proposal for marriage within the year. She was presently doubtful of her own vocation, but Thérèse never doubted that Céline too should one day come to Carmel. For now, however, in their evenings together in the belvedere they spoke about the power of prayer, of their father's health, of his tender willingness to give Thérèse permission to enter Carmel, and of how Thérèse might eventually approach her uncle for his permission, which was still required. Thérèse was confident. All was well.

CHAPTER 18

I Knew Jesus Was There Sleeping in My Boat

Having received from her father permission to enter Carmel, Thérèse felt a new surge of joy in her spirit. Convinced that her vocation to religious life was not simply her desire but the divine call in her, she was determined to follow it. Her willingness to take her place beneath the cross prepared her to endure the painful obstacles she was to meet on the path to her vocation.

By requesting entry into the Carmelite convent in Lisieux where two of her sisters, Marie and Pauline, were already nuns, and by requesting that she be received in her fifteenth year, Thérèse was asking for special treatment on two counts. One rule of Carmel stated that no one was to be accepted before the age of twenty-one. Exceptions to this age restriction were sometimes made, but very rarely.

Another rule of Carmel, dating back to the time of St. Teresa of Avila, stated that no more than two members of the same immediate family should be accepted into the same convent. In this regard, also, exceptions were sometimes made. For Thérèse to have anticipated that in her case exceptions would be made to both of these rules was hardly realistic.

Thérèse needed the permission of her uncle Isidore because he had become deputy guardian of the five Martin girls following the death of their mother, so she sought out the best occasion to make her request. Her father had responded graciously, but she was not so sure about her uncle. Graciousness was not a word she ever associated with him. Isidore was of a completely different temperament from her father. Whereas her father, although strong in integrity, was quiet and unassuming, even vulnerable and shy, Isidore was blustery and powerful, self-assured and domineering.

Thérèse's relationship with her uncle had been most seriously affected four years before when she was ten and he had brought up the topic of her mother's death. At that time, Isidore had seen Thérèse as a melancholy little girl, overly sensitive and holding on to the pain of her mother's death in a self-indulgent way. His intrusive manner had precipitated Thérèse's frightful illness, and then during her serious sickness he had even tried to distract her from thinking of Carmel when such thoughts alone gave her life. Also during her time at school, although she was considered intelligent by her teachers and classmates, *it wasn't like that at Uncle's house,* Thérèse remembered; *where I was taken for a little dunce, good and sweet, and with right judgment, yes, but incapable and clumsy* (SS 82). All these memories weighed on Thérèse as she prepared to meet with him.

Dreading to ask her uncle's permission, yet wanting to make the request herself in a forthright way, she waited for four months after her father's approval so she could find both the courage and the right moment. When the day came, she was trembling as she spoke with him.

Isidore had not previously noticed Thérèse's psychological and spiritual growth since the months after her Christmas conversion. Trying to respond kindly to her request, he nevertheless followed his usual abrupt style and bluntly said no. Furthermore, he explicitly forbade Thérèse to speak with him about the matter again until she was seventeen years old.

The reason for his decision, he announced to Thérèse, was that she was just too young and immature for the life of Carmel. He spoke of "human prudence." He suggested that he himself would be eminently embarrassed if, after granting his permission, she were not to persevere in the convent. Léonie's behavior had made that a clear possibility—she had just left home in her second attempt at becoming a religious. A town filled with gossip about his lack of good judgment would not enhance his personal prestige or his income from his pharmacy business. He added that it would take a miracle to change his mind. That was the end of the matter as far as he was concerned.

Knowing that she could not reason with Uncle Isidore as she had with her father, and knowing that tears would have had the opposite effect on him as with her father, Thérèse felt defeated and was overcome with deep sadness. Whereas her father had also raised the same objection about her age, he had an empathy and sensitivity that she did not experience in her uncle.

Thérèse had come to Isidore frightened but with a certain amount of self-confidence, which was based on what she believed God wanted. If Isidore needed a miracle, he would get one. Twice before in difficult situations she had prayed for miracles; they had been granted. Now she turned to her loving Father with confidence.

Even though Thérèse knew that her sensitivity was being healed by her conversion, she still found feelings of separation and lack of support to be powerfully disturbing in her heart. In the following days she lived out the profound inner distress that flowed from Isidore's assault on her self-confidence and judgment. She continued to be in contact with him informally and socially, and continued to feel distraught, experiencing these casual meetings as having an air of artificiality and uneasiness. For Isidore's part it was business as usual. He apparently had had no trouble putting the matter out of his mind and assuming that all was finished.

Thérèse's inward suffering festered during those weeks. Pauline was informed of Isidore's refusal and promised to pray as well. The hope Thérèse had had was slipping away; she was experiencing *great sadness* of a degree she thought similar to the *sorrow of Mary and Joseph during their three-day search for the divine Child Jesus* (SS 109). Thérèse's own prayer was becoming more and more arid. God, whom she believed had inspired her with the desire to enter Carmel, seemed to have abandoned her.

For three days in particular during these weeks, her soul was in deep distress, a painful martyrdom. Thérèse felt as if she were in *a sad desert, or rather my soul was like a fragile boat,* she remembered, *delivered up to the mercy of the waves and having no pilot. I knew Jesus was there sleeping in my boat, but the night was so black it was impossible to see Him* (SS 109).

The dark night of the soul was the way Thérèse described these days. Being purified of her self-centeredness, she was under the cross again, or rather *all alone in the garden of Gethsemane like Jesus, and I found no consolation on earth or from heaven; God Himself seemed to have abandoned me.* The feelings of abandonment were again surfacing with all their fury. Thérèse even noticed that the weather during those days was miserable: *the sun did not shine and the rain poured down in torrents. . . . Nature seemed to share in my bitter sadness* (SS 109–10).

These very feelings and thoughts that were now inundating Thérèse were the very kinds of emotions and ideas that her uncle Isidore, for all his goodwill, would probably have found childish, sentimental, immature, even self-indulgent, and certainly excessive. But Thérèse was living at a different level of reality in which God was ever present and active.

Thérèse decided that she could not go on like this. She was frightened of her uncle, it was true, but she did not have to be intimidated. As she had in her Christmas experience with her father, she could take the next step. She would not die. She could take courage, endure the pain of fear, and act in faith. If God were giving her this desire for Carmel, then divine grace would give her the courage. She would make a second appeal to her uncle.

Praying to Mary, Queen of Heaven, and to her own mother, Thérèse decided to see Isidore again, with or without a miracle. So distressing had been this time that to her it had seemed like an eternity since his refusal; it had been only two weeks.

Probably accompanied by Céline or her father, Thérèse came to the Guérin house on a routine visit, but hoping in particular to speak to her uncle. She had intended to take the initiative to see Isidore, but before she had a chance to ask to speak with him, he requested that she come into his study. Without Thérèse's knowledge, Pauline had written him the day before and had expressed to him what Thérèse had told her of her previous difficult visit with him. Pauline's letter had made Isidore conscious of his intimidating power over Thérèse and, being fond of her, he felt contrite.

Thérèse stood quietly before her uncle. *He began by making some gentle reproaches because I appeared to be afraid of him*, she later recalled (SS 110). Apparently he had taken Pauline's comments to heart, noticed his effect on Thérèse, and tried to make light of his overpowering style. Now he was more considerate and recognized that her *great sadness* that he had actually noticed during the casual meetings of the past weeks was not part of her old state of melancholy and self-indulgence. It was rather an appropriate sadness over the pain he had caused her by his abruptness and his dismissive manner; it was a sadness flowing from her feelings of being rejected and diminished, and from her sense of confusion over whether she had possibly misunderstood the divine will.

In an attempt at a disarming little joke, Isidore told his niece she did not need to continue to pray for a miracle. He himself had asked God and he himself had received an answer by being given a change of heart. Actually Thérèse had noticed the change in him. *Uncle was no longer the same. Without making any allusion whatsoever to human prudence, he told me I was a little flower God wanted to gather, and he would no longer oppose it.* It was a subtle reference to the approval that her father had given her as he so graciously handed her the tiny white flower from the garden wall. *This definitive response*, Thérèse later wrote in a humorous reference to her uncle's always bold and domineering manner, *was truly worthy of him.* And then Thérèse noted of her aunt that now *when Uncle gave his consent, she too gave hers* (SS 110). It was another light allusion to Isidore's controlling manner.

Joy filled Thérèse's heart. She experienced an entirely new attitude in her uncle. He was not the Isidore of just two weeks before. Pauline in conjunction with God had indeed worked the very miracle required. Furthermore, even the weather was better; the sun was shining as brightly as Thérèse could ever remember, *a beautiful sky, from which all the clouds were dispersed!* (SS 110). The next day she went to report all this to Pauline.

Thérèse at fifteen, photographed with her hair knotted on top of her head, the coiffure she adopted in order to appear older for her visit to Bishop Hugonin in October 1887. This photograph was taken in April 1888, a few days before Thérèse entered Carmel.

CHAPTER 19

I Wanted Carmel as Soon as I Knew about It

Pauline had carefully intervened with her uncle, and was delighted that Isidore had been converted and had given Thérèse his permission. Pauline had also carefully orchestrated all the approvals that were necessary from within the convent itself, countering her sister Marie's objections, gaining agreement from the community, and confirming the approval of the prioress, Mother Gonzague. Pauline thought that the matter had been settled and that Thérèse's entrance had been established. But when Thérèse arrived to tell her personally of her experience with Uncle Isidore, Pauline had some bad news to share.

Fr. Delatroëtte, the rather morose and perfunctory sixty-nine-year-old priest who had been ecclesiastical superior of the convent for the past seventeen years, had power in such matters and had decided against Thérèse's entrance. Even though he would not object to the third member of the same family entering the Lisieux Carmel, the entrance age fixed by the Carmelite rule, he determined, should not be abrogated in Thérèse's case (cf. GC II 1017).

His opposition, of course, was valid, even though legalistic. Pauline had been completely taken by surprise and was embarrassed and distressed. With the decision coming from such an authority, however, the matter was definitively settled. Thérèse could not enter Carmel until she was twenty-one. She was again burdened with feelings of confusion and sadness.

Faced with this new obstacle, however, Thérèse was not intimidated. Fortified by the feelings of empowerment from her conversion, feelings that were validated and strengthened by the initiative that she had taken with her uncle, she made a personal decision to take immediate action. Within the next few days arrangements were made, and with her father she went to address Fr. Delatroëtte directly. The weather was cloudy, a bad omen.

The priest received Thérèse coldly, and although her father added his words of support to Thérèse's argument, he dismissed them quickly, remarking as they left his office that he merely represented the bishop of Bayeux, Bishop Hugonin, who could override his decision. Thérèse left in tears and into a torrential downpour of rain, but she had already decided to do two things. Her intention was focused and she was determined. She was again in touch with that stubbornness of her childhood, now transformed into a willingness to endure whatever it would take to bring her to Carmel. She had decided to go to the bishop, and further, was even *determined to do all within my power, even saying I would go to the Holy Father if the Bishop did not want to allow me to enter at fifteen* (SS 111).

In the following days Thérèse prayed more intensely, and her prayer came alive. Her loving Father had not abandoned her after all, and she felt love flooding her heart. She was receiving divine love and reciprocating that love in the initiative she was taking to fulfill what she believed to be God's will.

As she prepared to meet with the bishop, life exteriorly continued as normal. She continued to read and study, to take care of her pet birds and her dog, Tom, and to take drawing lessons from Céline. She also took her turn caring for two little girls, the older not yet six, daughters of a relative of the family maid. The poor woman was dying, and the children needed attention.

Thérèse became, for several days, the little girls' daytime babysitter and for the first time saw young children at close hand, noticing how innocent, simple, and docile they were to her suggestions. Once she had to reconcile them after an argument, and she did that by talking to them about heaven and eternal rewards, as her mother had done when she and Céline were at odds. She saw that children are vulnerable and *soft as wax upon which one can imprint either virtue or vice* (SS 113). Once again she thanked her loving Father for her own family upbringing.

During these days Thérèse grew interiorly in prayer founded, as best she could, on receiving God's love and doing everything as an expression of divine love in her. Then the thought came to her that those in hell did not return divine love. They had resisted God's love, and so no act of love came to God from hell. So much did she want to have everyone everywhere please her loving Father that she thought she would be willing to be *plunged into hell so that He would be loved eternally in that place of blasphemy.* Immediately, however, she *realized this could not give Him glory since He desires only our happiness, but when we love, we experience the need of saying a thousand foolish things* (SS 112). It was a foolish and impossible idea, but the transports of love that Thérèse felt evoked images of the foolish and impossible. And now she was going to ask the impossible from Bishop Hugonin.

Thérèse again had feelings of fear, but also a deeper courage had awakened in her. She was strengthened by a thought she remembered from *The Imitation of Christ*, "Love never finds impossibilities, because it believes everything is possible, everything is permitted."

As she and her father arrived at Bayeux, rain was coming down in torrents, another bad omen. She *got her beautiful dress soaking wet* and, since they were early, her father adjusted their plans, taking her to the cathedral so that her dress might dry a bit, rather than going directly to the bishop's house. In the cathedral an important funeral was in progress with the bishop in attendance. Thérèse remembered the incident humorously. All the prominent ladies in mourning were wearing black. *I was in a bright frock and white hat.* As she walked down the aisle, directed by her father, obediently taking a seat in the front pew she was *stared at by everybody. . . . Not wishing to give* [her father] *any trouble, I executed this with great grace and thus procured this distraction for the good inhabitants of Bayeux, whom I would have preferred never to have known* (SS 115). In retrospect she told this story with charm and wit, but at the time she felt humiliated and simply miserable.

The weather cleared, but other unpromising omens continued. Monsignor Révérony, the vicar-general who had set up the meeting, was absent at the appointed time, and so Thérèse and her father roamed the streets for a while longer. Then with lunchtime nearing, *Papa brought me into a magnificent hotel where I did not do honors to the excellent cooking. Poor little Father's tenderness for me was incredible! He told me not to be sad, that certainly the Bishop would agree with me* (SS 115). But with the rain and all, Thérèse was not so sure anymore.

Bishop Hugonin had administered the Sacrament of Confirmation to her, but as they met in his office he gave no indication of remembering that encounter three years before. Never before had she been in this kind of a setting in the presence of a bishop; never before had she approached such an authority trying to make her own case. She was determined to overcome her timidity and act with confidence even if she did not feel that way. She was in the place of Joan of Arc before the ecclesiastic interrogators.

But already she felt mortified. Monsignor Révérony refused her excuses, and *telling me to show if I knew how to obey,* insisted that she sit in *a huge armchair which could hold four like me comfortably,* while he himself took a much smaller chair (SS 116). Her father, rather than assuming the lead in explaining the purpose of the visit, invited Thérèse to begin. She was at first taken off stride, but quickly regained herself and spoke with conviction of her great desire to enter Carmel.

Bishop Hugonin asked Thérèse if *it had been a long time since I desired to enter Carmel. Oh! Yes, Bishop,* Thérèse replied enthusiastically to a question she really knew the answer to, *a very long time* (SS 116). She was sitting up much straighter now. Monsignor Révérony, who seems to have actually been charmed by Thérèse, turned to her as she was beginning to resurrect herself from her burial in the huge armchair, and knowing she was only fourteen years old, said tantalizingly with a sly smile, "Come now, you can't say it is fifteen years since you've had the desire?"

Momentarily taken aback—this was a question worthy of the inter-rogation of Joan—Thérèse avoided the bait and swam gracefully with the current. *Smiling, I said: "That's true, but there aren't too many years to subtract because I wanted to be a religious since the dawn of my reason, and I wanted Carmel as soon as I knew about it. I find all the aspirations of my soul are fulfilled in this Order"* (SS 116). Thérèse spoke quietly, with a twinkle in her eye, and her smile was sly as well.

Bishop Hugonin was not impressed, especially since Fr. Delatroëtte had opposed Thérèse's entrance. He also believed that he was pleasing her father by having Thérèse remain at home for a few more years. His final words were that he would consult Fr. Delatroëtte before finally deciding. Thérèse broke into tears; things were hopeless. But to the tears, the bishop, unlike her uncle, actually responded with great kindness, hugging her in her sadness and telling her that all was not lost; after all, she was scheduled to be part of a pilgrimage to Rome and, the bishop suggested, that might give her an opportunity to pray to strengthen her vocation. It would also give her, she knew in her determination, an opportunity to follow through on her plan to ask the pope himself for what the bishop had withheld.

Thérèse and her father were dismissed with a promise from Bishop Hugonin that he would let them know his final decision in a month or so. As they were leaving, her father casually told the bishop that Thérèse had put up her hair for the occasion to make herself appear older. It was a gesture of openness and simplicity on the part of Louis, but also a stroke of unintended diplomatic genius since, although Thérèse was not amused, the bishop was. He was also taken by this young child's great determination. Subsequently *he never spoke about "his little daughter,"* Thérèse wrote, *without telling the story of the hair* (SS 117).

Thérèse was still crying as they left Bishop Hugonin's residence. *It seemed my future had been ruined forever. . . . My soul was plunged in sadness, but also in peace, for I was seeking only God's will* (SS 118). And now she would seek to fulfill God's will by addressing the highest religious authority on earth.

CHAPTER 20

Most Holy Father, I Have a Great Favor to Ask You!

With her father and Céline, Thérèse had been scheduled to take part in a pilgrimage to Rome. Her father had made the arrangements some time before. The pilgrimage, which was to celebrate the fiftieth anniversary of the ordination of Pope Leo XIII, was scheduled to depart just three days after Thérèse's interview with Bishop Hugonin.

The pilgrimage group consisted of almost two hundred people, including about seventy-five priests and some thirty laymen and laywomen of the nobility. This was Thérèse's first time traveling to such distant places, for such a long time, and with such a large and impressive group. Rumors flew through the small town of Lisieux that Thérèse was being taken to Paris and Rome by her father so that she would be distracted from entering the convent. Her uncle had been right; gossip was an important part of people's lives, and it was "human prudence" to take it into account. But the Martin family was not concerned.

Thérèse, Céline, and Louis first traveled to Paris to join the main pilgrimage. While there they visited the Church of Our Lady of Victories, and during Mass Thérèse had a religious experience so moving *that my happiness found expression only in tears, just as on the day of my First Communion.* During these last four years, since she had been so suddenly cured of her frightful and near-fatal illness, she had been burdened with anxiety about whether something special had really happened or whether she had only imagined the Virgin's smile. Now, attending Mass in the Church of Our Lady of Victories, the home, as it were, of the statue of the Virgin of the Smile, Thérèse became quietly convinced that something special had indeed happened at that time. She had not just imagined the ravishing smile of the Virgin. *The Blessed Virgin made me feel it really was her who had smiled at me and cured me. I understood she was watching over me, that I was her child* (SS 123). Thérèse came to a deep sense of peace in the arms of her only real mother. This was the first of many graces of the pilgrimage.

Another grace Thérèse received as the pilgrimage moved from Paris was discovering that regarding the nobility, titles did not change people, and that regarding priests, *their dignity raises them above the angels,* [yet] *they are nevertheless weak and fragile men.* All kinds of people could be selfish and critical, judgmental and petty, vindictive and sarcastic, and given to hurting one another. Except for her sad time at the Benedictine school, Thérèse had lived and associated with people who were not prone to that type of attitude and behavior. She had somehow imagined that, perhaps, only inconsiderate children like herself had these weaknesses, but now she saw them in older people of all walks of life: those of noble class and cultural dignity, those of religious longings and priestly status, and everyone else in between. Thérèse was learning that no human being, even a priest, even one who seemed to be seeking God, was without the weaknesses of human nature. *If holy priests, whom Jesus in His Gospel calls the "salt of the earth"* [Matthew 5:13], *show in their conduct their extreme need for prayers,* she learned, *what is to be said of those who are tepid?* (SS 122).

The pilgrims, traveling by train, stopped in Milan, Venice, and Loreto before reaching Rome. Thérèse loved the beauty of the landscape, was inspired by some of the places she visited, and had some humorous incidents to recount to her sisters Pauline and Marie in the cloister. In Bologna Céline and Thérèse were harassed by students who lined the streets in a sporting mood. At the train station a group of young men, searching for such an occasion, noticed Céline and Thérèse standing alone, having been momentarily separated from their father. One young man ran to Thérèse, took hold of her, and was ready to carry her off. *I gave him such a look he soon let go!* (SS 128, note 141), Thérèse reported. *Besides, Céline had seen what happened and was coming to my rescue.* This pilgrimage was the first time Thérèse had associated with young men; she was not impressed.

In Rome at the Colosseum, Thérèse and Céline, like *two fugitives,* boldly disregarded the prohibitions of the guide and their father's admonitions and crossed a police barrier, climbing *down over the ruins* to reach the *tiny bit of pavement marked with a cross as the place where the martyrs fought.* The two knelt and kissed *this sacred soil.* Thérèse remembered, *I asked for the grace of being a martyr for Jesus and felt that my prayer was answered!* (SS 130–31).

At the Catacombs, in another act of boldness, Thérèse and Céline *slipped down together to the bottom of the ancient tomb of Saint Cecilia* and there scooped up some holy dirt as a relic and souvenir. Thérèse had never before had any devotion to St. Cecilia, but when she visited the site of the saint's martyrdom and learned of her courage and *the virginal song she sang to her heavenly Spouse hidden in the depths of her heart, I felt more than devotion* for her; it was the real tenderness of a friend. She became my saint of predi-lection, my intimate confidante. Everything in her thrilled me, especially her abandonment, her limitless confidence (SS 131). Thérèse was growing not only in piety but also in the courage to take appropriate initiatives, a quality she would need as she met with the pope.

Describing her adventures that followed the papal visit, Thérèse remem-bered another act of youthful boldness: when *visiting a Carmelite monastery, not content with following the pilgrims in the outer galleries, I advanced into the inner cloisters* [an action that could incur excommunication], *when all of a sudden I saw a good old Carmelite friar at a little distance making a sign for me to leave. But instead of going, I approached him and showing him the cloister paintings I made a sign that they were beautiful. He undoubtedly understood by the way I wore my hair and from my youthful appearance that I was only a child, so he smiled at me kindly and left. He saw he was not in the presence of an enemy* (SS 140).

From this and other experiences, Thérèse speculated more philosophi-cally, *I still cannot understand why women are so easily excommunicated in Italy, for every minute someone was saying: "Don't enter here! Don't enter there, you will be excommunicated!" Ah! Poor women, how they are misun-derstood! And yet they love God in much larger numbers than men do and during the Passion of Our Lord, women had more courage than the apostles since they braved the insults of the soldiers and dared to dry the adorable Face of Jesus. . . . In heaven, He will show that His thoughts are not men's thoughts, for then the last will be first* (SS 140).

During these days, Thérèse also reflected on the beauty she had encoun-tered. She later wrote,

When I saw all these beauties very profound thoughts came to life in my soul. I seemed to understand already the grandeur of God and the marvels of heaven. The religious life appeared to me exactly as it is with its subjections, its small sacrifices carried out in the shadows. I under-stood how easy it is to become all wrapped up in self, forgetting entirely the sublime goal of one's calling. . . . Riches don't bring happiness, for I would have been much happier under a thatched roof with the hope of Carmel in the offing, than in the midst of these sumptuous dwellings,

these marble staircases, and silk tapestries. . . . Joy isn't found in the
material objects . . . but in the recesses of the soul. (SS 125, 137)

The pilgrimage, far from distracting her from her vocation, only brought it into clearer focus. The primary reason that Thérèse was on this pilgrimage took place on November 20, 1887, two weeks after the departure from Paris. The meetings with her uncle and with the bishop had been upsetting, but the audience with Pope Leo XIII raised Thérèse's anxiety to new heights.

The ambiance of the audience was itself daunting: the magnificence of the architecture, the ceremonies designed to arouse wonder and worship, as well as the preliminary prayers of reverence and unworthiness. And then into the midst of the silence and respect of the pilgrims entered the seventy-seven-year-old pontiff himself, so noble in bearing and garb, so encompassed in the splendor and dignity of his personal prestige, surrounded with the veneration of his obliging attendants. In this setting of awe stood the fourteen-year-old Thérèse, harboring a secret and hatching a plan that only three people in the vast room knew anything about. Her heart was pounding with nervousness, but also with expectation.

The pope, looking emaciated, was somber but gracious in receiving the pilgrims. He was not in good health, and this fact was proclaimed to the pilgrims to inspire reverence and caution. No one was to talk to the Holy Father; all were to simply give their obeisance and move on silently. Thérèse was anxious, but she was also keenly observant, and later she amusingly described the aging pope as *so old that one would say he is dead* (GC I 353). Yet in the matter of who was really closer to death, the final irony was that Leo XIII outlived Thérèse by six years; he died in 1903.

As the ceremonies of the audience progressed, the pilgrims were again warned not to speak personally to the pope. Having been part of the pilgrimage and noticing Thérèse throughout all these days, Monsignor Révérony, who had chided her on her longtime desire to enter Carmel, now stood in attendance at the pontiff's right side. He was to direct the pilgrims from the Bayeux diocese as they approached the pontiff, preventing any from lingering or altering the protocol. He was a powerfully built man, and although he had warmed to Thérèse's hopes, no smile for her was in evidence at the moment. Thérèse's courage began to falter. Besides, it had been raining heavily all day.

However, Thérèse had not come all this way geographically, spiritually, and emotionally to be thwarted now. She had been encouraged by her father, by her sisters, and particularly by Pauline, who, having vacillated over the weeks, had recently written a letter supporting the idea of Thérèse's directly addressing the pope. Now, at the decisive moment, Céline whispered, "Speak."

When her turn came to pay her respects, Thérèse knelt and kissed the pope's slipper as was protocol, but as he extended his hand for a kiss as well, Thérèse spontaneously took his hand in hers and with tear-filled eyes said sincerely and without self-consciousness, *Most Holy Father, I have a great favor to ask you!* (SS 134). This was not protocol and demanded an explanation.

Pope Leo XIII, Monsignor Révérony, the papal guards, the others in attendance, as well as the pilgrims standing reverently nearby—all were startled. The pope, however, did not fuss; he leaned toward Thérèse, surprised and fascinated by the boldness of this young girl. Thérèse spoke with the clarity of conviction but with some hesitancy under the curious glances of the disturbed pilgrims as well as the critical eyes of Monsignor Révérony and the papal guards. *Holy Father*, she said quietly but clearly, *in honor of your Jubilee permit me to enter Carmel at the age of fifteen* (SS 134).

The pope turned to Monsignor Révérony and said, "I don't understand very well." "Most Holy Father," the vicar-general replied in embarrassment tinged with irritation and sarcasm, "this is a child who wants to enter Carmel at the age of fifteen, but the superiors are considering the matter at the moment." "Well my child, do what the superiors tell you!" the Holy Father replied kindly. *Oh! Holy Father*, Thérèse responded spontaneously and with the enthusiasm that surged from her intense desire, *if you say yes, everybody will agree!* (SS 134–35). She could not have put the matter better, more simply, more compellingly, more pleadingly, more rightly. "Go, go. You will enter if God wills it," the pontiff replied with a trace of irritation and admiration.

Pope Leo XIII knew that this young girl before him had spoken the truth. The pope had also spoken the truth, but in a sense Thérèse's truth was deeper, more relevant, and more cogent. The pope's truth, that things will happen if God wills, was applicable to all manner of situations, and he did not have to know much about this young girl to pronounce it: obedience was virtuous, and the divine will would prevail. But Thérèse's truth was both more particular and more universal: that the pope's will would prevail in this situation and in most others to which he applied it. The reality that carried the day, however, was simply that Pope Leo XIII could not and would not get involved.

Thérèse gazed into the dark eyes of the kindly old man and was about to offer one final word, but she had been dismissed. The papal guards now moved into action. One touched her shoulder politely; but this was not enough to make Thérèse take her hands from the pontiff's lap and rise, so, with the help of Monsignor Révérony, the guards lifted her up. The pope reached with his hand to touch her lips, then blessed her as she was dragged forcibly from his feet. Two guards carried Thérèse to the door and, giving her a medal of the pontiff, ushered her from the audience. Thérèse wept; she felt *completely crushed and abandoned* (GC I 353).

That same evening one of the guards who had helped remove Thérèse described the scene to his own family, secretly acknowledging his admiration for the young girl's boldness. His young daughter, who subsequently entered religious life, remembered at that time that he had admitted, "Oh! it would be impossible ever to see a more charming girl asking for something so difficult" (GC I 354, note 5).

Thérèse's father had been with the men's group and had not actually seen Thérèse's interaction with the pope, but when he joined his little queen she was inconsolable as she described the "fiasco, the shameful humiliation," as Céline called it (GC I 350).

If Louis had not noticed Thérèse's transformation at the time of her Christmas conversion, his experience of her determination and courage during her adventures in this pilgrimage, as well as when she had pursued her desire to enter Carmel with her uncle, with Bishop Hugonin, and now with the pope himself, must have shocked him into awareness. His little queen was no longer a baby, shy and insecure, intimidated by her feelings and needing to please everyone. She had become a mature woman, her own person, who knew herself, her desires, and her convictions, and was willing to suffer in doing what she believed to be God's will. She wept, but her tears were no longer those of a child.

Thérèse had originally experienced her conversion as a breakthrough in enlightenment and empowerment. Refined and further deepened by illuminations and courageous initiatives over this last year, her heart had expanded. She was a now a young woman of desire, of faith, and of love. Jesus' love made her powerful, and she was obeying and manifesting that love in ways that must have surprised even herself.

The pilgrimage would be departing from Rome shortly, but Thérèse's father wanted to renew his friendship with Br. Siméon, a seventy-three-year-old distinguished member of the Brothers of the Christian Schools whom Louis had visited two years before during a pilgrimage he had made to Constantinople. During the last years, Louis Martin had been associated with the brothers who staffed two schools in Alençon and one in Lisieux. He and Isidore Guérin were especially supportive of the school that had been operating in Lisieux for over a hundred years. Br. Siméon, himself a Frenchman, was the founder and president of the premier Catholic secondary school for boys in Rome, that educated the relatives of some of the most prominent officials in the Vatican, including the grandnephews of the pope.

In the course of Louis' visit with Br. Siméon the conversation naturally turned to the just-completed papal audience and specifically to Thérèse's desires and her plight. Siméon had never met Thérèse, but when her father, usually so quiet and reserved, talked powerfully about her great love for God, of her wish to enter Carmel, and of her embarrassing experience with the pope, Br. Siméon listened intently and took notes as if for future reference. Moved by the description of Thérèse's religious spirit, he responded out of his own spiritual sense. "One doesn't see this in Italy," he said, reflecting on the lack of enthusiasm among Italian girls for the religious life. Siméon may have spoken with a touch of nationalism, but he was truly impressed by the story of Thérèse.

As the conversation was finishing, another friend of Br. Siméon entered the residence. It was none other than Monsignor Révérony. In the course of their brief exchange, Thérèse's father, with uncharacteristic boldness, chided the monsignor for not having assisted Thérèse in her encounter with the pope. "You know very well that you had promised to help me," he said. Révérony accepted Louis' reproof in good spirits since he was actually secretly impressed with Thérèse's forthrightness and courage, even though he had seemed annoyed during the papal audience. He had also favorably observed Thérèse's simplicity, sincerity, and maturity on other occasions during the pilgrimage. Thérèse herself had noticed that he had *carefully studied all our actions, and I was able to see him do this at a distance. While eating, if I was not opposite him, he would lean over in such a way as to see me and listen to my conversation. He wanted to know me, undoubtedly, to see if I were really capable of becoming a Carmelite. And once on a bus, . . . he was even more friendly, promising to do all he could to have me enter Carmel* (SS 124, 139).

Thérèse's desires seem to have been well served by her father's exchange with Siméon and now with Révérony. Révérony's inclination to put in a good word for Thérèse with Bishop Hugonin may have been furthered by Louis' own remarks, and especially by the enthusiasm of Thérèse's newly acquired sympathetic friend and prestigious advocate, Br. Siméon.

In the following weeks Br. Siméon would also have had occasion, using the notes he had taken during his conversation with Louis, to speak on Thérèse's behalf to those church officials who might influence Bishop Hugonin's decision. A personal friend of the pope's secretary and respected by the most important people in the Vatican, Br. Siméon would not have hesitated to make his favorable impression of Thérèse known. He would have acted in Thérèse's favor not only because of his personal admiration for his new friend, but also for the sake of his countryman Louis Martin and as an expression of his own French religious sensibilities.

Br. Siméon never forgot his encounter with Louis Martin and Monsignor Révérony. At Thérèse's eventual entry into Carmel he rejoiced, and he remained in contact with her for the rest of her life. He became Thérèse's "Man in Rome." He would be available to obtain the pope's blessing for both her father and herself at the time of her profession, as well as to obtain other favors.

The remaining ten days of the returning pilgrimage involved much sightseeing in Naples, Pompeii, Assisi, Florence, Pisa, Genoa, Marseilles, and Lyons. For Thérèse, however, the most important part of the trip was over. With disappointment and sadness, she looked back on her encounter with Pope Leo XIII. She thought that God, whom she was sure wanted her in Carmel, could have at least smoothed the way.

During the following weeks in her prayer of detachment and availability to Jesus, Thérèse imagined herself as Jesus' little plaything, his little toy, his ball, that he could use in any way he wished. In her grief and distress she reflected that Jesus had heard her prayer, but in a way she had not expected. He had pierced his toy ball and cut it open to see what was inside of it. Then he had dropped it, and gone off to sleep (cf. SS 136, 142).

Thérèse had secretly hoped to attend Christmas midnight Mass as a new member of the Carmelite community, a postulant; but it was not to be. There had been no answer from the bishop. There were some consolations after the midnight Mass, however. Céline, ever sensitive and empathetic to Thérèse, had placed on her bed a basin of water in which floated a toy boat with the word "abandonment" painted on it; and in the boat, an image of Jesus asleep with a toy ball at his side.

Then, during her Christmas afternoon visit with Pauline in Carmel, Thérèse was also consoled as she was serenaded by the community of sisters with a hymn composed by her older sister. They also presented her with a statue of Jesus holding a toy ball in his hand. Thérèse reflected, *Though Jesus was not yet speaking to His little fiancée, and though His divine eyes remained closed, He at least revealed Himself to her through souls who understood all the delicacies and the love of His Heart* (SS 143).

Thérèse suffered deep distress during these days, yet she was also at peace at the most profound level of her soul. She had done all that God could have possibly wanted of her to further her entrance into Carmel. She had taken all the initiatives that she could; she had addressed all the opposition and had even pleaded with the pope himself. Even God could not have asked for more. There was no higher earthly source of permission. Now in a state of simply willing the divine will, Thérèse awaited the answer from Bishop Hugonin.

CHAPTER 21

I Want to Give Myself Totally to Him

Bishop Hugonin did not communicate directly with Thérèse, but on December 28 he wrote to Mother Gonzague, superior of the Lisieux Carmel. His answer was in Thérèse's favor. He overruled the objection of Fr. Delatroëtte and allowed Mother Gonzague to make the final decision. Mother, who had an affection for Thérèse, had already agreed that the young girl did indeed have a vocation to Carmel and had even designated a religious name for her. Her answer was clearly that Thérèse should be permitted to enter. But a few days later, on January 1, 1888, when Thérèse herself first received word of the decision, the word that she received was negative. She was not to enter just yet. From another source within the convent itself, a new objection had arisen.

Pauline had been ceaseless in encouraging Thérèse in her path to Carmel. She had originally brought her little sister to the convent, she had been crucial in obtaining Uncle Isidore's consent, she had countered Marie's objection that Thérèse was too young, and she had plotted with Thérèse to request the pope's permission. But now she backed down. Concerned about Thérèse's welfare, she had an objection, not about Thérèse's vocation or age, but about the timing of her entrance. Since the Lenten season involved some of the most rigorous physical penances of the year, she thought it would be in Thérèse's best interest if she were not to enter Carmel until after Lent. Pauline wanted to spare Thérèse pain during her first months in Carmel, and the delay might also help to placate the overruled Fr. Delatroëtte.

From Thérèse's point of view, Pauline, her second mother, had again emotionally abandoned her, just when she was finally sensing victory. Even her father was angrily upset with Pauline, and as Marie (who was present during their father's visit) recalled, "He pointed his finger, saying: 'She is always the same; she says something, then she takes it back'" (GC I 389–90). But Pauline had convinced Mother Gonzague of the appropriateness of her concern for Thérèse, and the matter was settled.

This was the last and in some ways the saddest obstacle for Thérèse, coming as it did from her own sister. Thérèse had experienced the several weeks following the pilgrimage while awaiting the bishop's decision as a *trial . . . very great for my faith*. Now, on January 1, she received Pauline's objection in a flood of tears, with feelings of disappointment and abandonment. *It was all the more painful,* she remembered, *as I did not understand it* (SS 143). She was being asked to wait for three months for her own good.

During these months Thérèse might have plunged into self-pity and moodiness; she could have indulged herself in distractions of trivial reading, or travel. Those feelings and thoughts did arise in her, but now Thérèse was a stronger person. *At first the thought came into my mind not to lead a life as well regulated as had been my custom,* she recalled, *but soon I understood the value of the time I was being offered. I made a resolution to give myself up more than ever to a serious and mortified life* (SS 143). With the strength of her conversion just one year before, she decided to make these months into a personal retreat. She decided that she would not hold on to her troubling feelings; she would not allow any feelings of disappointment or resentment against Pauline to linger. Her feelings would not control her as before. She was seeing an important connection between managing her feelings and finding her spiritual path.

Thérèse again allied herself with Pauline, allowing her older sister to direct and assist her in using well these three months of waiting. Under Pauline's guidance, Thérèse promptly wrote to Bishop Hugonin, thanking him for his permission, which she called *the beautiful New Year's gift you sent me.* Then she wrote to Monsignor Révérony, thanking him as well for his help in securing the bishop's permission. And finally, again under Pauline's supervision, she also wrote to Fr. Delatroëtte, telling him that during these months she was *working to prepare her soul for the life of Carmel* and requesting his prayers. He still harbored some bitterness that Thérèse had actually gone over his head to ask the bishop's permission. His reply to her letter lacked the graciousness of Monsignor Révérony's response. Whereas the vicar-general wrote to say that he would "gladly share in your joy," Fr. Delatroëtte assured Thérèse that he would pray "with my whole heart to make you worthy of being" a Carmelite. But he felt it his duty to add the caveat that "I cannot refrain from regretting that you pressed for your entrance with so much insistence. I fear that later on you and your own sisters will have to regret it" (GC I 390, 392, 393).

Pauline knew the attitude of Fr. Delatroëtte and directed Céline not to speak with him about Thérèse. She also told Léonie, who had just returned on January 6 from a half-year stay as a postulant at the Visitation convent in

Caen and who was going to confession to him, to avoid the topic. Any talk with him about Thérèse "would cause trouble and all is useless. We can see that he imagines we are trying to make him change his mind," Pauline wrote to her little sister (GC I 398).

Thérèse, meanwhile, resumed her weekly lessons with her tutor, and Pauline gave her a book of readings on the lives of several Carmelites who entered the cloister only after many years of trials. Taking the book seriously, Thérèse assured Pauline, *I am very fortunate that God has given me a sister like you. . . . I want to give myself totally to Him,* she added. *I want to live no longer but for Him* (GC I 399).

In preparation for her entrance, Thérèse focused her attention primarily on being faithfully loving in her daily obligations. Convinced that she had done everything she could do to enter Carmel, she was now confident that God would bring about his own purposes for her. She was being led by her loving Father into God's house, her home. *I believe that . . . this trial was very great and made me grow very much in abandonment and in the other virtues* (SS 143). The month of March became *one of the most beautiful months of my life,* Thérèse remembered years later (GC I 390). Pauline's decision to postpone Thérèse's entrance was for her another grace in disguise.

Thérèse was inspired to give attention to the third resolution she had made at her First Communion. At that time she had resolved *to try to humble my pride.* Initially as a child she had thought of humility as a personal project that she could attain by trying to forget herself. Then she discovered that trying to forget herself was impossible. The effort to forget herself made her remember herself; the whole project of self-forgetfulness was, in itself, an impossible, self-centered activity.

By now she had matured into a spiritual path that would truly lead to humility: that of abandoning herself into the arms of her loving Father and responding to the ordinary ups and downs of life without the need of self-satisfaction. This disposition helped her also address her willfulness in a new way, as well as the more subtle self-centeredness of spiritual ambition.

Thérèse moved further away from the practice of imposing acts of penance on herself that seemed to be self-punitive. Such practices had been suggested to her as a young child by Pauline and Marie, and she noticed Céline still doing similar acts. *I made a resolution to give myself up more than ever to a serious and mortified life,* she remembered. But *when I say mortified,* she quickly explained, *this is not to give the impression that I performed acts of penance. Alas, I never made any. Far from resembling beautiful souls who practiced every kind of mortification from their childhood, I had no attraction for this. Undoubtedly this stemmed from my cowardliness, for I could have, like Céline, found a thousand ways of making myself suffer* (SS 143).

Instead of walking the way of *making myself suffer,* however, Thérèse began to adopt the attitude of simply not cultivating her own preferences, of not drawing any attention to herself, and of not seeking any personal recognition. She began, on the one hand, to focus on secret, inconspicuous acts of service to others; and, on the other hand, she refrained from imposing herself on others or putting herself forward in conversations, and especially she refused to harbor thoughts and feelings that she sensed were self-centered. Addressing her own capacity for self-indulgence and self-love, she did small physical acts of self-denial to keep herself mindful of her Beloved's presence.

Thérèse was familiar with St. Paul's description of charity: "Love is patient; love is kind. Love is not jealous; it does not put on airs; it is not snobbish. Love is never rude; it is not self-seeking; it is not prone to anger; neither does it brood over injuries. Love does not rejoice in what is wrong but rejoices with the truth. There is no limit to love's forbearance, to its trust, its hope its power to endure" (1 Corinthians 13:4-7). She began to put these attributes of love into action, being kind and patient, and willing to endure the discipline of not brooding, not being rude or snobbish, not nurturing jealousy or moodiness, not holding on to anger. She would forget herself not by willful effort but by not fostering any form of self-indulgence, self-promotion, or self-pity. This was going to be Thérèse's way of cultivating humility and love, as well as her way of dealing with her feelings of rejection, betrayal, and being abandoned. And all would be done inconspicuously and to please her Beloved; no one would notice, but God would know. *It was through the practice of these nothings,* she later wrote, *that I prepared myself to become the fiancée of Jesus* (SS 144; cf. GC I 504).

Thérèse's new way of addressing her pride required a willingness and a capacity to bear the pain of the feelings of disappointment and separation. She would go to God on his own timetable, confidently bearing the pain of her difficult feelings. This spiritual insight had grown in Thérèse over several years, and it was among the most important that she would bring to Carmel. To Pauline she wrote, *I hope that you will pray for your poor little girl so that she will correspond with the graces that Jesus wants to give her; she has a great need of your help, for she is far from what she would like to be* (GC I 401).

Thérèse was now fifteen years and three months old, a young age for a Carmelite postulant, but she had already lived more than half her life. The question of age implied the question of maturity. In Thérèse's case, if she had not received the grace of her complete conversion, as she herself acknowledged, she would not have been ready for Carmel. *I really don't know how I could entertain the thought of entering Carmel when I was still in the swaddling clothes of a child!* (SS 97). Just fifteen months before she had been, in many ways, just a young child, a baby; now she was a mature young woman in the most fundamental ways. She was understanding more deeply what love was all about.

Thérèse had the self-knowledge and the willingness, the inner strength and the experience, of enduring sufferings that made her ready for a life that was at once God-centered and penitential, enclosed in a cloistered convent away from the world but open in spirit to share divine love with the whole human race.

CHAPTER 22

Suffering Opened Wide Its Arms to Me

As Thérèse stepped across the threshold of Carmel on April 9, 1888, the feast of the Annunciation, the first experience she had was a sense of sweet, *deep peace impossible to express* that confirmed her vocation (SS 148). This inexpressible peace arose from having finally attained a great achievement after many struggles, but fundamentally it was a great grace freely given her by her Beloved. It was a peace that flowed from Thérèse's small and inchoate sense of her Beloved's love for her, and it never left her even in the midst of the greatest sufferings over the next years.

At the very brief ceremony as Thérèse passed through the doorway into the cloister of Carmel, the thwarted Fr. Delatroëtte was present. He had a final word of reservation about this matter of a fifteen-year-old entering the convent. His remarks were directed to the prioress, but spoken loudly enough for Thérèse, her father, and members of her family, as well as the sisters present, to hear. "As the delegate of . . . the bishop," he said in his morose style, "I present this child of fifteen whose entrance you so desired. I trust she will not disappoint your hopes." Attempting to relieve his own conscience, he added pointedly, "I remind you that if she does, you alone will bear the responsibility" (GC I 408, note 1). Tears filled the eyes of Thérèse as well as those of her father, but the priest's words did not really matter.

Thérèse was led by Mother Gonzague into the chapel where the Blessed Sacrament was exposed for the adoration of the nuns, but *what struck me first,* Thérèse remembered, *were the eyes of our holy Mother Geneviève which were fixed on me. I remained kneeling for a moment at her feet, thanking God for the grace He gave me of knowing a saint* (SS 148). Mother Geneviève of St. Teresa, sub-prioress at the time, was one of the original founders of the Lisieux Carmel in 1838. Thérèse saw Mother Geneviève, now in her mid-eighties, as a holy woman, a model of how the spiritual life could be lived in the day-to-day routine of the convent. In both her living and her dying, Mother Geneviève would be a continual inspiration and consolation to Thérèse.

In deep peace she walked with Mother Gonzague through the cloister areas, noticing the statue of the child Jesus and the picture of the Holy Face with the small lighted candle. But in addition to feeling at peace, Thérèse also had the sense that she was being welcomed into a state of suffering. *Suffering opened wide its arms to me and I threw myself into them with love* (SS 149). Thérèse believed she was being invited into the loving arms of Jesus crucified, into a love that was real and therefore a love that would involve suffering and sacrifice. Her attitude of willingness to embrace the suffering required by love was not masochistic; it was, rather, the attitude that she had learned particularly from her mother. Given Thérèse's tendency to self-consciousness, self-centeredness, and codependency, that suffering for the sake of authentic love would inevitably be for her both transformative and solitary.

From all outward appearances Thérèse made a smooth transition from the family home into Carmel, but indeed suffering had opened its arms and trials awaited her almost immediately. Having made significant spiritual and emotional progress in the last sixteen months, she still had lived a protected and extremely comfortable life. She had been routinely spared by Céline and the family maid from doing any of the common household chores at home, and she was unprepared for her first convent assignments of helping in the linen room and sweeping a corridor. The physical rigor of the lifestyle of Carmel immediately overwhelmed this young, pampered teenager.

Thérèse was now in a "small and poor" convent, as Marie had described it when she had entered. She was expected to endure the poor quality and small portions of food, the lack of heat throughout the building (there was only one fireplace, and that in the common gathering room), the cramped and cold bedroom cell, the close quarters without privacy, the extensive physical work, the long hours in prayer, the deadening, unrelenting daily routine with its complete lack of "creature comforts," the brief time for sleep, and the total absence of youthful fun. Thérèse was young and had become used to living like a "little queen." Pauline had been right in wanting to delay Thérèse's entrance so that the even more difficult regime of the Lenten season would be over, and the winter cold, from which Thérèse would suffer physically more than from anything else in her life, would be subsiding (cf. TLMT 98). The poor food would also become an issue for her, but with food as with the cold and other inconveniences, she followed her childhood resolution of never complaining. For now, Thérèse wrote, *everything thrilled me; I felt as though I was transported into a desert* (SS 148).

The usual daily timetable outside of the Lenten routine was rigorous enough. It required the sisters to rise at 4:45 a.m. to begin the day with an hour of private prayer and then the recitation of the Divine Office, the official prayer of the church that included Scripture readings and the choral recitation of the psalms. Mass was celebrated at 7:00 a.m., followed by breakfast and a period of work. A short personal examination of conscience at 9:50 a.m. was followed by the midday meal at 10:00 a.m., then an hour of community recreation, then an hour of personal time that could include a siesta, and at 1:00 p.m., an hour of work and the Divine Office. A half hour of spiritual reading at 2:30 p.m. was followed by two hours of work, an hour of personal prayer, and, at 6:00 p.m., supper. After the evening meal there was another period of community recreation, the Divine Office, and an hour of personal time. A final recitation of the Divine Office was at 9:00 p.m., and a personal examination of conscience ended the day. The sisters retired at 10:30 p.m. The schedule rarely varied: six and a half hours of personal and communal prayer together with five hours of work, two hours of community recreation, and two hours of free time.

The sisters spent some of the day in solitude and most of the entire day in silence, speaking only when strictly necessary, except for the periods of community recreation, when they conversed while knitting or doing arts and crafts projects or other handiwork. From her first day in the community Thérèse deeply appreciated the usual silence and solitude of the lifestyle as an invitation to prayer, and adhered to the schedule and rule as a way of fulfilling what her loving Father wanted of her. She became noted among the sisters as never seeking exemptions even during the very painful physical and emotional episodes that were to come upon her in the following nine years.

Thérèse was sometimes physically exhausted at day's end. However, the trial that most deeply troubled her came not in the area of her physical weakness but in the area of her emotional strength, that is, in her ability to relate and to please, and in particular in her capacity to bond. Her experience at the boarding school had challenged that ability, but she now had a level of confidence that she would be welcomed into the group of twenty-six nuns, who had already often given her signs of affection. In addition, she had already connected well with the superior, Mother Gonzague.

Thérèse was only nine years old when she first met Mother Gonzague, and from the first the two had bonded in mutual admiration. Years before when Thérèse had learned in so painful a manner of her sister's decision to enter Carmel, Pauline, in a gesture of appeasement, took her to visit Mother Gonzague. Pauline intended that Thérèse would feel some personal consolation in sharing with the prioress her own youthful desire to join Carmel as well. Mother Gonzague performed the best service she could for little Thérèse; she took her seriously and affirmed her vocation. For Thérèse it was an act of uniting with yet another mother, and that afforded great comfort to the young girl, who already had lost one mother and, at the time, was about to lose Pauline, her second mother.

Two months after the first meeting with the prioress, the child Thérèse, paying her first visit to Pauline now in Carmel, took with her a secret that she wanted to share, not with Pauline but with Mother Gonzague. That particular morning, as she often did, Thérèse had rested in bed praying. She was considering in her own heart what name she would take as a future Carmelite. The name *Thérèse of the Child Jesus* came to her, and she wanted to share that insight with Mother Gonzague (SS 71).

During the visit but before Thérèse could say anything to the prioress about this idea, the prioress spontaneously told Thérèse that she herself in consultation with the community had been considering the name that Thérèse might be called when she would some day enter Carmel. Mother Gonzague then announced the name that she as prioress had decided on: "Thérèse of the Child Jesus." Not only had Mother Gonzague originally taken Thérèse's vocation seriously, but the prioress, with all her duties and responsibilities, had found time to think about Thérèse and the religious name she would have. That name was the very same name that Thérèse herself had conceived. Thérèse, astonished, had already begun then to feel the joy of belonging and the hope of finding both a mother and a home in Carmel. And these feelings now returned as Mother Gonzague escorted her through the convent.

After showing Thérèse into the chapel and through the various other areas of the cloister, one of the first things that Mother Gonzague did was to bring Thérèse to her office and ask her to recite a chapter of *The Imitation of Christ*. The superior had heard that Thérèse had memorized the book, so she simply read the first sentence from the chapter entitled "One must love Jesus above all things," and asked her to finish the three hundred words of the text. Thérèse was delighted to recite one of her favorite chapters, the very chapter she had marked in her own copy with the little white flower her father had given her. The superior was impressed and pleased. It was the kind of affirming interaction that Thérèse had expected from Mother Gonzague.

But in the days that followed, the superior's attitude seemed to fluctuate. The support and encouragement that Thérèse could have expected, the warm relationship with the prioress that she would have personally found so comforting, seemed suddenly thwarted. In the daily interactions of convent living, she experienced Mother Gonzague acting quite ambiguously toward her.

As the weeks went on there were numerous occasions when Mother Gonzague was not impressed and not pleased, and acted coolly, even harshly, to her. The superior found fault with the way Thérèse responded to her routine responsibilities. Without having done ordinary housework at home, Thérèse brought no reserve of common knowledge to the daily chores of convent life. Her incompetence quickly became obvious, and Mother Gonzague let none of her mistakes go unnoticed or uncorrected. The superior actively criticized and humiliated the young postulant.

All the customs of the community had to be learned, and Thérèse learned most by trial and error. She was reprimanded many times a day. She could do nothing quite right; neither sweep the floor, nor kill the spiders, nor dust the steps, nor cut the bread, nor even walk through the house with proper posture, gravity, and decorum. Mother Gonzague seemed to have taken as her personal mission the obligation of correcting her. Thérèse later wrote that *I know that she loved me very much and said everything good about me that was possible, nevertheless, God permitted that she was very severe without her even being aware of it* (SS 150).

Privately and publicly, Mother Gonzague reprimanded Thérèse for her many shortcomings and mistakes. Following the prioress' lead, some of the sisters became "critical mothers" as well. Over the previous years all the sisters had come to know Thérèse as the charming child who had visited her sister Pauline, as the privileged child who had such a wonderful family and so loving a father, and as the specially graced child who had seen the statue of the Virgin smile—a miraculous event that cured her illness. But some perceived her as the child who had demanded special privileges, requesting entrance into their convent before the proper age and with two blood sisters waiting and ready to give her special attention.

While most of the sisters were generally impressed with Thérèse, some began to feel that she was disturbing the community's life by failing to uphold the community customs. She was the child who evoked in them upsettingly ambiguous feelings: the warmth of motherliness, the attraction of sisterliness, the burden of their own perfectionistic spirit, and the embarrassment of their envy and jealousy. If this pleasing child were given special attention, it would subvert the rigor of the convent life and distract from whatever status they themselves had managed to achieve.

In this convent situation where every item had its proper place, where rules applied to the least procedure and gesture, where everything big and small had to be fussed over, arranged just so, done properly, straightened out, and fixed up, where everything needed to be right because custom demanded it—in such a place an attitude of making things perfect was inevitable, and spirituality was easily interwoven with perfectionism.

The "critical mothers" may have thought that they had perfect intentions and motives; they may have been simply trying to enforce the rule or to strengthen this obviously weak, young recruit; or they may have been protecting themselves from the annoyances of accommodating change. But in all this, Thérèse was confused and disappointed, bewildered and hurt. She had really expected a different reception from this community of sisters who had sung to her a song of consolation and encouragement just a few short weeks before and who had received her on the first day with warm embraces.

Years later Thérèse would write that the calm happiness of entering Carmel found expression in the words that at the time she had repeated with deep joy. *I am here forever and ever! This happiness was not passing. It didn't take its flight with "the illusions of the first days." Illusions, God gave me the grace not to have a single one when entering Carmel,* Thérèse wrote. *I found the religious life to be exactly as I had imagined it . . . no sacrifice astonished me,* she said simply (SS 148–49).

Yet, if Thérèse could honestly say that she had no illusions about the religious life of Carmel, it must have been because she did not count—could not count—as illusions her own expectations, hidden and personally unknown even to herself at the time. She consciously knew that following a commitment of love would inevitably bring suffering and the purification of any self-centered expectations she might have. She also knew that she may not have been completely aware of all these expectations. She was, however, willing to bear whatever was required and to do whatever was needed to follow her calling. She had had no illusion about that. And, indeed, over the years her self-centered expectations, hidden in all their subtle forms, were inevitably consumed in a crucible of suffering.

Thérèse could not, however, possibly have known the details of the community life that she was entering, with its small and petty aspects. Nor could she have known the details of the difficult feelings that community life with strangers would evoke in her. And she could not possibly have known that "the pain is in the details." Over the years she adopted the personal attitude of allowing her expectations to be purged and her hopes to blossom.

Thérèse as a novice, January 1889

CHAPTER 23

Love Is Nourished Only by Sacrifices

Mother Gonzague was one of the few nuns in the convent who was cultured and educated. She was fifty-four, about seven years older than the average age of the sisters, most of whom were of normal intelligence and limited education. She had come from an aristocratic family and had a powerful aura about her. She was self-confident and determined; but she was also sometimes moody, arbitrary, and capricious. For Thérèse she was fascinating, charming, and alluring. Even as a child, from their first encounter, Thérèse had been attracted by the prioress' personality.

She felt drawn to Mother Gonzague and had taken from her the unsaid communication that she had an affirming mother and an understanding confidante in the superior. The young child had received the silent message that she was being invited into Carmel with the implicit assurance that she would receive the special name that they had both been inspired to know. She also must certainly have believed that she would be privileged to have her affection returned by a mother and superior who would care for her and provide her with a home that would be forever. These were extremely comforting messages, and they had become subtle and not fully conscious expectations in Thérèse's thinking about Carmel and Mother Gonzague.

These unsurfaced assumptions had an impact on Thérèse that was not unlike the influence Pauline's entrance into religious life had had on Thérèse's choice of vocation. As Pauline had been, so Mother Gonzague had also been a human instrument of God's providence in arousing Thérèse's faith and bringing her to Carmel. Thérèse wanted to enter Carmel for *Jesus alone*, and that was certainly her true conscious motivation of faith, but as she already knew and would come to relearn often in the years ahead, motivation often goes beyond the conscious and is rarely singular (SS 58).

In these first years in Carmel Thérèse was being invited to continue on the lifelong spiritual journey of honestly facing and then dismissing as unnecessary or even as unhealthy the currents of motivation that had previously been hidden from her. She had already started on this path before her fourteenth birthday when she noticed that, although she had in faith *a great desire to practice virtue*, as she said, *I went about it in a strange way* (SS 97).

And she had taken further steps on this path of self-awareness in the experience of her complete conversion itself.

In the actual daily presence of Mother Gonzague and under her harsh direction, Thérèse was confused by conflicting feelings. On the one hand, she was feeling rejection and separation; on the other hand, she was feeling more and more personal attraction to the prioress. The fascinating appeal that Mother Gonzague had over several of the other sisters was also overcoming Thérèse.

So strong did her need to be close to Mother Gonzague grow, that Thérèse had *violent temptations to satisfy myself and to find a few crumbs of pleasure. . . .* She remembered years later in writing to Mother that *I was obliged to walk rapidly by your door and to cling firmly to the banister of the staircase in order not to turn back. There came into my mind a crowd of permissions to seek. . . . I found a thousand reasons for pleasing my nature* (SS 237).

On one occasion a year after her entrance and during her novitiate, Thérèse had good reason to visit Mother Gonzague in the prioress' cell. Mother Gonzague was ill with a bronchial attack, and Thérèse had keys to return to her. Her desire to be in contact with the superior was so compelling that when another sister, fearing that Thérèse would awaken Mother, wanted to take the keys, Thérèse resisted. She humorously tells the story: *I was too stubborn to give them to her and to cede my rights. As politely as I could, I told her that it was my duty to return the keys. . . . Very soon the thing we feared most happened: the racket we were making made you* [Mother] *open your eyes.* The sister blamed Thérèse, and Thérèse knew *that if I began to justify myself I would not be able to retain my peace. . . . My last plank of salvation was in flight* (SS 223–24).

As a young religious Thérèse felt a need to be connected to Mother Gonzague and was experiencing toward the superior the same dangerous magnetism of the schoolgirl crushes she had experienced at the abbey school in her relationships with some of the teachers and with her particular classmate friend. At that time, as she said, she had not *allowed myself to be taken.* Actually, she had been spared attachment not so much by her own doing as by the unresponsiveness of the teachers and by the indifference of her classmate. Now, with that same dangerous dynamic surfacing, the more mature Thérèse had the awareness and courage to bear the pain and step away.

Several years later Thérèse was assisting Mother Gonzague as "senior novice." This assignment required her to be in close contact with the superior, but by now, after much soul-searching and prayer, Thérèse had managed to become detached from Mother Gonzague's powerful attraction. Her own experience, however, had enlightened her to notice that an older sister in the novitiate, Sr. Martha of Jesus, had also fallen into the same trap of emotional attachment to the superior. Knowing the darkness of such an entanglement, Thérèse also knew the pain that the light of truth would cause Martha when she was told what she needed to hear to be freed. Thérèse understood that for Martha's own good she needed to be confronted, and, since she was responsible for the novices, Thérèse decided to address Martha forthrightly.

Thérèse prayed for several months to have the inner freedom and creativity to speak without fear and with compassion so that Sr. Martha could hear the truth and bear the pain. *I begged God to place sweet and convincing words in my mouth, or rather that He speak through me* (SS 236).

Thérèse understood that she was taking a personal risk. If Sr. Martha were to become defensive and tell Mother Gonzague that Thérèse was trying to damage their relationship, Thérèse could be expelled from the convent. To Pauline, who knew of her plan and of the danger it put her in, Thérèse said, *I am now certain that it is my duty to speak; I must not worry about the consequences* (GC II 758).

Thérèse's own experience with Mother Gonzague had prepared her to be empathetic; her own sensitive nature allowed her to be disarmingly gentle. She told Sr. Martha simply that her affection for the superior had nothing supernatural about it. It was not real love; it was dangerous infatuation; she was actually loving herself. Thérèse told the sister, *your fondness for Mother Prioress is too natural. She is doing your soul a great deal of harm, because you love her passionately, and those kinds of feelings displease God; in nuns they are poison. You did not become a Carmelite to satisfy your natural longings; you did so to mortify them and die to yourself.* Thérèse bluntly suggested that this kind of relationship was really like *a dog . . . attached to its master* (SS 237).

To soften the sting, Thérèse told Sr. Martha of her own personal struggles in her relationship with Mother Gonzague. Sr. Martha was embarrassed, then enlightened, and finally overwhelmed by young Thérèse's insight into her feelings and behavior. Martha suddenly understood that she had been hiding the truth from herself. The two sisters wept together, and Martha was freed from her attachment.

When Thérèse wrote, *Love is nourished only by sacrifices, and the more a soul refuses natural satisfactions, the stronger and more disinterested becomes her tenderness*, it was as if she were speaking to Martha, but she herself needed to know all this, as well (SS 237). In these early years in Carmel the truth of Thérèse's words had been planted in her own heart but had not yet fully ripened. Thérèse still had aspects of her own motivation to discover.

In light of Thérèse's personal and sometimes dark needs for closeness, Mother Gonzague, it seems, had her own wisdom in her overly strict and critical manner. Had the prioress allowed Thérèse to become the favorite, the pampered little one of the community, had she not personally distanced herself from the young postulant, Thérèse may have gone down the side path of attachment and self-indulgence. She may never have reached the depth of spiritual maturity that she finally attained.

When Thérèse later reflected on her relationship with the prioress, she wrote, *What would have become of me if I had been the "pet" of the community as some of the Sisters believed? Perhaps, instead of seeing Our Lord in my Superiors, I would have looked upon them as ordinary persons only and my heart . . . would have become humanly attached in the cloister. Happily I was preserved from this misfortune. I loved Mother Prioress very much, but it was a pure affection* (SS 150–51). Mother Gonzague knew Thérèse's personal and spiritual potential; she also suspected her capacity for self-indulgence and emotional attachment.

Perhaps, too, in her relationship with Thérèse, Mother Gonzague rediscovered in herself the true depth of her own spiritual calling that had become overshadowed. Seeing in this young woman the potential of her own missed psychological and spiritual development, the prioress may have offered to Thérèse what she herself had needed but did not receive: a firm hand to prevent her from squandering her personal gifts by chasing after human affirmations and consolations.

At a deep personal and spiritual level, Mother Gonzague respected and loved Thérèse. Just a little over a month after Thérèse had entered Carmel and while criticizing her for her many mistakes, Mother Gonzague wrote to

Thérèse's aunt, Céline Guérin, "never would have I expected to find such sound judgment in a fifteen-year-old. Everything is perfect." And, many months later, describing Thérèse at the time of her profession of vows, Mother Gonzague wrote, "This angelic child is seventeen and a half, and she has the judgment of one of thirty, the religious perfection of an old perfected novice, and possession of herself; she is a perfect religious. Yesterday, not an eye remained dry at the sight of her great and entire immolation." Mother Gonzague seems to have actually admired and appreciated Thérèse more than any of the other members of the community (GC I 430, note 4; 678).

Years later Mother Gonzague told one of the sisters in confidence that "if a prioress were to be chosen from the whole community, I would unhesitatingly choose Sister Thérèse of the Child Jesus in spite of her young age. She is perfect in everything; her only fault is to have her three sisters with her" (STL 253; TLMT 115).

Mother Gonzague described herself at the end of her life as a failed religious. She outlived Thérèse by seven years and felt consolation in knowing that Thérèse, the "perfect nun," had loved her in life and was interceding for her in her last days as she died of cancer.

At the end of her own life, Thérèse, wiser and more mature, knowingly thanked Mother Gonzague for her firm treatment, especially during those early years. She appreciated the prioress for her *strong . . . education,* and for *not sparing* her (SS 206). Thérèse understood that her Beloved, using whatever may have been the personal motives of the prioress and the sisters, had protected her during those first years in Carmel in the same way that her loving family had cared for her during the early years at home. The parable that she had made up about the father who was also a doctor and who had taken the stone out of the path of the son was unfolding for her in Carmel. She could so easily have been spoiled.

Thérèse never knew Mother Gonzague's motivation in their ongoing relationship, but even in her youthful confusion and hurt, Thérèse never felt anger or resentment toward the prioress. She had simply taken that relationship for what it was and turned it into gold. The ability to transform her relationships into precious jewels became for Thérèse a consummate skill and a great grace.

CHAPTER 24

I Didn't Come to Carmel to Live with My Sisters

Marie and Pauline had not been expecting what they perceived to be the insensitive, even harsh reception that some of the sisters, and particularly Mother Gonzague, gave to their beloved little sister. Both of Thérèse's older sisters had naturally thought that Mother Gonzague's behavior was reprehensible in its severity. They themselves now leaned in the other direction; they tried to make Thérèse feel at home in Carmel. Thérèse had had a premonition during her three-month personal retreat before her entrance into Carmel that she might have to struggle against her older sisters' cuddly, intrusive behavior toward her, and she was correct in this fear.

Marie and Pauline wanted to reconstitute the relational bonds they had had with Thérèse when they had all been at home. Thérèse, however, saw the emotional and spiritual dangers in this and did not want to make any concession to what would have been her natural inclination to indulge in special attention and comforting relationships with her sisters. She had come to Carmel for *Jesus alone* and not to foster family connections.

Thérèse had also come to Carmel with the open-hearted wish to love all the nuns, and she knew that advancing family connections would be exclusive. She wrote, *"No one," Jesus said, "lights a lamp and puts it under a measure but upon the lampstand that it may give light to ALL in the house"* [Matthew 5:15]. *It seems to me that this lamp represents charity which must enlighten and rejoice not only those who are dearest to us but to "ALL who are in the house" without distinction* (SS 220).

Less than a year after her entrance into Carmel, Thérèse was assigned to work daily in the dining room managing the meal preparation of the beer and water. She also had the care of the bread, which was kept in an unlighted recess under the stairs. This was where the spiders hid and frightened her whenever she met them (cf. GC I 526). As a child Thérèse had always been afraid of spiders and also had a fear of the dark. Now these reawakened childhood fears became an embarrassment in her new assignment.

In performing her duties Thérèse was constantly judged and corrected by various sisters for her little mistakes. She found herself in so many little ways fulfilling her First Communion resolution of addressing her pride:

The refectory, which I was given charge of immediately after I received the habit, furnished me, on more than one occasion, with the chance of putting my self-love in its proper place, that is, underfoot, she remembered. Also, in ordinary circumstances *I applied myself to practicing little virtues, not having the capability of practicing the great* (SS 159).

But in particular, this assignment gave her physical closeness to Pauline, who also worked in the dining room. They now worked side by side, and Thérèse, neither feeling free to confide in her "second mother" as she had at home nor wanting to offend her by appearing cold and distant, entered into a daily inner struggle. Pauline wanted to deepen the family bond and the spiritual relationship she had had with her little sister from their earlier years. Thérèse was grateful, but knew that she could easily be drawn into Pauline's desires and compromise her own unique calling. She had to be constantly attentive about her feelings and reactions to Pauline.

This same watchfulness, Thérèse discovered, must also be applied to her relationship with her sister Marie. Marie, too, had a special bond with her little sister, having been her teacher, confessor, and confidante. She had even introduced Thérèse to her own spiritual director, Fr. Pichon. Marie had been Thérèse's "other mother" after Pauline had gone to Carmel, and Thérèse knew that she could not afford to be drawn into receiving Marie's support now in any similar way. In her relationships with Pauline and Marie, and also with the other nuns, Thérèse profited by her adherence to the convent's rule of silence and solitude.

If Thérèse had a weakness of attraction in her relationship with Mother Gonzague, in her dealings with Pauline and Marie she manifested a self-discipline and maturity beyond her years. She appreciated her sisters' love and encouragement, and she used all her skills to please them. It was with delicate tact and exquisite finesse that she withdrew from them without offending them. *I didn't come to Carmel to live with my* [blood] *sisters but to answer Jesus' call,* she wrote at the end of her life. *Ah! I really felt in advance that this living with one's own sisters had to be the cause of continual suffering when one wishes to grant nothing to one's natural inclinations* (SS 216).

In particular with Pauline, during all her years in Carmel, Thérèse had to manage a certain distance that would allow her to follow her own spiritual path and become her own person. Thérèse owed so much to Pauline, but she also owed to herself the fulfillment of her own calling unencumbered by the desires and preferences of anyone, even her "second mother." Pauline, for her part, in some personal way, needed the acceptance and admiration—even approval, indeed the intimate confidence—of her little sister. Having sacrificed to her vocation the fulfillment of her maternal needs, Pauline, it seems, still felt the need to be Thérèse's "mother."

Thérèse had a deep love and closeness to Pauline, a debt of gratitude to her, and a pull to fulfill Pauline's need. Over the next years, Thérèse would use all her skills of relationship to walk the narrow path that did not deviate into the indulgence of her own feelings or those of Pauline. Thérèse needed to maintain a constant yet discreet vigilance in her relationship with Pauline, and the only way she could do that was to turn more and more to prayer.

Her relationship with Pauline and Marie became a further impetus for Thérèse to find her own spiritual path, indeed, to establish her identity, her deepest friendship, and her home in her relationship with Jesus. Not her sisters but her Beloved who called her to Carmel would have to become the guiding support of her Carmelite life. Embracing the tradition of prayer as the focus of the Carmelite vocation, she threw herself into her relationship with Jesus. Yet, to her great astonishment and distress, Jesus, who had welcomed her into Carmel with an initial brief burst of elation, seemed to have left her alone. The deep sense of peace remained, but was now overshadowed by a palpable aridity. Jesus seemed to have abandoned her, and Thérèse's prayer was filled with emptiness.

Two months after her entry into Carmel, Thérèse had the opportunity to make a general confession to Fr. Pichon. Having been Marie's confessor before she entered Carmel, he had now been invited to celebrate the liturgy as Marie received the veil and as the community commemorated the fiftieth anniversary of founding of the Lisieux Carmel. Thérèse knew Fr. Pichon from previous meetings. As a young girl of ten, she had welcomed him when he had been invited by Marie to the family home. She always felt, however, that he, like her uncle, thought she was a bit childish, and she never got the impression from him that he took her seriously.

Several years later, after Fr. Pichon had gone to Canada as a missionary, Thérèse continued a relationship with him through her correspondence. Each month she wrote him a letter from Carmel, hoping that he would continue to serve as her spiritual director. On one occasion he acknowledged his desire to write more faithfully: "If you only knew what my life is! I don't understand myself any longer in the whirlwind in which my dear apostolate engulfs me." But he replied rarely, about once a year, and although he wrote that "there is not one of your little sheets that hasn't failed to touch me sweetly and console me interiorly," he destroyed all her letters (GC I 559). Nonetheless, over the years, through the retreats that he gave at Carmel, and through his infrequent replies, Thérèse learned much from Fr. Pichon.

The general confession she made to him was a source of great consolation. Finally, in the reassuring presence of Fr. Pichon, she calmed the last inner disturbances that lingered from the experience of her nearly fatal illness. Her visit to the shrine of Our Lady of Victories in Paris had assured her that the Blessed Mother had brought about her cure, but she was still haunted by the fear that she may have deceptively played a role in the origin of the illness itself, and that she may have seriously displeased God by telling Marie about the experience of the Virgin's smile.

Now Fr. Pichon assured her, "I declare that you have never committed a mortal sin." These words, Thérèse said, were *the most consoling words I ever heard in my life* (SS 149; cf. HLC 73). She was filled with joy and a profound sense of liberation and gratitude. She was confident now that she had never grievously offended God. If Jesus seemed to be absent in her prayer, she would now wait in a deep peace, knowing that despite her feelings he had not really abandoned her.

Fr. Pichon also told her to "thank God for what he had done for you, for if he had abandoned you, instead of being a little angel you would become a little demon." Thérèse knew what he meant. *I had no difficulty in believing it*, she wrote (SS 149). She was aware of her tendency to vanity and her need for closeness. She still remembered her early childhood dream about the *frightful little devils, dancing . . . on the barrel of lime, demons who are cowards,* inner demons and cowards before the honest *gaze of a little child* (SS 28). Ever conscious of her affinity with the struggles of Mary Magdalene, whose holiness was established solely in her friendship with Jesus, Thérèse sensed her own inner demons, and she was certain that her salvation also was to be solely founded in her honest gaze of self-awareness and in her loving relationship with Jesus. *If my heart had not been raised to God from the dawn of reason, if the world had smiled on me from my entrance into life, what would have become of me?* she had wondered. And she was thankful that *the Blessed Virgin, too, watched over her little flower and, not wanting* her to be tarnished by contact with worldly things, drew her to her mountain [the convent of Carmel] before she blossomed (SS 86).

"My child, may our Lord always be your superior and your novice master," the priest concluded, and Thérèse knew that that was true as well. Jesus was my Director, she wrote later (SS 151).

Under the shadow of the cross and in her honest search for intimacy with her Beloved, Thérèse extended her devotion to the Holy Face of Jesus. Pauline had earlier introduced her to this devotion, and now she found consolation in identifying with Jesus unknown, rejected, and suffering deep inner pain. Thérèse also began to understand more clearly her insights from her continued meditations on the life of Joan of Arc that, as the opposite of Joan, she would suffer the little pinpricks of feelings and be unknown. Devotion to the Holy Face and to Joan gave her awareness into her own hidden spiritual path. She identified with the "man of sorrows," unrecognized and alone, and with Joan, suffering desolation in prison. Thérèse was being drawn into a deeper detachment from her self-centeredness and into a more selfless love.

Two months after Thérèse had entered the convent, Céline told her father that she too wished to enter Carmel at the first opportunity. This announcement must have disturbed him deeply. In his strong faith he rejoiced in having already given three daughters to Carmel, but emotionally he suffered grief and loss. Léonie, who had been in and out of two convents, was still troubling him with her indecisiveness. Thérèse's leaving had been a difficult experience, and now, following his earlier paralytic stroke, he was feeling physically and emotionally weaker.

A week after Céline's announcement, her father, in great distress, disappeared from home for several days before the family learned that he was aimlessly walking the streets of Le Havre. Uncle Isidore and Céline escorted him home, and now he was obsessed with the idea of becoming a hermit. Céline knew that she would have to postpone her desire for Carmel and dedicate herself completely to caring for her father. Thérèse encouraged her sister in her resolve and self-sacrifice. She wrote to Céline, quoting Arminjon, that [God] wants to give us such a beautiful recompense, and His ambitions for us are very great. But how can He say: "My turn," if ours hasn't come . . . ? It does pain Him to give us sorrows to drink, but He knows this is the only means of preparing us to "know Him as He knows Himself and to become Gods ourselves" (GC I 450; cf. HF 129).

Two months after Louis Martin's disappearance, the rapidly aging man suffered another attack that temporarily paralyzed him. His condition was further complicated by a large cyst behind his left ear, which had originated from an infection caused by an insect bite some ten years earlier. His mind began to deteriorate, and a rumor began passing around the town of Lisieux that his distress over his beloved little queen's abandoning him had contributed to his breakdown. On hearing this news Thérèse was devastated. And among the sisters in the community, her father's name, once so highly respected, was now spoken only in a whisper as though it identified a man who had fallen into disgrace.

Deeply pained by her father's deterioration, Thérèse entered one of the most severe trials of her life. She had experienced the disappointment of Mother Gonzague's unexpected behavior toward her; she had begun to discretely distance herself from Pauline and Marie; her relationship with Jesus did not have the consolations she had expected; and now she felt that her father was leaving her, disappearing in the way that she had vaguely imagined when, as a child looking from the window onto the garden, she had seen the figure of the old, bent man disappear. Louis Martin, Thérèse's beloved king, was about to vanish into the inaccessible world of the mentally ill.

Devotion to the Holy Face as an expression of her detachment and selfless love now became the most important focus of Thérèse's prayer. She was to grow in this devotion as she came to see more and more deeply the features of the Holy Face of the suffering Jesus reflected in the face of her beloved, suffering father.

CHAPTER 25

We Have Only the Short Moments of Our Life to Love Jesus

Even though the ever-vigilant Fr. Delatroëtte advised against it, Thérèse's reception of the habit was approved by the community. Because of her father's condition, however, the ceremony, originally scheduled for October 1888, was delayed until January 10, 1889. Her private retreat preparing for the reception of the habit left Thérèse in spiritual dryness: *I believe Jesus' work during this retreat has been to detach me from all that is not himself.* She wrote to Pauline that her deepest desire, as she entered the Carmelite family, was to love Jesus *more than He has ever been loved* (GC I 511, 500).

The day Thérèse received her habit, nine months after she had entered Carmel, was a joyful one, filled with consolations and blessings for her. Although very weak, her father had made a slight recovery and was able to walk arm in arm with his beaming little queen down the chapel aisle. *Never had he looked so handsome, so dignified*, Thérèse later wrote (SS 155). Having feared that their father might suffer some sort of embarrassing mishap during the ceremony, Pauline had prayed the night before that "God . . . have pity on us and that Father would not weep in the chapel" (GC I 513). Bishop Hugonin, after presiding at the ceremony, entered the cloister to proudly introduce a radiant but embarrassed Thérèse as "his little girl" and to remark playfully about her hair (SS 156). And the snow, for which Thérèse had prayed, had fallen unexpectedly; *a small miracle,* she noted. These signs of hope Thérèse accepted as special gifts from her Beloved.

Now as a novice, Thérèse began signing her name *Sister Thérèse of the Child Jesus and of the Holy Face.* It would not be for more than a year, until her profession ceremony, that her name would officially include "of the Holy Face," but devotion to the loving Jesus, abandoned, unknown, and suffering, was becoming the most important aspect of Thérèse's devotional life. *Jesus is on fire with love for us. . . . Look at His adorable Face,* she wrote; *there you will see how He loves us.* Fr. Pichon, on learning of this addition to her name, wrote, "Jesus has given you his Childhood and His Passion. . . . What an incomparable dowry" (GC II 553, 720).

Thérèse's devotion to the Holy Face expressed her awareness of the role of suffering as a part of love, just as her devotion to the child Jesus expressed her understanding of the importance of simplicity and childlike reciprocity to her loving Father, who stooped down to embrace the human race in the incarnation, in the Eucharist, and in constant providence.

The next month Thérèse received word that her father, having brandished a revolver while suffering hallucinations, was hospitalized in the insane asylum of Bon Sauveur at Caen, with 1,700 patients. Thérèse was again in profound distress. That her king, still fully aware of his situation, would spend more than three years of his life wasting away in an asylum without a trace of personal dignity while she stood helpless evoked emotional turmoil in Thérèse. She would see him only once more in the next five years until his death.

The civil tribunal of Lisieux appointed an administrator to oversee Louis Martin's possessions. Thérèse felt not only loss and profound sorrow, but also inadequacy and shame. What was the real depth of her father's suffering and pain? Was there any truth to the rumor that had been circulating through the town? Was she in any way responsible for her father's condition? Would this mental illness appear at some time in herself or in her sisters? Under this crushing distress, that completely filled her capacity to suffer, she wrote, *Ah! That day, I didn't say I was able to suffer more!* (SS 157).

Encouraging Céline in her personal pain as their father lost more and more of his dignity, Thérèse wrote to her sister, *Now you are truly the Lily-Immortelle of Jesus. . . . Oh, I thank Jesus for having placed a lily near our dear father, a lily that fears nothing, a lily that wishes rather to die than to abandon the glorious field in which the love of Jesus has placed it!* (GC I 541–42).

In July, enduring great sadness over her father's quickly deteriorating condition, Thérèse nevertheless experienced a profound grace beginning during a private retreat. *It was as though a veil had been cast over all the things of this earth for me*, she remembered. *I was entirely hidden under the Blessed Virgin's veil. At this time, I was placed in charge of the refectory, and I recall doing things as though not doing them; it was as if someone had lent me a body.* This experience of *quietude,* as Thérèse called it, *remained that way for one whole week* (GC I 571; HLC 88). She was describing a mystical experience of grace that affirmed her sense that hiddenness was her path and that her Beloved would lead the way. She had never had an experience of affirmation and humility like this before and would never have another again.

Thérèse's spiritual consolation was short lived. Her father's condition was ever present to her, and now she received news that the family was not going to renew the lease on the family house, Les Buissonnets, which would expire in December 1889. The contents of the house needed to be disposed of and when the family clock and other items of family furniture were brought to Carmel, Thérèse's spaniel, Tom, visited the cloister and recognized Thérèse. Tom's tumultuous display of delight was another sad reminder for Thérèse of the kindness of her father.

At this same time Thérèse was beset with a brief attack of scruples, and her feelings so distressed her that sometimes *I no longer knew whether God loved me.* She shared her anxiety with Mother Geneviève, whom she regarded as the truly enlightened saint of the community, and with Fr. Pichon. Mother reassured her, "Remember, my child, 'Our God is a God of peace,'" and Fr. Pichon offered his firm reply, "Believe obstinately that Jesus loves you" (SS 169, GC I 585). At a deep level Thérèse felt at peace and knew that she was loved by Jesus, but she was still vulnerable to feelings of offending God, of loss, and of separation. She had to bear the intensity of her feelings until the day she died.

Now Thérèse, sixteen and a novice in Carmel, put to good use her personal learning about scruples and their cure. Her cousin Marie, who had supported her in the abbey school, was presently a young woman of nineteen and was suffering from the same *terrible sickness,* as Thérèse called it. Marie had visited the Paris Exhibition and wrote to Thérèse that "Paris was not made for healing the scrupulous. I no longer know where to turn my eyes. If I flee from one nudity, I meet another. . . . Neither does the demon fail [at night] to bring to my mind all these evil things that I saw during the day" (GC I 565–66). Marie feared for her soul. She did not want to receive Communion.

Thérèse quickly and with self-assuredness replied in a letter, *You did well to write me, and I understand everything, everything, everything, everything! . . . You haven't committed the shadow of any evil; I know what these kinds of temptations are so well that I can assure you of this without any fear, and, besides, Jesus tells me this in the depths of my heart* (GC I 567). Thérèse had prayed to the Blessed Mother when, in Paris before her trip to Rome, she too had experienced the distress of scruples.

She pleaded with Marie to return to Communion: *Go without any fear to receive Jesus in peace and love.* Thérèse wrote with uncanny spiritual maturity, addressing her cousin's lack of confidence not only in divine mercy, but more specifically in the truthfulness of her deep desire for God. Thérèse insisted that her cousin's personal doubt about her own capacity to make good moral judgments was a greater weakness and offense to Jesus than her fear of her supposed sin. Thérèse repeated that *I understand it all,* and bluntly told Marie, *You can go without any fear to receive your only true Friend* [in Communion]. . . . *What offends Him and what wounds His Heart is the lack of confidence.* . . . *Your heart is made to love Jesus, to love him passionately; pray that the beautiful years of your life may not pass in chimerical fears. We have only the short moments of our life to love Jesus!* (GC I 568).

From her own experience Thérèse was unfolding for her cousin not only wise advice concerning scrupulosity, but also profound teaching about the Blessed Sacrament, as well as deep insight about the spiritual path she herself was living. She would gradually articulate this path of confidence with increasing clarity. God is all mercy and love; Jesus' presence in the Blessed Sacrament is food for sinners; Jesus is present not so much to be adored as to be consumed, so that Jesus in his turn can transform us into himself. Jesus' eucharistic presence is a sign of his constant loving vulnerability and of his call to us to respond in repentance, with complete receptivity, in confidence and love even in our weakness and frailty.

This letter of Thérèse to her cousin in May 1889 was shown in 1910 to Pope Pius X by the priest in charge of the process of canonization for Thérèse. The pope finished reading it, saying, "It's a great joy for me." Then he added, "We must hurry this cause [of Thérèse's canonization]" (GC I 569, note 4). Thérèse's thoughts expressed in the letter helped Pope Pius X to decide that frequent reception of the Eucharist should be the norm rather than the exception in the life of the church.

At about this same time Céline also suffered from scrupulosity concerning purity. Thérèse offered Céline advice similar to the counsel she had given to their cousin Marie. *Céline, pure hearts are sometimes surrounded by thorns,* she wrote. *They are often in darkness, and then these lilies believe they've lost their whiteness, they think these thorns surrounding them have succeeded in tearing their petals. . . . The lilies in the midst of thorns are the loved ones of Jesus, and it is in their midst that He takes His delight. . . .*

Blessed is he who has been found worthy to suffer temptations (GC I 618; cf. GC II 1010).

Years later, now even more confident in her understanding of human nature and spiritual growth, Thérèse would tell one of the young sisters under her guidance,

It is amazing how easily souls lose peace when it comes to this virtue of purity! . . . However, there is no temptation less dangerous than that one. The means of being freed from these temptations is to regard them with calm, not to be astonished, much less, to fear them. . . . Be sure that one temptation of pride is by far more dangerous—and God is much more offended when we yield to that—than when one commits a fault, even a grave one, against purity, because God has consideration for the fragility of our corruptible nature, whereas for a fault of pride there is no excuse. Pride, however, is a fault that souls commit often and easily, without being upset! . . . Keep in mind the method used to make copper objects shine. You smear them all over with mud, with things that make them dirty and dull; after this operation, they will shine again like gold. . . . Temptations are like this mud for the soul; they serve for nothing less than to make the virtues which are opposed to these same temptations to shine forth. (TLMT 84–85)

CHAPTER 26

One Day We Ourselves Shall Have a Divine Existence

Now, as the late months of 1889 passed toward January 1890, Thérèse anticipated the profession of her taking vows, which, according to custom, should be a year after her reception of the habit. Again Fr. Delatroëtte intervened—it was his right to do so as the religious superior of the community—contesting that, at seventeen, she would be too young to take vows. Bishop Hugonin, however, gave his permission. Thérèse's profession was to be during her seventeenth year, but as a concession to Fr. Delatroëtte's original objection, the community postponed the ceremony eight months until September (SS 160). Once more Thérèse was able to experience delay as a grace. Surrendering to the will of her Beloved in the reality of this situation, she would *wait as long as you desire. . . . I want to be forgotten, not only by creatures, but also by myself. . . . The glory of Jesus that is all,* she wrote; *as for my own glory, I abandon it to him* (GC I 612).

Thérèse's cousin Jeanne Guérin was engaged to marry Francis La Néele, a medical doctor, in October. Thérèse challenged herself during the delay of her profession of vows to love and prepare for Jesus with the same fervor as Jeanne loved and prepared for her fiancé. She even whimsically designed invitations to her profession with the same language that a wedding invitation might have. She would wed Jesus, Son of the Father, becoming one in love with the Second Person of the Blessed Trinity, but on her Beloved's terms, which were "love for love" (cf. SS 168).

The months of delay also brought Thérèse to understand again her continuing struggle with mixed motives. She recognized that her *intense desire to make profession was mixed with great self-love* (SS 158), and therefore she still had need for a spirit of detachment that prompted a singleness of heart. At this time she had begun reading St. John of the Cross, in whom she found a perfect model for such a spirit.

For the next eighteen months or so, and as part of her preparation for her profession, John of the Cross became Thérèse's constant companion and teacher. She read and meditated on his works *The Spiritual Canticle* and *Living Flame of Love.* In these two books she saw her own state of soul reflected in the experiences of human darkness and divine consummation that the great saint of mysticism described so clearly. *I begged God,* she said, *to work out in me what he* [John of the Cross] *wrote, that is . . . to consume me rapidly in Love* (HLC 177).

Thérèse also discovered the text in the liturgy that focused on the "suffering servant" of Isaiah 53, the perfect example of abandonment to the divine will and an indispensable source of enrichment for her devotion to the hidden and holy face of Jesus. The words of Isaiah, *"Who has believed our report? . . . There is no beauty in him, no comeliness"* [Isaiah 53:1-2], she said, *have made up the whole foundation of my devotion to the Holy Face, or, to express it better, the foundation of all my piety* (HLC 135).

Moreover, she was growing in the awareness that her self-centeredness, personal ambitions, even spiritual ambitions motivated by self-love, were the straws that needed to be consumed in the divine fire of love. She shared the wisdom of her insights with Céline, sending her sister a page of excerpts from Isaiah and from St. John of the Cross that she had copied by hand.

At the end of August Thérèse entered her ten-day private retreat in preparation for her profession. The retreat *was far from bringing me any consolations since the most absolute aridity and almost total abandonment were my lot. Jesus was sleeping as usual in my little boat . . .* (SS 165). *My Fiancé says nothing to me, and I say nothing to Him either, except that I love Him more than myself, and I feel at the bottom of my heart that it is true, for I am more His than my own.* She wrote to Pauline, *Jesus took me by the hand, and He made me enter a subterranean passage . . . where I see nothing but a half-veiled light, the light which is diffused by the lowered eyes of my Fiancé's Face* (GC I 651–52).

On September 2, at the formal canonical examination preparatory for her profession presided over by Fr. Delatroëtte, Thérèse affirmed her Carmelite vocation: *I came to save souls and especially to pray for priests* (SS 149).

On the evening before her profession, while making the Way of the Cross, Thérèse suffered another bout with the little demons of scruples, a brief panic attack that questioned her own sincerity and that filled her with self-doubt and fear. *The darkness was so great that I could see and understand one thing only: I didn't have a vocation!* (SS 166). Could it be, she wondered, that she was misleading her superiors and that she did not really belong in Carmel? Believing that if she told her novice mistress about her anxieties she would be prevented from pronouncing vows, Thérèse nevertheless beckoned the nun out of choir after the evening recitation of prayers to confess her fears.

The novice mistress *completely reassured me*, and then later when Thérèse confided her doubts to Mother Gonzague, the prioress simply laughed at her and sent her away. Thérèse felt embarrassed and humiliated but was shocked into a sense of hope. Mother Geneviève further consoled her by assuring her that she too had passed through the same trial before pronouncing her vows (SS 170).

The next day, September 8, 1890, the nativity of Mary, Thérèse made her profession of the vows of poverty, chastity, and obedience in a private ceremony. *I felt as though I were flooded with a river of peace and it was in this peace "which surpasses all understanding"* [Philippians 4:7] *that I pronounced my Holy Vows. . . . I wanted to deliver all the souls from purgatory and convert all sinners. . . . I offered myself to Jesus in order to accomplish His will perfectly in me. . . . I placed my crown at the Blessed Virgin's feet.* The weather was radiantly clear, and throughout the day thousands of swallows were chirping on the rooftops of the convent building. In the evening Thérèse *gazed at the stars shining in the firmament* and thought *that soon this beautiful heaven would open up to my ravished eyes, and I would be able to unite myself to my Spouse in the bosom of eternal happiness* (SS 166–67).

Br. Siméon, Thérèse's friend and contact man in Rome, responded to a letter she had sent him, obtaining an apostolic blessing from the still reigning Pope Leo XIII for her profession and for "her venerable Father, the saintly old man, tried by suffering" (GC I 656). The blessing, as well as Br. Siméon's concern for her father, consoled and encouraged her.

The public veiling ceremony following her profession took place two weeks later. Thérèse had harbored the expectation that her father might be able to travel from the asylum to be present for the ceremony, but Uncle Isidore realistically squelched the notion. The ceremony was filled with relatives and friends—everyone but those whom Thérèse had really wished to be present: her father, increasingly debilitated, was absent; Fr. Pichon had gone to Canada to establish a ministry there; and Bishop Hugonin, who considered her "his little girl," was sick. *Everything was sadness and bitterness;* she wrote, *and still peace, always peace reigned at the bottom of the chalice* (SS 167).

As a special prayer at her profession, Thérèse prayed not that her father be cured but, *God, I beg you, let it be your will that Papa be cured!* (HLC 107). For Léonie, she asked that God would give her the vocation to become a Visitandine. *You cannot refuse me that,* she prayed. She also composed a prayer expressing her desire for *martyrdom of heart or of body, or rather . . . both* and to live a hidden, forgotten life, fulfilled in the image of *a grain of sand* that was a burden to no one. She asked for *love, infinite love without limits other than Yourself; love which is no longer me but You, my Jesus* (SS 275).

To Céline, who at that time was so distraught as their beloved father slipped out of their lives, Thérèse had written that *the martyrdom is beginning. Let us enter the arena together, the Lily-Immortelle . . . and the poor grain of sand* (GC I 537). In a burst of hope she wrote further, *We are greater than the whole universe, and one day we ourselves shall have a divine existence* (GC I 542). This truth that she had read about in Arminjon's book as a young child remained with her as the hope that even now, with all life's trials, the two spiritual sisters could live in a way that participated in the state of divine union awaiting them in eternity.

CHAPTER 27

I Want at Least to Tell Him Frequently That I Love Him

On the day Thérèse entered Carmel she experienced a deep peace, knowing that she was where her heavenly Father wanted her to be and that she was doing what he wanted her to do with her life. For the remaining nine years of her life, even as turbulence disrupted the surface of her thoughts, feelings, and images, that sweet peace never left her, residing at the core of her soul, in the deepest part of her person. Frequent times of confusion, touchiness, desolation, and sadness filled her with emotional distress. Her weaknesses and faults were not lessening, her prayer was not providing many consolations—*Jesus is not doing much to keep the conversation going!* she wrote. Yet she clung in faith to the core of peace, rejecting the path of fear, convinced that she was in her Beloved's arms despite all her doubts, all her distressing feelings. *I am far from being on the way of fear; I always find a way of being happy and of profiting from my miseries* . . . (SS 173).

Her relationships with God, her loving Father; with Jesus, her spouse; and with the Blessed Virgin Mary, her mother, were to become the foundations of her life, providing the comfort of bonding and mothering, the sense of security and home, and the certainty of self-worth and identity that she had craved since childhood. As an expression of these relationships and as a contributing element to their nurturance, constant prayer, even in aridity, was a central focus in her life.

The convent schedule called for times of communal and personal prayer, which Thérèse faithfully followed even though she experienced almost constant dryness. She participated in daily Mass and received Communion as often as she was permitted, but experienced few consolations. *I find this very understandable,* she said, *since I have offered myself to Jesus not as one desirous of her own consolation in His visit, but simply to please Him who is giving Himself to me. . . . He knows well that if he gave me a shadow of happiness I would cling to it with all my energy, all the strength of my heart* (SS 172).

Not sleeping well at night—the insomnia of her youth sometimes recurred—Thérèse would often fall asleep during her personal prayers and was overcome with drowsiness even after having received Communion. She did not, however, attribute her fatigue in a self-blaming way to a lack of fervor or a failing in fidelity, even though that would have been the logic of the spirituality of the times. Rather, with a creative spiritual boldness, she took a certain humorous delight in her weakness. She would *remember that little children are as pleasing to their parents when they are asleep as well as when they are wide awake; I remember, too, that when they perform operations, doctors put their patients to sleep. Finally, I remember that: "The Lord knows our weakness, that he is mindful that we are but dust and ashes"* [Psalm 103:14] (SS 165). Thérèse trusted that her loving Father knew her frailty and would continue to love her nevertheless. For Thérèse, God was not a harsh critic or a demanding judge, but a loving parent, a healing doctor. *Oh! Infinite mercy of the Lord, who really wants to answer the prayer of His little children,* she prayed.

She recited the Divine Office, the rosary, and other prayers in community, comforted in her drowsiness and lack of pious feelings by the hope that the fervor of her sisters would make up for her own deficiencies. Rather than blaming or condemning herself for the absence of a "felt" or "experiential" sense of devotion, she trusted in her own sincere desires and her willingness to be available to God. She was willing to live in surrender, gratitude, and trust.

Thérèse wished that she had more devotional feelings in her personal prayer, but when she lacked such feelings she was undaunted. She offered her weakness to Jesus and noted that *no doubt this* [way] *does not displease Jesus since he seems to encourage me on this road* (SS 173).

She imagined her aridity as a result of Jesus' sleeping, wearied with having always to take the initiative with souls as well as respond to their requests. In her case she would respect his repose and not make any demands. She would wait. She would simply let Jesus sleep, confident that he would *more quickly grow tired of making me wait than I shall grow tired of waiting for Him* (GC I 612).

After her mother's death, the young Thérèse, with her reserved, pensive disposition, had sometimes gone to her room and slipped *behind the bed in an empty space which was there,* [where] *it was easy to close myself with my bed curtain and . . . "I thought" . . . about God, about life, about eternity.* In the mornings before getting up, she had thought things *over in my bed,* just as she had done to discover the name she chose for the time when she would enter Carmel, *for it was there* [in bed] *I made my profound medita-*

tions, and, contrary to the bride in the Canticles, I always found my Beloved there (SS 74, 71).

When her father had taken his little queen fishing, she had sometimes preferred to *sit on the grass bedecked with flowers, and then my thoughts became very profound indeed! Without knowing what it was to meditate, my soul was absorbed in real prayer* (SS 37). *I loved God very much,* she remembered about herself as a six-year-old, *and offered my heart to him very often, making use of the little formula Mother had taught me: My God, I give you my heart, take it, please, so that no creature may possess it, but you alone, good Jesus* (SS 38).

As she had grown older, and certainly after she entered Carmel, Thérèse did not think of prayer as something she did just as she lay in her bed, or as something necessarily consisting of profound thoughts, or even as something to be done for several hours each day. Thérèse's prayer, particularly her drowsy thanksgiving after Communion, extended with more attention throughout the entire day. Keeping mindful of God's love, she received more spiritual insights during her ordinary daily occupations than she received at the fixed times of prayer. It seemed to Thérèse that instead of allowing her to store up insights from her time of prayers, Jesus provided in each successive moment during the day the grace and insight that she needed.

Never have I heard Him speak, she wrote, *but I feel that He is within me, at each moment. He is guiding and inspiring me with what I must say and do. I find just when I need them certain lights that I had not seen until then, and it isn't most frequently during my hours of prayer that these are most abundant but rather in the midst of my daily occupations* (SS 179). She also noted, *I believe it is Jesus Himself hidden in the depths of my poor little heart . . . giving me the grace of acting within me, making me think of all He desires me to do at the present moment* (SS 165). This convinced her that the state of prayerfulness, a spirit of being mindfully available and self-disposed to her Beloved at every given moment throughout the day, would be her prevailing attitude supplementing her formal times of prayer.

Although often meditating on readings from *The Imitation of Christ* or on the writings of St. John of the Cross or St. Teresa of Avila, Thérèse was particularly drawn again and again to the sacred Scriptures and especially to the gospels. *The Gospel . . . sustains me during my hours of prayer, for in them I find what is necessary for my poor little soul. I am constantly discov-*

ering in them new lights, hidden and mysterious meanings (SS 179). Other books of piety and prayer were of little help to her and sometimes distracted her with their tendency toward Jansenism and perfectionism.

On one occasion Thérèse whispered to one of the novices as she stood in front of the convent library, *Oh! I would have been sorry to have read all those books. . . . If I had read them, I would have broken my head, and I would have wasted precious time that I could have employed very simply in loving God* (HLC 261). She experienced that *all books left me in aridity. . . . If I open a book composed by a spiritual author (even the most beautiful, the most touching book),* she wrote, *I feel my heart contract immediately and I read without understanding, so to speak. Or if I do understand, my mind comes to a standstill without the capacity of meditating* (SS 179).

At the same time, Thérèse was convinced that *Jesus has no need of books or teachers to instruct souls; He teaches without the noise of words . . .* (SS 179; cf. TLMT 76). *Without showing Himself, without making His voice heard, Jesus teaches me in secret; it is not by means of books, for I do not understand what I am reading. Sometimes a word comes to console me such as this one, . . . "I want to make you read in the book of life, wherein is contained the science of LOVE"* [words of the Lord to St. Margaret Mary in *Little Breviary of the Sacred Heart*] (SS 187). She was certain that Jesus was teaching her by the experiences of her own *book of life.*

Thérèse was persuaded that to pray,

> *It is not necessary to read from a book some beautiful formula composed for the occasion. If this were the case, alas, I would have to be pitied! Outside the Divine Office which I am very unworthy to recite, I do not have the courage to force myself to search out beautiful prayers in books. There are so many of them it really gives me a headache! And each prayer is more beautiful than the others. I cannot recite them all and not knowing which to choose, I do like children who do not know how to read, I say very simply to God what I wish to say, without composing beautiful sentences, and He always understands me.* (SS 242)

On one occasion Thérèse was asked what she did when, during her private prayer time, her mind was filled with distractions. She responded, *I have a lot of these, but as soon as I perceive them I pray for the persons that occupy my imagination and this way they benefit from my distractions* (TLMT 25).

Desiring to combine her love for God with her love for her sisters, despite some feelings of apathy and even antipathy toward certain nuns, she took steps to make her prayer permeate her entire day. Thérèse wrote,

> *When I am feeling nothing, when I am incapable of praying, of practicing virtue, then is the moment for seeking opportunities, nothings, which please Jesus more than mastery of the world or even martyrdom suffered with generosity. For example, a smile, a friendly word when I would like to say nothing, or put on a look of annoyance, etc., etc. . . . It is not for the purpose of weaving my crown, gaining merits, it is in order to please Jesus. . . . When I do not have any [such] opportunities, I want at least to tell Him frequently that I love Him; this is not difficult, and it keeps the fire going. Even though this fire of love would seem to me to have gone out, I would like to throw something on it, and Jesus could then relight it. . . . Jesus is really powerful enough to keep the fire going by Himself. However, He is satisfied when He sees us put a little fuel on it. The attentiveness pleases Jesus, and then He throws on the fire a lot of wood. We do not see it, but we do feel the strength of love's warmth.* (GC II 801)

Thérèse was in love with Jesus, and *to please Jesus* was the constant motive in her consciousness to which she continually returned. *Everything I did was done to please God,* she said (HLC 118). Some of the other sisters mentioned to Thérèse that their motivation for prayer and good works was more to make reparation for their sins or to gain a reward in heaven. Each morning as part of the morning prayer, a translation of a verse from the psalms was prayed by the community: "I have set my heart on keeping your commandments always because of the reward that might be merited" (Psalm 119:12; cf. Psalm 19:11b). Thérèse was embarrassed to say this verse and confided to a novice, Sr. Marie of the Trinity, *Within myself I hastened to say: "Oh Jesus, you know very well that I don't serve you for the reward, but solely because I love you and to save souls"* (TLMT 93).

The convent's annual preached retreats, except for those preached by Fr. Pichon and one other retreat preacher, were *more painful to me than the ones I make alone,* she noted (SS 173). The preached retreats reminded her of the retreats of Fr. Domin at the preparation for her First Communion in their similar disturbing, Jansenistic focus on sin and damnation.

To Fr. Blino, a Jesuit retreat preacher and director who had given the retreat several months before her profession, she confided, *I want to become a saint.* Seeing only an immature, pious young sister in her first fervor, the priest responded paternalistically, "What pride and what presumption! Confine yourself to correcting your faults, to offending God no longer, to making a little progress in virtue each day, and temper your rash desires" (GC I 623, note 8). Thérèse knew she was on a completely different path from the one that such a response implied.

Sanctity, for Thérèse, was not a matter of tempering her desires but of cultivating them, since she experienced them as coming from her Beloved and was confident that the Holy Spirit would give her only desires that could be fulfilled. As she neared her death she would write with confidence, *When I shall appear before my Beloved Spouse, I shall have only my desires to offer Him* (GC II 1054). But for now she replied, *Father, I don't think that these are rash desires; I can aspire to sanctity* (GC I 623, note 8). The sanctity to which Thérèse aspired was not to be achieved by getting rid of faults. If sanctity were a matter of being without faults, she would have despaired long ago. She knew she had many weaknesses and defects. She was also aware that striving willfully to get rid of even one fault would have involved, for her, a self-centeredness and possibly a self-violence that would have resulted in a state worse than the first.

For Thérèse, holiness was a matter of being more and more available to her Beloved, who might or might not give her the grace to overcome a fault. Getting rid of her faults was the Lord's business; the willing surrender to the divine will was her business. Her availability to God, her loving closeness to Jesus, would be her sanctity. As she matured, Thérèse would finally come to pray, *I desire . . . to be a saint, but I feel my helplessness, and I beg you, O my God! To be Yourself my sanctity* (SS 276).

Her openness to an ever-closer union with her Beloved would be her path of holiness in this life, extending even into eternal life. She had no inclination to moderate her desires; truly they were not her own desires anyway, they were God's desires in her. *The more you want to give us,* Thérèse was convinced, *the more you make us desire* (SS 276). Thérèse, like her mentor

Teresa of Avila, was a woman of desire, moving toward fewer and fewer attachments and more and more conviction.

She had implicitly asked Fr. Blino, the retreat director, for confirmation of her path and instead had been given a pious admonition to temper her fervor. Thérèse left his presence unsupported but also undeterred.

For a long time now, from even before she had entered Carmel, she had been confident *that Jesus was my Director.* She believed that she *needed no other guide but Jesus. I compared directors to faithful mirrors, reflecting Jesus in souls, and I said that for me God was using no intermediary; He was acting directly!* (SS 105). But the year following this retreat, in October 1891, as she approached her nineteenth year, Thérèse found the priest-director who did reflect Jesus to her. He was an intermediary that she really needed.

CHAPTER 28

For Me, Prayer Is a Surge of the Heart

Fr. Alexis Prou, a Franciscan renowned for his preaching to large groups and for his ministry of reconciliation to great sinners, was asked to give the October 1891 community retreat at the Lisieux Carmel. He was not the convent's first choice. By default he was available, and later the other sisters confessed that they were not impressed with his preaching. But for Thérèse he was the only retreat director besides Fr. Pichon, her Jesuit confidant, that she appreciated during her entire time in Carmel.

Not suggesting that holy desires be moderated or that fear be given the final word, Fr. Prou made a singularly important contribution to Thérèse's spiritual awareness. She had always been prone to a certain scrupulous fear of offending God—a tendency that had on occasion poisoned her first years in Carmel—and was still plagued by the thought that no one knows whether they are worthy of love or hatred—an idea that Fr. Domin had sown in her heart as an eleven-year-old. Now Thérèse was suffering from *great interior trials of all kinds, even to the point of asking myself whether heaven really existed* (SS 173).

She at first felt that she would make her confession to Fr. Prou but *say nothing of my interior dispositions since I didn't know how to express them* (SS 173). But in the presence of the Franciscan she felt her soul expand, and she opened her heart. She explained that she was in the confused state of wondering whether she might be offending God by her feelings and faults, and was suffering from dark forebodings about the afterlife.

Fr. Prou understood her immediately, better than she understood herself. He assured her *that my faults caused God no pain; . . . and that God was very much pleased with me.* With his assurance she was convinced that *Jesus gives us the grace of feeling at the bottom of our heart that we would prefer to die rather than to offend Him,* and knew that this conviction reached a richer truth than whatever truth there was in the statement that "no one knows whether they are worthy of love or hatred." Three years earlier Fr. Pichon had responded to Thérèse's general confession by telling her that she had never committed a serious sin, and even more recently, in the face of her continued concerns, had written to her, "No, no, you have not committed any mortal sins. I swear it. . . . Banish, then, your worries. . . . Never, never, never, have you committed a mortal sin" (GC II 767). And now Fr. Prou's *assurance filled me with joy.* Thérèse was completely confirmed in what she had intuitively known in her heart, that *God is more tender than a mother* (SS 174).

Thérèse's encounter with Fr. Prou was a high-water mark in Thérèse's spiritual voyage. *He launched me full sail upon the waves of confidence and love which so strongly attracted me, but upon which I dared not advance.* She would be nineteen years old in three months, and she was convinced more than ever that *my nature was such that fear made me recoil, with love, not only did I advance, I actually flew* (SS 174). Thérèse had hoped to have a second interview with Fr. Prou, but Mother Gonzague, in one of her moods, would not permit it.

Yet, for all her new spiritual impetus, Thérèse still did not achieve any level of competence at a method of private prayer. Rather, being confident in her desire to please Jesus, she trusted her spiritual intuitions and prayed the way she could. At times she simply followed the desire of her heart to be completely and willingly available to Jesus, reciprocating his love in her charity toward the sisters. At other times she struggled in God's presence to understand the meaning of her immediate experiences. When she could, she lingered on thoughts of heaven and eternity, as she had as a child when she was alone at home in her room behind the curtains or when she was with her father as he fished. Even as a child she had begun to live out what she finally came to formulate in her maturity as her definition of prayer. *For me,* she later wrote from her experience, *prayer is a surge of the heart; it is a simple look turned toward heaven, it is a cry of recognition and of love, embracing both trial and joy; finally, it is something great, supernatural, which expands my soul and unites me to Jesus* (CCC 2558; cf. SS 242).

When during her private prayer times she was having difficulty keeping awake or arousing feelings of piety, Thérèse would recite the Our Father very slowly, and then the Hail Mary in the same slow fashion. She found the private recitation of the rosary very difficult. *When I am alone (I am ashamed to admit it),* she did admit, *the recitation of the rosary is more difficult for me than the wearing of an instrument of penance. . . . I force myself in vain to meditate on the mysteries of the rosary; I don't succeed in fixing my mind on them. . . . For a long time I was desolate about this lack of devotion that astonished me, for I love the Blessed Virgin so much that it should be easy for me to recite in her honor prayers that are so pleasing to her. Now I am less desolate; I think that the Queen of heaven, since she is my mother, must see my good will and she is satisfied with it* (SS 242–43). At the end of her life Thérèse sighed, *When I think of how much trouble I've had all my life trying to recite the rosary!* (HLC 160).

Throughout her years in the convent she prayed for the sisters with whom she lived, particularly those for whom she had a natural antipathy. She prayed for priests, for the salvation of all souls on earth, and for the liberation of souls in purgatory. At the end of her life as she herself experienced a trial of faith, Thérèse identified with those who did not believe, and she prayed especially for atheists and nonbelievers. She prayed for her family. She prayed for everyone who asked for her prayers. She prayed for so many people that she sometimes grew weary of remembering each individually.

At first Thérèse attempted to be specific about the intentions of those who had requested her to pray for them, but she found that she simply could not remember all her *treasures,* as she called those who asked her prayers. Trying to find a solution to this little dilemma, one day at prayer she suddenly had an insight. She was captured by the words of the Song of Songs, "Draw me, we shall run after you" (Song of Songs 1:4). She took special notice that the Scripture prayer requested that the Lord *draw me,* but that in doing so *we shall run; we* were all swept up by *one soul* being attracted to God (SS 254, 257).

She understood that when a soul allows itself to be captivated by the love of God, the soul cannot run alone; all those whom it loves are also swept along with it. Thérèse, in opening her heart to Jesus and being drawn to God, took with her to her Beloved all those who were in her heart. Her intuitive conclusion was consoling: *The more the fire of love burns in my heart, the more I shall say "Draw me." And the more the souls who will approach me (poor little piece of iron, useless if I withdraw from the divine furnace), the more these souls will run swiftly in the fragrance of the perfumes of their Beloved, for a soul that is set on fire with love cannot remain inactive* (SS 257).

Draw Me became her simple prayer: *I ask Jesus to draw me into the flames of His love, to unite me so closely to Him that He live and act in me.* Thérèse wanted to be plunged into the fire as Joan of Arc had been—*the fire of the Divine Love* (SS 257).

From her teenage study of science, Thérèse knew that Archimedes had said that he could lift the world if he had a fulcrum and a lever. At the end of her life she recalled that image and described prayer as the lever and God as the fulcrum. Prayer was the way that the whole world could be lifted up to Jesus: by *prayer which burns with a fire of love* (SS 258). She was willing to allow her whole life to become one act of burning, loving prayer.

She had come to Carmel to pray, and to pray especially for priests. One particular priest for whom Thérèse began to pray just six months before her retreat with Fr. Prou was Fr. Hyacinth Loyson. Loyson had been a Carmelite priest of highest standing in his community, a famous preacher, and a personal friend of Cardinal Newman. He had, however, abandoned the priesthood and the church more than twenty years before, married a Protestant widow, and founded a sect that rejected papal infallibility. A continuing scandal to the Carmelites in France, he was in Normandy at this time on a preaching tour against the church.

The Catholic press demonized Loyson as a "renegade monk," but Thérèse prayed for him as a *brother*. Knowing that he had a keen mind and was highly educated, Thérèse acknowledged that *he is really culpable, more culpable than any other sinner ever was who was converted. But,* she asked in a letter to Céline, requesting her prayers as well for him, *cannot Jesus do once what He has not yet ever done?* Thérèse was as faithful to her *brother* as she was to her *first child*, continuing to pray for Loyson, as she did for Pranzini, for the rest of her life. She offered her last Communion on her deathbed for Loyson (GC II 728).

Years later, having read *Story of a Soul* and some poems of Thérèse sent to him by Céline, Loyson assured Céline that he was deeply touched by Thérèse's life and concern for him, that he admired her and was grateful to her. He was, however, never publicly reconciled to the church, but may have been so privately at the time of his death.

In November Bishop Hugonin presided at the Mass in Carmel in honor of the centenary of St. John of the Cross. Again he entered the cloister to celebrate with the sisters, and again he expressed delight to be with Thérèse, whom this time he called "his little daughter." Taking her head in his hands he bestowed on her, she remembered, *a thousand caresses* (SS 156). Delighted and somewhat embarrassed, she nevertheless experienced in the bishop's affection a faint image of God's own tender embrace.

Encouragement in her prayerful spirit came to Thérèse from the example of some of the sisters, especially Mother Geneviève, one of the founders of the Lisieux Carmel. This elderly nun, whom Thérèse especially loved, became for Thérèse a model of simplicity, humility, and inconspicuous virtue. Thérèse knew that these characteristics were to be the stepping-stones for her own spiritual path. Mother Geneviève's words illuminated and consoled her. "Our God is a God of peace" (1 Corinthians 14:33), she had confided to Thérèse during a difficult time when Thérèse *was in such a night that I no longer knew whether God loved me* (SS 169). Thérèse had been overcome with joy.

The saintly old nun died on December 5, just two months after Thérèse had received Fr. Prou's assurance. Like that assurance, Mother Geneviève's death was a healing and sacred moment for Thérèse. She assisted in the nun's preparation for death, taking a place at the foot of the dying nun's bed, noticing all her last movements, and secretly touching a cloth to the nun's cheek, claiming her last tear as a treasured relic. She placed the cloth in the little container that held the formula of her vows, which she wore around her neck.

This was the first time Thérèse had been present to a dying person, and she found the entire experience, especially the actual moment of death, to be in some way an experience of joy. *It was as though Mother Geneviève had imparted to me a little of the happiness she was enjoying, for I was convinced she went straight to heaven* (SS 170). It was an experience Thérèse had not had with the death of her own mother.

Thérèse had been sheltered during those last days of her mother's life, but she did see her mother's body lying in a coffin. As she now stood by the coffin of Mother Geneviève, that childhood scene returned:

I imagined myself back once again in the days of my childhood and all those memories flooded into my mind. . . . The day of Mamma's departure or the day after, Papa took me in his arms and said: "Come, kiss your poor little Mother for the last time." Without a word I placed my lips on her forehead. I don't recall having cried very much, neither did I speak to anyone about the feelings I experienced. I looked and listened in silence. No one had any time to pay any attention to me, and I saw many things they would have hidden from me. For instance, once I was standing before the lid of the coffin which had been placed upright in the hall. I stopped for a long time gazing at it. Though I'd never seen one before, I understood what it was. I was so little that in spite of Mamma's small stature, I had to raise my head to take in its full height. It appeared large and dismal. (SS 33–34)

Thérèse's childhood feelings—dismal feelings of confusion, alienation, and separation, of being of no consequence and of being overwhelmed in her littleness—all these feelings returned now in the experience of Mother Geneviève's death. But now the childhood feelings were enveloped in Thérèse's maturity of faith and wisdom, and they no longer had an intimidating impact. Rather, Thérèse experienced something *ravishing* about the death of Mother Geneviève, healing and transforming the childhood feelings she had at the death of her mother that had lingered all these years (SS 170).

Now she could bear the emotional pain of losing a loved one, and more important, she could look into the face of death, stand her ground emotionally, and not be intimidated. She saw Mother Geneviève take the next natural step of life. Death was really not the end, but rather a natural passing into an experience of peace. Death did not need to be shrouded in mystery, coldness, and alienation. Thérèse was now able to embrace the inevitable feelings of fear and sadness in the presence of death, yet also feel *inexpressible joy and fervor* (SS 170). She had more of the strength and courage of Joan of Arc than she had imagined.

Thérèse had learned much about death, as well as much about her own inner strength in the face of death and of her capacity for faith, courage, and constancy as loved ones died in her presence—and all this learning and self-awareness she would especially need in the weeks ahead.

After Mother Geneviève's death Thérèse *had a very consoling dream: I dreamed she was making her last will and testament, giving each of the Sisters something which she possessed. When my turn finally came, I thought I would get nothing as there was really nothing left to give; however, she said: "To you I leave my heart." She repeated this three times with great emphasis* (SS 171). Nothing could have been more consoling and reassuring to Thérèse than to be one in heart with the nun she was convinced had lived a simple, holy life of love.

CHAPTER 29

I Am Not Always Faithful, but I Never Get Discouraged

Receiving few consolations during the scheduled times of prayer, Thérèse now directed more and more of her attention to simplifying her prayer. She followed her daily routine in the mindful attitude of simply pleasing Jesus by being prayerfully available to his love and present to the sisters in charity. She was especially attentive to accommodating the sisters and expressing little acts of kindness. Inspired by the memory of Mother Geneviève, Thérèse was deliberately inconspicuous about these small acts of charity, which were also often acts of bearing in peace her own inner confusion as well as the little pinpricks of community life. Even in distressful encounters, when she could do nothing more helpful, she simply extended a small courtesy, a knowing smile, or a kind hand to a sister in need. Thérèse would later confide to one of the novices,

> *Before I entered Carmel, when I woke up in the morning I used to think about what the day could possibly have in store for me, happy or troublesome, and if I foresaw only troubles, I got up depressed. Now it is the opposite. I think only of the pains and sufferings that await me, and I get up so much more joyful and full of courage when I think of the opportunities that I will have to prove my love to Jesus. . . . After that I kiss my crucifix, . . . and I say to him: "Jesus, you have worked and wept long enough during the thirty-three years of your life on this poor earth! Today, you rest . . . It is my turn to fight and to suffer!"* (TLMT 104)

An epidemic of influenza had been raging in Europe during the past year, 1891, claiming seventy thousand victims. The disease broke out in the Carmelite community the day after Christmas. Thérèse, the youngest among the professed nuns and just about to celebrate her nineteenth birthday, had been in the convent only three and a half years. She, her sister Marie, and one of the younger sisters were the only ones who were not brought down by the illness. Having assisted at Mother Geneviève's death earlier in December, just before the epidemic hit the convent, she had received the grace to courageously face death. Now as sisters began to die around her, she drew on that grace.

Sr. Saint Joseph, eighty-three and now the oldest member of the community, died on Thérèse's birthday, January 2. Two days later Sr. Febronie, seventy-three and the subprioress, also died. It was to this mature superior that the youthful Thérèse, in a recent exchange of opinions on God's justice and mercy, had said with confident boldness, *My Sister, you want God's justice, you shall have God's justice. The soul receives from God exactly what it hopes for* (FGM 121; cf. GC II 737). Thérèse was confident that it is the person who chooses. She was also confident that God's justice was enfolded in divine mercy, and that the subprioress would be surprised in death by the boundlessness of divine mercy, mercy that *reaches to the heavens* [Psalm 36:6] (SS 181).

Thérèse found Sr. Madeleine of the Blessed Sacrament dead in bed three days later. In the face of the continuing spread of the disease and despite her youth, Thérèse assumed more and more of a leadership role in the community, taking the initiative at every turn, making many small but crucial decisions in the care of the sisters and in the daily business of the convent. *Now I ask myself*, Thérèse wrote several years after the experience, *how I could have done all I did without experiencing fear. Death reigned supreme.* Working alone in the sacristy since Sr. Saint Stanislaus, the sacristan, had taken ill, Thérèse *was the one who had to prepare for the burials, open the choir grills for Mass, etc. God gave me very many graces making me strong at this time.* Her Beloved also blessed her in a special way: *I had the unspeakable consolation of receiving Holy Communion every day* (SS 171–72).

During the epidemic, the sisters experienced Thérèse's spirit of compassion and her fresh directness, faith, and courage. They appreciated her practical, simple, holy way, her self-giving, her wisdom and integrity, and they were beginning to delight in her youthful joy and energy. The older sisters especially were amazed and touched by Thérèse's poise and selflessness, her peace and fearlessness. Even Fr. Delatroëtte was impressed and finally acknowledged her maturity; nonetheless, the best compliment he could manage was to say that Thérèse showed great promise for the community.

Sr. Saint Stanislaus, who loved Thérèse, had the year before given her the nickname of "Little Sister Amen" as a humorous nod to Thérèse's spirit of humility and self-effacement. The pet name also became a playful acknowledgement that Thérèse, as she matured in Carmel and having finally managed to proceed slowly in her way of walking, now seemed always, like an "amen," to arrive at the end of any gathering of the sisters.

Another sister called her affectionately, if with some ambiguity, "the big nanny goat" (TLMT 13). She was taller now, and more playful than her older sisters Pauline and Marie. She had become known for her humorous stories and her ability, which she seems to have acquired from her father, to playfully mimic others without being offensive.

In May 1892, after thirty-nine months in the asylum, Thérèse's father, paralyzed in both legs, was returned to Lisieux to be cared for by the Guérins, by Céline, and also by Léonie until she reentered the Visitation convent the following year.

Two days after Louis Martin's return, the family brought him to Carmel to see his three daughters. It was an especially sorrowful meeting for Thérèse, who must have known that it was the last time she would ever see her beloved king. He was physically spent, emaciated, unable to support himself, emotionally distressed, and mentally struggling. He sat almost motionless in his wheelchair. He could hardly speak, and when he attempted his final farewell, he simply mouthed the words "in heaven" as he gestured with his hand and gazed longingly into Thérèse's eyes. Thérèse was deeply moved, recognizing her father's hope that all the family would one day be reunited in heaven. Céline wheeled him from the convent parlor. Pauline, Marie, and Thérèse wept together.

During a private retreat in October following her father's last visit, Thérèse received the spiritual insight that the downward path of Zacchaeus, who had been invited by Jesus from his treetop perch, would be her own path. Writing to Céline, she shared with her sister that by the slow deterioration of their father, *Jesus has stricken us in the most sensitive exterior part of our heart; now . . . what Jesus desires is that we receive Him into our hearts. No doubt, they are already empty of creatures, but, alas, I feel mine is not entirely empty of myself, and it is for this reason that Jesus tells me to descend* (GC II 762).

The election for the position of prioress, delayed a year because of the epidemic, was held in February 1893. Thirty-two-year-old Pauline was elected superior of the convent, becoming "Mother" to the community, but in a new and deeper sense "Mother" for Thérèse. Thérèse wrote that evening to Pauline, *Dear Mother, how easy it is for me to give you this name! . . . Today God has consecrated you . . . You are truly my Mother and you will be for all eternity. . . . Oh! How beautiful this day is for your child!* (GC II 781).

Even though canon law prevented Mother Gonzague, who had served the previous two terms, from being reelected, she was of two minds about Pauline. On the one hand she worked for Pauline's election, but on the other hand she had feelings of irritation and disappointment when Pauline won the vote. She felt that Pauline and the Martin sisters had been exerting too much influence in the convent and resisted Pauline's exercising any authority. The balloting had not been completely secret, and Pauline also was upset because the vote had been far from unanimous in her favor.

Pauline, now Mother Agnès, showed no resentment, however. Following the custom of appointing the former prioress as novice mistress, she designated Mother Gonzague to that role and then appointed Thérèse as Mother Gonzague's assistant. Thérèse had just celebrated her twentieth birthday in January, but despite her youth, the community, with only one or two exceptions, appreciated the appointment (cf. TLMT 73).

Distressed that Pauline was trying now as prioress to assert her rightful and independent influence over the community, Mother Gonzague could have been equally unnerved at having Pauline's "little girl" as her assistant in the novitiate. However, she found in Thérèse the support that she needed. Thérèse's sensitivity and her capacity to accommodate, as well as her deep and purified affection for Mother Gonzague, helped the former prioress regain her equilibrium, even though she would continue to have clashes of character with Pauline. Thérèse extended signs of care and concern toward both her "mothers," pouring oil on their wounds and calming the troubled waters that separated them. *I love you, dear Mother, with tenderness,* she would later write to Mother Gonzague; *and I love my sisters too,* she added discreetly (SS 216).

Having obediently assumed the role, but because of canonical restrictions, not able to assume the title of assistant novice mistress, Thérèse would remain, at her own request, as a "senior novice" in the novitiate. This was a gesture of acknowledgment and gracious accommodation to the prescription of the Carmelite rule that prevented her, given the presence in the community of her sisters Marie and Pauline, from taking a place in the community legislative chapter, voting for the prioress, or being named to any official community position. She remained in this role of simplicity, docility, dependence, and subjection to others as the community customs described the virtues applicable to such a role, for the next four and a half years—the rest of her life.

At first Thérèse was the senior mentor, guide, and teacher for one postulant and one novice, each older than herself. Mother Gonzague had almost died of an asthma attack in April, just two months after Pauline's election, and her health was failing. Out of respect for her new assistant's ability and also out of necessity, she left to Thérèse most of the religious instruction of the young religious. In this work Thérèse *felt that the only thing necessary was to unite myself more and more to Jesus. . . . In fact, never was my hope mistaken, for God saw fit to fill my little hand as many times as it was necessary for nourishing the soul of my Sisters* (SS 238).

Sr. Marie of the Angels, now the subprioress, had been Thérèse's novice mistress. She knew Thérèse well and described her as the

> Jewel of the Carmel . . . tall and strong, with the appearance of a child, a tone of voice, an expression hiding within her a wisdom, a perfection, a perspicacity of a fifty-year-old. [Her] soul always calm and in perfect possession of itself in all things and with everybody. Little innocent thing, to whom one would give God [Communion] without confession, but whose head is full of mischief to play on anyone she pleases. [She is a] mystic, comic, everything. . . . She can make you weep with devotion and just as easily split your sides with laughter during our recreations. (GC II 778)

Having reassigned Thérèse from sacristy work to assist as senior in the novitiate, Pauline also put her in charge of the artwork in the convent. One sister gossiped that Thérèse apparently had come to Carmel to do nothing but simply amuse herself. Another sister, having become aware of Thérèse's capacity for self-centeredness, referred to her as "the grand lady," spreading the word that since she was not gifted at manual work she would probably never be of much use to the community. These remarks, sometimes said to be overheard, were a source of pain to Thérèse, who deeply wanted to please her Carmelite sisters and to be bonded with them.

Thérèse had no formal or extensive training in painting or any other art form, although she had begun to express drawing and painting skills even as a child and had taken some drawing lessons from Céline. She had not pursued her artistic interest, even though her father might have encouraged her as a child to take painting lessons if she had put herself forward when he made the same suggestion to Céline.

In June, having been asked by Pauline to paint a fresco in the prayer room of the convent oratory, Thérèse completed the work with the inscription *If you knew the gift of God* [John 4:10] (GC II 787). A quotation from the gospel, it was also an expression of her personal gratefulness to God for Pauline's election and a subtle reference to her belief that Pauline's leadership as prioress would be a grace for the entire community.

In addition to painting, at this time Thérèse was asked to compose a poem. To please one of the sisters, she wrote "The Divine Dew," a Marian poem, in February 1893, just before the election of Pauline as prioress. Pauline actually advised Thérèse against trying to write poetry, thinking that she would not be successful since in this art form, as in painting, she had almost no formal education. As a first attempt, the poem is notable in its bold and striking images, images that were to appear in many subsequent poems. This was really a prayer-poem, a love poem, as were all her poems:

You, Jesus, are the Flower just open new—
I watch your first awaking and see this.
You, Jesus!—That delightful Rose is You:
In that vermilion bud, what grace there is!
Your sinless Mother, rocking You to rest,
Makes of her arms a royal throne for You.
What is Your gentle sun but Mary's breast?
What other than the Virgin's milk, Your dew?
(*Collected Poems of St. Thérèse of Lisieux*, translated by Alan Bancroft, 3)

Thérèse continued to write poetry for the rest of her life at the request of some of the sisters, out of a sense of duty, and to give pleasure to sisters on their feast days. Poetry gave expression to her love, her own original ideas, and the outpouring of her heart in prayer. Writing to musical tunes and intending that the poems be sung, Thérèse composed them during the day as she worked. Then she wrote them down from memory during the free time in the evenings, making corrections as time permitted. Her second poem was written a year later, in February 1894. Then in a burst of creative expression she wrote fifty-two more in just over three years, until her last in May 1897.

In June 1893, at the time Thérèse was painting the fresco, Léonie entered the Visitation convent in Caen for the second time, causing a wave of disturbance to her ill father as well as to Céline and the Guérins. However, to

Céline's surprise, Uncle Isidore supported Léonie, and later Thérèse wrote to her, *If you only knew, dear little Léonie, the thanksgivings I am sending to heaven for the favor that God has granted to you* (GC II 816).

Without Léonie, Céline felt deserted and alone in caring for her dying father. In a letter to console her sister, Thérèse used the word *abandonment* for the first time, not to describe just a passing religious sentiment or virtue but to identify a fundamental aspect of an entire way of spiritual life. Just before she entered Carmel, Thérèse had been pleased to receive from Céline the gift of a little toy boat on which Céline had written the word "abandonment." Now Thérèse began to incorporate the notion of abandonment to God's will as a central concept in her spiritual understanding.

Thérèse wrote these words of self-revelation as words of support to Céline:

> *Merit does not consist in doing or in giving much, but rather in receiving, in loving much. . . . It is said, it is much sweeter to give than to receive* [Acts of the Apostles 20:35], *and it is true. But when Jesus wills to take for Himself the sweetness of giving, it would not be gracious to refuse. Let us allow Him to take and give all He wills. Perfection consists in doing His will and the soul that surrenders itself totally to Him is called by Jesus Himself "His mother, His sister," and His whole family* [Matthew 12:5]. *. . . What* [Thérèse] *must do is abandon herself, surrender herself, without keeping anything, not even the joy of knowing how much the bank* [of love] *is returning to her. . . . But this is done in peace, in abandonment.* (GC II 794–95)

Echoing one of the resolutions of her First Communion that she would never get discouraged, she wrote again to Céline a few days later, *I am not always faithful, but I never get discouraged; I abandon myself into the arms of Jesus* (GC II 801). She also tried to encourage Céline with memories of their courageous adventures in Rome. *Let us sing a melodious canticle in our hearts to our Beloved*, she wrote, inviting Céline to imitate St. Cecilia, whom the two had first encountered during their pilgrimage to Italy and whom Thérèse now identified as *the saint of abandonment* (GC I 553; GC II 850).

CHAPTER 30

O My God, You Have Surpassed All I Have Hoped For

For Thérèse, the election of her sister Pauline as prioress in 1893 was the culmination of a series of events that brought a new and deeper sense of peace to her. Her early years in the convent were laced with difficulties: the physical hardship of the cloistered life, the tension in the personal relationship with Mother Gonzague and with some of the other nuns, her need to distance herself from Pauline and Marie, her doubts about the validity of her spiritual way, her aridity in prayer, and the painful sense of losing her father: *This was my way for five years; exteriorly nothing revealed my suffering which was all the more painful since I alone was aware of it*, she would later write (SS 149).

Now, although saddened by her father's condition, Thérèse was at peace with his approaching death, knowing that he himself was at peace. The childhood feelings associated with the death of her mother had been healed, and she was one in heart with Mother Geneviève. Fr. Prou's reassurance had transformed her; she was gaining confidence in her own spiritual path and becoming more and more her own person. Her self-centeredness was being purified into peace, and now her "second mother" had been elected prioress. All these experiences contributed to the beginning of a new time in Thérèse's life.

All my trials had come to an end and the winter of my soul had passed on forever, she wrote of this time (SS 34). Additional blessings were to come, chief among which were the peace of her father's death, Céline's entry into Carmel, and the discovery of her Little Way. But her trials were far from being over forever.

For now, Thérèse joyfully celebrated her twenty-first birthday on January 2, 1894. In this, her sixth year in Carmel, she was blossoming into one of the main contributors to the community of aging nuns and was referred to as the "jewel" of the community. She was physically vigorous and was gaining emotional balance. She was contributing significantly to the community by her work in the novitiate and was increasingly respected for her quiet wisdom. Some of the older nuns now came to ask her advice on spiritual matters. She was more at peace with her emotional relationship with Marie and especially with Pauline. She was becoming more independent of her older sister, and this was indicated in a very small but significant way by her finally abandoning at this time the handwriting style that Pauline had taught her as a child.

Just a few weeks after her birthday, she presented her first play, *The Mission of Joan of Arc,* as a pious recreational piece for the enjoyment of the community. Those in the novitiate were expected to provide community recreations at Christmas and on special feasts, so Thérèse began to write, produce, direct, and often act in her original plays, eight of which she wrote over the next three years.

To the admiration and delight of the nuns, in this first play she acted the part of her beloved Joan of Arc. The two young sisters in the novitiate played the other roles and did the sound effects. Coincidentally, and to the delight of both the community and Thérèse herself, just a week after the play Pope Leo XIII authorized the beginning of the canonization process for Joan and conferred on her the title of Venerable.

Yet even in her vigor and creativity, as the flowers came to bud on the convent grounds, Thérèse—who from infancy had struggled with bouts of whooping cough and frail health—began to suffer a soreness in her throat that persisted in an ominous way. By July she had a continuous sore throat, a hoarse voice, and some pains in her chest. Without actually examining her at this time, Dr. Francis La Néele, husband of her cousin Jeanne Guérin, prescribed some medication. The irritation subsided but did not completely leave her. During the next months, Thérèse sensed that she was beginning to lose strength. It was at this time that she began to express more explicitly in her correspondence with her cousins and with Céline an intuition that she had had for many years: that she would die young. *If I die before you,* she wrote at this time to Céline, *do not believe that I will be far from your soul.* Then she added, *But above all, do not worry, I am not sick* (GC II 871).

Her father continued to suffer repeated heart attacks and strokes, especially during the winter and spring months of 1894. His left arm was now completely paralyzed; he was bent over and could swallow food only with difficulty.

Offering support to Céline in her care for their father and knowing that she was additionally burdened by the frequent episodes of intoxication suffered by her father's personal assistant, Thérèse wrote to her sister, using the words and sentiments that she had discovered in Arminjon's book years before: *Soon the day will come when Jesus will take His Céline by the hand and will have her enter her little house which will have become an eternal palace. Then He will say: "Now, it is my turn." You have given me on earth the only home that every human heart is unwilling to renounce, that is, yourself, and now I am giving you as a dwelling my eternal substance, that is, "Myself"* (GC II p. 841; cf. HF 129).

Gradually losing his strength and mental functioning, Louis Martin suffered what was to be a fatal heart attack on June 5, 1894. He died at the end of the following month. His death was both expected and a shock to the family, and especially to Thérèse, a blessing and a deep sadness, a time for mourning and a time for giving thanks. She recalled the vision she had had as a child of the old man disappearing behind the trees in the garden. *Why had God given me that light? Why did He show such a small child a thing she couldn't understand . . . ? He parcels out trials only according to the strength he gives us. Never . . . would I have been able to bear even the thought of the bitter pains the future held in store for me. I wasn't even able to think of Papa dying without trembling* (SS 47–48). But now she wrote to Léonie in the convent, *Papa's death does not feel like death to me, but like true life. I have found him again after six years' absence. I am conscious of him around me, looking at me, protecting me* (GC II 884). She composed a prayer-poem for her father that began,

Recall that here on earth your happiness
Lay in your looking after us! We pray
That you who go on loving us, will bless
Your children—will protect us still today.
You've reached your Homeland, where
      you're met and greeted by
Our mother dear—there, long
      before you, up on high:
   In Heaven now you reign
   Together. Both again,
      Watch over us! (CP 28)

Having recently become more conscious of the spirit of abandonment growing in her, Thérèse now would draw on that spirit in her prayer.

Her assigned duties in the novitiate were Thérèse's main concerns, and not her father, whom she remembered fondly and for whom she prayed daily, or her own health, to which she gave scant attention. Sr. Marie of the Trinity, transferring from the Paris Carmel, had entered the postulancy in June at the age of twenty and became the third young woman under Thérèse's formative direction. She was a year younger than Thérèse herself and so became the youngest member of the community. This rather bold and feisty postulant, "the little mischief" of the community, as one of the sisters playfully called her, was to become Thérèse's best student, her treasured friend and confidante. Thérèse, herself as a child "the little imp" and "the little rascal," resonated with the postulant's spirit and affectionately called her *my little doll*. Their relationship became a test and expression of Thérèse's maturity in firm and truthful love.

Within a week of Louis Martin's death, Céline requested entry into Carmel. Fr. Delatroëtte, still the clerical superior of Carmel and ever conscious of legality, spoke against it. The community had to consider that Céline's entrance would bring to four the number of blood sisters in the same convent, a number that was strictly forbidden by the spirit and letter of the Carmelite rule and would require an exception that St. Teresa of Avila herself would not have granted.

However, with Pauline in her role as prioress, with Thérèse in her role as prayer intercessor and consummate diplomat, and with the support of Mother Gonzague, the community and the priest finally agreed to Céline's request. But one sister, who was continually annoyed at the cultured mannerisms of the Martin sisters and who thought that "Carmel had no need of artists; it has a much greater need of good nurses and good menders," opposed her entrance. Praying against the final resistance of this sister, Thérèse asked God to give a sign that her father had gone straight to heaven by dissolving the sister's opposition. Thérèse prayed during Mass, and after the Mass the sister called her aside and affably withdrew her opposition. Céline's entry into Carmel, although delayed for four weeks, fulfilled Thérèse's final dream and was an emotional and spiritual gift, consoling her that her beloved king was, indeed, with her Beloved in heaven.

For Céline, who entered in September at the age of twenty-five, the road to Carmel had not been an easy one. To counter her father's earlier suggestion that she go to Paris to study art, Céline had expressed a desire to enter

Carmel. That was just two months after Thérèse had left home. Céline had also been considering a marriage proposal. Much to the chagrin of Thérèse, who could not bear the thought that *the sweet echo of my soul* might not join her in Carmel, the vivacious and attractive Céline had continued her social life. She was especially enamored of a young attorney who lavishly expressed his love for her.

Moreover, to complicate matters, two years prior to Céline's entry into Carmel, Fr. Pichon had asked her to come to Canada to work with him and to become the founder of a new secular institute (cf. SS 177, note 215). He had told Céline to keep his request secret, and she did so, toying with the idea that "she was a great soul, a saint in the making." "Why not go far way to Canada!" she asked herself whimsically (GC II 870, note 5). The playful, seductive thoughts of being a privileged soul and of going to an exotic foreign land were all innocent enough on Céline's part. However, when Thérèse learned of Fr. Pichon's plan and discovered that her sister, with whom she shared all her most personal thoughts, had kept this secret from her all this time, she was shocked and deeply troubled. *My heart is torn apart,* Thérèse wrote to Céline (GC II 878). Together with Marie and Pauline, she was indignant and hurt.

Thérèse had never doubted that Céline was called to be with her in Carmel. However, on hearing about Fr. Pichon's plans for her sister—he was, after all, now Céline's spiritual director—Thérèse seems to have suffered some momentary misgivings about her own certainty. Thérèse later confessed, Céline remembered, that "in all her life she had not wept so much; she had such a violent headache that she wondered if she were not on the verge of becoming ill" (GC II 878).

A few days later, feeling more confident once again, Thérèse wrote to Céline, telling her that she was willing to write to Fr. Pichon to tell him what she thought about his plan, and *I shall not be embarrassed!* [but] *I am heavy of heart!* (GC II 878). Céline herself promptly wrote to Fr. Pichon with her decision. She finally concurred with Pauline, Marie, and Thérèse that Fr. Pichon was mistaken and that her vocation was to Carmel.

Fr. Pichon quickly responded to Céline, "Yes, yes, I give my Céline to Carmel. God wills it! I have no doubt, I hesitate no longer. God's will appears evident to me" (GC II 879). To Thérèse, when she later chided him about his plan, he responded, "No, no, the secret imposed on Céline was not a lack of confidence. One day I will explain it to you. Take revenge by praying very much for my little work which appears to me destined to save many souls" (GC II 901).

Knowing that Fr. Pichon would never explain things to her, Thérèse rejoiced without feelings of revenge in what she considered a miracle of prayer. Together with Pauline and Marie, she led the community in welcoming their sister, who still had some misgivings, into Carmel.

Céline's very presence in the convent was a blessing for Thérèse, but Céline also brought with her several items that were to prove to be significant gifts for her younger sister. One was the statue of Our Lady of the Smile that had proved so important in Thérèse's cure as a child. It was placed on a stand in the antechamber of Thérèse's room, and before it she would often kneel in prayer. Gazing on this image of Mary became a source of consolation to her in her final days as she lay dying.

Other items that Céline brought were from her personal collection of photographic materials. Artistic from an early age, sketching and painting with much skill, and having taught drawing to Thérèse as a child, Céline had nonetheless refused her father's invitation to study painting in Paris, fearing that living in that city might endanger her spiritual life. Instead she pursued her interest in the newly developing art of photography and acquired enough photographic experience and equipment to develop pictures herself. She became a skilled photographer and one of the first persons to record Carmelite life inside the cloister. Her forty-five or so photographs of Thérèse and the community still possess an artistic and fascinating quality today.

But for Thérèse, the most significant item Céline brought to Carmel was a notebook in which she had copied some passages of the Old Testament from the Bible that Uncle Isidore kept in his home. She shared these texts with Thérèse. Having never had access to the complete Bible before (a situation common to most Catholics in this era), Thérèse was overjoyed to be able to read passages of the Old Testament that she had never known. Several texts, especially from Isaiah, now became an important source of personal inspiration for Thérèse, helping her understand her Beloved's way with her and forming a foundation for her teaching in the novitiate.

Studying these texts of the Old Testament, Thérèse gained insight into what she called the *science of love* (SS 148). She was delighted to read in the Book of Proverbs that God treasured especially the little ones: "Whoever is a little one, let him come to me" (Proverbs 9:4). She had always considered herself to be numbered among the little ones in the reign of God. She read in the passages of Isaiah and also rejoiced to know that "As one whom a mother caresses, so will I comfort you; you shall be carried at the breast, and upon the knees they shall caress you" (Isaiah 66:12-13). *Ah! Never did words more tender and more melodious come to give joy to my soul*, Thérèse said. She now knew for certain that it was true: God was like a mother, and her own mother's love and her father's *maternal love* had been but faint images of the divine infinite love. *After having listened to words such as these . . . there is nothing to do but to be silent and to weep with gratitude and love. O my God, you have surpassed all I have hoped for, and I want to sing of your mercies* (SS 188). Fr. Prou's assurances were validated.

Two other passages were especially inspirational for Thérèse. The words of the Book of Wisdom "For to him that is little, mercy will be shown" (Wisdom 6:7) brought Thérèse to silence and to tears of joy. She loved to imagine herself in the arms of her loving Father, knowing that, as Isaiah wrote, "God shall feed his flock like a shepherd; he shall gather together the lambs with his arm, and shall take them up in his bosom" (Isaiah 40:11).

In her inadequacy and littleness, Thérèse desired mercy and understood that to receive divine mercy was really to participate in the life of the Holy Spirit, the Spirit who would sanctify her. Experiencing herself as a little one in need of mercy and in need of being held and supported, Thérèse settled into these truths as she had settled securely into the arms of her parents as a child.

During the months after Céline's entry, especially with the illumination of these four texts from Proverbs, Wisdom, and Isaiah, Thérèse matured considerably in her discovery and understanding of what she was later to teach as her Little Way of spirituality. Insight also into the downward path of Zacchaeus, the call for mercy of the publican, the spiritual richness of the spirit of abandonment, the purifying role of bearing serenely for love of God and neighbor her feelings and the sacrifices imposed by everyday life, the growing sense of God's love even in her most difficult times, together with her continual awareness of her own littleness and weakness—all brought Thérèse into a further appreciation of God's mercy and the need for her to remain little in the spiritual life. As a gesture to remind herself of this developing awareness and to celebrate it, and not as a cute pretension, she began to sign her name *Tiny Little Thérèse*.

CHAPTER 31

The Elevator Which Must Raise Me to Heaven Is Your Arms, O Jesus!

Thérèse began to reflect more on the reality of divine mercy during the last three months of 1894. Her father had, in the end, died peacefully, and she had no doubt that he was in heaven, reunited with his beloved wife and the four children who had died in infancy. Léonie had persevered during the last year and a half in the Visitation convent, finding at least temporary peace and happiness in her vocation. Pauline was becoming an effective pastoral leader in her role as prioress, guiding the sisters with grace and care. Céline was now even more her sister in Carmel, and Thérèse herself was being blessed with insights of truth and confidence into herself and into her path of spirituality. She felt more inner freedom from her emotions. God's mercy was more tangible, and Thérèse began to share her spiritual way more confidently with the young sisters in the novitiate and with the entire community.

In these final months of the year 1894, Thérèse came to understand more clearly and formulate more confidently what she would come to call the Little Way. The Scripture passages that Céline had brought with her a few months before were decisive in confirming for Thérèse that her image of God as a loving father and as a loving mother extended back into the Old Testament. That the texts even spoke specifically of God's special love for the "little one" had delighted Thérèse, who had always considered herself to be little. Meditating on these texts was a source of great inspiration for her in understanding how her Beloved had been active in her life all these years.

Trying to understand and explain her Little Way of spirituality, Thérèse used the image of the elevator, the lift. Stairways and ladders reaching up to levels of perfection were among the favorite images of writers and preachers of the time. Struggling upward was one of the dominant images of holiness: climbing the steps of perfection, climbing the ladder of prayer, scaling the stages of virtue—climbing laboriously step by step. These images confirmed that holiness was not for the weak and the little.

The stairway of perfection, or *the rough stairway of fear* as Thérèse once referred to it, had originally seemed to her to be similar to the actual "rough stairway" that she had faced when, as a two-year-old, she had tried to climb to the second floor of her family home. At that time her mother had described

Thérèse attempting the impossible: *She will not climb the stairs all alone, but cries at each step: "Mamma, Mamma!"* (GC II 1152; SS 18; cf. GC II 1218).

This image of personal inadequacy had returned to Thérèse as an adult. She simply could not, by her own effort and willfulness, overcome her weaknesses and climb that rough, fearful stairway of perfection. She needed the help of a loving parent, and she was willing to receive that help from her loving Father.

Once before, on the Christmas night of Thérèse's conversion, she had received God's help on a stairway. At that time she had learned the important truth that she could physically climb the steps even in great distress, but that it was grace that was the source of her empowerment and enlightenment. Then her loving Father had given her the help she needed, and now she was asking again to receive aid in whatever form it might take.

In the course of her pilgrimage to meet Pope Leo XIII, Thérèse experienced a new invention, the elevator, the lift, in the hotel where she stayed in Rome. Thérèse was delighted to learn from experience that elevators made it possible not to need to climb stairs laboriously step by step. If an elevator could replace the *rough stairway of perfection,* everything would be different. If there were an elevator in the spiritual life, she thought, then the weakness of the little child could be addressed in a *totally new* way (SS 207).

Was it possible that the spiritual life had an elevator? Thérèse knew immediately that it did, and she knew that *the elevator which must raise me to heaven is Your arms, O Jesus!* (SS 208). She would abandon herself into the arms of her loving Father, and all her concern about holiness and perfection would be solved. It would be that simple: God would do the heavy lifting; Thérèse would remain spiritually the little child. With the image of the elevator, Thérèse had captured an image of the fundamental mystery and the essential message of the gospel.

Already in her prayer Thérèse had known an important secret of her Beloved's love, a secret that often escaped the wise and learned who could and did climb a certain distance on the stairway of perfection. It was the secret revealed to the little children, too small to do any climbing. Thérèse's secret was in knowing that it is of the nature of divine love to *stoop down* and to lift us up and transform us.

Reflecting on her life, she understood that it was to the little ones who were inadequate in the spiritual life—the child *who knows only how to make . . .*

feeble cries; [and] *the poor savage, who has nothing but the natural law* [and who doesn't even know about stairways or ladders]—*it is to their hearts that God deigns to lower Himself.... When coming down in this way,* she wrote, *God manifests His infinite grandeur. Just as the sun shines simultaneously on the tall cedars and on each little flower as though it were alone on the earth, so Our Lord is occupied particularly with each soul as though there were no others like it.... Yes, in order that Love be fully satisfied, it is necessary that It lower itself, and that It lowers Itself to nothingness and transforms this nothingness into fire* (SS 14, 195).

Her Beloved had reached down in love, as love, because God is love and such is the nature of love to stoop down and love gratuitously—that awareness was Thérèse's joy. The image of being embraced by her loving Father who scoops her up was the answer to Thérèse's desire to be holy.

To rest in Jesus' arms had been, for Thérèse, since early childhood, an image in which she had found great consolation. Now that image took on new meaning. Not only could she rest secure in Jesus' arms, she could also be carried, in fulfillment of her loving Father's desire in her, to the perfection of holiness that he wished for her. She no longer needed to struggle up a difficult, frightful stairway; she could be lifted up by divine love. And further, to be lifted meant that the entire need to grow up and to grow out of inadequacies in order to reach holiness was transformed.

If Thérèse were to be carried in the elevator of God's arms, then, as she said, *for this I had no need to grow up, but rather I had to remain little and become this more and more.* It was not, then, that being weak and little she needed to become strong; it was rather that she needed to remain little so as not to be a burden when God reached down to lift her. *I can,* she now knew, *despite my littleness, aspire to holiness* (SS 208, 207).

Her totally new way would mean becoming more humble in conformity to the divine will, becoming willing to remain little in her weaknesses and imperfections, but with total confidence in love and with complete abandonment in the arms of her loving Father. It would be divine love that transformed her and raised her in the perfection of holiness; it would not be her doing. Her Beloved's love and her willing response would be her sanctity. God himself would be her holiness.

In order to be raised up by God, Thérèse needed to die to herself, to her self-love. She now understood Jesus' invitation in the gospel and the paschal mystery of everyday life: to die daily to her self-centeredness and her willfulness, even to the self-will that might be hidden in the spiritual ambition of being perfect. It was a matter of allowing the divine will to unfold in the very ordinary, everyday experiences of life and of responding with generosity, confidence, and love. In this way God would stoop down and lift her to that degree of perfection that her Beloved had prepared for her.

At the end of her life she wrote that she has *only to cast a glance in the Gospels* to immediately know that she will not go to God like the Pharisee. *I don't hasten to the first place but to the last; rather than advance like the Pharisee, I repeat, filled with confidence, the publican's humble prayer* (SS 258).

The parable of the Pharisee and publican (cf. Luke 18:9-14), which Jesus proclaimed to those who believed in their own righteousness and perfection, became an important teaching for Thérèse regarding the nature of the spiritual life and the call to authentic gospel holiness. Thérèse saw in this parable that the Pharisee and publican each personified a radically different way of spirituality. Each went to the temple to pray, to contact God; one was successful, the other was not.

The Pharisee thanked God for his religious successes and achievements—that is, for his own perfection. The publican, however, desirous of holiness but keenly aware of his sinfulness and his complete inability to attain the perfection prescribed by the law and by the spiritual leaders of his day, simply prayed that God would have mercy on him, a sinner. The publican was justified; the Pharisee was not.

Thérèse saw in the publican's prayer, "O God be merciful to me, a sinner" (Luke 18:13), a simple and honest acknowledgement of weakness and sinfulness and, at the same time, a humble request that God be the source of mercy and love in her life. These became the sentiments of Thérèse's Little Way: that the God of mercy would reach down and enfold her in mercy and love.

This parable completely illumined Thérèse's spirituality (cf. SS 258). She now fully understood that holiness, her union with her Beloved, was being achieved not by herself and her efforts but by God being God in her life, that is, by Love, by the Holy Spirit, reaching down in mercy and raising her up in her weakness and sinfulness to holiness and true perfection. She completely rejected the Pharisee's prayer of self-centeredness and self-promotion and fully embraced the publican's simple plea for mercy. Thérèse saw that Jesus' teaching in this parable was unfolding in her own spiritual life. Her Little Way was the way of the publican, Jesus' own image of the person of gospel holiness.

Seeking at the end of her life a prayer that would embody her way, Thérèse made her plea an echo of the prayer of the publican: *Jesus, draw me into the flames of your love; unite me so closely with you that you live and act in me* (SS 257). *I always feel,* she wrote, *the same bold confidence of becoming a great saint because I don't count on my merits since I have none, but I trust in Him who is Virtue and Holiness. God alone, content with my weak efforts, will raise me to himself and make me a saint, clothing me in his infinite merits* (SS 72).

Now she could go to her loving Father with *confidence and love. I entrust to Jesus my failings; I tell Him all about them; and I think, so bold is my trust, that in this way I acquire more power over His heart and draw to myself in still greater abundance the love of Him who came to call sinners, not the righteous* (HF 337). Echoing St. John of the Cross, Thérèse told her novice Sr. Marie of the Trinity, *Hold on tight to your confidence. It is impossible for God not to respond to that, because He always measures His gifts by how much confidence we have* (TLMT 86). *One obtains from God what one hopes for* (STL 233).

Nothing is more fundamental in the gospel message that the Holy Spirit revealed to Thérèse than that it is of the nature of divine love *to stoop down* in merciful love, and to draw into Love everyone, not just the "good" and the "just." It was in the willingness to participate in that flow of divine love that Thérèse's perfection would consist. Jesus himself is, of course, the personification of this very truth. The mystery of the incarnation is nothing other than God reaching down, coming in the person of Jesus, to draw all things to himself. Jesus' life of love and compassion is the expression of this truth, and Jesus' death and resurrection are the completion of the paschal mystery on which Thérèse's teaching was focused. Thérèse's Little Way is the very heart of the message of gospel revelation seen in a fresh and compelling vision.

Although Thérèse spoke of searching for a *totally new* way, the way of spirituality that the Holy Spirit was inspiring in her was actually the gospel way of holiness, the fundamental Christian way, needing to be rediscovered. Thérèse's genius was that she recognized and rediscovered authentic gospel holiness, which had begun to be lost to ordinary Christians of her time.

CHAPTER 32

If You Are Willing to Bear Serenely the Trial

As Christmas 1894 approached, Thérèse composed a play for the community recreation, *The Angels at the Crib*. It was a reflection on God's stooping down in mercy to the human race in response to weakness and need.

Céline had been surprised on that Christmas night some eight years before to see Thérèse managing her feelings of hurt at her father's remark. Now as a postulant, Céline was truly amazed to experience her sister at the center of community life, deeply engaged in the workings of the novitiate and bearing so courageously the daily rigors of the convent. Nor was it many years before at the boarding school that Céline had had to carefully defend "her little girl," and now as a new member of the community, she herself was being shepherded into the depths of the spiritual life by that same little sister.

Céline experienced her sister as having a self-awareness and a self-confidence, an inner freedom, peace, creativity, and faith, a love and wisdom that came from a deep spiritual and psychological maturity. She saw Thérèse as remarkably capable of humbly accepting her strengths and weaknesses, as creatively handling her feelings, and as being a loving presence to the community. Céline was especially challenged in living now with her little sister because she herself was so impetuous and often had outbursts with the other sisters. Céline was experiencing her weakness in the way she reacted to the pinpricks of community life and was distressed at not being able to handle the difficult interactions of community with the same inner peace and charity as Thérèse did.

Thérèse's work with the young sisters required her to give not only good example but also precision and simplicity to her instructions about her developing insights. She based her teaching on the Scriptures, on the teaching of the church (after all, she had been proclaimed a "little doctor" by Fr. Domin even before she was a teenager), on the Carmelite tradition, and now especially on her own experience as she came to reflect on her life overall. In the poems and plays she was writing, as well as in her letters, she expressed various truths that she considered important in the spiritual life. Some of her insights deviated from the conventional thinking of the times, contradicted some of the attitudes of the sisters with whom she lived, and even diverted from some of the notions stressed by the retreat directors she had heard over the years.

The common notion at the time was that to become holy, one had to attain perfection, and that perfection was usually achieved through strength of will-fulness and sometimes violence to self. The holy person was free of personal defects, a master of ascetical practices who achieved an extraordinary level of prayer and virtue, at times had experienced visions and revelations, and no longer committed sin. The text of Matthew 5:48—"Be perfect as your heav-enly Father is perfect"—was sometimes used to substantiate that the call to gospel holiness was indeed a call to flawless perfection. The saints' constant cry for God's mercy because of their weaknesses and sins was discounted as further confirmation of their heroic humility. These common notions reserved holiness to the "great saints." Thérèse knew that she could never attain that kind of perfection.

With a focus on divine wrath, even the newly popular and widespread devotion to the Sacred Heart emphasized not so much God's love, but rather the need to placate God's justice and was thus a call for additional ascetical achievements. *You know,* Thérèse wrote, expressing the sense of her own devotion, *I do not see the Sacred Heart as everyone else, I think that the Heart of my Spouse is mine alone, just as mine is His alone, and I speak to him then in the solitude of this delightful heart-to-heart, while waiting to contemplate Him one day face to face* (GC II 709).

Some of the distortions in the common notion of spirituality were, no doubt, a misunderstanding of some Scripture texts, and some were due to the influence of Jansenism and Pelagianism, heresies that continued despite their condemnation centuries earlier. Thérèse heard during her lifetime that holiness and human weakness were incompatible. Knowing that this kind of "holi-ness" was simply beyond her, she would have to find another way to holiness, and that way would have to be *totally new,* as she said. The "old" way of perfection was inaccessible to her.

In her search for a new way in the prevailing climate of perfectionism and Jansenism, Thérèse had not been assisted by the usual spiritual helps. The preached retreats at Carmel were of little benefit to her, and most of the sisters in the convent were living out of the perfectionist model and the Jansenist image of God. The spirituality of Pauline and Marie had been a source of important learning, and the example of Mother Geneviève had been a singular help, as had been the insights of the Carmelite tradition and her more recent understanding of the Scriptures, especially the gospels and the writings of St.

Paul, but she was constantly being challenged by the conventional understanding of spirituality of her day.

From St. John of the Cross Thérèse had heard that God's love was like fire. The fire of the Holy Spirit consumed the imperfections and sins of those who loved. She understood further that it is the nature of divine love to humble itself, and therefore to *stoop down to nothingness* and to draw that nothingness to God. She was fully aware that she was weak and inadequate, like a child, like a *little grain of sand* (SS 275; cf. GC I 406), like *nothingness*. She was confident that her Beloved, like a loving parent, like fire, like a spouse, evoked in her the very longings whereby she loved and became united to God. Her weakness and divine love—she as beloved child, God as merciful, loving parent—this twofold truth became the centerpiece of her Little Way.

In the following months Céline continued to complain to Thérèse that she was not able to act with as much piety and charity as she would have liked. "Oh, when I think how much I have to acquire!" Céline said to Thérèse. Thérèse responded wisely from the recent experiences that had been nourishing her in the spirit of abandonment: *Rather, how much you have to lose* (*My Sister St. Thérèse* by Sister Geneviève of the Holy Face, 28). At first Céline did not fully understand what she needed to lose. Thérèse's clarification came only many months later.

By that time, Céline had been more than two years in Carmel, but was still frustrated in her efforts to appear good to the sisters, to curtail her impetuosity and to contain her outbursts. She continued to be disheartened that she had not yet achieved a certain level of virtue and had not yet conquered her faults, especially her failings in charity. She was not the holy person that she willed to be, and she was not being acknowledged by the other sisters. She wrote a despondent note to Thérèse. Sensing Céline's discouragement and willfulness, Thérèse shared with her a profound secret that she herself had discovered. It was Christmastime and Thérèse wanted to encourage her sister to welcome the Christ child into her heart despite her faults. Thérèse wrote to Céline: *If you are willing to bear serenely the trial of being displeasing to yourself, then you will be . . .* [for Jesus] *a pleasant place of shelter* (*Collected Letters of Saint Thérèse of Lisieux*, translated by F. J. Sheed, 303; cf. GC II 1038 for a slightly different translation).

Thérèse was expressing a truth from the deep wisdom of her own experience: that divine love enfolded Céline in her weakness. Her sister did not need to acquire; rather, she first needed to lose what prevented the Holy Spirit from fostering virtue in her. In this case, Thérèse saw that Céline needed to lose her discouragement, which was self-centered, and particularly to lose her willfulness, which drove her to strive for self-improvement. That harsh willfulness was itself a kind of violent obstacle to the power of the Holy Spirit in her. If Céline would be willing to lose her attachments to herself and enter the path of humility, serenely bearing the pain of honestly being herself, that willingness, humility, and honesty would put her on the path of transformation.

Thérèse was telling Céline that her weaknesses provided an opening for grace, and that her willingness to bear them peacefully would allow her to do the good works that God wished her to do at each moment. But Thérèse did not expect Céline even to be successful at bearing her faults in peace; she only invited her to be willing as best she could and not to become disturbed with herself for being disturbed with the sisters.

Thérèse was suggesting that what Céline needed to lose was her self-promotion, her attachment to feelings of perfectionism, her desire to be more than she was, and her self-condemnation. Thérèse was trying to move her sister from the violence to herself that was implicit in her attitude of self-criticism and the willfulness of trying to be who she was not. Thérèse was encouraging her to simply be *willing to bear serenely the trial of being displeasing to* herself. That attitude of nonviolent willingness, Thérèse was revealing to her sister, would be a primary step on the path to welcoming Jesus into her heart.

The truth contained in the words *how much you have to lose* and in the invitation to be *willing to bear serenely the trial of being displeasing to yourself* had been germinating in Thérèse for many years. She had begun to sense something of its power as she bore, as best she could, the difficulties during her school years. She had also gotten a glimpse of it after the Christmas midnight Mass as she climbed the steps to her room, courageously enduring her father's words of criticism without guilt or resentment. She had grasped this truth even more deeply as she overcame her disappointment and purposefully made her personal retreat preparing to enter the convent. She had lived this truth and been purified by it during all these years in Carmel, as she bore the idiosyncrasies of the sisters. Now it flowered in the eloquent and profound advice she gave to her beloved sister. Thérèse felt confident in sharing this truth with her soul mate, knowing that it was the gospel truth that would lead Céline to happiness, to holiness, to Jesus. This truth was becoming the cornerstone of Thérèse's spirituality, and she would express it often in various ways.

She recognized that the way in which she was being led flowed from Jesus' teaching on the quality of a person's loving relationships with God, with oneself, with one's neighbor, and with the world. Jesus' teaching did not concern itself essentially with a person's willful attainment of a certain level of asceticism and prayer, nor with the gift of visions, nor with the achievement of a level of perfectionism. Thérèse understood that Jesus' teaching of holiness was not driven by fear of a wrathful and vindictive God waiting to entrap the weak; nor were spiritual accomplishments necessary to win divine approval. She saw that the gospel way of holiness had to do essentially with love: God's primary and continual love for us and our reciprocating in willing love.

She was convinced that the text of Matthew "Be perfect as your heavenly Father is perfect" was not a call to moral perfectionism; but in its immediate context, and in the wider context of the complete gospel, the text clearly was about inclusive love, love even for enemies (cf. Matthew 5:44; Luke 6:27). The parallel text of Luke 6:36 enjoins, "Be compassionate as your heavenly Father is compassionate." Thérèse understood that these passages spoke of the Father's love for all, particularly for those who are not perfect. They were also a call to share that love with others, especially "the enemy" outside, that is, precisely those who are judged to be evil and unjust. They were also a call to share that merciful love with "the enemy" within, that is, our own weaknesses and sinfulness.

The spiritual thoughts that Thérèse appreciated most were ones that John of the Cross also treasured: *Love is repaid by love alone* (SS 195; cf. GC I 546). And *Love works so in me that whether things go well or badly, Love turns all to one sweetness transforming the soul into itself* (SS 179). *Jesus is teaching her,* she said of herself, *to learn to draw profit from everything, from the good and the bad she finds in herself* (GC II 795). This thought resonated with what Thérèse had read in the epistles of St. Paul: "If I glory in anything it will be in my weakness" (2 Corinthians 12:5).

Thérèse knew that a high level of morality and self-mastery, prayer, penance, detachment, and zeal would indeed flow from divine love's permeating the human heart as that heart also responded in love. But moral perfectionism, self-mastery, and even great works—which could be egotistical accomplishments—did not of themselves guarantee cooperation in the flow of compassion and love that Jesus identified as the "perfection of the heavenly Father." Thérèse was in love with Jesus and desired to be consumed by divine love, and in that love she would find a holiness that expressed itself in works of virtue.

Thérèse allowed Jesus to direct her and to teach her a new way: *Directors have others advance in perfection by having them perform a great number of acts of virtue, and they are right; but my director, who is Jesus, teaches me not to count up my acts. He teaches me to do all through love, to refuse Him nothing, to be content when He gives me a chance of proving to Him that I love Him. . . . It is Jesus who is doing all in me, and I am doing nothing* (GC II 796).

The governing orientation of Thérèse's life had become more and more clearly the depth and purity of her loving relationship with Jesus, expressed in her willingness to bear her weaknesses, to receive divine love, and to be loving toward others. It was all now a matter of abandoning herself into the arms of her loving Father in confidence and love. *I do not ask you, Lord, to count my works,* Thérèse prayed. *All our justice is stained in Your eyes. I wish then, to be clothed in Your own Justice, and to receive from Your Love the eternal possession of Yourself* (SS 277). It was no longer a matter of her efforts or strivings or accomplishments; it was all a matter of divine love. She would be mindful and vigilant, not allowing the least opportunity to love God and others to pass her by.

Thérèse was on the path of reaffirming the gospel truth that Christian perfection consists not of attaining moral perfectionism but of reciprocating God's love, allowing Jesus to do *all in me,* specifically motivating the good acts that expressed God's love. She was coming in her own way to a fresh vision of St. Paul's understanding of Christian holiness: "It is no longer I who live, but Christ lives in me" (Galatians 2:20).

These last three months of 1894 were a time of great spiritual growth for Thérèse. Céline's entry into Carmel had reunited Thérèse with her spiritual sister and was for Thérèse a great source of joy and encouragement. The Scripture passages that Céline had shared with Thérèse had had a tremendously affirming and liberating affect on her. Pauline's role as prioress was a continuing blessing for the entire community, and this also gave much joy to Thérèse. These months and the following months of 1895 were among the happiest of her life.

CHAPTER 33

That I May Become a Martyr of Your Love, O My God

Thérèse's reflection on God's way with her was given a major impetus when, one day just before Christmas of 1894, Pauline asked her to write down her childhood memories. During a period of community recreation, Pauline, Marie, Thérèse, and Céline had been sharing anecdotes about their life at home, and Marie remarked to Pauline that it would be sad, since they had no written account, if they were to lose any of these stories. She suggested that Pauline as the superior require her youngest sister, who was such a good storyteller, to write as much as she could remember about the memories of her childhood (HLC 231).

Thérèse at first thought that Marie and Pauline were just joking, but Pauline, as prioress, made the formal request, and Thérèse responded in obedience. At the end of January 1895 she began her writing in a small school copybook during her brief periods of free time each day. Thérèse began to jot down her thoughts spontaneously, without an outline, as the memories came to her, musing as if she were on one of those fishing trips with her father. *It's as though I were fishing with a line; I write whatever comes to the end of my pen*, she later said (HLC 63).

A year later, on January 20, 1896, she gave to Pauline the completed work of about 170 pages in six small booklets sewn together. By then Pauline seemed to have forgotten she had made the original request, and she simply put the booklets aside.

In her opening reflections, Thérèse noted that at first she thought that writing about her life would play into her tendency toward self-preoccupation, but she knew that obedience was the most important virtue, and understood that in the writing *I'm going to be doing only one thing: I shall begin to sing what I must sing eternally: "The Mercies of the Lord"* (Psalm 89:1). She would be writing, then, primarily about *my thoughts on the graces God deigned to grant me* (SS 13, 15). The story of God's merciful graciousness unfolding throughout her life was to be the focus of Thérèse's attention.

As she wrote her memories, and also in her prayers at this time, Thérèse expressed with more certainty the thought that her Beloved was most grieved by those who were not aware of or were unwilling to receive and reciprocate divine love. She understood that God did not need achievements but longed for receptive hearts, for love. *He has no need of our works but only of our love,* she wrote. *He was thirsty for love. . . . Jesus is parched, for He meets only the ungrateful and indifferent among His disciples in the world; . . . alas, He finds few hearts who surrender to Him without reservations, who understand the real tenderness of His infinite Love* (SS 189).

She, therefore, would be totally available and reciprocal to divine love. She began to understand that reciprocity to the Father's love constituted Jesus' very life and that in the inner life of the Trinity love itself was the Holy Spirit. Thérèse wanted to participate in the life of the Trinity as fully as possible, allowing the Holy Spirit to live fully in her. The spirit of willingness and surrender in reciprocity to God's love, and sharing that love in charity with others, together with all the personal discipline that would be required—that way would be her way of love and reparation.

Thérèse had heard that a very holy nun in another French Carmelite convent had composed a beautiful prayer that inspired many in the community. The sister's prayer, following the piety of the times, was an offering of herself in reparation and expiation as a victim to God's justice. The prayer acknowledged that God's justice was being neglected and ignored, and needed to be appeased. It asked God to punish the one offering herself as a victim in place of the sinner who refused repentance. To placate God's justice, the punishment reserved for the sinner was welcomed by the one who prayed.

This offering seemed great and generous to me, but I was far from feeling myself drawn to making it (SS 180). Thérèse felt helpless attempting to duplicate severe austerities, but more important, she was convinced that her Beloved did not need to be placated. God was not vindictively reserving punishment for sinners. Her image of God was the image of one who thirsted and begged for love, who longed for the return of sinners so that the bond of love could be reestablished and extended into eternity, as had happened in the case of her *first child*, Pranzini. The sinner's punishment was not the act of a vengeful God but the pain of the sinner's own willful alienation from divine love, refusing to accept and reciprocate that love. For Thérèse, it was divine mercy more than divine justice that was unknown, ignored, and neglected.

When one of the novices told Thérèse that a psalm said divine justice "extended over the whole earth," Thérèse replied that the psalmist also said that *God's Mercy reaches to the heavens* [Psalm 36:6] (SS 181). This meant,

Thérèse told the novice, that God's mercy and love enfolded and surpassed justice. Jesus had promised that the peace he would give was not the same as the peace the world gives (cf. John 14:27), and Thérèse knew that the justice of God was not the same as the justice of the world. God's peace and justice were infinitely unique and creative, and emanated from the divine essence, that is, from love.

By now Thérèse was convinced that there were many different kinds of saints and many different kinds of vocations, but that her unique calling, flowing from her life experiences, was to honor *in a special way* the mercy of her loving Father:

> *I understand that all souls cannot be the same, that it is necessary there be different types in order to honor each of God's perfections in a particular way. To me He has granted His infinite Mercy, and through it to contemplate and adore the other divine perfections! All of these perfections appear to be resplendent with love; even His Justice (and perhaps this even more so than the others) seems to me clothed in love. What a sweet joy it is to think that God is Just, that is, that He takes into account our weakness, that He is perfectly aware of our fragile nature. What should I fear then? Ah! must not the infinitely just God, who deigns to pardon the faults of the prodigal son with so much kindness, be just also towards me who "am with Him always"?* (SS 180)

If you don't want to ever fear again do as I do, Thérèse told her novice, Sr. Marie of the Trinity, *take the means to force God not to judge you at all, by presenting yourself to him with empty hands. This means, don't hold onto anything for yourself, give all your merits to souls as you acquire them; in that way God can't judge something that is no longer yours!* The novice replied that if God doesn't judge good deeds, he will judge evil ones. Thérèse answered, *What are you saying! Our Lord, who is justice itself, can't judge your bad deeds if he doesn't judge your good ones! Be assured: for the victims of Love, there will be no judgment. God will hasten to repay with eternal delights his own love that he sees burning in their heart* (TLMT 80–81).

Directly opposed to the sentiment of the holy nun who, fearing that she did not have enough merit offered herself as a victim to bear the rigors of divine justice, Thérèse prayed,

O my God! Will your justice alone find souls willing to immolate themselves as victims? Does not your Merciful Love need them too? On every side this love is unknown, rejected; those hearts upon whom you would lavish it turn to creatures seeking happiness. . . . They do this instead of throwing themselves into your arms and of accepting your infinite Love. O my God! Is Your disdained Love going to remain closed up within Your Heart? It seems to me that if You were to find souls offering themselves as victims of holocaust to Your Love, You would consume them rapidly; it seems to me, too, that You would be happy not to hold back the waves of infinite tenderness within You. If Your Justice loves to release itself, this Justice which extends only over the earth, how much more does Your Merciful Love desire to set souls on fire since Your Mercy reaches to the heavens. O my Jesus, let me be this happy victim; consume Your holocaust with the fire of Your Divine Love! (SS 180–81)

Thérèse's heart surged with the passion of these sentiments. On the feast of the Holy Trinity, June 9, 1895, she felt drawn to compose a prayer that would express her great appreciation of divine love and her desire to reciprocate it. She would make an act of consecration to be a victim of holocaust, not to God's justice, but to divine love and mercy. Divine mercy flowed from God in waves of infinite tenderness, yet went unknown and unreceived by those who sought love only from creatures.

Her offering would use the same words found in the popular pious prayers of those who offered themselves as victims to God's justice, in the very words, in fact, of the holy nun's prayer: words like "martyr," "holocaust," and "victim." She would compose a prayer, offering herself as a victim of holocaust to God's merciful love, but in doing so she would subvert and transform the meaning of those words from images of violence into images of nonviolent love and devotion.

Thérèse's prayer would not be about the harshness of violence and victimization but about the intimacy of love and union. For Thérèse, to offer herself as a "victim" to God would not mean to be victimized by violence, but to be actively and totally available to divine love. To be a "martyr" would not mean to be destroyed in violence but to surrender in divine mercy. To be a "holocaust" would not mean to be consumed by the fire of sacrificial violence but to be united to God in the purifying and transforming fire of his tender and merciful presence.

Thérèse knew only a God of love who took no delight in the violence of punitive vengeance, even in the name of justice. She would be available to receive the overflow of the waves of infinite tenderness pent up within God, rejected by sinners. She would open her soul and become a martyr of divine love.

Thérèse was asking not to suffer pain from a vindictive god as a substitute for the sinner who may have deserved it, but to receive mercy in the embrace of a loving God and to share that love with those who did not deserve it. No one deserves divine love, Thérèse knew, just as a newborn does not deserve the parents' love. In the case of a newborn, as in the case of a child of God, to deserve or not to deserve love is not really the issue. It is a question of the parents' love, of God's love, as the prophet Isaiah had said, that first brought the child into the world, and that continues throughout life, even in the face of the child's weakness and resistance.

As Thérèse prepared to make her act of offering, she must have felt as she did when, a few months later, she helped Sr. Marie of the Trinity also make this offering. *Do you know what God requires of us by way of preparation?* she asked the novice rhetorically. *He requires us to admit our unworthiness. Since He has already given you this grace, give yourself up to Him without fear* (TLMT 87). *From this Oblation of self to God's love,* she said to Céline, *we can expect mercy alone. We have nothing to fear from this Act* (MSST 92). *I am only a child,* Thérèse prayed, *powerless and weak, and yet it is my weakness that gives me the boldness of offering myself as VICTIM of YOUR Love, O Jesus* (SS 195).

Thérèse asked Pauline, as prioress, for permission to make this *Act of Oblation to Merciful Love* in a formal way. So daring, original, and passionate did Pauline find Thérèse's prayerful sentiments that she later, just to be sure, submitted the prayer formula to a theologian for approval.

On June 11, kneeling before the statue of Our Lady, the same statue whose smile had cured her years before, Thérèse, with Céline at her side, recited her *Act of Oblation to Merciful Love:*

O my God! Most Blessed Trinity, I desire to Love You and to make You Loved, to work for the glory of the Holy Church by saving souls on earth and liberating those suffering in purgatory. I desire to accomplish Your will perfectly and to reach the degree of glory You have prepared for me in Your Kingdom. I desire, in a word, to be a saint, but I feel my helplessness and I beg you, Oh my God! To be Yourself my Sanctity.

Since You loved me so much as to give me Your only Son as my Savior and my Spouse, the infinite treasures of His merits are mine. I offer them to You with gladness, begging You to look upon me only in the Face of Jesus and in His heart burning with Love.

I offer You, too, all the merits of the saints (in heaven and on earth), their acts of Love, and those of the holy angels. Finally, I offer you, O Blessed Trinity! the Love and merits of the Blessed Virgin, my dear Mother. It is to her I abandon my offering begging her to present it to You. Her Divine Son, my Beloved Spouse, told us in the days of His mortal life: "Whatsoever you ask the Father in my name he will give it to you!" [John 15:16]. I am certain, then, that You will grant my desires; I know, O my God! that the more You want to give, the more You make us desire. I feel in my heart immense desires and it is with confidence I ask You to come and take possession of my soul. Ah! I cannot receive Holy Communion as often as I desire, but, Lord, are you not all-powerful? Remain in me as in a tabernacle and never separate Yourself from Your little victim.

I want to console You for the ingratitude of the wicked, and I beg of You to take away my freedom to displease You. If through weakness I sometimes fall, may Your Divine Glance cleanse my soul immediately, consuming all my imperfections like the fire that transforms everything into itself.

I thank You, O my God! for all the graces You have granted me, especially the grace of making me pass through the crucible of suffering. It is with joy I shall contemplate You on the Last Day carrying the scepter of Your Cross. Since You deigned to give me a share in this very precious Cross, I hope in heaven to resemble You and to see shining in my glorified body the sacred stigmata of Your Passion.

After earth's Exile, I hope to go and enjoy You in the Fatherland, but I do not want to lay up merits for heaven. I want to work for Your Love alone with the one purpose of pleasing You, consoling Your

Sacred Heart, and saving souls who will love You eternally.

In the evening of this life, I shall appear before You with empty hands, for I do not ask You, Lord, to count my works. All our justice is stained in Your eyes. I wish, then, to be clothed in Your own Justice and to receive from Your Love the eternal possession of Yourself. I want no other Throne, no other Crown but You, my Beloved!

Time is nothing in Your eyes, and a single day is like a thousand years. You can, then, in one instant prepare me to appear before You.

In order to live in one single act of perfect Love, I OFFER MYSELF AS A VICTIM OF HOLOCAUST TO YOUR MERCIFUL LOVE, asking You to consume me incessantly, allowing the waves of infinite tenderness shut up within You to overflow into my soul, and that thus I may become a martyr of Your Love, O my God!

May this martyrdom, after having prepared me to appear before You, finally cause me to die and may my soul take its flight without any delay into the eternal embrace of Your Merciful Love.

I want, O my Beloved, at each beat of my heart to renew this offering to You an infinite number of times, until the shadows having disappeared I may be able to tell You of my Love in an Eternal Face to Face! (SS 276–77)

To the text of her offering Thérèse signed her religious name preceded by her baptismal name, an acknowledgment that this act of oblation was about the action, *the fire*, of the Holy Spirit, fulfilling the grace of her religious vocation as well as the grace of her baptism. In her copy of the gospel that she kept over her heart in the pocket of her religious habit, she would carry a copy of the formula of this act together with the text of her religious vows.

A few days after having made her offering, while praying the Stations of the Cross, Thérèse was seized by a rapturous love that she had never known before. Consumed by peace and joy, she experienced a *wound of love . . . as though I were totally plunged into fire.* She felt her heart burning with love. *I was on fire with love, and I felt that one moment, one second more, and I wouldn't be able to sustain this ardor without dying.* Thérèse knew that this experience, although fleeting and never to reoccur, must have been similar to *what the saints were saying about these states which they experienced so often* (STL 63, HLC 77). She was certain that God had accepted her as a victim of love: *He would not inspire the longings I feel unless He wanted to grant them* (SS 181).

Several months later Thérèse wrote to Pauline in the booklet of her memories, *My dearest Mother, you allowed me to offer myself to God in this way, and you know the rivers or rather the oceans of grace which have flooded my soul. Oh! Since that happy day it seems that love penetrates and surrounds me, that at each moment this merciful love is renewing me, purifying my soul and not leaving any trace of sin in it, and I have no fear of purgatory* (SS 181).

The *Act of Oblation to Merciful Love* is the Little Way in prayer form, a prayer that the Holy Spirit had inspired in Thérèse. God had prepared Thérèse to receive this prayer by all the experiences of her life, particularly by the grace that had allowed her to place herself at the feet of Jesus crucified to receive divine love. The fire of merciful love would consume her, and the elevator of God's arms would envelop her. With her natural and supernatural gifts as well as her weaknesses and faults, she came by divine grace to the maturity to pray, from the center of her being and with all the passion of her heart, this act of oblation, of complete surrender and abandonment, of total availability and union, of immense faith and loving desire.

Thérèse wanted to invite her sister Marie to make the *Act of Oblation to Merciful Love*. Hearing the word "victim" and immediately thinking of the common violent notion of "victim of God's justice," Marie replied, "Certainly not. I am not going to offer myself as a victim; God would take me at my word, and suffering frightens me too much. In the first place, this word 'victim' repels me very much." Thérèse responded that she could well understand how her sister felt, but that *to offer ourselves as victims to the love of God is entirely different from giving ourselves over to His justice. It does not necessarily mean an increase of suffering but merely the ability to love the good God more, and to make up for those souls who do not want to love Him.* Marie finally agreed (MSST 90–91; GC II 1001).

Some saints have asked to die a martyr; some have prayed to die of love. Thérèse desired both. She desired to be loved by God all her life and finally to be loved to death. This desire became a source of immense consolation during her final illness, and on her deathbed she said, *Very often, when I am able to do so, I repeat my Offering to Love* (HLC 117).

CHAPTER 34

Jesus Does Not Demand Great Actions from Us but Simply Surrender and Gratitude

In the deepening maturity of her spiritual journey, Thérèse's prayer continued in a state of aridity; she was now purified of seeking any consolations. In pure faith she was confident of her Beloved's presence and love. *He will more quickly grow tired of making me wait than I shall grow tired of waiting for Him*, she had written earlier (GC I 612). Now she wrote, *I have understood more than ever how much Jesus desires to be loved.* She simply wanted to give Jesus the joy of being loved even if her feelings remained arid. She later advised a sister, *Do not fear to tell Him you love Him even without feeling it. That is the way to force Jesus to help you, to carry you like a little child too feeble to walk* (GC II 1117).

Thérèse's insights into the spiritual life had supported her courage and her willingness to abide the defects and inadequacies in herself that she could not overcome. She still experienced herself as weak and lacking in virtue. She still fell asleep during times of meditation; she was still impatient and had to deal with feelings of irritation and sensitivity; she was still prone to compromise herself with feelings of needing to please others. Jesus was more often than not still sleeping in her little boat. Spiritual insights ordinarily came to her through her usual experiences and often outside the official times of personal or communal prayer.

Her Little Way was based on her listening to the Holy Spirit. Thérèse noted a specific insight that she received from her own experience and not from books. It was near Christmastime, and she was with the sisters at recreation. The subprioress asked Thérèse to go and help bring in some tree branches for the crib. Since the request was a privilege, and noticing that the sister at her side really wanted to have the advantage, Thérèse purposely reacted slowly, wanting to allow the other sister to respond first. The community, however, interpreted the slowness as laziness and self-centeredness on Thérèse's part. *I cannot say how much good such a small thing did to my soul*, Thérèse later wrote, *making me indulgent towards the weaknesses of others. This incident prevents me from being vain when I am judged favorably because I say to myself: Since one can take my little acts of virtue for imperfections, one can also be mistaken in taking for virtue what is nothing but imperfections* (SS 221–22; cf. HLC 37 and GC II 1026).

But to be judged and appreciated by others was diminishing as a concern for Thérèse. Above all, she was now growing in love, not only in her intellectual understanding of the science of love, but in her willingness to participate in love: to fall more and more in love with Jesus. *It is only love which makes us acceptable to God,* she wrote, and the only road that leads to divine love *is the surrender of the little child who sleeps without fear in its Father's arms* (SS 188).

For Thérèse, to participate in love was not about self-centered effort or any kind of personal achievement. *Jesus does not demand great actions from us,* she wrote, *but simply surrender and gratitude* (SS 188). She did not negate *great actions.* She wanted to do great as well as small actions for God. She wanted simply to do all her actions in divine love. Indeed, she wanted to do the greatest of actions: she wanted to love Jesus more than he had ever been loved before. But she knew that any action was good and great only if it had been first inspired by God's great love. She viewed the spiritual life organically, as Jesus had suggested in his image of the vine and the branches. If the branch is attached to the vine, it will produce good fruit. Thérèse wanted to be united with the vine, and from that union with Jesus would come both the great and the small actions that her Beloved wanted of her.

At the beginning of my spiritual life when I was thirteen or fourteen, I used to ask myself what I would have to strive for later on because I believed it was quite impossible for me to understand perfection better, Thérèse wrote, recalling the time when she had thought that even the *learned . . . would have been astonished to see a child of fourteen understand perfection's secrets.* But now she knew that she did indeed understand gospel perfection better. *I learned very quickly since then that the more one advances, the more one sees the goal is still far off. And now I am simply resigned to see myself always imperfect and in this I find my joy* (SS 158). Gospel perfection, she was learning, had all to do with the willing spirit of humbly receiving divine mercy, and nothing to do with the willful spirit of acquisition or striving.

To her novice Sr. Marie of the Trinity, who was complaining that she had no courage in herself, Thérèse replied with words of encouragement and challenge:

You are complaining about something that should cause you the greatest happiness. Where would your merit be, if you could fight only when you feel courage? What does it matter if you have none, provided that you act as if you do! When you feel too weak to pick up a ball of yarn and you do it anyway for the love of Jesus, you have more merit than if you had accomplished something much more important in a moment of fervor. Instead of being sad when you get to feel your weakness, rejoice that God is providing you with the opportunity to save a greater number of souls for Him. (TLMT 104)

The way of love that Thérèse was entering into more deeply did not necessarily remove failures and weaknesses, as the retreat preacher Fr. Blino had implied that it should. Rather, Thérèse's Little Way summoned her to benefit even from her faults, because God was drawing profit from them. *How sweet is the way of love,* Thérèse wrote. *True, one can fail or commit infidelities, but, knowing how to draw profit from everything, love quickly consumes everything that can be displeasing to Jesus; it leaves nothing but a humble and profound peace in the depths of the heart* (SS 179).

In her state of abandonment and surrender she was learning to let her failures lead her into humility. *I am not disturbed at seeing myself weakness itself. On the contrary, it is in my weakness that I glory, and I expect each day to discover new imperfections in myself* (SS 224). Thérèse discovered from her experience the same truth that St. Paul had written about: "When I am weak, it is then that I am strong" (2 Corinthians 12:10).

She knew, of course, that surrender and abandonment to her loving Father did not mean being apathetic or slothful. Nor did it mean simply doing nothing in the spiritual life or, worse yet, wallowing in some kind of negativity or self-deprecation. Rather, the spirit of surrender had to do with poverty of spirit. Surrender to God was actually an expression of Thérèse's great desire to do actions that pleased her Beloved. It meant for her the willingness to appreciate being the person she was, with her gifts and her human weaknesses, and to reciprocate divine love.

Most importantly, surrender meant willingly enduring with serenity the pain and the real humility of not being able to overcome weaknesses by her own effort alone. Had she not tried for ten years to overcome her weaknesses after the death of her mother? She had failed; she had not given up but had prayed for a miracle. She surrendered, and the work of dealing with her feelings that she had not been able to do in those ten years after her mother's death was given to her in the little miracle of her complete conversion.

Thérèse now experienced this poverty of spirit, this spirit of surrender to divine love, as being an all-encompassing disposition that embraced the present, the past, and the future. Her spirit of surrender included abandonment to God's will, not only in those areas of her life that at present she could not change, but also in those early experiences of her life, the formative parts of her early childhood that contributed to her being the person she presently was, yet over which she had had no control. It also included the future as well, which was out of her hands. Surrender, for Thérèse, meant giving over her entire life to divine mercy.

To surrender herself meant, for Thérèse, to become who she was before God. She would not struggle to be someone else; nor would she even try to be better than she was. She did not obsessively compare herself with others and did not strive to reach the religious ideal of her time. She was confident that her Beloved loved her as she presently was with all her gifts and weaknesses. At the same time she knew that she was called to deeper union with God, and she was willing to be carried into that new area of holiness. But she also knew that she had to be carried as a little spiritual child, and that awareness and willingness were the bases of her spirit of surrender.

In not comparing herself with others and in not trying to reach a religious ideal, Thérèse allowed herself to be freed from a striving for perfection that would have been the trap of willfulness. She had known that she could not reach a state of being perfect in virtue and without failings; now she understood more clearly that the very attitude of "striving" for perfection injected the poison of self-centeredness into her will. It moved her will into an egotistical willfulness and away from a God-centered willingness to be open to divine providence. She was confident that her loving Father would draw her into the holiness that he wished for her if she were simply willing and available.

Thérèse understood that holiness consisted of loving, of reciprocating divine love. Loving was not a virtue that she could acquire; it was a gift that she would receive as she was willing to be united to the source of love, to Jesus, the vine, in a spirit of surrender.

In her pursuit of love, surrender would not have been complete for Thérèse without gratitude. Gratefulness naturally arose from the sense of surrender, because the sense of surrender was within a personal relationship of love. Thérèse was not surrendering to fate or to an impersonal force, but to the will of her Beloved, and that sense of surrender into the Beloved's arms evoked gratitude. In the arms of her Beloved, gratitude was the primary loving response. *Gratitude is the thing that brings us the most grace. . . . I have learnt this from experience,* she confided to Céline; *try it, and you will see. I am content with whatever God gives me, and I show him this in a thousand little ways* (STL 138).

When she was only about five years old, Thérèse had deliberately decided that she would never complain, and she had carried that determination with her through the years. Now her life in Carmel was filled with petty difficulties, the constant sense of inadequacy and the frequent little failures, the always-present physical and emotional austerity, the pressing routine of the daily convent schedule, the usual silence and solitude as well as the pinpricks of close, imposed relationships. Thérèse recognized that her call was to live all this in surrender and with gratitude. She would be grateful to God for the good times and the hard times. The flux of feelings became less and less important to her.

Her meditations on Joan of Arc had taught Thérèse that great actions that bring notice were well beyond her. Her great actions would consist of acting with as much fidelity to her call in the ordinary things of life as she could manage, in a spirit of love, patience, humility, and courage. But it was always with "as much fidelity as she could manage," for she knew she would not be perfect. Her kind of perfection would be to willingly surrender to the reality of who she was and to be grateful for what God was doing in her.

In January 1895, with her young sisters in the novitiate, Thérèse had presented to the community her play *Joan of Arc Accomplishing Her Mission.* Having just begun at that time also to respond to Pauline's assignment to write about her life, she wrote the script of *Joan of Arc* with some autobiographical references. She spoke on behalf of Joan's accepting martyrdom for love of God, but she was also speaking of herself, aware of her weakening physical condition and aware of her spiritual way:

My martyrdom! And I accept it, for Your love;
No more do I fear death or dread the burning fire.
For, Jesus, how my soul sighs now for You above–

Aspires to You alone, my God and my Desire!
I want to take my cross and follow You, to give
My life for love of You, sweet Saviour. This is why
I have one only wish. That I begin to live,
That He and I be one, is why I want to die. (CP 60)

She was sensing that she was dying; she was acknowledging her great desire to give all to Jesus; she was surrendering her life into the loving hands of her Beloved. Joan was her model in life and her spokesperson in the play. The play itself had a unique dramatic, near-martyrdom moment when, with Thérèse as Joan at the stake, the set caught fire. Pauline called out to Thérèse not to move while the fire was being extinguished. Thérèse obeyed and later said that she had been prepared to die like Joan.

In February Thérèse also spontaneously composed the fifteen stanzas of the poem "Living by Love." According to Céline, it was "the greatest of her poems"; it also contained some autobiographical references, particularly the last stanza:

Dying of Love! Behold my hope, when hence
I go, and see my bonds are broken: when
My God will be my Mighty Recompense—
I'm looking for no other Fortune then.
To see Him, to be one with Him! May He
Consume me (like a fire would do) above,
Always. Behold my Heav'n, my destiny:
   Living by Love!!! (CP 74)

Now, at the end of 1895, Thérèse was approaching her twenty-third birthday, and had been in Carmel seven years and five months. She had begun to develop a sore throat and a persistent cough, a condition that medication did not alleviate. She had a little over two years to live. In the last months of her life, Thérèse would pose the question, *How will this "story of a little white flower" come to an end? Perhaps the little flower will be plucked in her youthful freshness,* Thérèse wondered. *I don't know, but what I am certain about is that God's Mercy will accompany her always* (SS 181).

The community at recreation in the chestnut walk, February 1895, with Thérèse at upper left

CHAPTER 35

To Bear with One's Imperfections, That Is Real Sanctity

With growing confidence, Thérèse taught her Little Way to the novices and the other sisters through her example as well as in her conversations, and in her poems, plays, and correspondence. She was beginning slowly to influence the harsher, perfectionistic spirituality of the community.

The young sisters had been raised in the prevailing atmosphere of spiritual fear stemming from Jansenism and perfectionism. In their desire for self-improvement, they often complained to Thérèse about their flaws and deficiencies, deprecating themselves or even punishing themselves for these failings. Thérèse approached her own weakness differently. She experienced deep grief and repentance when she failed, but did not move to self-condemnation. *When I commit a fault that makes me sad, she said, I know very well that this sadness is a consequence of my infidelity, but do you believe I remain there? Oh! No, I'm not so foolish! I hasten to say to God: My God, I know I have merited this feeling of sadness, but let me offer it up to you just the same as a trial that You sent me through love. I am sorry for my sin, but I'm happy to have this suffering to offer to you* (HLC 71).

In directing the young sisters, Thérèse did not deny that corrections in their behavior and in their attitude needed to be made, but she emphasized the importance of the proper inner spirit necessary in addressing personal weaknesses and failings. She knew from her own experiences that she had grown spiritually not from the scolding or harshness of others, or from overhearing critical gossip about herself, or from doing violence to herself, but from patience and the firmness of love.

Especially during her first months in Carmel, Thérèse had made many mistakes that needed prompt correction for her own enlightenment as well as for the peace and proper functioning of the community. Mother Gonzague had acted quickly and decisively, and sometimes had scolded Thérèse into the needed changes of behavior. Thérèse could have done similarly with the young sisters, but she knew that in addition to behavioral changes, there was the more important aspect of attitudinal change. When Thérèse corrected the behavior of the young sisters under her care with firmness, it was with the intention of helping them develop a gospel consciousness.

Reflecting on the corrections that had been given to her, Thérèse knew that scolding and harsh reprimands might effect an outward behavioral change, but they could also evoke feelings of anger and resentment, or worse, feelings of self-loathing. Thérèse did not allow that to happen in herself, but in the face of the harshness of Mother Gonzague and some of the sisters, she did experience some of the feelings to which she had been especially vulnerable from her very earliest years: feelings of separation, self-pity, sadness, and inadequacy. Thérèse quickly turned these feelings into prayer and thus into stepping-stones for her own growth. *How easy it is to please Jesus, to delight His Heart*, she wrote to Céline. *One has only to love Him, without looking at one's self, without examining one's faults too much. Your Thérèse is not in the heights at this moment, but Jesus is teaching her to learn "to draw profit from everything, from the good and the bad she finds in herself"* (reference to St. John of the Cross; cf. SS 179; GC II 795). But she knew that the young sisters under her care would not always be able to have this spirit without further instruction in the spiritual life; she also knew that to provide that instruction was precisely her responsibility as assistant to the novice mistress.

Scolding and punitiveness were methods Thérèse saw as violent. She knew that both harsh correction and violent, willful self-effort to change behavior were incompatible with loving mercy; and the way of Jesus was the way of love and mercy.

Thérèse sometimes seemed to act sternly toward the young sisters as she tried to move them forward along the spiritual path, but she was really adapting her actions to fit their needs in order to meet them on their own terms. Her sternness was neither an expression of her anger or frustration, nor was it punitive. In her firmness she followed Jesus, who seemed to be uncompromising, but only as a way of accommodating his teaching to those who would not have understood if addressed in any other way.

Thérèse had a special point of view on how to deal with personal weaknesses and sins. She never scolded herself, and she never suggested to the young sisters that they reproach themselves for their misdeeds or punish themselves for their mistakes. She never suggested that they harbor thoughts or feelings that belittled themselves or that were self-critical. She constantly suggested that they acknowledge their mistakes but not become adversaries to themselves. Rather, she advised that they be patient with themselves, bearing *serenely the trial of being displeasing* to themselves and using their willpower not in an attitude of willfulness, but rather in a spirit of willingness to change.

To overcome faults, Thérèse emphasized the virtues of patient love for one-self, faith in the power of God, courage, and humility. And she knew that these virtues were attained not so much by willful self-effort as by self-awareness, vigilance, and a spirit of willingness to serenely persevere.

One day Sr. Marie of the Trinity, one of the novices, came to Thérèse to con-fess that she had been intolerant with some of the older sisters. In a self-criti-cal tone she added that she needed to become more patient. Thérèse studied Sr. Marie and told her that with that attitude she was becoming an enemy to herself. Instead, Sr. Marie, even in her failing, needed to properly love herself. Suppose, Thérèse said, *if God wants you to be weak and powerless like a little child, do you think you will be less worthy? Consent, then, to stumble at every step, even to fall, to carry your cross feebly. Love your powerless-ness; your soul will draw more profit than if, supported by grace, you achieve with a certain flair heroic acts which fill your soul with personal satisfaction and selfish pride* (TLMT 79). Can you bear the distress and personal trial of being an impatient person, Thérèse was asking, until God gives you the grace needed to be more patient? Can you accept your powerlessness without hat-ing yourself for it? Success in virtue is not the point. Love—love of the sisters in their weakness and love of yourself in your inadequacy, made possible by your willingness to receive divine love in you—that, Thérèse was trying to say, is the point. That patient love is also transformative, Thérèse knew, and would lead to deeper tolerance in action. The novice went away enlightened and remembered Thérèse's wisdom and advice years later.

On another occasion this same sister fell into fretting about her need to become better. Thérèse spoke again from her experience as a child:

You make me think of the very little child who starts to hold herself up but does not yet know how to walk. Wanting absolutely to climb to the top of the stairs to find her mother again, she lifts her little foot to finally climb the first step. Useless labor! She always falls without mak-ing any advance. . . . Consent to be this little child. Through practicing all the virtues, keep lifting up your little foot in order to clamber up the stairs of holiness. You will not even get to the first rung, but God asks nothing of you except your good will. From the top of the stairs he looks down at you with love. Soon, won over by your ineffective efforts, he will come down himself and, taking you in his arms, he will take you away into his kingdom forever where you will never have to depart from him. (TLMT 79–80)

God asks nothing of you *except your good will,* Thérèse said, knowing that one must pursue good in willingness, not willfulness. She had learned from her own experience as a child that willfulness was close to violence, and she knew that violence was not the gospel way.

If Sr. Marie of the Trinity were to continue sincerely, courageously, and patiently doing the best she could in any circumstance, aware of her weakness and enduring her faults until she received the grace to overcome them—that would be enough for God. That might not please herself, and it might not please the community, but it would please her Beloved. Thérèse was giving Sr. Marie the same advice she gave Céline: she was being called to willingly endure in peace the inner disturbance of not being as perfect as she would like.

With the young sisters, Thérèse echoed Jesus' teaching of conversion: a change of heart from the attitude of selfishness and of striving willfully in self-centeredness, to a spirit of humbly receiving divine love and willingly doing one's best without attachment to the results.

Thérèse also addressed the notion of personal discipline and sacrifice. While supporting the customs of the community, she changed those notions through her words and attitude from a form of violence to a form of love. The purpose of discipline, she directed, was not to inflict pain on oneself for the sake of correction or punishment, and certainly not in a spirit of self-retaliation for one's misdeeds.

Discipline, Thérèse understood in the spirit of St. Paul, was for the sake of being a disciple of Jesus. Paul, using the example of the athlete, made it clear that discipline consisted of doing and enduring all that was required to be completely available to the sport. In the spiritual realm, discipline consisted of doing and bearing all that was required to be completely available to God's will. Discipline was not a punitive activity. Athletic discipline required self-sacrifice, but it would be personally experienced by the athlete as simply what was needed to achieve the goal. It was not in any way self-punitive and not for the purpose of inflicting pain. Spiritual discipline would require self-sacrifice for the sake of the spiritual goal of being open to God, and not for the purpose of self-deprecation or as a form of emotional violence toward oneself.

To her postulants and novices, Thérèse's teachings sounded new, even bold. When Sr. Marie of the Trinity told Thérèse that she wanted to share some of Thérèse's wisdom with her parents, Thérèse cautioned her, *Be very careful how you explain it, because our "Little Way" badly understood could be taken for quietism or illuminism. Don't think that to follow the path of love means to follow the path of repose, full of sweetness and consolations. It is completely the opposite. To offer oneself as a victim to Love means to give oneself up without any reservations to whatever God pleases, which means to expect to share with Jesus his humiliations, his chalice of bitterness* (TLMT 89).

Thérèse's growing understanding of the spiritual path was clearly not founded on indifference or irresponsibility. Rather, it was founded on Jesus' teaching of responding to a loving Father with acts of justice and charity done in obedience and love—specifically, enduring the sacrifices and suffering that could not be avoided in the life of love. This would have separated it from quietism, which was commonly understood to mean doing nothing, and from illuminism, which claimed a secret revelation beyond the gospel. It would also have distinguished it from perfectionism and Pelagianism, both of which contaminated true spirituality with an assumption that holiness was a form of personal perfection and could be achieved by personal effort and willpower.

Thérèse's solution to the problem of personal failings and sins was not human effort of the will, much less self-condemnation or self-pity, but a willingness to move honestly, patiently, courageously, and confidently toward the source of all purification and virtue. In availability to God, in the arms of a loving Father, in the fire of divine love, all sin would be removed and all virtue established. She believed that the fire of divine love, into which the postulants and novices placed their faults by sincere and willing repentance, would cleanse and transform them. *When we cast our faults with entire filial confidence into the devouring fire of love,* she would later write, *how would these not be consumed beyond return?* (GC II 1134).

The transformation might not be manifested in their behavior immediately, but their Beloved would be pleased, and they would be changed in God's time. Thérèse advised her novices that until that behavioral change happened, they should humbly bear with themselves. As she expressed it, *Yes, it suffices to humble oneself, to bear with one's imperfections. That is real sanctity* (GC II 1122). In her Little Way of holiness, Thérèse abandoned completely an understanding that there was a form of positive violence in the name of good.

Understanding more clearly the path of nonviolent holiness on which she herself was being led by her loving Father, Thérèse became bolder in expressing her insights. She wrote to her sister Léonie, who the previous year had left the Visitation convent for the second time and was feeling discouraged, *I assure you that God is much better than you believe. He is content with a glance, a sigh of love. . . . As for me, I find perfection very easy to practice because I have understood it is a matter of taking hold of Jesus by His Heart* (GC II 965–66).

Thérèse probably adopted the expression *taking hold of Jesus by His Heart* from a letter she had received from Fr. Pichon the year before, but she had had similar sentiments since she had been a child in the arms of her parents. As she had run with open arms to them to be forgiven of her failings, she imagined herself in her weakness running with open arms *to take Jesus by caresses* (HLC 257; cf. GC II 900–901, note 4). She imagined taking Jesus, but at the same time being herself taken by Jesus. If her human brokenness and sins separated her from Jesus, she would be reunited to him not by her willful self-effort or punitive self-correction, but by running into the arms of Jesus in self-awareness and willingness.

Look at a little child who has just annoyed his mother by flying into a temper or by disobeying her, Thérèse continued in her letter to Léonie, perhaps reminiscing about her own childhood behavior. *If he hides away in a corner in a sulky mood and if he cries in fear of being punished, his mamma will not pardon him, certainly not his fault. But if he comes to her, holding out his little arms, smiling, and saying: "Kiss me, I will not do it again," will his mother be able not to press him to her heart tenderly and forget his childish mischief? . . . However, she knows her dear little one will do it again on the next occasion, but this does not matter; if he takes her again by her heart, he will not be punished* (GC II 966).

Thérèse had also found this idea expressed in the Book of Isaiah. *At the time of the law of fear,* Thérèse continued, *before the coming of Our Lord, the Prophet Isaiah already said, speaking in the name of the King of heaven: "Can a mother forget her child? . . . Well! Even if a mother were to forget her child, I myself will never forget you"* [Isaiah 49:15]. *What a delightful promise! Ah! We who are living in the law of love, how can we not profit by the loving advances our Spouse is making to us . . . how can we fear Him who allows Himself to be enchained by* [our smallest act of love]? (GC II 966).

Thérèse at twenty-two years old, in 1895, seated second from the left in the second row

CHAPTER 36

Lord, I Am Too Little to Nourish Your Children

Ongoing tension existed between Pauline, as prioress, and Mother Gonzague, who saw Pauline together with the other Martin sisters forming a powerful unit within the convent. Then Marie Guérin, the Martin sisters' cousin, entered the community in August 1895, about a year after Céline had entered, bringing to five the number of the same family in the convent—one-fifth of the community. This was a concern to the power-conscious Mother Gonzague.

As 1896 began, Thérèse too became personally involved in some tension with Mother Gonzague. As the mistress of novices, Mother Gonzague wanted to postpone the profession ceremonies of both Céline and Sr. Marie of the Trinity, and she was also considering sending Céline after her profession to the Carmel in Saigon, which had been a foundation of the Lisieux Carmel. A delay in the profession date would have meant that the sisters would have taken vows after the upcoming prioress election. If Mother Gonzague were to be elected, she would have the personal prestige of receiving the sisters' vows and thus depriving Pauline of the joy and privilege of presiding at her own sister's profession ceremony. Thérèse strongly opposed the delay, which she thought was arbitrary and totally unjustified, and she told Mother Gonzague directly that she did not agree with her.

One day in the laundry room, in January 1896, three months before the election, about fifteen members of the community had been working together and had begun discussing Mother Gonzague's proposal to delay the profession of Céline and Sr. Marie of the Trinity. The sister who had most opposed Céline's entry into Carmel remarked that Mother Gonzague as novice mistress had every right to impose this kind of humiliating trial on Céline. *There are some trials that should not be given,* Thérèse answered quite abruptly. Heads turned (TLMT 114).

It was one of the few times that Thérèse reacted sharply, and one of the very few times that she allowed her disagreements and annoyances with Mother Gonzague to surface. It was the adult equivalent of little Thérèse, empowered with appropriate anger, standing with dignity on the chair and telling Victoire in no uncertain terms that she was *a brat*. On that occasion

Thérèse had spoken and had *no need of repentance*. Now Mother Gonzague was also acting like a "brat."

A short time later at the formal assembly of sisters to vote on the proposal to postpone the profession date, Mother Gonzague, presiding at the meeting, used her power as novice mistress to exclude Pauline from the gathering. Céline, of course, was not present, nor were Thérèse or Marie, since they were sisters of Céline. Agreement was reached among the sisters attending the meeting not to defer Céline's profession, but to delay that of Sr. Marie of the Trinity. A sort of compromise had been reached.

Céline made her profession in February with Pauline presiding at the ceremony. Céline took the name of Sr. Geneviève, and Thérèse gave her a small gift for her profession. It was the cloth on which Thérèse five years earlier had gathered the last tear of the dying saintly Mother Geneviève, whom she had loved so dearly.

In March, the election for the superior was held, and Mother Marie de Gonzague was elected prioress once again, defeating Pauline, who was chosen simply as one of the community counselors. This time it was Pauline's turn to feel hurt and Thérèse's turn to be completely astonished and saddened that the community had not reelected her beloved sister. Thérèse, who could not attend the election, was described by one of the nuns as being "dumbfounded" by the results. With the election filled with tension and rancor, Mother Gonzague, at sixty-two and in ill health, seems to have harbored the mixed feelings of not wanting to be elected and yet not wanting Pauline to be reelected. The community had only these two leaders, however, and now Mother Gonzague felt hurt and bitter that she had been chosen only after seven ballots.

When the contentious process of the election had been completed, Mother Gonzague did not follow the usual custom of appointing the former prioress, Pauline, as novice mistress. Instead, she immediately moved to diminish the influence of Pauline and to exert her own authority by retaining the role of novice mistress herself. Then she announced that Thérèse would continue as her assistant in the novitiate. It was a snub to Pauline but an affirmation of the respect that Mother Gonzague and the community had for Thérèse. This arrangement continued to put Thérèse in a very delicate position of bridging the divide between Pauline and Marie Gonzague.

Mother Gonzague began to confide in Thérèse more openly, regarding her as an exception to many of the sisters whom she regarded as traitors

(GC II 958). The sisters had experienced Mother Gonzague's previous terms of leadership as more self-serving, lax, and capricious than the orderly and firm way the community had been led in these last years by Pauline. Mother Gonzague felt bitter that she was not as appreciated as she had been before, especially after having served six previous terms in office. To address Mother Gonzague's inner struggle, Thérèse composed a letter to her, telling a parable of a lamb conversing with the divine Shepherd about the plight of a shepherdess.

The divine Shepherd emboldens the lamb (Thérèse) to tell the shepherdess (Mother Gonzague) that *I do not want to take her trial away from her, I want only that she may understand the truth and recognize that her cross is coming from heaven and not from earth. . . . Your dear Mother must rejoice in having a share in My sorrows. If I am removing from her human support, it is only to fill her very loving heart!* (GC II 960–61).

Thérèse herself, over the years, had experienced the same withdrawal of human support and the same deep need for it. Thérèse's parable, written with genuineness and simplicity, was consoling to Mother Gonzague, who trusted Thérèse's wisdom.

Under Mother Gonzague, Thérèse became not just "senior novice" but the de facto novice mistress for the group of postulants and novices. In humility and discretion she would not allow herself the title, and besides, under the law of the church she was, at twenty-three years old, too young to be officially named. However, after Thérèse's death, Mother Gonzague, describing this time, would write that Thérèse "carried out the difficult charge of mistress of novices with a wisdom and perfection that was equalled only by her love for God" (GC II 943).

Even though admired and trusted by her superiors and her sisters for being wise and personally gifted, Thérèse had, from the start, undertaken her duties in the novitiate knowing *immediately that the task was beyond my strength. I threw myself into the arms of God as a little child and, hiding my face in His hair, I said: "Lord, I am too little to nourish Your children; if You wish to give through me what is suitable for each, fill my little hand and without leaving your arms or turning my head, I shall give your treasures to the soul who will come and ask for nourishment. . . ." From the moment I understood that it was impossible for me to do anything by myself, the task . . . no longer appeared difficult* (SS 238).

As the formal guide now to five young novices, four of whom were older than she and among whom were her sister Céline and her cousin Marie, Thérèse quickly came to understand *that to do good is as impossible without God's help as to make the sun shine at night.* In teaching the young sisters, she learned *that all souls have very much the same struggles to fight, but they differ so much from each other in other aspects.* She resonated with the truth of Fr. Pichon's expression, *There are really more differences among souls than there are among faces* (SS 238, 239).

One feels it is absolutely necessary, Thérèse concluded, *to forget one's likings, one's personal conceptions and to guide souls along the road which Jesus has traced out for them without trying to make them walk one's own way.* She deepened her capacity to listen and to be circumspect, carefully guarding her own feelings of attraction or antipathy to the sisters. *With the grace of Jesus never have I tried to attract their hearts to me; I understood that my mission was to lead them to God* (SS 238, 239).

Her biggest challenge, however, was the responsibility to correct the faults and imperfections of the young sisters. She continued to experience her need to please others, and at one level of her personality, Thérèse really wanted to be a friend of the young sisters. Having been given the responsibility to be their guide and director, she could not follow her personal preferences, and this proved to be very difficult for her.

What cost me more than anything else was to observe the faults and slight imperfections and to wage a war to the death on these. I would prefer a thousand times to receive reproofs than to give them to others. Thérèse learned that even when she corrected a young sister as diplomatically and meekly as she could, the sister saw *only one thing: the Sister charged with directing me is angry, and all the blame is put on me who am filled with the best intentions.* It took an interior struggle for Thérèse to become, as she expressed it, like a good shepherd, *running after them, . . . speaking severely to them when showing them that their beautiful fleece is soiled;* as well as being *the little sheep-dog* running about rounding up the lost sheep; and further to be *the watchman observing the enemy from the highest turret of a strong castle* (SS 239).

Without compromising her responsibility, Thérèse became creative in adapting her corrections and directives to the unique temperament and specific needs of each sister. *Some of them I have to catch by the scruff of the neck,* she said to Pauline, *others by their wingtips* (STL 31). Toward one she was very gentle and flexible, to another more firm and demanding. With one she shared her own inner struggles to offer encouragement; with another she concealed her own weaknesses and required conformity without undue words of support. To one she was stern, to another humorous. Thérèse's own self-awareness helped her enormously in understanding what the young sisters were experiencing and so what they most needed. She required Sr. Marie of the Trinity, who wept often, to drop her tears only in a small mussel shell that Thérèse supplied (TLMT 26). The situation became so ridiculous that the novice was cured of her frequent crying. Thérèse had been down these paths herself.

So clearly did Thérèse know a sister's feelings even before the sister expressed them, that on several occasions the young sisters thought that Thérèse could read their minds. When Thérèse did say something that came to her spontaneously without much thought and that was particularly help-ful to one of them, she *felt that God was very close, and that, without real-izing it, I had spoken words, as does a child, which came not from me but from Him* (SS 243).

The young sisters also found Thérèse's wisdom and practical sense a chal-lenge. "You have an answer for everything," one of the novices told her. "I believed I would embarrass you this time. Where do you go to get everything you say?" (SS 243). Thérèse developed great skills in dealing with the young sisters because she knew herself so well and could empathize so readily. But not all the young sisters responded well to Thérèse's style. One deliberately hid from her when the time came for her personal conference with Thérèse. Thérèse searched and sometimes found the sister, but at other times the sister managed to escape the shepherd, the sheepdog, and the watchman as well.

Meeting with the five young sisters each day for half an hour, Thérèse engaged them in discussion about the rule of Carmel and various aspects of the spiritual life. At a deeper level, it was truth that Thérèse was trying to con-vey in her guidance to the young sisters: the truth of their own motivations, the truth of the impact of their behavior on the community, and the truth of the gospel. And at the deepest level, she was teaching them the essence of the gospel by sharing with them the Little Way, the way of confidence and love.

If I'm not loved, that's just too bad! I tell the whole truth and if anyone does not want to know the truth, let her not come looking for me, Thérèse said. *We should never allow kindness to degenerate into weakness* (HLC 38). In loving the young sisters, she was completely honest with them and asked them to be completely honest with her. She did not want the sisters to take unduly into consideration her feelings, and she steeled herself not to take personally their criticism. *You understand*, she wrote to Mother Gonzague, *that everything is permitted to the novices; they must be able to say what they think, the good and the bad* (SS 243–44).

This openness with the young sisters made Thérèse vulnerable to their bluntness. *God lifts the veil which hides my imperfections, and then my dear little sisters, seeing me just as I am, no longer find me according to their taste. With a simplicity which delights me, they tell me all the struggles I give them, what displeases them in me.* On one occasion her own sister Céline was particularly abrupt with her, and Thérèse saw that that too was a grace to deepen her self-knowledge and humility: *Yes, it is the Lord who has commanded* [Céline] *to say all these things to me. And my soul enjoyed the bitter food served up to it in such abundance* (SS 244, 245).

In the eyes of the young sisters as well as the other members of the community, Thérèse seemed to be quite successful in her work. She understood that this road of success was dangerous because it exposed her to the temptation of self-love. She addressed her concern with faith. God allowed her to be admired in doing her work successfully, she considered, because this work would have been impossible if she had been seen by the community as she truly was, *filled with faults, incapable, without understanding or judgment.* It was her Beloved's work through her. *If He pleases to make me appear better than I am, that is none of my affair since He is free to act as He likes. . . .* God, Thérèse said, *has cast a veil over all my interior and exterior faults; . . .* [but] *there is always present to my mind the remembrance of what I am.* She told Mother Gonzague that *in the eyes of creatures I succeed in everything . . . but in the depths of my soul,* [Jesus allows] *many humiliations* (SS 244).

CHAPTER 37

When I Am Charitable, It Is Jesus Alone Who Is Acting in Me

In guiding the postulants and novices into the life routine and spirituality of Carmel, Thérèse had a responsibility to correct their behavior. In contrast, she was now happy to overlook the mistakes of the other members of the community. This attitude, however, had come only as she matured, for

> *formerly, when I saw a Sister doing something which displeased me and appeared to be against the Rule, I said to myself: Ah, if I could only tell her what I think and show her she is wrong, how much good this would do for me! Ever since I have practiced a little the trade of correcting, I assure you, dear Mother, that I have entirely changed my attitude. When it happens that I see a Sister perform an action which appears imperfect to me, I heave a sigh of relief and say: How fortunate! This is not a novice; I am not obliged to correct her. I then very quickly take care to excuse the sister and to give her the good intentions she undoubtedly has.* (SS 245)

When Thérèse was personally disturbed by a professed sister's behavior, even if that behavior was a fault, she rarely directly confronted the sister to request her to change her ways. Instead, Thérèse changed her own feelings about the disturbing behavior, regained her inner freedom, and then dealt creatively and compassionately with the situation.

Having had years of practice accommodating and pleasing others, Thérèse had learned early to avoid confrontation and to finesse her feelings to appear gracious and kind, even ingratiating, under almost all circumstances. The close living with personalities who struck her in the wrong way, however, made Thérèse conscious of the superficiality of merely appearing to be kind and charitable.

She had tried to act charitably toward the sisters, but her main focus in her early years in the convent had been on her relationship with Jesus and his Father. Now she came to understand more deeply the connection between love of God and love of neighbor, and to know more clearly that Jesus desired her to come to him in union with her sisters. In particular, she meditated on Jesus' directive at the Last Supper to love one another as he had loved us—the "new commandment" of love. And living out this new commandment of love became for Thérèse one of the final steps on her spiritual journey. During the last year of her life she recognized that *God has given me the grace to understand what charity is* (SS 219).

First Thérèse noticed that the original commandment of charity from the Old Testament was to "love your neighbor as yourself" (Leviticus 19:18). To love others as she loved herself, however, lacked the depth of the call in the new commandment of Jesus, "love one another as I have loved you" (John 13:34). The reference point of the new commandment caught her attention and challenged her: Jesus had said to love "as I have loved." She was not to love others as she loved herself, but as Jesus loved. She quickly came to understand that her own love for her sisters certainly did not have the breadth or depth of Jesus' love.

The second element Thérèse noticed was that Jesus' love for his disciples was not diminished by their faults and sinfulness. Thérèse was aware, however, that she did discriminate in her love, and that those personalities who were more to her liking received more of her attention and affection. Now she felt herself drawn to respond to these two challenges.

The seeds of the response to the first challenge, the call to love others as Jesus himself loved them, had already found a place in Thérèse's heart when she had learned to position herself at the foot of the cross. She knew then that her place was to receive Jesus' love and share that love with sinners. But only now did it come to her with forceful clarity that this sharing of Jesus' love was the very essence of the fulfillment of the new commandment. She could love her sisters as Jesus loved them only with Jesus' own love. *Ah! Lord, I know that you do not command the impossible,* she wrote. *You know better than I do my weakness and imperfection. You know very well that never would I be able to love my Sisters as you love them, unless you yourself, Jesus, still loved them in me* (SS 221).

The fact that Jesus had given this new directive to his disciples precisely at the Last Supper consoled her. That was the time of Jesus' self-giving in love, and this truth *gives me,* Thérèse said, *the assurance that Your Will is to love in me all those you command me to love!* (SS 221).

When Thérèse remembered the times during the past years when her heart went out in real charity to her sisters, she became aware that on those occasions Jesus, in fact, was actually loving through her. *Yes, I feel it, when I am charitable, it is Jesus alone who is acting in me, and the more united I am to Him, the more also do I love my sisters* (SS 221). Thérèse would respond to the new commandment only by becoming more and more united to Jesus, the source of love. In this way she could become more lovingly available to her sisters in service.

But Thérèse also noticed that in her heart she was blocked from being lovingly available to the sisters by some of her negative feelings about them. Whereas Jesus extended his love to all, she discriminated in her love. This was the second challenge.

In particular, she recognized that Jesus loved his disciples even though they were rough and crude and sinful. *Why did he love them?* Thérèse asked herself, as she meditated on the gospels. Then she answered, *Ah! It was not their natural qualities which could have attracted him* (SS 220).

So if she were to love the way Jesus loves, she would have to love even those sisters for whom she felt natural antipathy and whom she found, at least on occasion, repugnant or even contemptible. To purify her motivation when she did feel antipathy, Thérèse imagined herself on the one hand imitating Jesus, and on the other hand acting toward the difficult sister in the same loving manner in which she would act to please Jesus himself. *I understand now that charity consists in bearing with the faults of others, in not being surprised at their weakness, in being edified by the smallest acts of virtue we see them practice*, Thérèse wrote at the end of her life (SS 220).

Years before, Fr. Pichon had confirmed one of her intuitions about loving Jesus: "Yes, you are right," her confessor had written in reply to one of her letters, "it is better to love Jesus on His terms" (GC I 559). This idea now became part of her thinking about love for her sisters. *Love does not seek its own interest* (TLMT 108), she said, and she understood that to love her sisters as Jesus loved them would also imply that she love them on their terms and in light of their weaknesses and needs.

Accommodating others on their terms and disregarding herself had been Thérèse's practice in her early life, and it had been a trap. She had found herself *practicing virtue . . . but in a strange way*. Pleasing others had not always actually flowed from real charity; it had trapped her in a form of codependency that had undermined her own inner freedom. Now more aware of her own strengths and weaknesses, she began to explore creative ways to accommodate her sisters by acts of charity on their terms, yet without falling into her earlier pattern of doing violence to herself by disregarding her own integrity. Her sense of humor helped her.

In her final months of life, Thérèse on occasion sat outside under the chestnut trees, confined by her illness to a wheelchair—the very wheelchair that her dying father had used. There, writing her recollections, she was sometimes distracted by sisters who, passing by, wanted to say a word of encouragement or kindness to her. These well-intentioned interruptions became a burden to her, and so she regarded them with humor, adapting her response in order to meet the needs *of more than one good charitable sister* (SS 227). She began to amuse herself by anticipating each annoyance:

> *I want it; I count on it . . . so I am always happy. . . . I don't know if I have been able to write ten lines without being disturbed. This should not make me laugh nor amuse me; however, for the love of God and my sisters (so charitable towards me) I take care to appear happy and especially to be so. For example, here is a hay worker who is just leaving me after having said very compassionately: "Poor little Sister, it must tire you out writing like that all day long." "Don't worry," I answer, "I appear to be writing very much, but really I am writing almost nothing." "Very good!" she says, "but just the same, I am very happy we are doing the haying since this always distracts you a little." In fact, it is such a great distraction for me.* (SS 228)

Thérèse became much more flexible in adjusting to the needs of others, not standing on principle or on her position as "novice mistress." She adapted herself to respond to the sisters' needs and desires inconspicuously, creatively. Her love of others became eminently practical, combining a spirit of detachment and a spirit of charity, especially in small things. On one occasion a sister mistakenly took her lamp, which at that particular time she desperately needed. After an initial feeling of annoyance at the sister, she recognized the situation as a disguised grace: *I was really happy, feeling that poverty consists in being deprived not only of agreeable things but of indispensable things too* (SS 159).

Detachment from material things had always been clearly a spiritual value for her, and now she further understood that *the goods of heaven don't belong to me either; they are lent to me by God, who can withdraw them without my having a right to complain.* These goods were *the goods which come directly from God, inspirations of the mind and heart, profound thoughts, all this forms a riches to which we are attached as to a proper good which no one has a right to touch* (SS 233).

Thérèse became conscious of her own attachment to these *goods of heaven* when, having confided to a sister some spiritual insights that she had received during prayer, the sister in turn shared the insights with another sister as if they had been her own. Thérèse was irritated but managed her feelings. On a similar occasion during recreation, she whispered to her companion a witty remark, and her companion spoke it aloud to the community as if it had been her invention. All the sisters were amused, but Thérèse felt the theft in the situation and became aware of her own attachment to the goods of intellect and spirit. She did not retaliate, but rather grew in the awareness of her own weakness and in her need to love in a spirit of detachment.

The day came when Thérèse would *find it very natural* that she was able to let others *steal* what she had said. She amused herself, again noting that she was *the donkey.* God *is free to use me to give a good thought to a soul; and if I think this inspiration belongs to me, I would be like "the donkey carrying the relics" who believed the reverence paid to the saints was being directed to him* (SS 234).

In her deepest desire, wanting to respond to Jesus' new command, she came to see that her charity could not consist just in superficially pleasing her sisters, much less in muted resentment. Nor could her love be simply actions that made herself feel good or made others praise her for appearing charitable. To be genuinely charitable, Thérèse saw that she would have to love with Jesus' love, with the detached generosity of God, and that her own contribution would be the sensitivity, inner freedom, and creativity that would allow her to share herself on the sisters' terms rather than her own. That would require a self-forgetfulness and a capacity to endure some trials and suffering. She had become practiced in all this over many years, and at the end of her life she knew that her charity was now the love of Jesus in her and through her.

CHAPTER 38

We Don't Have Any Enemies in Carmel, but There Are Feelings

Thérèse's great capacity to be aware of her own feelings gave her an equally great capacity to be empathetic to others. As a child, when she had attempted to connect with others, she drifted into self-love and a kind of codependency. But as she grew older and moved into deeper prayer, she began to grasp what charity really meant. She began to live more fully the real charity that had entered her heart at the time of her Christmas conversion; now this charity was beginning to blossom in her capacity to share Jesus' love with others.

She meditated on Jesus' words "Love your enemies" (Matthew 5:44; Luke 6:27). How, she wondered, might that admonition of Jesus apply to her in the convent? *No doubt,* Thérèse said wryly, *we don't have any enemies in Carmel.* Then she added simply, with a disarming honesty, *but there are feelings* (SS 225). Thérèse's heart was telling her that her hidden feelings of animosity could be blocking her from loving as Jesus loved. She was also making a significant connection between her feelings and the identification of "the enemy."

"The enemy," Thérèse was beginning to understand, was the label she placed on any person who aroused in her feelings of repugnance, distress, or threat. In that sense, she recognized that her emotions actually invented enemies; that "the enemy" was a unique creation of her own thoughts and feelings. *One feels attracted to* [one] *sister, whereas with regard to another, one would make a long detour in order to avoid meeting her. And so, without even knowing it, she becomes the subject of persecution . . .* (SS 225). *I have noticed,* she wrote, *that the most saintly sisters are the most loved. We seek their company; we render them services without their asking. . . . On the other hand, imperfect souls are not sought out. No doubt we remain within the limits of religious politeness in their regard, but we generally avoid them fearing lest we say something which isn't too amiable* (SS 245–46).

When I speak of imperfect souls, she noted, *I don't want to speak of spiritual imperfections since the most holy souls will be perfect only in heaven.* She was, rather, speaking of those who were simply irritating and repulsive. Several of the sisters did have habits and traits that were naturally unattractive to Thérèse's sensitivities. She experienced them as having *a lack of judgment, good manners, touchiness; . . . all these things which don't make life very agreeable. I know very well that these moral infirmities are chronic, that there is no hope of a cure* (SS 246). Thérèse was noticing that the world is divided into "good" people and "bad" people, into "friends" and "enemies," according to one's own tastes.

Thérèse further understood that if she could be aware of her feelings of repugnance that made her label a sister as "the enemy," she could take the first step toward responding to Jesus' command to "love your enemy." If she could let go of her adversarial feelings and her antipathies, perhaps she would be able to retain her inner freedom and act creatively and compassionately. In that way, even though she did not feel love, she would nevertheless actually be loving and be able to act lovingly. As she reflected on her difficult relationships with some of the sisters in Carmel, she said, *I told myself that charity must not consist in feelings but in works* (SS 222).

One older sister who sat behind Thérèse during the communal prayers made a continuous clicking sound with her teeth, *a strange little noise which resembled the noise one would make when rubbing two shells, one against the other.* Thérèse became extremely annoyed; *it would be impossible for me to tell you how much this little noise wearied me.* In her agitation Thérèse felt the urge to confront this "enemy" sister. *I had a great desire to turn my head and stare at the culprit who was very certainly unaware of her "click." This would be the only way of enlightening her. However, in the bottom of my heart I felt it was much better to suffer this out of love for God and not to cause the Sister any pain* (SS 249).

A self-righteous glare might have stopped the sister's disturbing habit, but it would not have been the charitable and honest thing for Thérèse herself to do. She could not in love *stare at the culprit* in a reprimanding way. Perhaps another sister could respond in both love and agitation, but Thérèse knew that she simply could not. She had matured since her experiences with Victoire as a child, when her agitation had overcome her capacity to love. How, then, was Thérèse to act in love toward the "culprit," the "enemy"? With a sense of simplicity and humor, Thérèse tells her story:

I remained calm, therefore, and tried to unite myself to God and to forget the little noise. Everything was useless. I felt the perspiration inundate me, and I was obliged simply to make a prayer of suffering; however, while suffering, I searched for a way of doing it without annoy-

ance and with peace and joy, at least in the interior of my soul. I tried to love the little noise which was so displeasing; instead of trying not to hear it (impossible), I paid close attention so as to hear it well, as though it were a delightful concert and my prayer (which was not the Prayer of Quiet) was spent in offering this concert to Jesus. (SS 249–50)

In her capacity to acknowledge and deal with her feelings, Thérèse had discovered a way of loving the "enemy" and spiritually profiting from the enemy's actions, as well.

A similar experience occurred when a sister with whom Thérèse was doing the laundry inadvertently splashed water on Thérèse's face. The sister herself did not notice and had no intention of being unpleasant to Thérèse. Thérèse could have harangued or embarrassed the sister, or simply asked her to change her behavior. If Thérèse had had other gifts of personality, she might have been able to directly and charitably challenge the offending sister; but respecting her own limitations, Thérèse quickly recognized an opportunity to profit from the sister's actions.

She described her handling of the situation again with awareness and a sense of humor. *My first reaction,* she wrote, *was to draw back and wipe my face to show the sister who was sprinkling me that she would do me a favor to be more careful. But I immediately thought I would be very foolish to refuse these treasures which were being given to me so generously, and I took care not to show my struggle. I put forth all my efforts to desire receiving very much of this dirty water, and was so successful that in the end I had really taken a liking to this kind of aspersion* (SS 250).

Without denying that the sister's action was inconsiderate, Thérèse nevertheless avoided becoming disdainful or condemnatory. She also refused to parade a self-indulgent attitude of being a victim or to respond with self-righteousness to the sister's inappropriate actions. Thérèse received the experience as another grace in disguise.

Although Thérèse herself was not argumentative, she did see some of the sisters at odds with one another, scolding, arguing, and gossiping. Later she advised Céline that even when she was wronged or given reason to argue, not to let the power of her feelings against another sister move her to justify herself or seek vengeance: *When you tell someone, even Mother Prioress, about some argument, never do it to have the sister who caused it corrected or so that the thing you're complaining about might stop; rather, speak with detachment of heart. When you don't feel that detachment, if there is still even a spark of emotion in your heart, it is more perfect to keep quiet and wait . . . because talking about it often only aggravates it* (FGM 188).

With great sensitivity Thérèse avoided irritating other sisters; yet, she knew that, especially when she had first entered the convent, she herself had evoked disturbing and antagonistic feelings in several sisters. At that time, to some sisters Thérèse seemed to have lacked good judgment and proper convent decorum. She had made frequent mistakes in the convent customs and often had done her house chores in ways that the sisters thought sloppy and careless. She had aroused the irritation of Mother Gonzague and other sisters by her oversights and blunders.

Even now, at the very time she was reminiscing and writing about these insights regarding charity, Thérèse was ill, and by her tuberculosis—her coughing, raspy breathing, and physical limitations—she was disturbing and annoying to some of the sisters. This had also been the case many years ago when she had been ill as a child and needed the miracle of the Virgin's smile. At that time she had been a severe burden to her family at home, but she had been cared for with love; now as she was ill in the convent, her superior and the sisters were kind and tolerant to her. Why could she not be kind and tolerant to the sister who was not well in her character development? *I told myself that I should be as compassionate towards the spiritual infirmities of my sisters as you are, dear Mother* [Gonzague], *when caring for me with so much love* (SS 245).

A sister may be troublesome because she herself was troubled, Thérèse began to recognize. A sister may be disturbing because she herself was disturbed. *If a sister is sick spiritually, disagreeable in everything, everyone stays away from her, frowns on her, instead of seeking to relieve her,* Thérèse noticed. To be charitable to such a sister, "to love your enemy," "to bear one another's burdens," she thought, it would not do to lose patience with the disturbed sister, much less become her adversary. Rather, the needy sister needed to be cared for in a creative and empathetic way that took into consideration her condition. *That is what I consider to be true charity*, Thérèse said (cf. *The Little Way* by Bernard Bro, 27).

There was an older nun, Sr. Saint Pierre, who for Thérèse, then still a novice, was particularly irritating and demanding—another "enemy." Because this sister was so critical and complaining, Thérèse's natural feelings were fear, inadequacy, and antagonism. As she took the initiative to serve this sister, Thérèse knew that she would have to cope with these feelings and even the feeling of being rejected. In telling the story of her interactions with this sister Thérèse acknowledged her resistance:

Each evening when I saw . . . [her] shake her hour-glass I knew this meant: Let's go! It is incredible how difficult it was for me to get up, especially at the beginning; however, I did it immediately, and then a ritual was set in motion. I had to remove and carry her little bench in a certain way, above all I was not to hurry, and then the walk took place. It was a question of following the poor invalid by holding her cincture; I did this with as much gentleness as possible. But if by mistake she took a false step, immediately it appeared to her that I was holding her incorrectly and that she was about to fall. "Ah! my God! You are going too fast; I'm going to break something." If I tried to go more slowly: "Well, come on! I don't feel your hand; you've let me go and I'm going to fall! Ah! I was right when I said you were too young to help me."

Finally, we reached the refectory without mishap; and here other difficulties arose. I had to seat. . . [her] and I had to act skillfully in order not to hurt her; then I had to turn back her sleeves (again in a certain way), and afterwards I was free to leave. (SS 247–48)

Thérèse had feelings of repugnance, even feelings of being a victim in the face of the sister's cantankerous, demeaning attitude. By taking the initiative, however, Thérèse maintained her inner freedom, and her feelings quickly changed. Instead of this troublesome, potential enemy, she saw a troubled, suffering sister.

Thérèse noticed that Sr. Saint Pierre could not easily break her bread at meals. She had not asked for help with this little task, but nevertheless, Thérèse, with her *most beautiful smile* (SS 248), simply and inconspicuously assisted her. Experiencing the genuine, spontaneous kindness of someone to whom she had been demanding and harsh, Sr. Saint Pierre was deeply touched. Thérèse's love had won over her "enemy."

Excessively sensitive at times, Thérèse had found her feelings to be both a blessing and a curse. Now her sensitivity helped her to become conscious of dynamics within herself that were blocking her from being charitable. Her feelings of antipathy, she knew, were not of themselves wrong; those feelings helped her understand herself and evaluate situations. But if her feelings became strong enough to block her inner freedom and prevent her from being available to the sisters with kind service, then those feelings had to be addressed, not harbored or fostered.

Thérèse told a story about *a sister who has the faculty of displeasing me in everything, in her ways, her words, her character, everything seems very disagreeable to me* (SS 222). Here, for Thérèse, was a prime candidate for the label "enemy." Yet she recognized that this sister was a holy person and was loved by Jesus. Thérèse also knew that she herself could not love this woman on the level of feelings but only on the level of faith.

Thérèse accepted the spiritual challenge *to bear serenely* her feelings of repugnance, and moved to the level of action in faith. *Each time I met her I prayed to God for her, offering Him all her virtues and merits. . . . I wasn't content simply with praying very much for this sister who gave me so many struggles, but I took care to render her all the services possible and when I was tempted to answer her back in a disagreeable manner, I was content with giving her my most friendly smile* (SS 222–23).

On these occasions Thérèse managed not to let her feelings overcome her own deepest truth or prevent her charitable acts. She did not deny or over-ride her feelings, nor did she ignore them; instead, she tried not to let them manipulate her. In this she was sometimes successful, sometimes not.

So difficult was this particular sister that Thérèse admitted that she was not always successful at controlling her strong feelings of hostility. On certain occasions, when the sister's outbursts of anger became particularly violent and out of control, Thérèse, her own reactive feelings also especially strong, simply had to leave the sister's presence. *Frequently, when I . . . had occasion to work with this sister, I used to run away like a deserter whenever my struggles became too violent* (SS 223). She may have felt like a deserter, but Thérèse was really acting with the greatest prudence; greater prudence than she had had in a similar encounter with Victoire as a young child. She could not endure the violence to herself, yet she could not respond with her own disturbed feelings, and so she left the presence of the disturbance. This was the most honest, non-violent, and charitable thing she could do both for the sister and for herself.

Thérèse became so adept at managing her distressing feelings that this particular sister never became aware of them, but only noticed Thérèse's successful accommodations. Thérèse tells the story again with awareness and humor. *As she was absolutely unaware of my feelings for her,* Thérèse recounts, *never did she suspect the motives for my conduct and she remained convinced that her character was very pleasing to me. One day at recreation she asked in almost these words: "Would you tell me, Sister Thérèse of the Child Jesus, what attracts you so much towards me; every time you look at me, I see you smile?" I answered that I was smiling because I was happy to see her,* Thérèse wrote, then added playfully in parentheses, *(it is understood that I did not add that this was from a spiritual standpoint)* (SS 223).

A further irony to this story developed when her sister Marie, seeing how Thérèse treated this difficult sister so graciously with her words and notes of encouragement, became jealous of the relationship, convinced that Thérèse loved this sister more than Thérèse loved her. When Marie complained that Thérèse's love for this sister was not fair to her, Thérèse realized that she had a new problem to solve, and responded again with humor. She smiled her mischievous smile and then laughed good-naturedly, but she did not explain or justify herself. Yet inwardly Thérèse struggled (STL 97–98).

Thérèse's accommodating relationship with troublesome sisters helped not only the individual sister, but also helped to smooth the difficult interactions throughout the community. After Thérèse's death this particularly difficult sister, now without sufficient support, was overburdened by her severe psychological problems, left the community, and had to be committed to a mental institution.

Thérèse understood clearly the connection between feelings and faith. While bearing in peace those feelings of antipathy and repugnance, she needed to take initiatives of faith. Her feelings did not always support faith, but in faith she tried to bear her feelings, letting go of those that she could not harbor in charity. She could not allow herself the luxury of having "enemies" in Carmel.

Taking the initiative of faith and charity toward the "enemy," she wrote,

Well, Jesus is telling me that it is this [enemy] *Sister who must be loved, she must be prayed for even though her conduct would lead me to believe that she doesn't love me. . . . I must seek out in recreation, on free days, the company of the sisters who are the least agreeable to me, in order to carry out with regard to these wounded souls the office of the Good Samaritan. A work, an amiable smile, often suffices to make a sad soul bloom; but it is not principally to attain this end that I wish to practice charity, for I know I would soon become discouraged; a word I shall say with the best intention will perhaps be interpreted wrongly. Also, not to waste my time, I want to be friendly with everybody (and especially with the least amiable Sisters) to give joy to Jesus.* (SS 225, 246)

Thérèse understood that, on the one hand, the new command of Jesus was not a command to override her own sensitivities in an attempt to be charitable to her sisters. When she could not cope, she had to leave the scene so as not to do violence to herself or to do violence to the other sister out of a sense of self-defense or self-righteousness. Desertion was not cowardliness; it was a realistic understanding of her own weaknesses and an awareness of her need to maintain her inner freedom.

On the other hand, when Thérèse could cope, she understood that she needed to be charitable in a creative way that would respect her own weaknesses by not forcing herself to do more than she could, while at the same time adapting her own abilities to accommodate the needs and terms of the sister. At the end of her life, Thérèse told Céline simply, *Charity consists in bearing with those who are unbearable* (MSST 229). And Sr. Marie of the Angels, who had been her novice mistress, described Thérèse simply: "She was an angel of peace for everybody" (STL 207).

There may be one final dimension to Thérèse's charity in her telling these stories of trying to fulfill Jesus' command to love even our enemies. Thérèse was writing these examples of love in action in the manuscript that Mother Gonzague had requested her to write. The emphasis on bearing minor inconveniences and feelings of antipathy without retaliating as well as with an emphasis on correcting by loving actions rather than by harshness were exactly the patterns that the superior herself needed to cultivate. Perhaps among the reasons Thérèse wrote these examples of charity was to subtly enlighten Mother Gonzague to move from her usual critical, capricious ways to creative ways of loving the troubled sisters under her care in Carmel. If this be the case, it is another example of Thérèse's great capacity to respond creatively to others' needs on their own terms.

CHAPTER 39

Everything Has Disappeared; I Am Left with Love Alone

Never had Thérèse felt so emotionally and physically strong as during the Lenten season of February and March 1896. She had begun to live more confidently in the truth of her Little Way. Holy Week was approaching, and she was enjoying such a vital, clear faith that the thought of heaven had become the source of deep happiness. Thérèse's awareness of divine love filled her heart. She had made her *Act of Oblation to Merciful Love* in June 1895, and *since that happy day, it seems to me that Love penetrates me and surrounds me. . . . O, how sweet is the way of Love!* (SS 181).

At about midnight on the night of Holy Thursday, April 2, 1896, after ending her time of adoration before the Blessed Sacrament, Thérèse lay in bed.

> *I had scarcely laid my head upon the pillow when I felt something like a bubbling stream mounting to my lips. I didn't know what it was, but I thought that perhaps I was going to die and my soul was flooded with joy. However, as our lamp was extinguished, I told myself I would have to wait until the morning to be certain of my good fortune, for it seemed to me that it was blood I had coughed up. The morning was not long in coming; upon awakening, I thought immediately of the joyful thing that I had to learn, and so I went over to the window. I was able to see that I was not mistaken. Ah! my soul was filled with a great consolation; I was interiorly persuaded that Jesus, on the anniversary of His own death, wanted to have me hear His first call. It was like a sweet and distant murmur that announced the Bridegroom's arrival.* (SS 210–11)

In the morning she reported to Mother Gonzague what had happened, but she described the situation in such a way so as not to alarm the superior. Although she had a chronic sore throat—it had begun two years before and still persisted even after her throat had been cauterized—Thérèse was still young, and recently her health had been good. Now she assured Mother Gonzague that, despite her coughing blood, she did not feel ill and could continue with her duties as before. *I am not in pain, Mother,* she told the prioress, *please do not give me anything special.* Mother Gonzague complied.

Later that day Thérèse, "her face shining with happiness," according to her novice Sr. Marie of the Trinity, shared her joy about the possibility of her *going soon to see God.* She also made the novice promise not to reveal the situation to Pauline. Thérèse fasted as prescribed by the rule on that Good Friday, eating nothing but a little dry bread and drinking only water at noon and at 6:00 p.m. She attended the hours of prayer, did her housework, and in the afternoon climbed a ladder to wash windows. Sr. Marie observed that by now Thérèse was pale and tired, and so she volunteered to help Thérèse finish her work. Thérèse refused, reminding her that this was Good Friday, the day Jesus had endured so much (cf. TLMT 101–2).

That night Thérèse experienced more hemorrhaging: *Jesus gave me the same sign that my entrance into eternal life was not far off* (SS 211).

The next morning, Holy Saturday, Thérèse did not feel excessively weak, and no one except Sr. Marie of the Trinity seemed to notice. When Sr. Marie forthrightly asked Mother Gonzague to dispense Thérèse from at least the obligatory attendance at the earliest morning Divine Office, the superior replied that if Thérèse needed that dispensation, she should ask for it herself. Thérèse continued in her habit of never complaining and never asking for anything special (cf. TLMT 102).

Even though she was physically beginning her decline, Thérèse's faith that she would soon be in the arms of her Beloved gave her a sense of peace that her life might be drawing to a close. She was not alarmed at the prospect of dying; on the contrary she experienced a certain joy. Then, suddenly and with no warning, on Easter Sunday the certainty of faith completely left her, and a thick, dense darkness of confusion and torment inundated her soul. The sense of an existence beyond this life—the security of heaven—suddenly vanished.

This experience of alienation was a totally different feeling from anything that Thérèse had ever known before. Descending over her heart was a blanketing fog of nothingness—the inner distress and terrible pain of deep isolation that was to last almost eighteen months, until the very moment she died.

The surety of her final home in heaven where she would never again feel separation or abandonment, where she would be eternally face to face with her loving Father, secure in his arms, had always been a profound source of hope and consolation. She had hoped that, in heaven, she would finally be in the total embrace of her Beloved Jesus and in the eternal love of Mary, her mother. She had hoped that, in heaven, she would again rejoin her beloved human family, her mother and father together with her two brothers and two sisters who had preceded her. She had hoped that, in heaven, she would continue to share God's love with those on earth. Now, even the thought of heaven became a source of torment.

Was there an afterlife at all? Thérèse was utterly distressed. Would she ever see Jesus face to face? Was she to be separated from her beloved family forever? Was the hope of being eternally in the arms of her Beloved a mere illusion? In her imagination she heard the mocking voices of those who had no faith. The voices of sinners were saying contemptuously to her, *You are dreaming about the light; . . . You believe that one day you will walk out of this fog that surrounds you! Advance, advance; rejoice in death which will give you not what you hope for but a night still more profound, the night of nothingness* (SS 213). Except for a few brief flashes of light, the fog of darkness totally and continuously covered her soul. She was not going to die of love; her life had been meaningless; her way, an illusion.

Thérèse was entering a profound spiritual trial, beginning a long walk through a dark underground cavern, a tunnel with no end. It would be a slow, laborious walk of months and months of dark emotional and spiritual desolation, devoid of hope, barren and empty. The dense fog of the absurdity of faith had encompassed her heart. She was seized by a radical, existential sense of nothingness. This experience of an endless night of darkness, coming upon her so suddenly and so unexpectedly, was not like the aridity of prayer and the loss of the sense of the presence of God that Thérèse had experienced before. This was more profound, more ominous, more pervasive, more compelling, more devastating.

Throughout her eighteen-month-long trial of faith, Thérèse's physical health gradually but continuously deteriorated. Her worsening physical suffering, her deepening emotional distress, and her spiritual desolation formed an impenetrable wall of pain, a wall that surrounded and isolated her.

After the hemorrhage on the night of Holy Thursday, Thérèse continued to live the daily routine of her religious life in a spirit of dedication and obedience, fulfilling all her obligations with the novices and the community in as faithful a way as her physical condition permitted. She carried out her responsibilities, but without any feelings of contentment. *I do not have the joy of faith,* she wrote. *I am trying to carry out its works at least* (SS 213).

The sisters did not notice her inner turmoil. She was as kind and congenial as she had always been. She continued to write religious plays for the community. She continued to compose religious poetry for any sister who asked. Her writings, filled with religious sentiments and expressions of faith, edified the sisters with sublime ideas and vivid images of spiritual truths.

Although Thérèse continued to speak of the joys of heaven, now she spoke only of what she desperately wanted to believe. *When I sing of the happiness of heaven and of the eternal possession of God, I feel no joy in this, for I sing simply what I WANT TO BELIEVE* (SS 214). To her novice Sr. Marie of the Trinity, she confided, *I sing what I want to believe, but it is without any feeling. I couldn't even tell you to what degree the night is dark in my soul, for fear that I would make you share my temptations* (TLMT 33).

As she entered the darkness of this night, she reflected on a poem by St. John of the Cross and composed this one herself:

I suffer, yes! From lack of Light
(Life here is short and fugitive),
At least, though, in this earthly night
In Love Celestial I live. . . .
Though on this path which leads above
Unnumbered perils may appear,
My will is to endure, by Love,
The Darkness of my exile here. (CP 144)

It is true that at times, Thérèse acknowledged, *a very small ray of the sun comes to illumine my darkness, and then the trial ceases for an instant, but afterwards the memory of this ray, instead of causing me joy, makes my darkness even more dense* (SS 214).

In May there was a moment of consolation. Thérèse had a dream in which three Carmelite sisters from heaven appeared; one was Venerable Sr. Anne of Jesus, a companion of St. Teresa of Avila and founder of the Carmelites in France in the early seventeenth century. In the dream the joyful Thérèse boldly asked Sr. Anne,

"O Mother! I beg you, tell me whether God will leave me for a long time on earth. Will He come soon to get me?" Smiling tenderly, the

saint whispered: *"Yes, soon, soon, I promise you."* I added: *"Mother, tell me further if God is not asking something more of me than my poor little actions and desires. Is He content with me?"* The saint's face took on an expression incomparably more tender than the first time she spoke to me. Her look and her caresses were the sweetest of answers. However, she said to me: *"God asks no other thing from you. He is content, very content!"* . . . *My heart was filled with joy* (SS 191).

Thérèse awoke from sleep, and *the storm was no longer raging, heaven was calm and serene. I believed, I felt there was a heaven and that this heaven is peopled with souls who actually love me, who consider me their child* (SS 191). The dream, a glimpse of a beacon in the expanse of darkness, was an important flash of light that faded just as quickly as it had come.

She, who as a child had pointed out to her father a constellation of stars that formed her own initial T in the dark night, now saw only *a wall which reaches right up to the heavens and covers the starry firmament* (SS 214). She was experiencing what it must be like for those who have no faith, who reject the light of Christ. She could identify with those who were agnostics and atheists. *It's the reasoning of the worst materialists, which is imposed upon my mind,* she said; but *I never cease making acts of faith* (HLC 257–58).

Even though she still clung to faith, she knew emotionally and intellectually what the torment of the absence of faith actually was. She was suffering vicariously, enduring the trial of unbelief, for those who did not believe, for those who refused to believe, who rejected divine love through their own choices. The atheists were her new *brothers,* as she said, to whom she had been introduced in this experience by divine providence. She no longer was separated from the impious. Rather, now she knew what it was to be one of them; she could pray for them and with them from her own experience. Instead of being at heaven's eternal banquet, Thérèse found herself at the table of sinners.

Courageously Thérèse resigned herself to be in this state of spiritual darkness for as long as God willed it. She prayed for those who sat alone at the same table and asked God that they be brought to the heavenly banquet. She was willing to share this table with the atheist and the agnostic and all those who had no faith. I am ready and willing, she prayed, *to eat the bread of sorrow as long as You desire it* (SS 212).

In empathy with her unbelieving brothers and sisters, she begged pardon and mercy, asking her Beloved to give them, together with her, a participation in God's presence in heaven. In her own name and in the name of all those who suffered the pain and distress of unbelief, she prayed the prayer of the publican, *"Have pity on us, O Lord, for we are poor sinners!"* [Luke 18:13]. *I am happy not to enjoy this beautiful heaven on this earth, so that He will open it for all eternity to poor unbelievers. . . . The only grace I ask of You is that I never offend You!* (SS 214, 212).

Seeking some support and relief from the temptation to doubt and the *frightful thoughts* that enveloped her, Thérèse confided her struggles to the rather stern and severe Fr. Youf, her ordinary confessor. Over the years, when she had reported that she had fallen asleep during prayer, he had scolded her (GC I 659, note 5); now, responding to her plea with his usual fearful, Jansenistic style, he told her, "Don't dwell on these thoughts! It is very dangerous." Thérèse was further distressed, but later joked that *this is hardly consoling to hear* (HLC 58). Of course, it was not that she wanted to dwell on these *frightful thoughts*, as her confessor warned; it was rather that these thoughts were inundating and overtaking her heart and spirit. She felt even more isolated and alone.

Thérèse never argued about the existence of heaven with those mocking voices that told her that all was meaningless and nothingness. In this spiritual combat, she knew that, like the physical duels touted in her time, a direct confrontation would actually have involved more bravado than bravery, coming from arrogance and false self-confidence. Incessantly she struggled, but her struggle took the form of flight. *When my enemies come to provoke me, I conduct myself bravely. Knowing it is cowardly to enter into a duel, I turn my back on my enemies. . . . But I run towards Jesus. I tell Him I am ready to shed my blood to the last drop to profess my faith in the existence of heaven* (SS 213).

Previously she had imagined herself standing under the cross, catching the blood of Christ on behalf of sinners and unbelievers. Now she was participating in Jesus' own experience of darkness, from which he had cried out, "My God, my God why have you abandoned me?" (Matthew 27:46). Thérèse was suspended between heaven and earth, hanging with Christ in the void of darkness and nothingness. Her Carmelite vocation to pray had reached, in her own experience, a final degree of purity and inclusivity.

Purifying her of all attachments, even those associated with faith, this inner darkness and distress became a manifestation for Thérèse of divine providence—another experience of grace in disguise. *Never have I felt before this,* she wrote, *how sweet and merciful the Lord really is, for He did not send me this trial until the moment I was capable of bearing it. A little earlier I believe it would have plunged me into a state of discouragement. Now it is taking away everything that could be a natural satisfaction in my desire for heaven* (SS 214).

It was during this time that she marked over the lintel of the door of her room the words *Jesus is my only love* (STL 128). In love, with all the power and courage of her mighty will, she clung to faith. This was the battle she had been preparing for over the years, when she had honed her willpower in her many personal struggles and spiritual combats. She had imagined herself a warrior like Joan of Arc, and now she was in the conflict of faith, with love her major weapon—her only weapon.

He knows very well that while I do not have the joy of faith, I am trying to carry out its works at least. I believe I have made more acts of faith in this past year, Thérèse said, *than all through my whole life* (SS 213). Even if the sun were blocked from her view, she knew its reality. Even so, her loving Father was absent to her feelings. She acknowledged to one of the sisters, *If you only knew what darkness I am plunged into. I don't believe in eternal life; I think that after this life there is nothing. Everything has disappeared on me, and I am left with love alone* (STL 195).

CHAPTER 40

What Good Does It Do to Defend or Explain Ourselves?

Thérèse was slowly dying, deteriorating physically while enduring the emotionally and spiritually distressing trial of faith. At this very time a series of events plunged Thérèse into a new depth of emotional suffering. She became associated in a most personal way with a particular unbeliever, one of the impious whom Thérèse had never before personally known but with whom, through her trial of faith, she had begun to identify.

In June 1895, the year before Thérèse had begun her slow descent into the dark tunnel, she made her *Act of Oblation to Merciful Love*. Coincidentally just a short time after that, Thérèse heard of Diana Vaughan, a new convert to Catholicism. In May Diana had also offered herself to God, but in keeping with the tradition of the times, her offering was to divine justice.

Through the intercession of Joan of Arc, Diana had just converted from Satanism as well as from Freemasonry, both of which were notoriously opposed to Catholicism. Diana's name appeared in the Catholic newspapers, and she was the talk of the Catholics of France. Diana had even written a eucharistic novena of reparation, which Leo XIII himself had read with pleasure and approval.

Thérèse's uncle Isidore Guérin, having sold his pharmacy some years before, was now working as a journalist for the local Catholic newspaper and probably gave the sisters at Carmel copies of Diana's pious writings. Thérèse had the opportunity to read them. She was so impressed that she copied by hand long sections from Diana's eucharistic novena. Pauline, still prioress and also fascinated by Diana's story, asked Thérèse to write something, a prayer perhaps, that might be inspired by the conversion of this "new Joan of Arc." In response, in June 1896 Thérèse composed the play *The Triumph of Humility*. In it she acknowledged her respect for Diana by using the same names for the evil spirits that Diana had given them in her eucharistic novena of reparation.

Shared devotion to Joan of Arc also bonded Thérèse with Diana. Joan's cause for beatification had been introduced just the year before Diana had converted, and Thérèse had written two plays about Joan. Thérèse was deeply touched by Diana's piety and said that *my greatest desire would be*

. . . to see her united with Jesus in our little Carmel. The thought of the possibility of this once notorious sinner—who had participated in Satanic rituals and devil worship—now entering Carmel, delighted the entire community.

Pauline also asked Thérèse to compose a poem in honor of Diana, but Thérèse was not inspired. Instead, Pauline wrote a letter to Diana and included a copy of a photograph from the play Thérèse had written the year before, *Joan of Arc Accomplishing Her Mission*. Thérèse herself added a few words of encouragement. The photograph showed Thérèse portraying Joan imprisoned in chains, in deep sadness and pain, with Céline as St. Catherine comforting her.

Pauline, Thérèse, and all the sisters at Carmel saw Diana as a kind of new Joan of Arc, battling the forces of evil at war with the church. During this historical time, many saw the pope as a prisoner of the Vatican fighting against the civil powers that had overrun the Papal States. On the occasion of Thérèse's profession of vows in 1890, Br. Siméon, Thérèse's friend in Rome who had obtained for her an apostolic blessing, had written her requesting prayers for the pope. "Hell is triumphing in Rome," he warned. The pope is being persecuted, "afflicted and humbled" by civil enemies. And now God had raised up Diana, the modern-day Joan. In the struggle between good and evil, Diana stood against the devil and the impious.

Taking time from her writings defending the church against the Freemasons, Diana replied to Pauline's letter with an expression of appreciation for her encouragement and for the photograph.

So famous was Diana becoming among Catholics throughout Europe as an apologist for truth and as an adversary of Freemasonry, that a Roman commission was established to investigate her conversion and validate the orthodoxy of her writings. The report of the commission would also address some mounting skepticism. Thérèse herself now expressed reservations after she had learned that Diana had criticized an Italian bishop.

Meanwhile the religious and national press of France had been publicizing Diana and her story for almost two years, without having ever actually interviewed her. Taking sanctuary in convents to prevent retaliation from the Freemasons, she had managed to avoid all personal appearances.

Responding to increasing insistence that Diana be available to the press, Léo Taxil, a confidant of Diana and her spokesperson, made arrangements for a public press conference to be held during April 1897 in Paris. Taxil himself, a former notorious Freemason, had also converted to Christianity. He appeared on stage at the conference, seated with a large photograph projected behind him. It was the very photograph of Thérèse portraying Joan of Arc, with Céline as St. Catherine, that Pauline had sent to Diana. The picture added a note of drama and piety, proclaiming the presence of the modern Joan.

Convening the conference, which included about four hundred members of the press and guests, Léo Taxil announced that he had an important preliminary statement to make before Diana would be introduced. Then, to the hushed and expectant audience, he bluntly announced that the reason Diana Vaughan had never before appeared personally for a press conference was that she, in fact, did not exist!

In the stunned silence that followed, Taxil revealed to the astonishment of his audience that he himself had invented Diana's identity as well as her history, her conversion, and her writings. Diana Vaughan was Taxil's elaborate hoax, a deception that had extended in various guises over the previous twelve years. Furthermore, Taxil himself had not converted from Freemasonry. He was more than ever an opponent of the Catholic faith and had fabricated Diana's story simply to embarrass the church and to show plainly how superficial Catholic piety really was. The press conference ended in total chaos.

Taxil had succeeded in a plot that had deceived everyone from the simple faithful to the pope himself. Thérèse and the sisters of Carmel had been completely hoodwinked and totally embarrassed. They had been personally implicated as part of the lie, because the image of Thérèse and Céline had formed the dramatic backdrop for Taxil's revelations. During the news conference itself, but without mentioning them by name, Léo Taxil pointedly mocked the pious and stupid faith of the Carmelites who portrayed Joan and Catherine, as well as "the poor imbecile" who had so naively sent Diana the photograph projected behind him. The photograph appeared in the press coverage of the incident throughout France.

The Catholic press and particularly *La Normand*, the newspaper for which Isidore worked, denounced Taxil as a "wretched buffoon" and a "disgusting swindler." Through the news releases passed to the convent by her uncle, Thérèse came to know this infamous atheist. A year before, as she had entered into her inner darkness, she had identified with the impious and atheists and willingly prayed for them, calling them *her brothers*. At that time, however, her prayer was not focused on anyone with whom she was actually acquainted. A distant relative by marriage was a proclaimed atheist, but Thérèse had never met him and really did not personally know anyone who had completely rejected the faith. Even Pranzini, her *first child,* was a believer; and Hyacinth Loyson, although separated from the church, was still a Christian.

Until Taxil, Thérèse had always thought that those who denied the faith and the afterlife were actually knowingly lying. She had written, *I was unable to believe there were really impious people who had no faith. I believed they were actually speaking against their own inner-convictions when they denied the existence of heaven, that beautiful heaven where God Himself wanted to be their Eternal Reward* (SS 211).

Until Taxil, she had not personally known anyone who with malice denied and ridiculed the faith, nor had she known how ignoble and how vicious such a person could actually be. Now she had encountered a person who had deliberately chosen to remove himself from God and whose life testified to the real possibility of unbelief, agnosticism, atheism, and self-deception. Thérèse was shaken to her depths.

Céline, also sickened by the experience, wrote a few days after Taxil's press conference that "one sees so many contemptible things, so many defections in the world, that disgust fills one's soul." Thérèse may have had similar sentiments.

Clinging to faith and putting her feelings behind her, Thérèse tore up the letter that she had previously received from Diana gratefully acknowledging her picture, threw the pieces on the compost pile, and never spoke of the matter again.

In her physical pain and spiritual suffering, she was desperately struggling in her own heart with the very truth that Taxil was mocking. As she continued to live in the shadow of the *wall which reaches right up to the heavens* and to walk the *dark tunnel* toward her death, Thérèse must have wondered: if Taxil, in the name of the fictitious Diana, could have fabricated from his imagination such beautiful descriptions of spiritual realities to deceive others, then could it be equally possible to deceive oneself in one's own imagination about heaven, about God, about eternal life?

Thérèse had heard her own inner darkness, *borrowing the voice of sinners, say mockingly to me . . . you are dreaming about the eternal possession*

of the Creator of all these marvels; . . . death . . . will give you . . . [only]
the night of nothingness (SS 213). The voice of Taxil was the voice of one of
those mocking sinners.

Taxil had tried to show in a theatrical way what Freud, at this same
period, was trying to prove in a more scientific way: that heaven, indeed all
of religious faith, is an illusion. A year before, Thérèse had written about
her own personal sentiments, and similar thoughts must have lingered in her
mind through this period, even until her death: *Is pure love in my heart? Are*
my measureless desires only but a dream, a folly? Ah! If this be so, Jesus,
then enlighten me, for You know I am seeking only the truth. If my desires
are rash, then make them disappear, for these desires are the greatest mar-
tyrdom to me (SS 197).

Thérèse's desires were a martyrdom because they were being confronted
with the psychological reality of her experience of nothingness. Thérèse
was experiencing the sort of darkness Taxil must have known as the result
of his willfully rejecting the light. The struggle between darkness and light,
which was to continue at the core of Thérèse's being until her final hour, had
now taken on a further dimension. If, for Thérèse, there had been anything
abstract or theoretical about this struggle between darkness and light, it had
been completely removed by her encounter with Taxil.

Through her meeting with Taxil she had been drawn into deeper regions
of darkness and doubt, yet she continued to cling to radical faith, to confidence, and to love. Although Thérèse never again mentioned Diana Vaughan
or Taxil, and although she must have humanly felt great repugnance toward
him, perhaps even experiencing him as an "enemy,'" she welcomed him as
a special brother with whom she hoped to spend heaven thanking God for
his divine mercy.

With Taxil, who was living out the sentiments of her own trial of faith,
Thérèse wanted to share God's love in the mutual pain of darkness. Willingly,
desperately clinging to faith, she would pray for him, *begging pardon for her*
brothers: "Have pity on us, O Lord, for we are poor sinners!" [Luke 18:13].
Oh! Lord, send us away justified. May all those who were not enlightened
by the bright flame of faith one day see it shine. O Jesus! If it is needful that
the table soiled by . . . [nonbelievers] *be purified by a soul who loves You,*
then I desire to eat the bread of trial at this table . . . filled with bitterness at
which poor sinners are eating until the day set by You (SS 212).

Just a few weeks before the humiliating exposé of Diana, Thérèse had told Pauline, *When we're misunderstood and judged unfavorably, what good does it do to defend or explain ourselves? Let the matter drop and say nothing. It's so much better to say nothing and allow others to judge us as they please!* (HLC 36). These sentiments, too, continued to linger in her heart, but for Thérèse the possibility of self-deception would always be a greater trial than the pain of being misunderstood and judged unfavorably.

A month after Taxil's news conference, Thérèse wrote another poem identifying with the inner sufferings of Joan of Arc:

When God, the Lord of Hosts gave you the victory.
. . . .
A fleeting glory, though! You needed to possess
That aureole, a saint's which never can grow dim,
Your Love held out to you His cup of bitterness—
You drank; and human kind rejected you, like Him,
For, in a lightless cell, weighed down by heavy chains,
There then were rained on you the strangers' cruel jeers.
No friend of yours was found to share with you your pains—
None was there to step forth and wipe away your tears. (CP 206)

Thérèse, who saw herself in a similar trial of faith, had experienced in the Taxil episode one of Joan's deepest sufferings, as new to Thérèse as it was unexpected by Joan: betrayal. Thérèse's identification with Jesus, who had suffered betrayal, gave her deep consolation, but nothing in her experience relieved the continuing deep inner distress, the dense fog of doubt, darkness, and nothingness that continued to crush her heart. She was plunged into a profound solitude that was to become more and more excruciating in the weeks ahead.

CHAPTER 41

He Sees the Blind Hope That I Have in His Mercy

Five months after Thérèse first coughed up blood on that late Holy Thursday night, April 2, 1896, Marie asked her to take time during her annual private retreat to explain her religious teaching in writing. Marie was not aware of what had happened that Holy Thursday night or that her little sister was suffering a severe trial of faith. But Marie did have an intuition that Thérèse might not have long to live, and she wanted to more fully understand her spiritual wisdom. Knowing that her Little Way was meant for many beside herself, Thérèse responded by writing to her sister a short three-page cover letter and a twelve-page manuscript. These two documents—which has come to us as Manuscript B of *Story of a Soul*—plus the letter Thérèse wrote subsequently to Marie constitute what has been called the charter of the Little Way.

Thérèse entered the time of her private retreat in September 1896. It was the sixth anniversary of her profession and her eighth year in Carmel; this next year would be the last of her life. As she wrote her reply to Marie's request, her thoughts turned to that time of her consecration to Jesus. On that occasion her desires had been to be a spouse of Jesus, to be a Carmelite, standing under the cross beside Mary, the mother of all souls. Thérèse had expected that those relationships of spouse, Carmelite, and mother, carried to fulfillment, would be the essence of her vocation. But now Thérèse found herself desiring something more.

She had deep desires to express her love by participating more fully in Jesus' redemptive work. She desired to be a martyr giving her blood as a testimony of her love; to be a priest who would preach the gospel and make the Eucharist available to those seeking Jesus' love; to be a doctor of the church who would proclaim the teaching of the gospel; to be an apostle who would be a missionary throughout the world. The list seemed to be endless.

Thérèse, who had chosen all as a child, now once again wanted to *choose all* for God. She did not want to be a saint by half measures; in fact, she wanted to extend her vocation to include the vocations of all the members of the mystical body. Her desires seemed to be infinite; her capacities, so limited. She was perplexed. *O my Jesus! What is your answer to all my fool-*

ishness? Is there a soul more little, more powerless than mine? (SS 193).

Thérèse again went to the Scriptures, again to St. Paul, and read about the most excellent way of love (1 Corinthians 12:27–13:13). She had read this passage many times before, but now as she reflected prayerfully, in a flash of grace she understood that every vocation could be fulfilled only if they were expressions of love. If any works were done without love, the members of the mystical body would not be realizing their vocations. She came to find peace in these thoughts:

> *I understood that if the Church had a body composed of different members, the most necessary and most noble of all could not be lacking to it, and so I understood that the Church had a Heart and that this Heart was BURNING WITH LOVE. I understood it was Love alone that made the Church's members act, that if Love ever became extinct, apostles would not preach the Gospel and martyrs would not shed their blood. I understood that LOVE COMPRISED ALL VOCATIONS, THAT LOVE WAS EVERYTHING, THAT IT EMBRACED ALL TIMES AND PLACES. . . . IN A WORD, THAT IT WAS ETERNAL!* (SS 194)

Love was the most excellent way, and the smallest act done under the impulse of pure love was of more value than all other acts. Thérèse wanted to share in that pure love. In that way she would participate in all the vocations of all the members of Christ's body, and her desire to *choose all* would be fulfilled. As her vocation in the mystical body she would choose to be at the fountain of love, at the heart itself. In that flash of grace she delighted. *Then, in the excess of my delirious joy, I cried out: O Jesus, my Love; . . . my vocation, at last I have found it. . . . MY VOCATION IS LOVE! Yes, I have found my place in the Church and it is you, O my God, who have given me this place—in the heart of the Church, my mother, I shall be LOVE. Thus I shall be everything—and thus my dream will be fulfilled!* (SS 194).

These spiritual revelations, *the greatest graces* of her retreat, brought to a deeper fruition the graces of her being called to stand at the foot of the cross. Even as she continued to experience the desolation of faith in the tunnel of darkness, she experienced herself called to be at the center of the mystical body, at the heart of all humankind, at the still point of the dynamism of love, indeed, at the confluence of the union of all creatures with the creator, and thus to participate in divine love flowing throughout the entire universe.

It was a moment of *delirious joy* for Thérèse; more importantly, it was a moment of deep calm and peace in the midst of the thick, dense fog of confusion, torment, and nothingness that was filling her soul. It was a brief flash of light, assuring her of the truth of her path and calling her home into God's heart. Then Thérèse's awareness quickly returned to the reality constantly before her: the spiritual darkness that now permeated her life together with her pervading sense of littleness. Where would her weakness fit into this splendid imagery? Well, her weakness would actually give her a certain boldness to cry for the assistance of all who participated in her desires, the angels, the saints, and especially the Blessed Virgin.

Thérèse's weakness also made her understand again that, while the proof of love consisted in acts, especially acts of sacrifice, these acts would be very small, very simple. They would be like the little flowers that adorned the notebook Pauline had given her in preparation for her First Communion. They would mean nothing to anyone except her Beloved. *I have no other means of proving my love for You*, she wrote, addressing Jesus, *other than that of strewing flowers, that is, not allowing one little sacrifice to escape, not one look, one work, profiting by all the smallest things and doing them through love* (SS 196).

She would continue to do her simple acts, her *nothings*, in union with Christ, inconspicuously serving others, enduring the inner darkness as well as the ongoing difficulties of her ordinary life, but now out of a deeper awareness of the nature of love, at the heart of the mystical body, and with a more ardent desire to please Jesus in his work of redemption. She would move more and more deeply into the disposition of abandoning herself to the will of her loving Father. Her life was like a rose being unpetalled for Jesus' pleasure. She composed a love poem:

> *Delightful Child! The rose can deck Your Feast-days when*
> *   It's at its height.*
> *The rose, un-petalled though—thrown to the wind's will, then*
> *   Blown out of sight!*
> *That rose gives up itself—all artless—that it may*
> *   No longer live.*

Child Jesus! I, to You give myself up that way—
   Joyously give!
Upon such petals then one walks without regret:
   And their debris
Are ornaments by no deliberation set—
   This now I see.
For You, I've strewn my life—my future, with what's gone:
   To mortal eye,
A rose that always will be withered from now on,
   I ought to die. (CP 209)

Other saints were like great eagles, but Thérèse compared herself to *a weak little bird* [that] *dare*[s] *to gaze upon the Divine Sun, the Sun of Love . . . and wills to fly toward the bright Sun. . . .* She knew more and more with each passing day as she entered these last months of life that *alas! The only thing it can do is raise its little wings; to fly is not within its little power!* (SS 198). If she were to fly to the source of divine love, she would need the intercessory assistance of the great eagles. In particular she would need the *Divine Eagle's own wings.* To enter the divine love, she was ready to receive that love in surrender and gratitude in the simple experiences of her life.

Thérèse was certain that this would happen because of her loving Father's great condescension. He would stoop down to fetch this little bird, and draw it into himself. And not only would her Beloved stoop to her, God would stoop to all little souls, those poor in spirit who opened their hearts to receive divine assistance. These were the legion of little souls throughout the world and throughout the ages that Thérèse wished to bring to the fire of divine love.

Yet for all her expressions of fervor, inwardly Thérèse continued her long, slow walk. *Do not think that I am swimming in consolations,* Thérèse wrote to Marie from her darkness; *oh, no! My consolation is to have none on this earth. Without showing himself, without making his voice heard . . . Jesus deigned to show me the only road that leads to this Divine Furnace, and this road is the surrender of the little child who sleeps without fear in its Father's arms* (SS 187–88).

When she read the manuscript in which Thérèse shared all these thoughts and images of her desires and fervor, Marie was taken aback. "You are possessed, absolutely possessed by God," she wrote to Thérèse. "I would like to be possessed, too, by the good Jesus," Marie added in a surge of passion; but, in truth, she was frightened and embarrassed by Thérèse's intensity.

Among all the various roles Thérèse desired to fulfill in the mystical body, Marie focused on Thérèse's desire to be a martyr. She responded to Thérèse that "like the young man in the Gospel, a certain feeling of sadness came over me in view of your extraordinary desires for martyrdom" (GC II 997). Marie felt shame. She could not ask God for martyrdom; she was afraid.

Thérèse replied immediately, in a letter trying to accommodate Marie's feelings, by inviting her to consider again the imagery of the little bird that needed the wings of the Divine Eagle. That story told it all: it was all God's work. My *desires of Martyrdom are nothing;* Thérèse told her sister, *they are not what give me the unlimited confidence that I feel in my heart. . . . These desires are a consolation that Jesus grants at times to weak souls like mine, but when He does not give this consolation, it is a grace of privilege* (GC II 999).

Are you not ready to suffer all that God will desire? Thérèse asked Marie rhetorically, addressing her feelings of fear and shame. *If you want to feel joy, to have an attraction for suffering, it is your consolation that you are seeking.* Spiritual good feelings, Thérèse wrote from her own inner darkness, could in fact be a stumbling block, because one could secretly take self-centered delight in them as a kind of spiritual *sparkle.* With this understanding, Thérèse wrote confidently to Marie that she, without spiritual good feelings, was more open to grace than Thérèse herself. Faith needed to supersede feelings. If you do not feel great desires, Thérèse reminded Marie, you still have faith and can actually rejoice in feeling nothing, since then you are truly *poor in spirit* (GC II 999).

Thérèse reassured Marie with great tact:

Understand that to love Jesus, to be His victim of love, the weaker one is, without desires or virtues, the more suited one is for the workings of this consuming and transforming Love. The desire alone to be a victim suffices, but we must consent to remain always poor and without strength, and this is the difficulty, for "The truly poor in spirit, where do we find him? You must look for him from afar," said the psalmist. He does not say that you must look for him among great souls, but "from afar," that is to say in lowliness, in nothingness. Ah! let us remain then very far from all that sparkles, let us love our littleness, let us love to feel nothing, then, we shall be poor in spirit and Jesus will come to look for us and however far we may be, He will transform us in flames of love. (GC II 999)

What really pleases Jesus, Thérèse wrote to Marie, is that He sees me loving my littleness and my poverty, the blind hope that I have in His mercy. . . . This is my only treasure, dear Godmother, why would this treasure not be yours? (GC II 999). Thérèse was inviting her sister to accept and rejoice in her own spiritual poverty, to surrender and be grateful to divine love.

Then Thérèse appealed to Marie's own words, when Marie had written, "I would like to be possessed, too, by the good Jesus." She assured Marie that even in her fear, if she really wanted to be possessed by God, then I am sure that God would not give you the desire to be POSSESSED by Him, by His Merciful Love if He were not reserving this favor for you, or rather He has already given it to you, since you have given yourself to Him, since you desire to be consumed by Him, and since God never gives desires that He cannot realize (GC II 1000).

When Thérèse had been a young child, Marie, her godmother, had led her into the divine mysteries. When Thérèse had struggled with scruples and her fear of displeasing God, Marie had been at her side, guiding her young sister through her anxieties and worries and helping her put her concerns into the perspective of divine love. Now it was Thérèse's turn. She was leading Marie into those same mysteries of God's love, the foundation of her Little Way, with the surety of a mature spiritual guide.

CHAPTER 42

Perfection Seems Simple to Me

As she was coming to the end of her human journey, Thérèse was now reaching the deepest stages of her spiritual purification and transformation. The continuing trial of faith, purifying her of all self-seeking and all attachments, even to her image of heaven, made her totally available to divine love and completely willing to love. By challenging everything in her natural desire for heaven in the future, her trial led her to involve herself more deeply in life's present moment. Profoundly conscious that everything in life was passing, Thérèse accepted the present moment as the only available time to give herself freely to her Beloved in love. Referring to her death, she said, *I shall see God, true; but as far as being in His presence, I am totally there here on earth* (HLC 45). *I no longer have any great desires except that of loving to the point of dying of love*, she wrote (SS 214).

At about this time Thérèse received two great consolations that brought her joy and fulfillment in her missionary zeal and in her need for human relationships. She developed relationships with two young men: one a newly ordained priest, the other a seminarian soon to be ordained. Knowing that the special ministry of Carmel was to pray for priests, each of these young men had requested prayers from Carmel. Each had written separately to the mother prioress, asking contact with a nun who would pray especially for him.

As it happened, just two months after that fateful Easter Sunday when Thérèse entered the dark tunnel of faith, Mother Gonzague had called Thérèse into her office to announce that Fr. Adolphe Roulland, twenty-six years old, had requested that one of the nuns be a spiritual companion, praying especially for him. He was newly ordained and was about to move to China as a missionary. Thérèse hesitated to accept, not because of her inner turmoil but because Pauline, less than a year before, when she was still prioress, had also asked Thérèse to accept the responsibility of being a spiritual sister to a seminarian. Maurice Bellière, twenty-two, was just about to finish seminary training and move to Africa, also as a missionary.

Thérèse wondered, in view of her commitment to Maurice Bellière, if another sister might be a better spiritual companion to Fr. Roulland. Mother Gonzague simply said, "No, the zeal of a Carmelite should set the world on fire." Thérèse "could have several brothers," Mother Gonzague announced.

In fact, Thérèse was delighted. She had a great missionary desire, and two missionaries were not too many to fulfill her own zeal. Also, Thérèse had always wanted to have a brother priest, now she had two to replace her two brothers who had died in infancy. When Zélie Martin was pregnant with Thérèse, Zélie had hoped that the baby would be a boy who might become a priest and a preacher. Moreover, Thérèse herself had always wanted to be a priest and a missionary. Now circumstances were allowing Thérèse to fulfill vicariously her own desires as well as those of her parents (cf. GC II 1094). *I would really have to go back to my childhood days to recapture once more the memory of joys so great,* she later wrote (SS 251).

With these two men, Thérèse became more a spiritual mother than a sister or mere spiritual companion. In the letters she wrote to them, she shared moments of deep spiritual intimacy and some of her most profound religious insights. They were men who needed prayers, but they also needed spiritual instruction, and Thérèse gave them both. She, who throughout her life seldom revealed her pain to others and was reluctant to mention her difficulty of faith lest she scandalize her sisters, now began to write to her *spiritual brothers* about her trials, but more so about what she had come to know in faith. She opened to them a rich and profound gospel vision of holiness and of her loving Father's gentleness and merciful love.

Maurice Bellière, her first spiritual brother, was a year younger than Thérèse. He was in his second year of seminary training in 1895 when he first wrote to the Lisieux Carmel to say that, for all of his good intentions and efforts, he was having a "hard time absorbing the spirit of the church and holding myself to all the demands of the seminary rule." He pleaded that one of the nuns "devote herself particularly to the salvation of my soul, and obtain for me the grace to be faithful to the vocation God has given me, that of a priest and missionary" (*Maurice and Thérèse: The Story of a Love* by Patrick Ahern, 15–16).

Pauline, the prioress at the time, immediately asked her little sister to be the spiritual companion that Bellière needed. Delighted, Thérèse began praying for him, and Pauline wrote to the seminarian informing him that a special saintly nun would be his spiritual sister. He wrote back promptly, expressing his gratitude, but then delayed for almost a year before writing again to say that he had been obliged to leave the seminary to fulfill his military service.

"I am a soldier," he wrote. "I have had many a fall, many unheard of stupidities, in the midst of this world which has taken hold of me again. I have just committed the most beautiful [contemptible] of all. . . . I am plunged into a deplorable situation, and my dear sister, Thérèse of the Child Jesus, must tear me away from it at all costs. . . . She must or I am lost. . . . Tell her she must" (GC II 972).

Thérèse's reply, her first letter to Bellière, expressed her empathy and sorrow for his spiritual distress, and, with touching sensitivity, she assumed some responsibility for his failings by attributing them to her own lack of fervor. He was, after all, her *spiritual brother.* Her own experience with disguised graces had prepared her to write to him about his failings: *When Jesus calls a soul to direct and to save multitudes of other souls, it is necessary that He have him experience the temptations and trials of life.* She prayed that *you may be not only a good missionary but a saint all on fire with the love of God and souls; I beg you to obtain also for me this love so that I may help you in your apostolic work* (GC II 1010).

Having felt understood and encouraged by Thérèse, Fr. Bellière spoke honestly in subsequent letters of his struggles and weaknesses, of his need to break himself away from some strong attachments and habits of "easy" living. Thérèse's replies always reminded him of God's great mercy, and that, as she knew so well, human efforts do not guarantee success in dealing with difficult feelings and resisting human weaknesses.

It is very consoling, she wrote to him, *to think that Jesus, the Strong God, knew our weaknesses, that He trembled at the sight of the bitter chalice, this chalice that He had in the past so ardently desired to drink.* And she acknowledged to him that she herself was *no angel,* but was *very imperfect—yet who in spite of her poverty wants, like yourself, to work for the glory of God* (GC II 1042–43).

Do not think that it is humility that prevents me from acknowledging the gifts of God, Thérèse wrote. *I know He has done great things in me, and I sing of this each day with joy. I remember that the one must love more who has been forgiven more* [Luke 7:47], *so I take care to make my life an act of love, and I am no longer disturbed at being a little soul; on the contrary, I take delight in this.* She would never be ready, she added, *if the Lord does not see fit to transform me* (GC II 1085).

Fr. Adolphe Roulland, her second spiritual brother, was three years older than she. As a priest of the Foreign Missions, he embarked in September 1896 for China. Despite all of Roulland's formal education, which far exceeded her own, Thérèse did not hesitate to correct his Jansenistic thinking and to share with him her Little Way of spirituality. She led the future missionary on a path that completely subverted the conventional notion of perfection and opposed the spirituality of fear that he had learned in the seminary:

I know one must be very pure to appear before the God of all holiness, but I know, too, that the Lord is infinitely just; and it is this justice, which frightens so many souls, that is the object of my joy and confidence. To be just is not only to exercise severity in order to punish the guilty; It is also to recognize right intentions and to reward virtue. I expect as much from God's justice as from His mercy. It is because He is just that. "He is compassionate and filled with gentleness, slow to punish and abundant in mercy, for He knows our frailty, He remembers we are only dust. As a father has tenderness for his children, so the Lord has compassion on us" [Psalm 103:8, 14, 13]. . . . How would He allow Himself to be overcome in generosity? (GC II 1093)

She continued to press the point:

This is, Brother, what I think of God's justice; my way is all confidence and love. I do not understand souls who fear a Friend so tender. At times, when I am reading certain spiritual treatises in which perfection is shown through a thousand obstacles, surrounded by a crowd of illusions, my poor little mind quickly tires; I close the learned book that is breaking my head and drying up my heart, and I take up Holy Scripture. Then all seems luminous to me; . . . perfection seems simple to me, I see it is sufficient to recognize one's nothingness and to abandon oneself as a child into God's arms. Leaving to great souls, to great minds the beautiful books I cannot understand, much less put into practice, I rejoice at being little since children alone and those who resemble them will be admitted to the heavenly banquet. I am very happy there are many mansions in God's kingdom, for if there were only the one whose description and road seem incomprehensible to me, I would not be able to enter there. (GC II 1093–94)

Expressing herself with simplicity and conviction, Thérèse invited her spiritual brothers to be among the first to join her on the path of the Little Way.

Both priests were concerned about their lack of perfection and feared God's vindictiveness. Both needed Thérèse's way of confidence and love. When Fr. Bellière spoke of himself as a "miserable person," telling her of the "beautiful years . . . I wasted, sacrificing to the world and its follies the talents God was lending me," Thérèse brushed aside the violence implicit in his self-deprecation and self-hatred:

> Do not think you frighten me by speaking "about your beautiful, wasted years," I myself thank Jesus, who has looked at you with a look of love as, in the past, He looked at the young man in the Gospel. Ah! Brother, like me you can sing the mercies of the Lord, they sparkle in you in all their splendor. . . . You love Saint Augustine, Saint Magdalene, these souls to whom "many sins were forgiven because they loved much." I love them too; I love their repentance, and especially . . . their loving audacity!
>
> When I see Magdalene walking up before the many guests washing with her tears the feet of her adored Master, whom she is touching for the first time, I feel that her heart has understood the abysses of love and mercy of the Heart of Jesus, and, sinner though she is, this Heart of love was not only disposed to pardon her but to lavish on her the blessings of His divine intimacy, to lift her to the highest summits of contemplation. (GC II 1133)

When Thérèse referred to St. Mary Magdalene, she subtly moved her thoughts into a more personal area. Identifying with Magdalene more than with any other saint, Thérèse wanted Fr. Bellière to know that she had personally experienced the same dark impulses of heart that he and Magdalene had. She, as did Magdalene, understood the depth of Jesus' love, and in *loving audacity* allowed her relationship with Jesus to transform her. Thérèse followed Magdalene's path in her relationship with Jesus, and she now invited her spiritual brother to do likewise.

Ah! Dear little Brother, Thérèse continued, acknowledging that she too had faults and often remembered them, but did not allow her thoughts and feelings to move into the violence of self-hatred. *Ever since I have been given the grace to understand also the love of the Heart of Jesus, I admit that it has expelled all fear from my heart. The remembrance of my faults humbles me, draws me never to depend on my strength which is only weakness, but this remembrance speaks to me of mercy and love even more* (GC II 1133).

I know, Thérèse added with confidence, *there are some saints who spent their life in the practice of astonishing mortifications to expiate their sins, but what of it: "There are many mansions in the house of my heavenly Father," Jesus has said* [John 14:2], *and it is because of this that I follow the way He is tracing out for me. I try to be no longer occupied with myself in anything, and I abandon myself to what Jesus sees fit to do in my soul, for I have not chosen an austere life to expiate my faults but those of others* (GC II 1134).

Then, as if to caution her little brother as she had cautioned her novice about the need to understand the fullness of her thoughts, she wrote, *I just read over my note, and I wonder if you are going to understand me, for I have explained myself very poorly. Do not think that I condemn the repentance you have for our faults and your desire to expiate them. Oh, no! I am far from doing so, but, you know, we are now two, the work will be done more quickly (and I with my way will do more than you), so I hope that one day Jesus will make you walk by the same way as myself* (GC II 1134).

Thérèse admired Mary Magdalene's audacity and familiarity toward Jesus. Magdalene was confident that her faults were consumed in the devouring fire of Jesus' love, and Thérèse expressed her own similar audacity and confident love. Self-hate or any self-violence as an expression of repentance and guilt was not Thérèse's way. Rather, her way was to throw herself into the arms of her loving Father, acknowledging her weaknesses. She must have startled the timid and fearful Fr. Bellière.

He replied, "Do you realize you are opening up new horizons for me? In your last letter especially, I find some insights on the mercy of Jesus, on the familiarity He encourages, on the simplicity of the soul's relations with this great God which had little touched me until the present because undoubtedly it had not been presented to me with this simplicity and unction your heart pours forth" (GC II 1143–44).

"No, dear little Sister," he assures her, "you did not explain yourself poorly. You are right. . . . I am relying fully on Our Lord and on you. This is the surest way. I consider, as coming from Jesus Himself all that you say to me. I have full confidence in you and am guiding myself according to your way which I would like to make my own" (GC II 1144).

We must go to heaven by the same way, that of suffering united to love, Thérèse replied. *Ah! How I would like to make you understand the tenderness of the Heart of Jesus, what He expects from you* (GC II 1152).

I understood more than ever the degree to which your soul is sister to my own, she assures him; *since it is called to raise itself to God by the elevator of love and not to climb the rough stairway of fear,* she says in an explicit reference to her Little Way (GC II 1152).

Then she paints for Fr. Bellière this compelling image of the spiritual life, a complementary image of God as the loving mother annoyed by the little child flying into a temper, which she had suggested to Léonie in a letter some time before:

I picture a father who has two children, mischievous and disobedient, and when he comes to punish them, he sees one of them who trembles and gets away from him in terror, having, however, in the bottom of his heart the feeling that he deserves to be punished; and his brother, on the contrary, throws himself into his father's arms, saying that he is sorry for having caused him any trouble, that he loves him, and to prove it he will be good from now on, and if this child asks his father to punish him with a kiss, I do not believe that the heart of the happy father could resist the filial confidence of his child, whose sincerity and love he knows. He realizes, however, that more than once his son will fall into the same faults, but he is prepared to pardon him always, if his son always takes him by his heart. . . . I say nothing to you about the first child, dear little Brother, you must know whether his father can love him as much and treat him with the same indulgence as the other. . . . (GC II 1153)

Thérèse repeats what she had said to him in a previous letter. *I explain myself so poorly that I must wait for heaven in order to converse with you about this happy life. What I wanted to do today was to console you* (GC II 1153). She knew that her teaching on holiness would sound bold, even unorthodox to him, trained in the popular fear-filled, violent spirituality of the day. But she was confident of her path, and she knew he trusted her wisdom. She had based her teaching on the life and parables of Jesus, particularly the parable of the prodigal son, but she did not simply refer to that parable. She invented a new one especially to accommodate him. *I can't fear a God who made Himself so small for me,* she wrote; *love Him! For He is only love and mercy!* (FGM 153)

Anticipating her imminent death as well as trying to deepen Fr. Bellière's assurance of the truth of her message, she wrote, *When I am in port, I shall teach you, dear little Brother of my soul, how you must sail the stormy sea of the world with the abandonment and the love of a child who knows that his Father loves him and would be unable to leave him in the hour of danger. . . . I shall help you much more to walk by this delightful way when I shall have been delivered from this mortal envelope* (GC II 1152–53).

When he continued to express feelings of guilt and the fear of Jesus as well as shame of sharing with his little sister in the face of his weakness, Thérèse wrote words of consolation and correction. *You must know me only imperfectly to fear that a detailed account of your faults may diminish the tenderness I have for your soul! Oh, Brother, believe it, I shall have no need "to place my hand on the lips of Jesus,"* she wrote in a reference to his plea that she help him placate Jesus. *He has forgotten your infidelities now for a long time. . . . I beg you, do not drag yourself any longer to His feet; follow that 'first impulse that draws you into His arms.' This is where your place is, and . . . you are forbidden to go to heaven by any other way except that of your poor little sister. . . . Regarding those who love Him and who come after each indelicacy to ask His pardon by throwing themselves into His arms, Jesus is thrilled with joy. . . . How little known are the goodness, the merciful love of Jesus* (GC II 1164–65).

In her last letter, after which the dying Thérèse could manage to write no more than a line or two, she appealed once again to Fr. Bellière, who had not yet understood fully the depth of divine mercy. Still filled with fear of God, he was also filled with embarrassment and fear of Thérèse herself, that once in heaven she would not understand or overlook his faults. Thérèse, continuing to endure the pervading darkness of her trial of faith, nevertheless, again attempted to admonish and console her spiritual brother with words she desperately *wanted to believe*:

I tell you, Little Brother, we do not understand heaven in the same way. It seems to you that sharing in the justice, in the holiness of God, I would be unable as on earth to excuse your faults. Are you forgetting, then, that I shall be sharing also in the infinite mercy of the Lord? I believe the Blessed have great compassion on our miseries, they remember, being weak and mortal like us, they committed the same faults, sustained the same combats, and their fraternal tenderness becomes greater than it was when they were on earth, and for this reason they never cease protecting us and praying for us. (GC II 1173)

As the *Act of Oblation to Merciful Love* was the Little Way in prayer form, and the fifteen pages that Thérèse wrote to her sister Marie forming Manuscript B constituted the charter of the Little Way, these last letters to her priest-brothers were Thérèse's expressions of the Little Way accommodated to those who were misled, fearful, and ashamed.

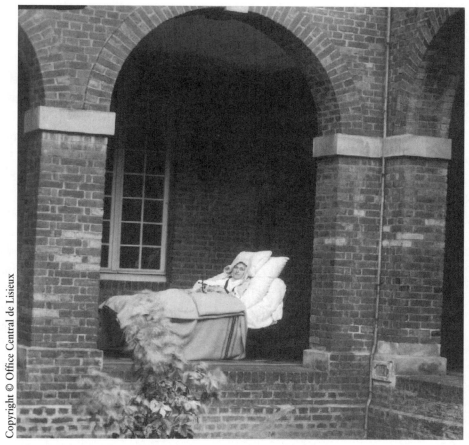

Thérèse lying ill in the cloister, August 30, 1897

CHAPTER 43

Everything Is Grace

Mother Gonzague recognized Thérèse's deteriorating condition and on June 5, 1897, had a novena of Masses begun in honor of Our Lady of Victories to obtain the miracle of a cure. However, by this time, fourteen months after Thérèse had first coughed up blood and just four months before she was to die, it would indeed have required a miracle for Thérèse to survive. Although in her exhausted state she still followed the Carmelite rule and the community schedule, particularly finding consolation in attending daily Mass, Thérèse had been relieved of some of her responsibilities in the community. She no longer came to the dining room for her meals or attended the periods of community recreation. She was being treated medically by blistering and puncturing the skin on her back, horribly painful and senseless procedures that in Thérèse's era were thought to be remedies for tuberculosis. She knew now for certain that an intuition she had had since she was a child would be fulfilled: that she would not live beyond youth (cf. HLC 94).

Earlier in the year, Thérèse had written to Br. Siméon in Rome that *I believe that my course here below will not be long.* Prior to that she had written, *Never have I asked God to die young, this would have appeared to me as cowardly, but he, from my childhood, saw fit to give me the intimate conviction that my course here below would be short . . .* (GC II 1152). *I never did ask God for the favor of dying young, but I have always hoped this be His will for me* (SS 215).

In January she wrote a poem she entitled "My Joy":

When Heaven's blue grows dark, and so
Seems to have left me cast aside,
My joy's to see myself brought low—
To stay within the shade, to hide.
My joy's, His Holy Will (so dear
Is Jesus!)—that I shall obey.
And so I live devoid of fear:
I love the night as much as day. (CP 191)

The following month, in honor of one of her spiritual heroes, Théophane Vénard, a priest of the Foreign Mission Society who had been martyred in Annam (present-day Vietnam), she wrote,

Soldier of Christ! ah, now lend me your arms,
I'll suffer much for sinners. How I long
To fight, in shadow of your victory-palms—
Protect me! Hold me, so that I'll be strong. (CP 198)

Before I die, she had confided to Céline, *I want to write a poem which will transcribe my whole thought on the life and virtues of the Blessed Virgin* (MSST 122). In May she fulfilled that dream in the long poem of twenty-five stanzas "Why I Love You, O Mary!" It was her final major poem, and expressed *all that I think and all that I would preach about the Blessed Virgin if I were a priest,* she told her sisters (STL 97). It manifested her great love for the only mother who never abandoned her.

I want to follow you each day, my Mother dear—
To live with you, though I still wait my Home above,
I plunge into your heart; enraptured, I revere,
O Mother, seeing there, such an abyss of love!
Beneath that mother's-gaze I never fear; in turn
It teaches me to weep and then rejoice with you.
My pure and holy joys you're never going to spurn;
You want to share them, and you deign to bless them too. (CP 226)

Also in May Thérèse finally revealed to Pauline that she had coughed up blood the year before, and Pauline finally recognized the gravity of her sister's condition. Thérèse had kept this secret from Pauline, just as Pauline had kept from Mother Gonzague the secret that her little sister had written her childhood memories for her two years before. Now Pauline was fearful that with Thérèse's condition worsening, she would die and her story would be incomplete. What Thérèse had already written described much about her early years at home, as Pauline had asked her to do, but not much about her experiences since coming to Carmel.

Pauline, convinced at this time that her little sister was a saint with a message to share, had begun writing down Thérèse's words, a practice she would continue until her sister's death. These words, edited by Pauline, have come to us as the document *Her Last Conversations*. But Pauline also wanted Thérèse to complete her own story and had, in fact, just recently suggested that Thérèse ask the prioress to continue writing. Thérèse, sensitive to her sister's feelings but not needing to please, discreetly said no.

Pauline, no longer prioress, could not require Thérèse's obedience; now only Mother Gonzague could do that, so Pauline approached the superior and with calculated shrewdness revealed that Thérèse had written some memoirs for her when she was prioress. The writing was good, Pauline told Mother Gonzague, but it was not adequate for an obituary, suggesting that maybe Thérèse could be put under obedience to finish her story and produce for Mother Gonzague something much better and more complete. The conversation played into Mother Gonzague's sense of power, conceit, and rivalry. Also she as prioress would now acquire the previous manuscript Thérèse had written for Pauline.

Mother Gonzague, whose respect and fondness for Thérèse had continued to grow over the years, agreed with Pauline's suggestions and asked Thérèse to continue to write her memoirs. Mother Gonzague may have been prompted by some personal vanity, relishing the idea that now the earlier manuscript as well as the new writing would be addressed to her, but she may also have had a real desire to understand more deeply Thérèse's spirituality that she was glimpsing from reading the letters Thérèse was writing to her priest-brothers.

Thérèse's new manuscript, written during the month of June as she was dying, was addressed to *my dear Mother* [Gonzague]. *You told me . . . of your desire that I finish singing with you the Mercies of the Lord* [Psalm 89:1], Thérèse wrote. *I began this sweet song with your dear daughter, Agnès of Jesus* [Pauline] *who was the mother entrusted by God with guiding me in the days of my childhood. . . . It is with you that I am to sing of the happiness of this little flower now that the timid glimmerings of the dawn have given way to the burning heat of noon. Yes, dear Mother, I shall try to express, in answer to your wishes, the sentiments of my soul, my gratitude to God and to you* (SS 205).

With this new mandate to continue writing about her life, Thérèse also reflected on the fact that some holy men and women had deliberately intended not *to leave anything of themselves behind after their death, not the smallest souvenir, not the least bit of writing.* And then there were others, Thérèse wrote, thinking of St. Teresa of Avila, *who have enriched the Church with their lofty revelations, having no fears of revealing the secrets* [God had entrusted to them], *in order that they may make Him more loved and known by souls* (SS 207). It comes down to obedience, Thérèse reflected, and to following the inspiration of the Holy Spirit. She would write in obedience, to please Jesus and to make God loved.

Thérèse had always wanted to write a commentary on the Canticle of Canticles (the Song of Songs), a book of the Old Testament that had been a treasure for her, but now Pauline suggested that she write about charity. After writing some reflections on her relationship with Mother Gonzague and sharing some insights about her Little Way, Thérèse wrote about her current trial of faith. Then she wrote about charity, about the novices, and about her spiritual brothers. Her reflections of a few pages on the Canticle of Canticles and on prayer were written as she neared the point of sheer exhaustion. The manuscript addressed to Mother Gonzague now constitutes the final fifty-five pages of *Story of a Soul.*

On June 7 Céline took three photographs of her sister, who stood with some difficulty in the same pose in each, holding side by side pictures of the Holy Face and of the Infant Jesus, images testifying to the essence of her spirituality.

One month later, on July 8, Thérèse was brought to the infirmary, carried on a mattress. She had written all she could; she had finished the manuscript in pencil, being no longer able to handle a pen and ink. She had been vomiting and was so weak that she could no longer manage to feed herself. By now it was clear to everyone that Thérèse was beyond help.

The previous day, July 7, Céline had written to Br. Siméon, Thérèse's friend in Rome, informing him simply but with great sadness that Thérèse was dying. Céline asked him to obtain for her sister the blessing of Pope Leo XIII. Within a week, Br. Siméon replied to Céline, telling her that through his friend, the pope's private secretary, he had fulfilled the request. This would be Br. Siméon's final gift to his beloved Thérèse.

The next day everything had been prepared for Thérèse's death. She was told that she might not last through the night, and she received extreme unction, the last rites of the church. But she rallied, and on July 12 she spontaneously composed her last lines of poetry as she prepared to receive Communion:

You, knowing I'm as small as I can be,
Are glad in stooping down, You little too:
O white Host, whom I Love! Oh come to me,
Come to me, for my heart aspires to You!—
And (after such a favor) grant that I
May die of love—I beg You—and depart . . .
Hear, Jesus, as in tenderness I cry:
    "Come to my heart!" (CP 234; cf. HLC 91–92)

Mother Gonzague, fearing that Thérèse's disease might be contagious, tried to limit the contact that the younger sisters had with Thérèse (cf. HLC 264). She relieved the young Sr. Marie of the Trinity of her duty as assistant infirmarian, but did assign Céline to help her sister. Céline would be at Thérèse's side for the remaining two and a half months of her life. Pauline and Marie were also given special permission to be with their little sister, and their cousin Marie Guérin sometimes joined them. Thérèse had always kept a discreet distance from her blood sisters in Carmel; now as she slowly died, they were reunited in a special bond of tender affection. *How can anyone say it is more perfect to separate oneself from one's blood relatives?* Thérèse had written. *When the human heart gives itself to God, it loses nothing of its innate tenderness; in fact, this tenderness grows when it becomes more pure and more divine* (SS 216).

As the days passed, Thérèse warned her sisters that they might find her dead anytime. They would have liked her to die in some notable way, certainly immediately after receiving the last rites and the Eucharist. To this kind of talk, she replied simply, *Oh, that wouldn't resemble my Little Way . Dying after receiving Holy Communion would be too beautiful for me; little souls couldn't imitate this. . . . Without a doubt, it's a great grace to receive the sacraments; but when God doesn't allow it, it's good just the same; everything is a grace* (HLC 98, 57).

Her sisters hoped that she would die on some special feast day, perhaps that of St. Teresa of Avila or St. John of the Cross. Thérèse responded, *To die after Communion! On a great feast day? Oh no, this isn't how I wish* to die! This would be an extraordinary grace that would discourage all the little souls, because they couldn't imitate that. They must be able to imitate everything about me (TLMT 37). And when Pauline insisted, "Surely, you will die on a feast day," she responded with a smile, It [my death] will be a beautiful enough feast day in itself! (HLC 180).

Ever mindful of the feelings of others and trying to diminish the distress of her sisters, she also joked about the ugliness of the candlestick that was being prepared for her wake and playfully mimicked the girth of Dr. de Cornière, a friend of the Martin family and the ordinary physician of the Carmelite community who attended her. And she mischievously nicknamed her three sisters "Peter, James, and John" (HLC 122) after they had fallen asleep watching at her bedside.

Thérèse even joked about her continuing desire to be a priest. She told Céline she knew why she had become ill and would die during her twenty-fourth year. Don't you see that God is going to take me at an age when I would not have had the time to become a priest, she said with her sly smile. If I had been able to become a priest, it would have been in this month of June, at this ordination that I would have received holy orders. So in order that I may regret nothing, God is allowing me to be sick (HLC 260; cf. MSST 118). While being totally at peace with her vocation in Carmel as love at the heart the church, Thérèse nonetheless saw humor in the thought that God had granted her this illness and an early death so that she might not suffer feelings of exclusion on reaching the age at which priests were usually ordained. I truly believe, she encouraged Céline, that those who have so lovingly desired the priesthood and have not attained to it in this world will enjoy all its privileges in the next (MSST 118–19).

During the last months of her life, she continued to suffer the physical pain of gangrene of the intestines, fevers, insomnia, constipation, bedsores, and gradual suffocation from tuberculosis, as well as the inner trial of the sense of darkness in her relationship with God. If you only knew to what state of powerlessness illness reduces you, she had whispered to her novice Sr. Marie of the Trinity during one of the last times she could come to community recreation. Last night I needed more than half an hour to go back up to my cell; I had to sit down on almost every step of the stairs to recover my breath (TLMT 35).

CHAPTER 44

It Is Love Alone Which Attracts Me

In all of her physical pain and inner sufferings as she lay on her deathbed, Thérèse continued to give the external appearance of calm. She shared little of her inner distress even with Pauline or Céline, and almost nothing with Marie, as they stayed near her during her last weeks in the infirmary. Marie learned of her sister's temptations against faith only after her death, when reading her writings. Thérèse did not want to reveal what was happening within her lest she might inadvertently share something that could seem blasphemous to her sisters and the other nuns (cf. SS 213). She did not want to alarm them. *I tried not to make anyone suffer from my pains.* Nor did she want *to offend the good God.*

One sister with whom Thérèse did share some of her feelings later commented, "I was strangely surprised to hear of this temptation against faith, for her soul seemed peaceful and serene as ever; one would have thought that she was flooded by consolation, so easily and naturally did she practice virtue."

In her suffering, Thérèse was isolated emotionally from some of the nuns who could not understand what was happening within her. One sister, coming into the infirmary in the evenings, would place herself at the foot of the bed and simply laugh at Thérèse. *It's painful to be looked at and laughed at when one is suffering,* Thérèse confided in Pauline, *but I think how Our Lord on the Cross was looked at in the same way in the midst of His sufferings* (HLC 167).

"If you only knew how little you are liked or appreciated!" one sister visiting her during her last illness insensitively remarked to her. And another comment that had been made at recreation was thoughtlessly repeated to her: "I don't know why they talk so much about Sister Thérèse; she doesn't do anything remarkable. We never see her practicing virtue; in fact she could hardly be called even a good religious!" *Oh! Just imagine hearing that I was not a good religious, just when I am on my deathbed.* Thérèse responded with an indifference born of simplicity and humility, and reminiscent of Francis of Assisi: *what joy! Nothing could have given me greater pleasure* (STL 197). *My soul feels utterly exiled. I am well aware that others do not believe I am seriously ill, but that comes from God.* And reminiscent of her childhood determination never to complain, she said simply, *It gives us so much strength not to speak of our troubles* (HLC 135). She had dropped all self-concern, all self-protection, all attachment to herself, and was completely free to be who she simply was.

Thérèse's physical sufferings continued to be compounded by her spiritual trial and her emotional isolation. Even Pauline seemed not to have fully understood her little sister's Little Way. "I was telling her," Pauline recounted of an exchanged that she had with her little sister, "that she must have had to struggle a lot in order to have become perfect." Thérèse replied with a muted sense of exasperation, *Oh, it's not that!* (HLC 129). It was similar to the sense Thérèse had had when Céline had spoken of "how much I have to acquire," and Thérèse had advised her of how much rather she had to lose. For Thérèse, holiness was not a struggle to become perfect, rather holiness was being *willing to bear serenely the trial of being displeasing* to herself, and thereby letting herself be *for Jesus, a pleasant place of shelter.*

Thérèse considered her willingness to bear in peace the suffering of her immediate situation as the supreme proof of her love as well as the most important way of identifying herself with Jesus, assisting him in the salvation of souls. Standing beneath the cross, participating with Jesus on the cross in abandonment to the divine will: this understanding of suffering had allowed her to endure willingly all the suffering of her life and now gave her meaning in dying. She had mentioned to her novice Sr. Marie of the Trinity that no suffering *can be too much for me, because we have only this one lifetime in which to prove our love!* (TLMT 94). Not seeking pain but enduring in peace the inevitable pain of the moment, in faithful union with the pain of the crucified Jesus, was for Thérèse the primary way of being in love with God.

One evening, Thérèse recounted to Sr. Marie,

The infirmarian came to put a hot-water bottle on my feet and a tincture of iodine on my chest. I was consumed with a fever, a burning thirst was devouring me. When submitting to these remedies, I couldn't resist complaining to Our Lord: "My Jesus, You are my witness, I am burning and they bring me still more heat and more fire! Ah! If only I had in place of all this a glass of water! . . . My Jesus! your little girl is very thirsty! However, she's happy to find the opportunity of lacking what is necessary in order to resemble You better and to save souls."

Soon the infirmarian left me, and I didn't expect to see her again except the next morning, when to my great surprise she returned a few minutes afterwards, bringing me a refreshing drink. . . . Oh! how good our Jesus is! How sweet it is to confide in Him! (HLC 263–64)

When you are not given something you have asked for, Thérèse advised her novice, *That is a grace; it is because* [God] *has confidence that you are strong enough to suffer something for him* (TLMT 103).

Inevitable and unavoidable sufferings were now fully upon Thérèse. *If He increases them, I will bear them with pleasure and with joy because they will be coming from Him. But I'm too little to have any strength through myself. If I were to ask for sufferings, these would be mine, and I would have to bear them alone, and I've never been able to do anything alone* (HLC 145).

As a child Thérèse had willfully and aggressively reached for the basket of doll-things that Léonie had held out, and cried, *I choose all!* That gesture and those words, Thérèse had said, were a symbol for her whole life. She wanted to embrace all that her Beloved asked of her. Now in deep physical pain, when asked if she would rather live or die, she replied, *As God wills.* "And if you could choose?" she was asked. *I would not choose.* She spoke to Céline at her bedside, *I choose nothing; my path is abandonment into God's hands.* All of her willfulness had been transformed into an active willingness to abandon herself in simplicity to her loving Father. Thérèse's choosing had been enfolded into God's choosing. Thérèse was being chosen, being drawn into the embrace of divine love, the *flames of His love* (SS 257).

At the end of May, Thérèse had written a poem she entitled "Abandonment Is the Sweet Fruit of Love":

And from its branches fair
(The tree is Love) there came
A fruit, that's sweet and rare—
Abandonment is its name.
. . . .
You've come here, from the Height,
Celestial Flame whose heat
Has warmed me! By its light
Abandonment is complete. (CP 212–13 slightly altered)

Having prayed to Joan of Arc for courage and fidelity and having experienced her own mother's great capacity to suffer patiently, Thérèse now at the end, in an act of courageous desire and faith-filled love, had written the creed in her own blood (GC II 986); she so desperately *wanted to believe*. At the deepest level of her being, Thérèse did have faith, confidence, and trust, but on the surface she was in a dark, desolate night. *If I did not have faith,* she had previously told Sr. Marie of the Trinity, *I could never bear so many sufferings. I am surprised that there aren't more atheists who take their own lives* (TLMT 39).

Like her mother, who for many years had kept hidden the increasingly intense pain of her breast cancer, Thérèse suffered mainly in silence and alone. Thérèse dutifully reported the progress of her illness to Mother Gonzague, but she did so in a spirit of nonchalance and even with some cheerfulness. The doctor made periodic visits and was aware of Thérèse's physical condition, but no one really knew the extent of her total physical and spiritual suffering during the weeks leading up to her last days. As she suffered inner loneliness, those early feelings of isolation and unattachment were again surfacing.

Thérèse's physical condition deteriorated inexorably. And as it did, this young woman who had lived her emotional life with a tendency to excessive sensitivity and a great need to please her way into some kind of bond with others, found herself purified of all feelings and enduring darkness in her relationship with God. Her faith was active, her trust constant, her love unshakable; but her feelings were as dark as the blackest night. *Why should I be protected more than anyone else from the fear of death?* she said. *I won't say like St. Peter: "I will never deny you"* [Matthew 26:35] (HLC 83).

"Pray," her sister Céline invited Thérèse. *I am,* Thérèse replied, *but I can say nothing to Jesus; I just suffer. I'm just loving him,* she sighed (STL 160). Thérèse had prayed in her *Act of Oblation to Merciful Love* the year before, *I want, O my Beloved, at each beat of my heart, to renew this offering to You an infinite number of times, until the shadows having disappeared I may be able to tell You of my love in an eternal face to face!* (SS 277). It was the beating of her suffering heart that now alone carried her prayer. She had prayed, *O God, to be with you, to be in you, that is my one desire, and your assurance of its fulfillment helps me to bear my exile as I await the joyous eternal day when I shall see you face to face.*

Throughout her life, Thérèse had always had *immense desires*. She had actually spoken of her *infinite desires* and had originally included that phrase in her *Act of Oblation to Merciful Love: I feel in my heart* [infinite] *immense desires and it is with confidence I ask you to come and take possession of my soul.* But the word "infinite" had offended Pauline's censuring theologian, and it was replaced (cf. GC II 1102, note 4). But now, the issue wasn't the intensity of her desire—that was still infinite—what was important was the object of her desire:

And now I have no other desire except to love Jesus unto folly. . . . Neither do I desire any longer suffering or death, and still I love them both; it is love alone that attracts me, however, I desired them for a long time; I possessed suffering and believed I had touched the shores of heaven, that the little flower would be gathered in the springtime of her life. Now, abandonment alone guides me. I have no other compass! I can no longer ask for anything with fervor except the accomplishment of God's will in my soul without any creature being able to set obstacles in the way. . . . For a long time I have not belonged to myself since I delivered myself totally to Jesus, and He is therefore free to do with me as He pleases (SS 178, 218). *How happy I am to die! Yes, I am happy not at being delivered from sufferings here below. . . . I am happy to die because I feel that such is God's will.* (GC II 1139)

Fortunately, I didn't ask for suffering, Thérèse said a short time before her death, in the midst of her greatest distress; *if I had asked for it I fear I wouldn't have the patience to bear it. Whereas, if it is coming directly from God's will, He cannot refuse to give me the patience and the grace necessary to bear it* (HLC 290).

After Thérèse's death and canonization, the church offered official prayers as part of the liturgical office to be recited in her honor. One such prayer began, ". . . inflamed with the desire of suffering, she offered herself . . . as a victim to the merciful love of God." Pauline immediately saw the error of this interpretation of Thérèse's way. She promptly and then relentlessly petitioned the Sacred Congregation of Rites to change the wording from "inflamed with the desire of suffering" to "on fire with divine love" (MSST 85). Pauline clearly understood that aspect of Thérèse's spirit, and the correction finally prevailed.

With her life slipping away, Thérèse saw her path as the spirituality of Zacchaeus and of the publican in the gospel parable. It was a spirituality not of doing great things, acquiring merit, and being perfect; rather, like the way of Zacchaeus, the Little Way was the way of descending, of responding to Jesus' call to "come down" (Luke 19:5), of being with Jesus and then letting Jesus' love transform her as he wished. Like the publican, as a sinner eating at the table of sinners, she would go to her loving Father by way of his mercy. *Our sins serve to glorify the mercy of God*, she boldly confided to Sr. Marie of the Trinity. She had never kept a ledger of deeds, good or bad; much less did she keep an account of her sacrifices. Thérèse was in love, and a person in love does not keep account of such things. *There is a science God doesn't know*, she said: *arithmetic* (TLMT 74–75; cf. GC II 1122).

CHAPTER 45

I Want to Spend My Heaven Doing Good upon Earth

In her *Act of Oblation to Merciful Love* Thérèse had prayed, *In the evening of this life, I shall appear before you with empty hands, for I do not ask you, Lord, to count my works. All our justice is stained in your eyes. I wish, then, to be clothed in your own Justice and to receive from your Love the eternal possession of Yourself* (SS 277). In a letter to her sister Léonie, she wrote, *Since I am putting forth all my efforts to be a very little child, I have no preparations to make* [for dying]. *Jesus himself will have to pay the expenses of the journey and the cost of entering heaven* (GC II 967).

I am not afraid of what happens after death, she said. She no longer feared purgatory, confident that, like the publican in Jesus' parable, divine mercy would purify her. She prayed that she would be consumed by divine love, not in the sense of being simply changed, but in the sense of being transformed into God *like a fire that transforms everything into itself* (SS 276). Death would consume her in divine love, she believed.

She had written to Fr. Roulland, suggesting that he not pray that she be delivered from purgatory. Following the example of St. Teresa of Avila, Thérèse thought that if she endured purgatory, she might, in that suffering, be able to save souls; her desire to do good after her death was more important than her own situation. *I do not want you to ask God to deliver me from the flames of purgatory*, she wrote. *I would like to save souls and forget myself for them; I would like to save them even after my death* (GC II 1072).

It was true that these sentiments expressed her desire to assist in Jesus' redemptive mission, but Thérèse really did not believe that her entry into the embrace of her loving Father would be delayed by purgatory. She believed that her role of saving souls would be in that divine embrace. She asked rhetorically in a letter to Fr. Roulland, *How would He purify in the flames of purgatory souls* [already] *consumed in the fires of Divine Love?* (GC II 1093). As part of her *Act of Oblation to Merciful Love* she had asked God, *May my soul take its flight without any delay into the eternal embrace of Your Merciful Love* (SS 277). *Without any delay*—that hope astonished her sisters.

Every soul, as was taught by the conventional spirituality, was destined to be delayed in purgatory. Even the saintly Mother Geneviève, as she died, had asked the sisters to pray that her purgatory would be short. The sisters understood that no one was worthy of going directly to heaven; Thérèse alone had been confident that Mother Geneviève would not need purgatory. Thérèse had heard the customary teaching that worthiness was needed to enter heaven, but she thought this teaching was irrelevant. She understood that worthiness or unworthiness could no longer be a factor where divine love was concerned. She had attempted to open herself completely to her loving Father in all the dimensions of her life; and now, in her agony, she was content to simply rest in his love, with her concerns turned toward others.

She knew that her Little Way of confidence and love, of willingness, surrender, gratitude, and charity, of reciprocity to divine love, had been inspired in her by Jesus, her teacher. It had been Jesus' own way of relating with the Father. It had been the way that Jesus had taught his disciples. Thérèse knew that this way was accessible to everyone. She had not done anything extraordinary. She had accepted all of her life experiences, even her brokenness and faults, as God's grace. She tried to reassure her sisters that they themselves were already receiving or capable of receiving the very same graces and blessings.

Thérèse told Sr. Marie of the Trinity, *If I am leading you in error with my Little Way of love, don't be afraid that I would let you follow it for very long. I would appear to you soon in order to tell you to take another route. But if I don't return, believe in the truth of my words: one can never have too much confidence in God, who is so powerful and so merciful! One receives from him quite as much as one hopes for!* (TLMT 77).

Now, in her last weeks, she began to understand that divine love could use her life as an example for ordinary people in their desire for union with God. *I beg You to cast Your Divine Glance upon a great number of little souls.* Thérèse prayed that all humanity be open to God: *I beg You to choose a legion of little victims worthy of Your Love!* (SS 200).

She had said, *I feel in me the vocation of the Priest* (SS 192), and now she prayed Jesus' prayer as high priest recorded in John's gospel, that *"the love with which you* [the Father] *have loved me may be in them, and I in them"* [John 17:26] (cf. SS 255).

When Fr. Roulland had written the year before, in June 1896, to say that he wished to visit the Carmel on his way to say good-bye to his family before he journeyed to the missions in China, Thérèse's missionary spirit was aroused.

She responded, *I shall be truly happy to work with you for the salvation of souls. It is for this purpose that I became a Carmelite nun; being unable to be an active missionary, I wanted to be one through love. . . . Ask for me from Jesus . . . to set me on fire with His Love so that I may enkindle it in hearts. For a long time I wanted to know an Apostle who would pronounce my name at the Holy Altar on the day of his first mass* (GC II 956).

Nine months later, in March 1897, she again expressed her missionary desire to Fr. Roulland: *If Jesus doesn't soon come looking for me for the Carmel of heaven, I shall one day leave for that of Hanoi* (GC II 1071). The Hanoi Carmel had been founded just two years before from the Carmel in Saigon, which was itself a foundation from Thérèse's own Lisieux Carmel. She wanted to go to Hanoi as a fulfillment of her desire to be a missionary and to be hidden with Jesus. She knew, of course, that she was too ill to fulfill that desire literally. Her real longing was to become a missionary after her death.

In this regard Thérèse's temptation to doubt the existence of heaven was especially distressing because she had been confident that heaven would be not so much a state of rest, but rather her Beloved's embrace, from which she could assist the continual flow of divine love to the world. *God would not give me this desire to do good on earth after my death if he did not want to realize it.* She had written to Fr. Roulland, *The thought of eternal beatitude hardly thrills my heart. . . . What attracts me to the homeland of heaven is the Lord's call, the hope of loving Him finally as I have so much desired to love Him, and the thought that I shall be able to make Him loved by a multitude of souls who will bless Him eternally. Ah! Brother,* she added, *I feel it; I shall be more useful to you in Heaven than on earth. . . . I really count on not remaining inactive in heaven. My desire is to work still for the church and for souls. I am asking God for this and I am certain He will hear me* (GC II 1141–42).

My mission is about to begin, Thérèse now told her sisters, who at her bedside were recording her words, *my mission to make God loved as I love Him, to give my Little Way to souls. If God answers my desires, my heaven will be spent on earth until the end of the world. Yes, I will spend my heaven doing good upon earth* (HLC 102). She had begun a novena to Théophane Vénard and to St. Francis Xavier, patron of the missions, for that intention. She was echoing the desire of Théophane and also that of St. Stanislaus Kostka, who was the subject of her last play. *I will come down,* Thérèse said simply (HLC 91; MSST 237). *I desire in heaven the same thing as I do on earth: to love Jesus and to make him loved* (GC II 1060; cf. GC II 1090).

Earlier she had written to Fr. Bellière, referring to herself, *I would be very happy if each day you would consent to offer this prayer for her which contains all her desires: "Merciful Father, in the name of our gentle Jesus, the Virgin Mary, and the Saints, I beg You to enkindle my sister with Your Spirit of Love and to grant her the favor of making You loved very much"* (GC II 1060).

During the month of May, Thérèse had heard a story, read in the dining room, about St. Aloysius Gonzaga, a young Jesuit. A sick man had prayed to Aloysius for a cure and saw "a shower of roses" falling on his sickbed. He was cured instantly. At recreation after the meal, Thérèse whispered to one of her sisters, *I, too, will let fall a shower of roses after my death* (STL 95).

In the eyes of Pauline, Marie, and Céline, as well as some of the other sisters, Thérèse was a saint. Pauline said as much to Thérèse a month before her death: "I think we are taking care of a little saint!" Thérèse replied simply, *Well, so much the better! However, I would want God to say it* (HLC 181).

When Pauline persisted in speaking of her as a saint, Thérèse responded, *No, I am not a saint. . . . I'm a very little soul upon whom God has bestowed graces; that's what I am. . . . I think God has been pleased to place in me things which will do good to me and to others* (HLC 143, 131).

One sister, echoing the common notion that the body of a holy person would not suffer decay, said to her, "You have loved God so much, that He will work a miracle for you, and we shall find your body incorrupt." To such remarks she replied, *Don't be astonished if I don't appear to you after my death, and if you see nothing extraordinary as the sign of my happiness. You will remember that it's "my little way" not to desire to see anything* (HLC 55).

A sheaf of corn was brought to her bedside; she detached the most beautiful ear and said to Pauline, *Mother, this ear of corn is the image of my soul: God has entrusted me with graces for myself and for many others. . . . I feel so much that everything comes from Him* (HLC 131–32). Thérèse regarded herself with a certain detachment so that she could rightly appreciate the Holy Spirit's gifts in her just as she appreciated them in others. *I think that "the Spirit of God breathes where He will"* [cf. John 3:8], she said (HLC 90).

Earlier Thérèse had noticed a white hen under a tree, sheltering her little chicks beneath her wing. She was moved to tears and later explained to Pauline, *I cried when I thought how God used this image in order to teach* us His tenderness towards us [cf. Matthew 23:37]. *All through my life this is what He has done for me!* (HLC 60).

Now, looking out the window at a particularly dark area in a grotto not far from the chestnut trees, where she had sat in her father's wheelchair doing her writing, Thérèse remarked, *Look! Do you see the black hole where we can see nothing; it's in a similar hole that I am as far as my body and soul are concerned. Ah! what darkness!* Then she added with a certain resignation, *but I am at peace* (HLC 173).

I really don't see what I'll have after death that I don't already possess in this life, she confided to her sister Pauline. *I shall see God, true; but as for as being in His presence, I am totally there here on earth* (HLC 45).

God will grow weary of testing me before I would ever doubt him, Thérèse had told Sr. Marie of the Trinity. Then she quoted a sentence from Job that she had discovered in a book she had read when, at about eleven years old, she had begun to read more widely for sheer delight (TLMT 86). *This saying of Job: "Although he should kill me, I will trust in him"* [Job 13:15], *has fascinated me from my childhood,* she said. *But it took me a long time before I was established in this degree of abandonment. Now I am there; God has placed me there. He took me into His arms and placed me there* (HLC 77).

A sister offered her a child's toy to distract her from her sufferings. Taken aback by the silliness of the situation, Thérèse said abruptly with irritation, *Whatever should I do with that?* Then she wept and begged the sister's pardon, *Oh, forgive me, forgive me, I was so rude.*

On another occasion after she had become irritated and impatient, she said to Pauline, *Ah, the good it does me for having been bad! . . . I am happier for having been imperfect than if, sustained by grace, I had been a model of meekness. . . . This does me much good to see Jesus is always so gentle, so tender to me!* (GC II 1100–1101).

Earlier in her life Thérèse had said, *The saints who suffer never make me feel pity! I know that they have the strength to bear their sufferings* (TLMT 105). But now from her own experience Thérèse changed her mind and knew that even holy people *lose patience. I would not have believed this formerly,* she sighed (HLC 130).

She never tried to conform herself to the perfectionistic model of sainthood of her day. She was willing to accept the reality of who she was. When Pauline suggested that she say something religiously pious and edifying to the doctor, she replied, *this isn't my little style. Let Doctor de Cornière think what he wants. I love only simplicity; I have a horror for pretence. I assure you that to do what you want would be bad on my part* (HLC 77).

Instead of the appearance of holiness, Thérèse preferred honesty and truth. *O my God, I really want to listen to you,* she said. *I beg you to answer me when I say humbly: What is truth? Make me see things as they really are. Let nothing cause me to be deceived* (HLC 105). *Yes, it seems to me I never sought anything but the truth.* Thérèse's humility was rooted in truth. *Yes, I have understood humility of heart* (HLC 205). *To me humility is truth,* she said to Céline. *I do not know whether I am humble but I do know that I see the truth in all things* (MSST 21). For Thérèse, truth was a name for her Beloved, Jesus, and truth had become the quest of her life.

Her sister Marie, trying to console her, told Thérèse that as she died she would surely see the Lord and the angels resplendent with light and beauty. *All these images do me no good,* Thérèse said; *I can nourish myself on nothing but the truth. This is why I've never wanted any visions. We can't see, here on earth, heaven, the angels, . . . just as they are. I prefer to wait until after my death.* And later she said, *Speak to me . . . about everything that is the truth* (HLC 134, 181).

The frankness of Thérèse as a child that had prompted her to run to her parents to confess her faults had grown in her so that as a woman she was now *resigned to seeing . . .* [herself] *always far from perfect, even glad,* and manifested itself in her profound desire for personal honesty and integrity.

My God, she prayed, *I beseech You to preserve me from the misery of being unfaithful to You! When I reflect on those words of Our Lord: "I come quickly . . . to render to them according to their works" I think that He will find my case a puzzle: I have no works. Well, He will reward me according to His own works.*

I can depend on nothing, on no good works of my own in order to have confidence, she said. *This poverty, however, was a real light and a grace for me. I was thinking that never in my life would I be able to pay my debts to God; this was real riches, real strength for me. . . . We experience such great peace when we're totally poor, when we depend upon no one except God* (HLC 137).

Now, in her extreme weakness, as she was pampered by her sisters, if any willfulness, self-love, or self-centeredness had remained in Thérèse it would surely have surfaced. The temptation to feel that she had achieved some degree of holiness; the pride of having been successful in acquiring merit to be rewarded; the secret self-satisfaction of having lived a notable life, of having made a good impression, and of having pleased her sisters; the self-love of having acquired some kind of virtue and status—all these traps were now lying in wait for Thérèse as she became more and more vulnerable. But she had grown into a spirit free of any self-consciousness, self-preoccupation, and self-importance, and this freedom allowed her to be even idolized without guardedness, resistance, or fuss. *I see only the graces I've received from God. . . . I have lights only to see my little nothingness. This does me more good than all the lights on the faith* (HLC 144, 148). She had attained a simplicity that was both completely engaging and totally disarming.

Reflecting on the time when Mother Gonzague had appointed her to be the guide for the postulants and novices, Thérèse wrote, *You did not hesitate, dear Mother, to tell me one day that God was enlightening my soul and that He was giving me even the experience of years. O Mother! I am too little to have any vanity now; I am too little to compose beautiful sentences in order to have you believe that I have a lot of humility. I prefer to agree very simply that the Almighty has done great things in the soul of His divine Mother's child, and the greatest thing is to have shown her littleness, her impotence* (SS 210).

Pauline had been recording Thérèse's every word as if she were recording sacred Scripture. Not puffed up, Thérèse was actually pained by this attention. With a sense of humor she responded to Pauline's many questions, *It reminds me of Joan of Arc before her judges. It seems to me I answer with the same sincerity* (HLC 104). Pauline noted that the attention, which amounted to a kind of reverence, "inhibited the outpourings of her heart, but [Thérèse] let me do it simply in order not to sadden me."

As she neared death, Thérèse, resonating with the strength of her mother, Zélie, prayed to the Blessed Virgin that she would not have to cough at night so that Céline, who was sleeping near her, would not be awakened. Later she said, *Here is what gives me the desire to leave: I tire out my little sisters, and then I give them pain when being so sick. . . . Yes, I would like to go.* Still later she prayed *to cause my sisters no more pain; and in order to do this, that I go very quickly* (HLC 174, 189). To the end, Thérèse, with her great gift of sensitivity, was ready to forget herself and to accommodate others in order to please and not disturb them.

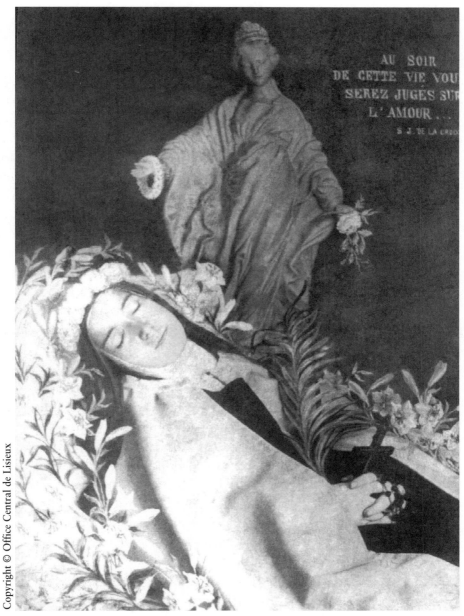

Thérèse in death in the infirmary, October 1, 1897

CHAPTER 46

I Go to Him with Confidence and Love

In the final weeks of Thérèse's life, Mother Gonzague did everything possible to assist and comfort her. She did not, however, permit Thérèse to receive the morphine injections recommended by the doctor to alleviate the agonizing pain. Such medication, the prioress believed, would not be proper for a Carmelite nun. In this decision she was following the common Carmelite view of the time, shared also by all the sisters, including Pauline, Marie, and Céline, as well as by Thérèse herself. Medication possibly would have relieved Thérèse's pain but probably would not have eliminated it. Mother Gonzague was to endure many years of suffering at the end of her own life, painfully dying of cancer of the tongue while refusing morphine in a spirit of religious simplicity. And Marie Guérin, the Martins' cousin, a novice under Thérèse, who would die eight years after Thérèse, also did not have pain remedies in her difficult sufferings from tuberculosis, which she may have contracted from Thérèse.

Tuberculosis, although at the time claiming 150,000 victims in France each year, was shrouded in fear and mystery. It was considered to be the sickness of the poor, the outcasts, and the marginalized. The middle and upper classes regarded the disease with repugnance and believed that it resulted from compromised behavior, much as some have viewed AIDS in modern times. Even naming the disease was regarded as indiscreet and taboo. During his early visits, the convent physician, Dr. de Cornière, would not acknowledge that Thérèse's illness was tuberculosis and described her condition as "a problem in the lungs, a real pulmonary congestion;" but then he prescribed the treatment used at the time for tuberculosis. He added that "only two percent" survive her condition.

Two months before Thérèse was to die, Dr. de Cornière was away on vacation, and Mother Gonzague finally agreed that Dr. Francis La Néele, the son-in-law of Uncle Isidore Guérin, could treat her. On August 17, just ʼʷ weeks before Thérèse's death, Dr. La Néele was the first to use the pro ᵈ word "tuberculosis." He told his father-in-law, Isidore, that Thérèse's ᵹ was totally lost, full of tubercles in the process of softening. The ˢ affected in its lower part. He shared the same diagnosis with

, thing Is Grace

Mother Gonzague. He knew there was no hope. He kissed Thérèse on her forehead on behalf of all her family who could not be with her.

The sisters positioned Thérèse's infirmary bed so that she could have the best view out of the window onto a patch of sky. A picture of Théophane Vénard was pinned to the drapery surrounding the bed. The statue of Our Lady Virgin of the Smile was placed at the foot of her bed. In her childhood cure Thérèse had experienced *the ravishing smile of the Blessed Virgin* (SS 66). Now as she lay dying, Thérèse glanced often in love and gratitude at Mary, the only mother who had stayed with her without fail. But Thérèse saw no smile.

It is to her, Thérèse had prayed, *I abandon my offering begging her to present it to You, . . . O my God!* (SS 276). The offering was no longer just the words of her *Act of Oblation to Merciful Love,* but was her very life ebbing away in utter darkness. The pain, Thérèse whispered, *it's enough to make one go out of one's mind.*

At one point, in complete distress, Thérèse said simply, *I can no longer pray. I can only look at the Blessed Virgin and say, "Jesus!"* Asked if Mary had ever been concealed from her these past months in her dark night of suffering, she replied spontaneously, *No, the Blessed Virgin will never be hidden from me, for I love her too much* (HLC 81).

In her last major poem, she prayed to Mary:

> *This music I shall hear and soon! And will arrive*
> *In Heav'n, to see you . . . you came down to see me—how*
> *You smiled upon me in the morning of my life.*
> *Come, smile on me again! For it is evening now.* (CP 229)

In her last note written on the back of a picture, she expressed her love of Mary: *O Mary, if I were Queen of Heaven, and you were Thérèse, I would wish to be Thérèse so that you would be Queen of Heaven* (PSTL 119).

I'm perhaps losing my wits, she moaned. *Oh! If they only knew the weakness I'm experiencing. Last night, I couldn't take anymore; I begged the Blessed Virgin to take my head in her hands, so that I could take my sufferings* (HLC 154).

I can't sleep; I'm suffering too much, so I am praying, Thérèse whispered to Céline at her bedside. "And what," her sister asked, "are you saying to Jesus?" *I say nothing, I just love Him!* (HLC 228; MSST 237).

The picture of the Holy Face, which Thérèse had often venerated, was also brought to the infirmary and positioned on a mantel with flowers and candles so that Thérèse could gaze upon it. Devotion to the Holy Face as well as her meditation on the Song of Songs had formed the core of Thérèse's devotions. Both in their own ways summoned her into a mystical spirituality of intimacy with God, of personal hiddenness, and of the acceptance of suffering and aridity as a participation in the love and pain of Jesus' dying in complete desolation.

Just after entering into her trial of faith, she had composed a Consecration to the Holy Face: *Lord, hide us in the secret of your Face,* she had written in personal darkness, desiring *to attain to the vision of Jesus, Face to Face.* Then she had added a reference to her inner desolation at the loss of a sense of heaven: *Your Veiled Look, that is our Heaven, O Jesus* (PSTL 91–92).

Thérèse never lost her desire for martyrdom that she had experienced so intensely when visiting the Colosseum and when befriending St. Cecilia during her pilgrimage to Rome. Her desire had been nourished by her devotion to Joan of Arc, expressed in the prayer she composed at the time of her profession of vows; now it arose again in her last days. But with her sense of humor Thérèse reflected, *And I who desired martyrdom, it is possible that I should die in bed!* (HLC 132).

"The martyrs suffered with joy," Fr. Pichon had preached in a community retreat at Carmel several years before, but, he noted, "the King of Martyrs suffered with sadness." This idea had resonated with Thérèse at the time, and she had shared that thought with Céline, who was then still at home with their father: *Let us suffer the bitter pain without courage! Jesus suffered with sadness; can the soul suffer without sadness? And we would like to suffer generously, grandly! Céline, what an illusion!* (GC II 557). Thérèse, without grand feelings, was willing now to join with the sad, suffering, dying Jesus on the cross of darkness. *I've been told so much that I have courage, and this is so far from the truth,* she lamented. Later she said, *I am suffering very much, but am I suffering very well? That's the point! . . . Suffering can attain extreme limits, but I'm sure God will never abandon me* (HLC 48, 152, 73; cf. GC I 557).

Our Lord died on the Cross in agony, and yet this is the most beautiful death of love. . . . To die of love is not to die in transports. I tell you frankly, she said to Pauline, *it seems to me that this is what I am experiencing* (HLC 73).

I do not count on the illness [to cause me to die]; *it is too slow a leader,* she said. *I count only on love. Ask Good Jesus that all the prayers being offered for me may serve to increase the Fire which must consume me* (GC II 1121; cf. TLMT 36).

On August 19, the feast of St. Hyacinth, Thérèse received Communion and prayed for Hyacinth Loyson, her renegade *brother*, whom she had promised never to forget. Due to her deteriorating condition this was to be her last Communion. Some of the sisters now became scandalized that she could no longer receive the Eucharist. She herself was distressed by this turn of events and in particular regretted not being able to receive communion from the hand of Sr. Philomena's nephew. Since her First Communion she had experienced God's love in the sacrament, but she also knew that she could find union with her Beloved and give him pleasure by now willingly surrendering to the overpowering agony of her dying.

On August 30, just a month before her death, she rallied again for about two weeks. Suddenly she regained her appetite and requested, to the surprise of the infirmarian and all the sisters, a chocolate éclair. On a rolling bed, she was taken outside in the cloister walk. There Céline photographed Thérèse for the last time; then she rolled her bed to the door of the chapel where Thérèse contemplated the Blessed Sacrament also for the last time.

The great saints have worked for God's glory, Thérèse said, *but I'm only a little soul; I work only for His pleasure* (HLC 102). *The only thing I beg . . . is the grace of loving Jesus and of making Him loved* (GC II 1055). Thérèse's great capacity to please others had turned completely and totally toward pleasing her loving Father.

I am suffering only for an instant, she said. *It's because we think of the past and the future that we become discouraged and fall into despair. . . . I myself suffer only at each present moment. So it's not any great thing. . . . No, God gives me no premonition of an approaching death, but of much greater sufferings. . . . But I don't torment myself; I don't want to think of anything but the present moment. . . . I'm without any thought, I suffer from minute to minute* (HLC 155, 241, 165, 170).

With surrender and a profound sense of peace Thérèse lingered in her final days, moment by moment. *God gives me courage in proportion to my sufferings. I feel at this moment I couldn't suffer any more, but I'm not afraid, since if they increase, He will increase my courage at the same time* (HLC 149).

We who run in the way of love, she said, *shouldn't be thinking of suf-*

ferings that can take place in the future; it's a lack of confidence. Then she added the profound and mysterious remark *It's like meddling in the work of creation* (HLC 106).

Oh, my sisters, Thérèse said to Pauline, Marie, and Céline, *how much gratitude I owe to you. If you had not brought me up so well, what a wretched thing you would have before you now—instead of what you see in me today!*

When told that Mother Gonzague and some other sisters were commenting about her being gracious and attractive, Thérèse responded, *Ah! what does that matter to me! It means less than nothing; it annoys me. When one is so close to death, one can't take any joy out of that* (HLC 173).

Thérèse whispered to those silently praying around her bed, *My sisters, pray for the poor sick who are dying. If you only knew what happens! How little it takes to lose one's patience! You must be kind towards all of them without exception. . . . Oh, how good God will have to be so that I can bear all I'm suffering. Never would I believe I could suffer so much. And yet I believe I'm not at the end of my pains; but He will not abandon me* (HLC 130, 164).

The excruciating pain of her failing body, the physical exhaustion, *the hissing of hideous serpents* that she heard in her imagination, the nightmares that tormented her sleep, the sense of a diabolic presence, the continuing spiritual desolation of walking the dark tunnel, the emotional isolation from some of the sisters—all had been driving her to thoughts of taking her own life. She shared her inner suffering discreetly. She simply begged for prayers. She had told Pauline, *Watch carefully, Mother, when you will have patients a prey to violent pains; don't leave near them any medicines that are poisonous. I assure you, it needs only a second when one suffers intensely to lose one's reason. Then one would easily poison oneself.* A few days before her death, Thérèse whispered to Pauline, *Yes! What a grace it is to have faith! If I had not had any faith, I would have committed suicide without an instant's hesitation* (HLC 62, 258, 196).

Despair was still a real possibility at this point for Thérèse, and Pauline, on the last day, prayed before the image of the Sacred Heart that Thérèse would not succumb.

A blessed candle was kept burning, and her bed and room were sprinkled with holy water. *I'll be falling into God's arms,* she sighed (HLC 191).

One stanza of Thérèse's poem "Living By Love" summarized the sentiments of her life:

"Living by Love—what folly, how bizarre!"
So says the world, "Stop singing," it will say;
"Don't waste your life, your perfumes as they are—
Learn how to use them in the proper way."
Loving You, Jesus—loss? But fruitful so!
My perfumes are for You alone, that's why—
All. And I'll sing, as from this world I go;
 "Of Love I die." (CP 74)

She had often meditated on the spiritual wisdom of her teacher St. John of the Cross, who had said, "In the evening of life, you will be examined on love." She had followed his advice: *Learn to love as God desires to be loved and forget yourself.* She had also assimilated his wisdom: *You will not arrive at what you desire by your own path, or even by high contemplation, but through a great humility and surrender of the heart* (FGM 227, note 2).

The evening before she died she said, *All is well, it is consummated: it is love alone that counts* (MSST 212).

We are greater than the whole universe, and one day, Thérèse had written some time earlier, *one day we ourselves shall have a divine existence.* Now that time was imminent.

Dear Mother, she said to Mother Gonzague, who was comforting her, *the chalice is full to overflowing! But God will not forsake me. He has never forsaken me. . . . Oh! My God . . . have pity on me! . . . O Mary, come to my aid! . . . My God, how I am suffering! . . . The chalice is full, . . . full to the brim! . . . never will I know how to die!* "Courage," Mother Gonzague tenderly replied, "you're coming to the end, a little while and everything will be finished." *No, Mother, it's still not finished,* Thérèse answered, *I feel that I'm going to suffer in this way for months* (HLC 267; TLMT 39–40). But she was mistaken; she was to die that evening.

"Death will come to fetch you," one sister had remarked some time earlier. Thérèse replied, *No, not death, but God! I am at the door of eternity.* She had written to Fr. Bellière, *I am not dying; I am entering into Life* (GC II 1128). That door of eternity, entering into eternal life, opened, and her Beloved welcomed Thérèse on September 30, 1897, at about twenty minutes after seven o'clock in the evening. Among her last words was a reaffirmation of her *Act of Oblation to Merciful Love: I am not sorry for delivering myself up to Love. . . . Oh no, I'm not sorry; on the contrary!* Her final sigh was an echo of her entire life: *Oh, I love Him! My God, I love You!* (HLC 205–6).

It had been raining all evening and now, just after seven o'clock, the rain ceased, the clouds parted, and the stars began to shine.

Her sisters noted that in her final moment, Thérèse raised her eyes and her face became transformed with an expression of radiant peace and sheer joy. She had begun a new chorus of that eternal song of praise to divine mercy that she had begun with her life, had reflected on in her writings, and now would sing for all eternity. At last she had been brought into the maternal embrace of her Blessed Mother and into the arms of her loving Father, in whom she found that love and that home she had so longed for during the whole of her life. *To love, to be loved,* was Thérèse's sole desire, *and to return to earth to make Love loved* (MSST 227; HLC 217).

Thérèse's final written words in the notebook to Mother Gonzague had been, *Yes, I feel it; even though I had on my conscience all the sins that can be committed, I would go, my heart broken with sorrow, and throw myself into Jesus' arms, for I know how much he loves the prodigal child who returns to Him. It is not because God, in his anticipating Mercy, has preserved my soul from mortal sin that I go to Him with confidence and love . . .* (SS 259; cf. GC II 1093).

Epilogue

On October 4 Léonie led Thérèse's funeral procession of just thirty people to the burial site, previously purchased by the Guérin family, in the municipal cemetery of Lisieux on a hill overlooking the city. There was no room in the community cemetery at Carmel. Uncle Isidore Guérin was unable to attend because of illness. Fr. Youf, Thérèse's confessor, was also too ill to be present; he died the following week.

In 1899, two years after Thérèse's death, Léonie reentered and this time persevered in the Visitation community at Caen. She lived to be seventy-eight. She became one of Thérèse's first and most faithful disciples outside of Carmel, living a saintly life in the spirit of the Little Way and dying a holy death in 1941.

Marie died at the age of eighty in 1940. She once spoke about the day, July 29, 1894, when word reached Carmel that their father had died: "I can still see Thérèse; she was pale, she followed behind us, without saying anything; in the speakroom, she said almost nothing either. This was her way; we did not pay any attention to her because she was the little one."

Pauline, having been directed by Thérèse to be custodian of her writings, edited them for publication, dividing them into chapters and correcting the spelling, as well as adding to and subtracting from the text as she saw fit, much in the same way she had corrected her little sister's work as her teacher at home. The original writings of Thérèse remained under the control of Pauline, who was reelected prioress in 1902 and, at the request of Pope Pius XII, remained prioress until her death in 1951 at the age of ninety. During her lifetime she prevented scholars from having access to Thérèse's original manuscripts. After Pauline's death, Céline, having been elected prioress, quickly made all of Thérèse's writings available.

Céline also lived to be ninety and died in 1959. She has provided the best physical portrait of the mature Thérèse through her forty-five or so photographs taken after she had entered Carmel. There are also several pictures professionally taken of Thérèse as a young girl and as a teenager. Photography was just coming into existence in her day, and Thérèse was among the first canonized saints to be photographed. In addition to being a photographer, Céline was also an artist, and she painted four or more portraits of her little sister. Although the paintings are based on some of the photographs and her own personal memory, they lack the strength, the vigor, and the pathos of the photographs themselves.

Mother Marie de Gonzague, to whom Thérèse gave her dying glance out of respectful obedience and affection (but only after having previously apologized to her blood sisters fearing they would not be pleased if she did not give them the loving look of final farewell), wrote in the convent register alongside Thérèse's act of profession, "The nine and a half years she spent among us leave our souls fragrant with the most beautiful virtues with which the life of a Carmelite can be filled. An accomplished model of humility, obedience, charity, prudence, detachment and regular observance. Sister Thérèse carried out the difficult charge of mistress of novices with a wisdom and perfection that was equalled only by her love for God. We call to witness the dear manuscript which will edify the whole world while leaving the most perfect examples to us all. This angel on earth had the happiness of taking flight to her Beloved in an Act of Love" (cf. GC II 943).

Thérèse's cousin, Marie Guérin, who had been a playmate, a friend, and then was one of her novices, remarked, "Hers is not an extraordinary sanctity, there is no love of extraordinary penances; no, only love for God. People in the world can imitate her sanctity, since she has tried to do everything through love and to accept all the little contradictions, all the little sacrifices that come at each moment as coming from God's hands. She saw God in everything and carried out all her actions as perfectly as possible" (HLC 281).

Is pure love in my heart? Are my measureless desires only but a dream, a folly? (SS 197). Thérèse had asked herself that question in her painful, final suffering. In death Thérèse surely received her answer, and that answer has reverberated throughout the world. The glorification of Thérèse in the life of the church, particularly among the little ones longing for God, as well as among all those seeking enlightenment, peace, and love, is the resounding affirmation of the truth that the *measureless desires* of the human heart are ultimately from God and for God. That glorification is also but a shadow of Thérèse's full glory and of what awaits all the poor in spirit who desire God and are willing to reciprocate divine love in their lives through works of peace and charity. The respect and honor extended to Thérèse from within the church and beyond are a testimony to the truth that union with God is possible to anyone who is open to the Holy Spirit, always available in the ordinary experiences of human life.

Select Bibliography

Ahern, Patrick. *Maurice and Thérèse: The Story of a Love*. New York: Doubleday, 1998.

Bro, Bernard. *The Little Way: The Spirituality of Thérèse of Lisieux*. London: Darton, Longman, and Todd Ltd., 1997.

Bro, Bernard. *Saint Thérèse of Lisieux: Her Family, Her God, Her Message*. San Francisco: Ignatius Press, 2003.

Catechism of the Catholic Church. Liguori, MO: Liguori Publications, 1994.

Day, Dorothy. *Thérèse*. Springfield, Illinois: Templegate Publishers, 1979.

de Meester, Conrad. *The Power of Confidence*. New York: Alba House, 1996.

de Meester, Conrad, ed. *Saint Thérèse of Lisieux: Her Life, Times, and Teaching*. Washington, DC: ICS Publications, 1997.

de Meester, Conrad, ed. *With Empty Hands: The Message of Saint Thérèse of Lisieux*. Washington, DC: ICS Publications, 2002.

Descouvemont, Pierre. *Thérèse of Lisieux and Marie of the Trinity*. New York: Alba House, 1997.

Divine Amoris Scientia: Apostolic Letter of His Holiness Pope John Paul II, October 19, 1997.

Gaucher, Guy. *The Story of a Life: Saint Thérèse of Lisieux*. San Francisco: Harper & Row Publishers, 1987.

Görres, Ida Friederike. *The Hidden Face: A Study of St. Thérèse of Lisieux*. San Francisco: Ignatius Press, 2003.

Jamart, Francois. *Complete Spiritual Doctrine of St. Thérèse of Lisieux*. New York: Alba House, 1961.

Merton, Thomas. *The Inner Experience*. New York: HarperSanFrancisco, 2004.

O'Donnell, Christopher. *Prayer: Insights from Saint Thérèse of Lisieux*. Dublin: Veritas Publications, 2001.

O'Mahony, Christopher, ed. and trans. *St. Thérèse of Lisieux by Those Who Knew Her*. Huntington, IN: Our Sunday Visitor, 1975.

Payne, Steven. *Saint Thérèse of Lisieux: Doctor of the Universal Church*. New York: St. Paul's, 2002.

Piat, Stéphane-Joseph. *The Story of a Family*. Rockville, IL: Tan Books, Inc., 1994.

Rahner, Karl. *The Practice of Faith*. New York: Crossroads, 1983.

Sister Geneviève of the Holy Face (Céline Martin). *My Sister Saint Thérèse*. Rockford, IL: Tan Books and Publishers, Inc., 1997.

Six, Jean-Francois. *Light of the Night: The Last Eighteen Months in the Life of Thérèse of Lisieux*. Notre Dame, Indiana: University of Notre Dame Press, 1998.

Thérèse of Lisieux. *Collected Letters of Saint Thérèse of Lisieux*. Trans. F. J. Sheed. New York: Sheed and Ward, 1949.

Thérèse of Lisieux. *Collected Poems of St. Thérèse of Lisieux*. Trans. Alan Bancroft. Herefordshire, England: Gracewing, 2001.

Thérèse of Lisieux. *General Correspondence, vols. I and II*. Trans. John Clarke. Washington, DC: ICS Publications, 1982, 1988.

Thérèse of Lisieux. *The Prayers of Saint Thérèse of Lisieux*. Trans. Aletheia Kane. Washington, DC: ICS Publications, 1997.

Thérèse of Lisieux. *St. Thérèse of Lisieux: Her Last Conversations*. Trans. John Clarke. Washington, DC: ICS Publications, 1977.

Thérèse of Lisieux. *Story of a Soul*. Trans. John Clarke. Washington, DC: ICS Publications, 1977.

von Balthasar, Hans Urs. *Thérèse of Lisieux*. New York: Sheed and Ward, 1954.

Index

Eucharist, 16, 28, 35, 82, 98, 103, 126, 128, 132–33, 186–87, 208, 286
  frequent reception of, 35, 103, 132–33, 188, 208, 286
  Jesus' lowering himself to sinners, 133, 186–88
  Thérèse's illness and death, 16, 306, 325
  See also **Thérèse of Lisieux,** First Communion

faith, 12, 23, 32–33, 46, 95, 132–33, 137, 143, 157, 161, 174, 194, 203, 206, 208, 226, 239–40, 259, 273–80, 283–87, 292–93, 299, 305, 307–8, 311, 324, 326
  holiness and, 119
  overcoming faults and, 249
  tension between feelings and, 26, 77, 270–72, 290, 311
  Thérèse's, 23, 32–33, 46, 95, 132–33, 137, 143, 157, 161, 174, 194, 206, 208, 226, 239–40, 259, 273–74, 326
  Thérèse's trial of, 12, 203, 274–80, 283–87, 292–93, 299, 305, 307–8, 311, 324
Febronie, Sr., 208
fire. *See* **love,** divine love and mercy
flowers, symbolism of, 82, 97, 134, 170, 186, 188, 223, 288–89, 317
forgiveness, divine. *See* **love,** divine love and mercy
forgiveness, human, 29, 67
Francis de Sales, 24, 34, 50–52
Francis of Assisi, 23, 308
Francis Xavier, 36
Freemasons, 281–82
Freud, Sigmund, 14–15, 284

Geneviève of St. Teresa, Mother, 24, 166, 187, 192, 205–7, 214, 227, 255, 314–15
Geneviève of the Holy Face, Sr., 255. *See also* **Martin, Céline**
God
  creativity of, 234
  not vengeful/not violent, 24, 67, 99, 112, 131, 233–34, 236
  source of our desires, 50, 199
  Thérèse's doubts about, 26, 201
  See also **love,** divine love and mercy
Gonzaga, St. Aloysius, 317
de Gonzague, Mother Marie, 13, 32, 35, 88, 134, 147, 161, 166, 168–70, 174–80, 184, 192, 202, 209–10, 214, 217, 247–48, 254–56, 259, 268, 272–74, 292–93, 302–6, 311, 320, 322–23, 326–30
  described, 174
  opinions of Thérèse, 13, 178, 330
  daily reception of Communion, 35
  relationship with Thérèse, 88, 147, 161, 168–70, 174–79, 180, 184, 254–56, 304
grace
  complete conversion. See **Thérèse of Lisieux,** conversion
  disguised, 55, 95, 107, 112, 119–20, 163, 263, 267, 279, 294
  enduring faults, 250
  everything is, 16–17, 306, 315
  faith and, 326
  God's descending by, 103
  gratitude and, 244
  human effort and, 96–97
  transforming relationships, 178
  sea as image of, 81, 239
  showered by Thérèse, 14

infatuation, 175–77, 106–9. *See also*
Thérèse of Lisieux, feelings, self-
indulgence

influenza epidemic, 207–8

Islam, 42

Jansenism, 24–25, 31, 37, 60, 96–98,
197, 227, 247, 278, 295. *See also*
Pelagianism; perfectionism

Joan of Arc, St., 23, 36, 113–16, 122,
149–50, 183, 203, 206, 215, 244–
45, 279–82, 285, 311, 320, 324
compared to Thérèse, 149, 183, 206,
279, 285, 320
influence on Thérèse, 23, 113–16,
122, 203, 244–45, 324
Thérèse's plays about, 215, 244,
281–82

John Damascene, St., 44–45, 47

John of the Cross, St., 24, 27, 41, 190,
306, 327

John Paul II, Pope, 12, 16, 20, 22,
39–41, 47, 48

Joseph, St., 52, 86, 143

justification. *See* holiness, human effort
vs. God's grace

Kostka, St. Stanislaus, 316

La Néele, Francis, 190, 215, 322

La Normand, 280, 282

Leo XIII, Pope, 11, 150–52, 154–57,
159, 192, 215, 222, 280, 305

Les Buissonnets, 75, 78, 117, 187

lift. *See* holiness, human effort vs.
God's grace, stairway vs. elevator

lilies. *See* flowers, symbolism of

Lisieux, France, 58, 75, 78, 152, 158,
184, 186, 209, 329

Lisieux Carmel. *See* Carmel, Lisieux

"little flower," 12, 15, 134, 144, 182,
245, 304, 312

"little doctor," 105, 109, 226

littleness. *See* Thérèse of Lisieux, characteristics

"little queen," 64, 76, 81–82, 89,
92, 104, 110, 124, 157, 167,
184–85, 196. *See also* Martin, Louis,
Thérèse's "king"

Little Sister Amen, 208

little souls, 9–10, 20, 22–23, 31, 36–
37, 46, 289, 306–7, 315. *See also*
poor in spirit; Thérèse of Lisieux,
characteristics, littleness

Little Way, 12–17, 20–38, 40–42,
47–48, 69, 116, 119, 123, 127, 129,
133, 199, 214, 220–21, 224–25,
227–29, 239–40, 242, 244, 247, 251,
258, 273, 286, 291, 295–96, 298,
300, 305–6, 309, 313, 315–17, 329
applied to today, 21–22, 38, 48
attitude of abandonment/availabil-
ity/willingness, 17, 20, 21, 23, 24,
27–31, 43, 46, 101, 116, 129, 137,
159–60, 163, 190–91 195, 199,
213, 216, 220, 222–23, 228, 230–
31, 233, 235, 239, 240–244, 250,
252, 288–89, 291, 295, 297, 299,
309–10, 312, 315, 318, 325, 327
cultivating desires, 199
first use of terminology, 213
gratitude and, 243–44
poverty of spirit, 23, 242–43,
291, 294, 319
never getting discouraged, 101,
139, 213
"victim" of God's love, 235–39

Notre Dame Church, 51
Notta, Dr., 51, 91

Orthodox Church, 42
Our Lady of the Smile, 219. *See also*
Mary, Blessed Virgin, smile/statue;
Our Lady of Victories smile/statue
Our Lady of Victories smile/statue,
92–94, 152. *See also* Mary, Blessed
Virgin, smile/statue

Papinau, Valentine, 117
Pasquier, Victoire, 78–80, 83, 94, 122,
254, 266, 270
Pelagianism, 24–25, 31, 37, 60, 96, 98,
227, 251. *See also* Jansemism; perfectionism
perfectionism, 24–25, 31, 37, 171, 197,
221–22, 224, 227, 229–31, 243,
247, 251, 295–96, 318. *See also*
holiness; Jansenism; Pelagianism
Philomena, Sr., 128
Pichon, Fr., 24, 118, 180–82, 185, 187,
192, 198, 201, 218–19, 252, 257,
262, 324
Pius X, Pope, 12, 188
Pius XI, Pope, 14, 36, 39
Pius XII, Pope, 36, 329
Poor Clares, 118, 142
poor in spirit, 14, 36, 133, 136, 289–
91, 330. *See also* little souls
Pranzini, Henri, 137–39, 204, 233, 283
prayer
    Catechism on, 44–45
    contemplation and, 30
    Divine Office, 38, 46, 168, 195,
        197, 274
    ordinary understanding of, 44
    Thérèse's, 10, 13, 28, 30–31, 40, 44–
        47, 76, 97–98, 101–2, 119, 131,

prayer, Thérèse's, *cont'd.*
    138–39, 144, 148, 153, 159, 168,
    176, 181–82, 193–98, 202–4, 207,
    212, 214, 216–17, 219, 222, 224–
    25, 233, 235–40, 248, 265–67,
    283, 305, 311
    abandonment/availability to Jesus,
        45, 159, 202, 207, 216
    Act of Oblation to Merciful Love,
        42–43, 235–36, 238–39, 273,
        280, 300, 311–12, 314, 323,
        328
    an attitude in ordinary experi-
        ences, 45–46, 195–98, 240
    aridity of, 10, 143, 181–82, 194–
        95, 214, 240, 275, 324
    books and, 197
    combination of forms, 45
    Consecration to the Holy Face, 324
    definition: *surge of the heart,* 202
    difficulty at/lack of devotion in,
        10, 20, 194–95, 197–98, 202–
        3, 207, 240, 278
    draw me, 203
    for nonbelievers, 203
    for Pranzini, 137–39, 204
    for priests, 191, 203–4, 292–99,
        314–17, 327
    for the salvation of souls, 203
    interreligious, 46–47
    "lever" metaphor, 204
    Marian, 101–2, 144
    motivation of, 198–99, 202, 233
    not restricted to formal times,
        195–96, 198, 240
    personal, 45
    poetry as, 212, 216
    the publican's, 224–25, 278
    receiving and reciprocating divine
        love, 148, 202, 235

prayer, Thérèse's, *cont'd.*
  remarkableness of, 45–47
  Scriptures and, 44–45, 196–97
  shift to feminine metaphor, 45
  shift from "prayers" to "prayer-
    fulness," 46
  turned feelings/faults into, 248
Protestant churches, 42
Prou, Fr. Alexis, 24, 201–2, 204–5,
  214, 220
psychoanalysis, 14
purgatory, 314–15. *See also* heaven
purity, 111, 188–89

Rahner, Karl, 27–29
Révérony, Msgr., 149–50, 155–59, 162
Rome, pilgrimage to, 150, 152–59
roses, shower of, 317. *See also* flowers,
  symbolism of
Roulland, Adolphe, Fr., 292–95, 314–16

Sacred Congregation of Rites, 36, 38
Saint Joseph, Sr., 207–8
Saint Pierre, Sr., 269
Saint Stanislaus, Sr., 208
sanctification. *See* holiness
Scripture, 20, 22, 37, 72, 226
  gospel, 12, 14, 16, 20, 22–26, 30–31,
    33–44, 47–48, 86, 105, 119, 130,
    136–37, 153, 196, 212, 222–25,
    227, 229–31, 238, 241, 247, 250,
    251, 258, 262, 286–87, 290, 293,
    296, 313, 315
  misunderstandings of, 227
  nonviolence and, 48
  Old Testament, 38, 48, 82, 110,
    191, 219–21, 236, 252, 261, 305
  Pharisee and publican, 97, 220,
    224–25, 278, 313–14

Scripture, *cont'd.*
  St. Paul's letters, 17, 23, 119, 121,
    123, 126, 164, 228, 230–231,
    242, 250, 287
  suffering servant, 191
  Thérèse's access to, 44, 219
  Thérèse's prayer and, 44, 196, 203
  Thérèse's spirituality and, 26, 40, 48,
    220–21, 227, 231, 287, 295
  Zacchaeus, 209, 220, 313
Siméon, Br., 11, 158–59, 192, 281,
  302, 305
Sisters of Charity, 56
Sisters of the Visitation, 23
The Spiritual Canticle, 190–91
Stein, Edith, 15
stigmata, 139, 237
suicide, 10, 25, 311, 326
surrender. *See* Little Way, attitude of
  abandonment

Taillé, Rosalie, 52–55, 57–58, 60, 62
Taxil, Léo, 281–85
Teresa of Avila, St., 24, 27, 39, 141,
  196, 200, 217, 276, 305–6, 314
Teresa of Calcutta, 15
Thérèse of Lisieux
  almsgiving, 76
  artistic endeavors, 104, 211–12
  beatification, 35, 36, 61
  biographies of, 15
  birthplace of. *See* Alençon
  canonization, 14, 36–37. *See also*
    Thérèse of Lisieux, miracles
    attributed to
  Carmel, 81, 88, 95, 133–135,
    147, 149–51, 155–62, 166–72,
    174–80, 184–85, 190–94, 208–9,
    211, 214–15, 217, 244, 247–51,
    254–59, 265–72, 304, 306, 308

Thérèse of Lisieux, *cont'd.*

feelings, *cont'd.*

Acknowledgments

Quotations from *Story of a Soul*, translated by John Clarke, OCD. Copyright © 1975, 1976, 1996, by Washington Province of Discalced Carmelites, ICS Publications, 2131 Lincoln Road, N.E., Washington, D.C. 20002-1199 U.S.A. www.icspublications.org. Used with permission.

Quotations from *St. Thérèse of Lisieux: Her Last Conversations*, translated by John Clarke, OCD. Copyright © 1977, Washington Province of Discalced Carmelites, ICS Publications, 2131 Lincoln Road, N.E., Washington, D.C. 20002-1199 U.S.A. www.icspublications.org. Used with permission.

Quotations from *General Correspondence, Volume One*, translated by John Clarke, OCD. Copyright © 1982 by Washington Province of Discalced Carmelites, ICS Publications, 2131 Lincoln Road, N.E., Washington, D.C. 20002-1199 U.S.A. www.icspublications.org. Used with permission.

Quotations from *General Correspondence, Volume Two*, translated by John Clarke, OCD. Copyright © 1988 by Washington Province of Discalced Carmelites, ICS Publications, 2131 Lincoln Road, N.E., Washington, D.C. 20002-1199 U.S.A. www.icspublications.org. Used with permission.

Quotations from the poems of St. Therese are taken from *Collected Poems of St. Thérèse of Lisieux*, translated by Alan Bancroft. Published and copyright © by Gracewing, Leominster, United Kingdom. Reproduced with the permission of the publisher.

Quotations from *Thérèse of Lisieux and Marie of the Trinity*, by Pierre Descouvemont, translated by Alexandra Plettenberg-Serban. Copyright © 1997 by the Society of St. Paul. Used with permission of Society of St. Paul/Alba House.

Quotations from the English translation of the *Catechism of the Catholic Church* for use in the United States of America, copyright © 1994, United States Catholic Conference, Inc.—Libreria Editrice Vaticana. Used with permission.